Programming Microsoft Dynamics® NAV 2013

A comprehensive guide to NAV 2013 development and design

David A. Studebaker

Christopher D. Studebaker

PACKT PUBLISHING

BIRMINGHAM - MUMBAI

Programming Microsoft Dynamics® NAV 2013

First published: February 2013

Production Reference: 1190213

Published by Packt Publishing Ltd.
Livery Place
35 Livery Street
Birmingham B3 2PB, UK.

ISBN 978-1-84968-648-8

www.packtpub.com

Cover Image by David Studebaker (das189@tigereye.com)

Credits

Authors
David A. Studebaker

Christopher D. Studebaker

Reviewers
Scott Barber

Daniel Rimmelzwaan

Kamil Sáček

Luc Van Dyck

Steven Renders

Acquisition Editor
Erol Staveley

Lead Technical Editor
Suchi Singhal

Technical Editors
Vrinda Amberkar

Nitee Shetty

Dominic Pereira

Project Coordinator
Joel Goveya

Proofreaders
Ting Baker

Joel T. Johnson

Mario Cecere

Indexers
Monica Ajmera Mehta

Tejal R. Soni

Rekha Nair

Graphics
Aditi Gajjar

Sheetal Aute

Production Coordinators
Aparna Bhagat

Nilesh R. Mohite

Pooja Chiplunkar

Cover Work
Nilesh R. Mohite

Foreword

Like many other enthusiasts in the NAV community, David runs a family business with his wife Karen. Their son Christopher got his start in NAV working in the family business. This is the kind of business which made NAV more successful than any other product in the ERP mid-market and we in the NAV R&D team can thank David, Karen and Christopher for their involvement in the product and the community which made NAV what it is today.

Like David I have had the pleasure of being part of the Dynamics NAV story for more than two decades — but on R&D team. Being a part of this for so long, I also have my favorite releases, each of which has meant something special to me:

- *Navigator 3.56: The "Last DOS version". With a full IDE, the AL language, multiplatform support and a high performing database (does anybody remember SCO Unix) this concluded an era with an extremely high quality release, which is still used by many customers today.*
- *Navision 2.60: The "Windows release" which matched 3.56 in terms of quality and in addition had COM support, new object oriented features in C/AL and a fantastic Windows UI. "The beauty of simplicity".*
- *Dynamics NAV 2013: The "New NAV runtime release" which introduces a completely new, highly scalable, managed runtime with deep integration into .NET, SQL, and Office. NAV 2013 also included an array of new client features using the same page definition, with more to come.*

David has written fantastic books about previous versions of NAV – but reading David and Christopher's new book reveals to me that NAV 2013 is their favorite too!

Michael Nielsen

Director of Engineering

Dynamics NAV at Microsoft

About the Authors

David Studebaker is Chief Technical Officer and a founder of Liberty Grove Software with his partner Karen Studebaker. Liberty Grove Software, a Microsoft Partner, provides development, consulting, training, and upgrade services internationally for Microsoft Dynamics NAV resellers and end user customers.

David has been recognized by Microsoft as a Certified Professional for NAV in all three areas: Development, Applications, and Installation & Configuration. He has been honored by Microsoft as a Lead Certified Microsoft Trainer for NAV.

David just celebrated his first half century of programming, having started programming in 1962. He has been developing in C/AL since 1996. David has been an active participant in each step of computing technology from the first solid state mainframes to today's technology, from binary assembly language coding to today's C/AL and C#.

David's special achievements include his role as co-developer of the first production multi-programmed SPOOLing system in 1967. David has worked on a diverse set of software applications including manufacturing, distribution, retail, engineering, general accounting, association management, professional services billing, distribution/inventory management, freight carriage, data collection and production management, among others. Prior to co-authoring this book, David was the author of Programming Microsoft Dynamics NAV (for the Classic Client) and Programming Microsoft Dynamics NAV 2009 (for the Role Tailored Client).

David has had a wide range of development, consulting, sales and management roles throughout his career. He has been partner or owner and manager of several software development businesses, while always maintaining a hands-on role as a business applications developer.

David has a BS in Mechanical Engineering from Purdue University and an MBA from the University of Chicago. He has been writing for publication since he was an undergraduate. David has been a member of the Association for Computing Machinery since 1963 and was a founding officer of two local chapters of the ACM.

Christopher Studebaker, a NAV Developer/Implementer, has 12 years' experience designing, developing, implementing and selling the NAV and SQL Server environments. He has specialized in retail, manufacturing, job shop, and distribution implementations, most in high user-count, high data volume applications. Chris has worked on many NAV implementations with integrations to external databases and third party add-on products. Some special applications have included high volume order entry, pick-to-light systems, procurement analysis and Web frontends.

Chris acts in a consulting and training role for customers and for peer NAV professionals. He provides training both in informal and classroom situations, often developing custom course material to support courses tailored to specific student group needs. Courses have included various NAV functional and development areas.

Before becoming a certified NAV developer, Chris was a certified environmental consultant working with manufacturing facilities to meet national and state regulations. His duties included regulatory reporting, data analysis, project management and subcontractor oversight. Accomplishments included obtaining several safety certifications and managing projects for hazardous material management and abatement.

Chris is a Microsoft Certified IT Professional, SQL Database Developer, as well as a Microsoft Certified Business Solutions Professional in NAV Development and NAV Installation and Configuration. He has a Bachelor of Science degree from Northern Illinois University and has done graduate work at Denmark Technical University.

Acknowledgements

David's Personal Acknowledgements

The work on this book would not have been possible without my co-author (and son) Christopher Studebaker. Chris' broad experience with and in depth technical knowledge of NAV made it possible for us to deliver this book. I'm a very lucky father to get to work with such a smart, knowledgeable son.

I would like to especially thank my partner in life and work, Karen Studebaker, for her unflagging support, patience, love and encouragement in all ways. No one could have a more wonderful partner or spouse. The first 50 years have been great; I'm looking forward to the next 50.

I would like to acknowledge the guidance and love that I received from my parents. They always were able to see the good in people. They expected their children to do their best and helped us to do so. Foremost, they expected us to treat others well and they led by their examples.

One of my life's treasures is the enthusiastic support and love of my wonderful children, Christopher and Rebecca, of whom I am very proud. Both Becky and Chris are high achievement professionals and managers who are thoughtful and caring of others in all aspects of their lives. Most importantly, they place the highest value on their roles as parents and spouses.

Much of my knowledge about NAV was developed while working with a terrific team of associates at Studebaker Technology and later at Liberty Grove Software. For many years I have had the good fortune to work with intelligent, dedicated people who are also my friends.

Finally, though there are far too many additional individuals to list, whatever I have been able to accomplish would not have been possible without the help of many, many friends, mentors and associates along the way. Life would be very poor without all the kind and generous folks I have met.

May you enjoy using this book as even a fraction as much as I enjoyed working on it with Chris.

Christopher's Personal Acknowledgements

First and foremost I would like to thank my parents, David and Karen Studebaker, for giving me the opportunity in starting in the NAV world, and allowing me the room to grow on my own. Of course I could not have participated in this book if it weren't for my wife, Beth. Having worked within the NAV community for the past decade, I have worked with many wonderful people, most notably my parents (of course), Betty Cronin, Kathy Nohr, Tommy Madsen, Susanne Priess, David Podjasek, Diane Beck, Hasse Nielsen, Ahmed Amini, Chris Pashby, and Joy Bensur. Without them, I would not be the NAV professional I am today.

Authors' Joint Acknowledgements

We wish to express our deep appreciation to the Dynamics NAV experts, the technical reviewers for this book. Scott Barber, Steven Renders, Daniel Rimmelzwaan, Kamil Sacek and Luc Van Dyck all generously contributed their time and immeasurable amounts of their expertise to the task of reviewing our work. Their combined store of knowledge about Dynamics NAV is amazing. The good qualities in this book are due in no small part to the contributions of these individuals. We appreciate their hard work and wish to thank each of them very much.

We want to offer special thanks to Michael Nielsen of Microsoft for his wholehearted support of this and the previous Programming NAV books.

We wish to thank the great people at Microsoft and the crew of editors and other professionals at Packt Publishing who patiently assisted us with their contributions throughout the creation of this book.

About the Reviewers

Scott Barber, as a MS NAV Developer/Consultant for Tectura, is responsible for designing and programming ERP systems to meet customer requirements. His responsibilities include system design and development, performing conversions, and supporting existing customers. Scott has been working with Navision since 1995 and has over 28 years of accounting software implementation experience.

Scott has worked with many of Tectura's customers in North America, as a result, he brings a depth of business knowledge to his development/consulting work. He is a skilled trainer and teaches courses in the classroom and on-site in all areas of Navision including the development environment.

Scott is currently implementing NAV in global environments in addition to working in the North American market.

Scott received his BS in Accounting at Utah State University.

Daniel Rimmelzwaan was born and raised in the Netherlands, and moved to the U.S. at the end of 1999 to be with his new American wife. In Holland he worked as a Microsoft Access and VBA developer. When looking for a job as a VB developer in the USA, he was introduced to Navision by a "VB Recruiter", and was intrigued by the simplicity of its development tools. He decided to accept a job offer as a Navision Developer, with the firm intention to continue looking for a "real" developer job.

More than 13 years later, having been involved in all aspects of NAV implementations, Daniel is still working with NAV. He currently owns his own business (RIS Plus), doing Business Analysis and Solution Design. He is enjoying his career more than ever.

Ever since he started working with NAV, Daniel has been an active member of the online communities, such as mibuso.com and dynamicsuser.net, and the online forums managed by Microsoft. For his contributions to these communities, Daniel received his first of eight consecutive Microsoft Most Valuable Professional Awards in July 2005, which was just the second year that the award existed for NAV. Microsoft gives the MVP Award to independent members of technology communities around the world, and recognizes people that share their knowledge with other members of the community.

Daniel has also served as a reviewer for *Microsoft Dynamics NAV 2009 Application Design* by Mark Brummel, and *Microsoft Dynamics NAV 2009 Professional Reporting* by Steven Renders.

He lives with his wife and two kids in Michigan in the U.S..

Kamil Sáček (Kine) graduated from the Brno University of Technology in 2001. After that he began work as a Navision developer with NAVERTICA a.s. (formerly FUTURE Engineering a.s.), where he works to this day, now as Department Manager of Software Development.

Working with computers since his first Atari 800XE, mostly without any available literature regarding computer science, he learned everything by trial and error in his early years. From Basic, Pascal, Assembler, C, C++, C#, MS SQL, Windows, and Linux administration to VoIP gateway configuration. As a technical geek he enjoys playing with all new technologies which are of use to him. His 30 years of experience with different technologies has given him a wide knowledge base, allowing him to solve nearly any problem which he encounters.

Since 2005 he has been consecutively awarded MVP (Microsoft Most Valuable Professional) status in Microsoft Dynamics NAV, mostly for his activities on the `mibuso.com` forum, where you can read his regular posts under the alias `Kine`.

Luc Van Dyck is active as a software consultant and works for a Belgian Microsoft partner. He started working with Microsoft Dynamics NAV in 1997 (at that time it was called Navision Financials 1.10).

In the year 1999, he started the website `http://myNavision.net` to provide a forum and downloads for users of the Dynamics NAV ERP system. When Microsoft bought Navision Software A/S in 2002, the site was renamed to `http://mibuso.com`; `mibuso.com` is one of the largest online communities of Microsoft Dynamics professionals.

This online community gives users and developers of products from the Microsoft Dynamics family (NAV, AX, CRM, and so on) a place to exchange ideas and tools, and to find business partners and products. The website provides a forum where you can ask questions about the different Dynamics products. It also contains a large selection of downloads, in different categories (code examples, demo versions, webcasts, factsheets, tools, and so on). Microsoft partners can submit their company details to the Business Directory and publish their add-ons or factsheets in the Product Directory.

`mibuso.com` also organizes two-day technical conferences, called NAV TechDays, for all Microsoft Dynamics NAV developers.

Steven Renders is a Microsoft Certified Trainer with skills spanning business and technical domains, specialized in Microsoft Dynamics NAV and Microsoft SQL Server.

He has more than 15 years of business and technical experience. He provides training and consultancy focused on Microsoft Dynamics NAV, Microsoft SQL Server, Business Intelligence Solutions, Microsoft SQL Server Reporting Services, and Database Performance Tuning.

Furthermore he is also an expert in Microsoft Dynamics NAV on which he has already delivered many training sessions. Steven was an author of some of the official training materials on Dynamics NAV Reporting, SQL Server performance tuning and development.

Steven is the author of the book, *Microsoft Dynamics NAV 2009: Professional Reporting* and was also a reviewer of the book, *Programming Microsoft® Dynamics™ NAV 2009.*

Steven has presented at various Microsoft MSDN and TechNet evenings, conferences, communities, events and the Microsoft MCT Summit.

In 2011 Steven started his own company, *think about IT,* which specializes in training and consultancy, helping companies learn, implement, understand, and solve complex business requirements related to IT, in Belgium and abroad.

His specialties are:

- Microsoft Dynamics NAV
- Microsoft SQL Server
- Business Intelligence and Reporting

www.PacktPub.com

Support files, eBooks, discount offers and more

You might want to visit www.PacktPub.com for support files and downloads related to your book.

Did you know that Packt offers eBook versions of every book published, with PDF and ePub files available? You can upgrade to the eBook version at www.PacktPub.com and as a print book customer, you are entitled to a discount on the eBook copy. Get in touch with us at service@packtpub.com for more details.

At www.PacktPub.com, you can also read a collection of free technical articles, sign up for a range of free newsletters and receive exclusive discounts and offers on Packt books and eBooks.

http://PacktLib.PacktPub.com

Do you need instant solutions to your IT questions? PacktLib is Packt's online digital book library. Here, you can access, read and search across Packt's entire library of books.

Why Subscribe?

- Fully searchable across every book published by Packt
- Copy and paste, print and bookmark content
- On demand and accessible via web browser

Free Access for Packt account holders

If you have an account with Packt at www.PacktPub.com, you can use this to access PacktLib today and view nine entirely free books. Simply use your login credentials for immediate access.

Instant Updates on New Packt Books

Get notified! Find out when new books are published by following @PacktEnterprise on Twitter, or the *Packt Enterprise* Facebook page.

Table of Contents

Preface

Congratulations on beginning your study of Microsoft Dynamics NAV, C/SIDE and C/AL. You are joining a high-quality, worldwide group of experienced developers. This is a collegial community of C/AL developers who readily and generously share their knowledge. There are formal and informal organizations of NAV-focused users, developers, and vendor firms on the Web and scattered around the globe. NAV is one of the best customizable ERP systems on the market. It continues to grow and prosper.

The information in this book will help you to shorten your learning curve on how to program for the NAV 2009 ERP system using the C/AL language, the C/SIDE integrated development environment and their capabilities. Welcome aboard and enjoy the journey.

A Business history timeline

The current version of Microsoft Dynamics NAV is the result of inspiration and hard work along with some good fortune and excellent management decision making over almost the last thirty years.

The beginning

Three college friends, Jesper Balser, Torben Wind, and Peter Bang, from Denmark Technical University (DTU) founded their computer software business in 1984 when they were in their early twenties. That business was Personal Computing & Consulting (PC & C) and its first product was called PC Plus.

Single user PC Plus

PC Plus was released in 1985 with a primary goal of ease of use. An early employee said its functional design was inspired by the combination of a manual ledger journal, an Epson FX 80 printer, and a Canon calculator. Incidentally, Peter Bang is the grandson of one of the founders of Bang & Olufsen, the manufacturer of home entertainment systems par excellence.

PC Plus was PC DOS-based, a single-user system. PC Plus' design features included:

- An interface resembling the use of documents and calculators
- Online help
- Good exception handling
- Minimal computer resources required

The PC Plus product was marketed through dealers in Denmark and Norway.

Multiuser Navigator

In 1987, PC & C released a new product, the multiuser Navigator and a new corporate name, Navision. Navigator was quite a technological leap forward. It included:

- Client/Server technology
- Relational database
- Transaction-based processing
- Version management
- High-speed OLAP capabilities (SIFT technology)
- A screen painter tool
- A programmable report writer

In 1990, Navision was expanding its marketing and dealer recruitment efforts into Germany, Spain, and the United Kingdom. Also in 1990, V3 of Navigator was released. Navigator V3 was still a character-based system, albeit a very sophisticated one. If you had an opportunity to study Navigator V3.x, you would instantly recognize the roots of today's NAV product. By V3, the product included:

- A design based on object-oriented concepts
- Integrated 4GL Table, Form, and Report Design tools (the IDE)
- Structured exception handling
- Built-in resource management

- The original programming language that became C/AL
- Function libraries
- The concept of regional or country-based localization

When Navigator V3.5 was released, it also included support for multiple platforms and multiple databases. Navigator V3.5 would run on both Unix and Windows NT networks. It supported Oracle and Informix databases as well as the one developed in-house.

At about this time, several major strategic efforts were initiated. On the technical side, the decision was made to develop a GUI-based product. The first prototype of Navision Financials (for Windows) was shown in 1992. At about the same time, a relationship was established that would take Navision into distribution in the United States. The initial release in the US in 1995 was V3.5 of the character-based product, rechristened Avista for US distribution.

Navision financials for Windows

In 1995, Navision Financials V1.0 for Microsoft Windows was released. This product had many (but not all) of the features of Navigator V3.5. It was designed for complete look-and-feel compatibility with Windows 95. There was an effort to provide the ease of use and flexibility of development of Microsoft Access. The new Navision Financials was very compatible with Microsoft Office and was thus sold as "being familiar to any Office user". Like any V1.0 product, it was fairly quickly followed by a V1.1 that worked much better.

In the next few years, Navision continued to be improved and enhanced. Major new functionalities were added:

- Contact Relation Management (CRM)
- Manufacturing (ERP)
- Advanced Distribution (including Warehouse Management)

Various Microsoft certifications were obtained, providing muscle to the marketing efforts. Geographic and dealer base expansion continued apace. By 2000, according to the Navision Annual Report of that year, the product was represented by nearly 1,000 dealers (Navision Solution Centers) in 24 countries and used by 41,000 customers located in 108 countries.

Growth and mergers

In 2000, Navision Software A/S and its primary Danish competitor, Damgaard A/S, merged. Product development and new releases continued for the primary products of both original firms (Navision and Axapta). In 2002, the now much larger Navision Software, with all its products (Navision, Axapta, and the smaller, older C5 and XAL) was purchased by Microsoft, becoming part of the Microsoft Business Systems division along with the previously purchased Great Plains Software business and its several product lines. The Navision and Great Plains products all received a common rebranding. Navision was renamed to Dynamics NAV.

Continuous enhancement

As early as 2003, research began with the Dynamics NAV development team planning moves to further enhance NAV, taking advantage of various parts of the Microsoft product line. Goals were defined to increase integration with products such as Microsoft Office and Microsoft Outlook. Goals were also set to leverage the functional capabilities of Visual Studio and SQL Server, among others. All the while, there was a determination not to lose the strength and flexibility of the base product.

This was to be a massive change that would require an almost complete rewrite of the underlying code, the foundation that's normally not visible to the outside world. To accomplish that while not destroying the basic user interface, the business application model or the development environment, turned out to be a larger, more complex effort than hoped for. The first public views of this new version of the system, a year or two later, were not greeted with universal enthusiasm from the NAV technical community. But the Dynamics NAV development team persevered and Microsoft continued supporting the investment, until NAV 2009 was released in late 2008 followed by NAV 2013 in late 2012. The biggest hurdles to the new technologies had been cleared.

A new user interface, the Role Tailored Client, was created as part of this renewal. NAV is now based on Microsoft's SQL Server and is well integrated with other Microsoft products such as Office, Outlook and SharePoint. The new product versions take increasing advantage of SQL Server technologies. Development is more integrated with Visual Studio and more .NET compliant. The product is becoming more open and, at the same time, more sophisticated, supporting features such as Web Services access, integration of third-party controls, and RDLC reporting. In our industry, it would be appropriate to say "To survive is to change." Change and survival are part of what Dynamics NAV does very well.

Microsoft continues to invest in, enhance, and advance NAV. More new capabilities and features are yet to come, continuing to build on the successes of the past. We all benefit.

C/AL's roots

One of the first questions asked by people new to C/AL is often "what other programming language is it like?" The best response is "Pascal". If the questioner is not familiar with Pascal, the next best response would be "C" or "C#".

At the time the three founders of Navision were attending classes at Denmark Technical University (DTU), Pascal was in wide use as a preferred language not only in computer courses, but in other courses where computers were tools and software had to be written for data analyses. Some of the strengths of Pascal as a tool in an educational environment also served to make it a good model for Navision's business applications development.

Perhaps coincidentally (perhaps not) at DTU in this same time period, a Pascal compiler called Blue Label Pascal was developed by Anders Hejlsberg. That compiler became the basis for what was Borland's Turbo Pascal, which was the "everyman's compiler" of the 1980s because of its low price. Anders went with his Pascal compiler to Borland. While he was there Turbo Pascal morphed into the Delphi language and IDE tool set under his guidance.

Anders later left Borland and joined Microsoft, where he led the C# design team. Much of the NAV-related development at Microsoft is now being done in C#. So the Pascal-C/AL-DTU connection has come full circle, only now it appears to be C#-C/AL. Keeping it in the family, Anders' brother, Thomas Hejlsberg also works at Microsoft on NAV. Each in their own way, Anders and Thomas continue to make significant contributions to Dynamics NAV.

In a discussion about C/AL and C/SIDE, Michael Nielsen of Navision and Microsoft, who developed the original C/AL compiler, runtime, and IDE, said that the design criteria were to provide an environment that could be used without:

- Dealing with memory and other resource handling
- Thinking about exception handling and state
- Thinking about database transactions and rollbacks
- Knowing about set operations (SQL)
- Knowing about OLAP (SIFT)

Paraphrasing some of Michael's additional comments, the goals of the language and IDE design were to:

- Allow the developer to focus on design, not coding, but still allow flexibility
- Provide a syntax based on Pascal stripped of complexities, especially relating to memory management

- Provide a limited set of predefined object types, reducing the complexity and learning curve
- Implement database versioning for a consistent and reliable view of the database
- Make the developer and end user more at home by borrowing a large number of concepts from Office, Windows, Access, and other Microsoft products

Michael is still working as part of the Microsoft team in Denmark on new capabilities for NAV. Another example of how, once part of the NAV community, most of us want to stay part of that community.

What you should know

This book will not teach you programming from scratch, nor will it tutor you in business principles. To get the maximum out of this book, you should come prepared with some significant experience and knowledge including the following attributes:

- Experienced developer
- More than one programming language
- IDE experience
- Knowledgeable about business applications
- Good at self-directed study

If you have those attributes, then by careful reading and performance of the suggested exercises in this book, it will help you become productive with C/AL and NAV much more rapidly. In addition, your knowledge will be broader and deeper than it would be otherwise.

For executives, consultants, managers and others who aren't developers, but want to learn about the development technology and capabilities of Dynamics NAV, this book is still an excellent resource. If you fit in one of those or similar categories, start by studying *Chapter 1, An Introduction to NAV 2013*, in detail for a good overview of what NAV is and its tools. Then review sections of other chapters as the topics apply to your areas of interest.

This book's illustrations are from the W1 Cronus database V2013.

Hopefully this book will smooth your path to knowledge of Dynamics NAV 2013 and shine a little light on challenges and opportunities alike. Your job is to take advantage of this opportunity to learn, to expand your knowledge of NAV, and then use your new skills productively.

What this book covers

Chapter 1, An Introduction to NAV 2013, starts with an overview of NAV as a business application system. This is followed by an introduction to the seven types of NAV objects, and the basics of C/AL and C/SIDE. Then we will do some hands-on work, defining Tables, multiple Page types, and a Report. We'll close with a brief discussion of how backups and documentation are handled in C/SIDE.

Chapter 2, Tables, focuses on the foundation level of NAV data structure — Tables and their structures. We will cover Properties, Triggers (where C/AL resides), Field Groups, Table Relations and SumIndexFields. We'll work our way through hands-on creation of several tables in support of our example application. We will also review the types of tables found in the NAV applications.

Chapter 3, Data Types and Fields, will help you learn about fields, the basic building blocks of NAV data structure. We will review the different data types in NAV. We will cover all the field properties and triggers in detail. We'll also review the three different Field classes. We'll conclude with a discussion of the concept of filtering and how it should be considered in database structure design.

Chapter 4, Pages – the User's Interactive Interface, covers the different types of pages, their structures (Triggers, Properties) and general usage. We'll build several pages for our example application using the Page Wizard and Page Designer. We will also study the different types of controls that can be used in pages. In addition we'll review how and where actions are added to pages.

Chapter 5, Queries and Reports, will help you learn about both Queries and Reports, two methods of extracting data for presentation to users. For Queries, we will study how they are constructed and some of the ways they are utilized. For Reports, we will walk through report data flow and the variety of different report types. We will study the two Report Designers, the C/SIDE Report Designer and the Visual Studio Report Designer and how a NAV report is constructed using both of these. We'll learn what aspects of reports use one designer and what aspect use the other. As in previous studied objects, we will discuss Properties and Triggers. We will review how reports can be made interactive and will do some hands-on report creation.

Chapter 6, Introduction to C/SIDE and C/AL, will help you learn about general Object Designer Navigation as well as the individual Designers (Table, Page, Report). We'll study C/AL code construction, syntax, variable types, expressions, operators and functions. We will then take a closer look at some of the more frequently used built-in functions. This chapter will wrap up with an exercise adding some C/AL code to report objects created in an earlier exercise.

Chapter 7, Intermediate C/AL, explores the C/AL development tools and techniques. We will review some more advanced built-in functions including those relating to dates and decimal calculations, both critical business application tools. We'll study C/AL functions that support process flow control functions, input/output, and filtering. Then we'll do a review of methods of communication between objects. Finally, we'll apply some of what we've learned to enhancing our example application.

Chapter 8, Advanced NAV Development Tools, we will review some of the more important elements of the Role Tailored User Experience, in particular the Role Center Page construction. We will dig into the components of a Role Center Page and how to build one. We'll also cover two of the powerful ways of connecting NAV applications to the world outside of NAV, XMLports and Web Services. To better understand these, we will not only review their individual component parts, but will go through the hands-on effort of building an example of each one.

Chapter 9, Develop, Debug, Deliver, covers in detail how NAV functions are constructed and learn how to construct our own functions. We learn more about tools and features built into C/AL and C/SIDE. We will study the new debugger, review the support for Test-driven Development, and take a look at the ability to integrate .NET Client Add-ins. We will integrate a .NET Add-in into our example applications. Finally, we will review tips for design efficiency, updating and upgrading the system, all with the goal of helping us to become more productive, high quality NAV developers.

Appendix A, Answers to Review Questions, contains answers for all the review questions that appear at the end of each chapter.

Appendix B, Review Questions with Answers, contains all the review questions along with the answers. This is not present in the book but is available as a free download from the following link: `http://www.packtpub.com/sites/default/files/downloads/6488EN_App_Final.pdf`.

What you need for this book

You will need some basic tools including at least the following:

- A license and database that you can use for development experimentation. An ideal license is a full Developer's license. If the license only contains the Page, Report, and Table Designer capabilities, you will still be able to do many of the exercises, but you will not have access to the inner workings of Pages and Tables and the C/AL code contained therein.

- A copy of the NAV Cronus demo/test database for your development testing and study. It would be ideal if you also had a copy of a production database at hand for examination as well. This book's illustrations are from the W1 Cronus database for V2013.

Access to other NAV manuals, training materials, websites and experienced associates will obviously be of benefit, but they are not required for the time with this book to be a good investment.

Who this book is for

This book is for:

- The business applications software designer/developer who:
    - Wants to become productive in NAV C/SIDE−C/AL development as quickly as possible
    - Understands business applications and the type of software required to support those applications
    - Has significant programming experience
    - Has access to a copy of NAV 2013 including at least the Designer granules and a standard Cronus demo database
    - Is willing to do the exercises to get hands-on experience
- The Reseller manager or executive who wants a concise, in depth view of NAV's development environment and tool set
- The technically knowledgeable manager or executive of a firm using NAV that is about to embark on a significant NAV enhancement project
- The technically knowledgeable manager or executive of a firm considering purchase of NAV as a highly customizable business applications platform
- The experienced business analyst or consultant or advanced student of applications software development who wants to learn more about one of the most widely used, most flexible business application systems available

The reader of this book:

- Does not need to be expert in object-oriented programming
- Does not need previous experience with NAV, C/AL, or C/SIDE

Conventions

In this book, you will find a number of styles of text that distinguish between different kinds of information. Here are some examples of these styles, and an explanation of their meaning.

Code words in text are shown as follows: "One is known as comma-separated value or comma-delimited files (usually having a .csv file extension)."

A block of code is set as follows:

```
IF Type = 'Resource' THEN No. := Resource.No.
    ELSE IF Type = 'Show' THEN No. := Radio Show.No.
    ELSE IF Type = 'Item' THEN No. := Item.No.
```

Any command-line input or output is written as follows:

```
"C:\Program Files (x86)\Microsoft Dynamics NAV\70\
RoleTailored Client\Microsoft.Dynamics.Nav.Client.exe"
 -configure -profile:"WDTU Test"
```

New terms and **important words** are shown in bold. Words that you see on the screen, in menus or dialog boxes for example, appear in the text like this: "We can set the Work Date by selecting the Microsoft Dynamics icon dropdown and navigating to the **Set Work Date...** option."

Warnings or important notes appear in a box like this.

Tips and tricks appear like this.

Reader feedback

Feedback from our readers is always welcome. Let us know what you think about this book—what you liked or may have disliked. Reader feedback is important for us to develop titles that you really get the most out of.

To send us general feedback, simply send an e-mail to feedback@packtpub.com, and mention the book title via the subject of your message.

If there is a topic that you have expertise in and you are interested in either writing or contributing to a book, see our author guide on www.packtpub.com/authors.

Customer support

Now that you are the proud owner of a Packt book, we have a number of things to help you to get the most from your purchase.

Downloading the example code

You can download the example code files for all Packt books you have purchased from your account at `http://www.PacktPub.com`. If you purchased this book elsewhere, you can visit `http://www.PacktPub.com/support` and register to have the files e-mailed directly to you.

Errata

Although we have taken every care to ensure the accuracy of our content, mistakes do happen. If you find a mistake in one of our books—maybe a mistake in the text or the code—we would be grateful if you would report this to us. By doing so, you can save other readers from frustration and help us improve subsequent versions of this book. If you find any errata, please report them by visiting `http://www.packtpub.com/support`, selecting your book, clicking on the **errata submission form** link, and entering the details of your errata. Once your errata are verified, your submission will be accepted and the errata will be uploaded on our website, or added to any list of existing errata, under the Errata section of that title. Any existing errata can be viewed by selecting your title from `http://www.packtpub.com/support`.

Piracy

Piracy of copyright material on the Internet is an ongoing problem across all media. At Packt, we take the protection of our copyright and licenses very seriously. If you come across any illegal copies of our works, in any form, on the Internet, please provide us with the location address or website name immediately so that we can pursue a remedy.

Please contact us at `copyright@packtpub.com` with a link to the suspected pirated material.

We appreciate your help in protecting our authors, and our ability to bring you valuable content.

Questions

You can contact us at `questions@packtpub.com` if you are having a problem with any aspect of the book, and we will do our best to address it.

An Introduction to NAV 2013

Your work is going to fill a large part of your life, and the only way to be truly satisfied is to do what you believe is great work. And the only way to do great work is to love what you do.
– Steve Jobs

Good design, like good painting, cooking, architecture or whatever you like, is a manifestation of the capacity of the human spirit to transcend its limitations.
– George Nelson

Microsoft Dynamics NAV has achieved one of the largest installed user bases of any full-featured ERP system in the market. Several years ago, the world-wide installed user base exceeded one million. There is an ever growing community of supporting organizations, consultants, implementers, and developers. Not only do the capabilities of the off-the-shelf product increase with every release, but the variety and depth of the add-on products and services continues to grow and prosper.

The release of Microsoft Dynamics NAV 2013 is the next step down that successful road. NAV 2013 not only has enhanced business functionality, it completes the move from the technology of the 90s and early 2000s, and begins the move to supporting ERP computing in the cloud.

In this chapter, we will take a look at NAV 2013, including the following:

- A general overview of NAV 2013
- A technical overview of NAV 2013
- A hands-on introduction to C/SIDE development in NAV 2013

Our goal in this chapter is to gain a big picture understanding of NAV 2013. We will learn enough to envision how NAV can be used by a business manager or owner to help manage the activities and resources of a business. (Note that NAV is used in many not-for-profits businesses as well as for-profits.) We will also be introduced to the technical side of NAV from a developer's point of view.

NAV 2013 – an ERP system

NAV 2013 is an integrated set of business applications designed to service a wide variety business operations. Microsoft Dynamics NAV 2013 is an **ERP** system where **ERP** stands for **Enterprise Resource Planning**. An ERP system integrates internal and external data across a variety of functional areas including manufacturing, accounting, supply chain management, customer relationships, service operations, management of human and other resources, and others. By having many related applications well integrated, a full-featured ERP system provides an *enter once, use many ways* information processing toolset.

NAV 2013 ERP includes the following (and more):

- Basic accounting functions (for example, general ledger, accounts payable, accounts receivable)
- Order processing and inventory (for example, sales orders, purchase orders, shipping, inventory, receiving)
- Relationship management (for example, vendors, customers, prospects, employees, contractors, and so on)
- Planning (for example, MRP, sales forecasting, production forecasting)
- Other critical business areas (for example, manufacturing, warehouse management, fixed assets)

The following diagram illustrates conceptually how the various functions integrate into a whole to form an ERP system:

A good ERP system, such as NAV 2013, is modular in design, which simplifies implementation, upgrading, modification, integration with third-party products and expansion for different types of clients, for Internet access, and so on. All the modules in the system share a common database and, where appropriate, common data.

The grouping of individual NAV 2013 functions that follows is based on the Departments Menu structure, supplemented by information from Microsoft marketing materials. Some of the groupings are a bit arbitrary; the important thing is to obtain a reasonable grasp of the overall components that make up the NAV 2013 ERP system.

NAV 2013 has two quite different styles of user interfaces. One UI, the Development Environment, is essentially similar to the previously used Classic Client and targets developers. The other UI style, the Role Tailored Client, targets end users. The example images in the following module descriptions are from the Role Tailored Client Departments menu.

Financial Management

Financial Management is the foundation of any ERP system. No matter what the business is, the money must keep flowing, and the flow of money must be tracked. The tools which help to manage the capital resources of the business are part of NAV's Financial Management module. These include all or part of the following application functions:

- **General Ledger**: Manages the overall finances of the firm
- **Cash Management and Banking**: Manages the inventory of money
- **Accounts Receivables**: Tracks the incoming revenue
- **Accounts Payables**: Tracks the outgoing funds
- **Analytical Accounting**: Analyzes the various flows of funds
- **Inventory and Fixed Assets**: Manages the inventories of goods and equipment
- **Multi-Currency and Multi-Language**: Supports international business activities

The Financial Management section of the Departments menu is as follows:

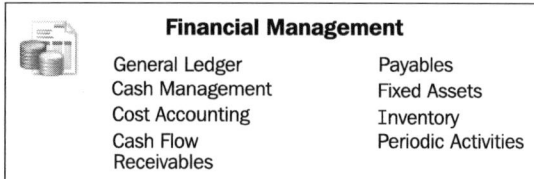

Manufacturing

NAV Manufacturing is general purpose enough to be appropriate for **Make to Stock (MTS)**, **Make to Order (MTO)**, **Assemble to Order (ATO)** as well as various subsets and combinations of those. Although off-the-shelf NAV is not particularly suitable for most process manufacturing and some of the very high volume assembly line operations, there are third-party add-on and add-in enhancements available for these applications. As with most of the NAV application functions, Manufacturing can be implemented to be used in a basic mode or as a full-featured system. NAV Manufacturing includes the following functions:

- **Product Design (BOMs and Routings)**: Manages the structure of product components and the flow of manufacturing processes
- **Capacity and supply requirements planning**: Tracks the intangible and tangible manufacturing resources

- **Production scheduling (infinite and finite), Execution, and tracking**: Tracks the planned use manufacturing resources, both on an unconstrained and constrained basis

The Manufacturing section of the Departments menu is as follows:

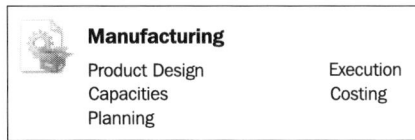

Supply Chain Management (SCM)

Obviously, some of the functions categorized as part of NAV Supply Chain Management (for example, sales, purchasing, and so on) are actively used in almost every NAV implementation. As a whole, these constitute the base components of a system appropriate for a distribution operation. The Supply Chain applications in NAV include all or parts of the following applications:

- **Sales order processing and pricing**: Supports the heart of every business, including entering, pricing, and processing sales orders

- **Purchasing (including Requisitions)**: Includes planning, entering, pricing, and processing purchase orders

- **Inventory Management**: Manages inventories of goods and materials

- **Warehouse Management including receiving and shipping**: Manages the receipt, storage, retrieval, and shipment of material and goods in warehouses

Even though we might consider Assembly part of Manufacturing, the standard NAV 2013 Departments menu includes it in the Warehouse section.

The Supply Chain Management section of the Departments menu is as follows:

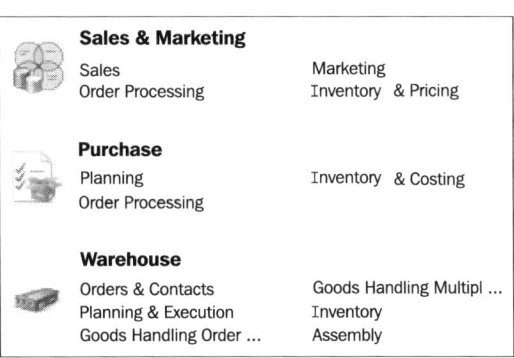

Business Intelligence and reporting (BI)

Although Microsoft marketing materials identify Business Intelligence and reporting as though it were a separate module within NAV, it's difficult to physically identify it as such. Most of the components that are used for BI and reporting purposes are (appropriately) scattered throughout various application areas. In the words of one Microsoft document, *Business Intelligence is a strategy, not a product*. Functions within NAV that support a Business Intelligence strategy include the following:

- **Standard Reports**: These are distributed ready-to-use by end users

- **Account schedules and analysis reports**: These use a very specialized report writer targeted only at General Ledger data

- **Query, XMLport and Report Designers**: These are developer tools to support the creation of a wide variety of report formats, charts, XML and CSV files

- **Analysis by dimensions**: This is a capability embedded in many of the other tools

- **Interfaces into Microsoft Office including Excel**: These support the communications of data either into NAV or out of NAV

- **RDLC report viewer**: This provides the ability to present NAV data in a variety of textual and graphic formats, includes user interactive capabilities

- **Interface capabilities such as Automation Controllers and web services**: These are technologies to support interfaces between NAV 2013 and external software products

Relationship Management (RM)

NAV's Relationship Management functionality is definitely the "little sister" (or, if preferred, "little brother") to the fully featured stand alone Microsoft CRM system. The big advantage of RM is that it's tight integration with the NAV customer and sales data. For those who need the full Microsoft CRM, a module connecting it to NAV 2013 is available.

Also falling under the heading of Customer Relationship module is the NAV **Service Management (SM)** functionality. While the RM component shows up in the menu as a part of sales and marketing, the SM component is identified as an independent function in the menu structure.

- Relationship Management:
  - **Marketing campaigns**: Plans and manages promotions
  - **Customer activity tracking**: Analyzes customer orders
  - **To do lists**: Manages what's to be done and tracks what's been done

- Service Management:
  - **Service contracts**: Supports service business operations
  - **Labor and part consumption tracking**: Tracks the resources consumed by the service business
  - **Planning and dispatching**: Manages service calls

Human Resource management (HR)

NAV **Human Resources (HR)** is a very small module, but relates to a critical component of the business, the people. Basic employee data can be stored and reported via the master table (in fact, one can use HR to manage data about individual contractors in addition to employees). A wide variety of individual employee attributes can be tracked by use of the following dimensions fields:

- **Employee tracking**: Maintains basic employee description data
- **Skills inventory**: Maintains an inventory of the capabilities of employees
- **Absence tracking**: Maintains basic attendance information
- **Employee statistics**: Tracks government required employee attribute data such as age, gender, length of service, and so on

Project Management

The NAV Project Management module consists of the jobs functionality supported by the resources functionality. Projects can be short or long term. They can be external (in other words billable) or internal. This module is often used by third parties as the base for vertical market add-ons (for example, for construction or job-oriented manufacturing). This application area includes parts or all of the following functions:

- **Budgeting and cost tracking**: Manages project finances
- **Scheduling**: Plans project activities
- **Resource requirements and usage tracking**: Manages people and equipment
- **Project accounting**: Tracks the results

Significant changes for NAV 2013

In some ways, NAV 2013 is as notable for what is no longer included in the product as what is new. The old Classic Client user interface and Classic Database have been left behind along with the associated two-tier system. NAV 2013 is no longer constrained by the technology limitations those required. All user and development focus is now on the Role Tailored Client.

There are added capabilities in terms of functionality, development tools, Internet compatibility, and increased integration to other Microsoft products along with other improvements. Information on the minimum hardware and software requirements to install and run Microsoft Dynamics NAV 2013 are found in the *Developer and IT Pro Help Microsoft Dynamics NAV 2013 Requirements*.

Following are some of the specific areas where NAV 2013 contains significant changes (this list is representative, not comprehensive).

Application changes

- Cash Flow Forecasting
- Cost Accounting Budgeting, Tracking, and Analysis
- VAT Management
- Warehouse Inventory Movement
- Supply Planning
- Assembly Management (an expanded version of the previous Kitting functionality)
- Jobs WIP and Service Usage
- HR Time Sheets
- Dimensions data structure (major revision for efficiency)
- RapidStart Services (implementation tools to help set up a new company)

Client enhancements

- New SharePoint Client
- New Web Client
- Increased control over user interface
- Increased Office compatibility, both look and feel, and Excel integration
- New filtering capabilities

- Copy and Paste between documents
- Two-way Copy and Paste with Excel
- Additional Page layout design control
- Enhanced extensibility and charting
- Customizable User Help documentation
- OneNote integration

Development tools

- New Query object for data view definition and data extraction
- New Page Design immediate preview capability
- New Debugger with state-of-the-art functionality and RTC compatibility
- New Report Data Designer
- Enhanced integration with Visual Studio for report layout design

Other areas

- All development work is done in the Development Environment (formerly the Classic Client) combined with Visual Studio for report layout; all of the user work is done in one of the Role Tailored Clients
- OData support
- 100 percent 64-bit server
- NAV Application Server enhanced and runs on the Service Tier
- Internal data coding is done in Unicode

A developer's overview of NAV 2013

From the point of view of a developer, NAV 2013 consists of several thousand potentially customizable off-the-shelf program objects (consider these as building blocks) plus the Integrated Development Environment (the C/SIDE development tools), which allow us to modify those objects and create new ones.

The NAV 2013 system is an object-based system made up of the seven different object types available in NAV. NAV does not have all of the features of an object-oriented system. A full-featured object-oriented system would allow for the definition and creation of new object types, while NAV only allows for the creation and modification of instances of the seven pre-defined object types.

NAV object types

Let's start with basic definitions of the NAV 2013 object types. They are as follows:

- **Table**: Tables serve both to define the data structure and to contain the data records.

- **Page**: Pages are the way data is formatted and displayed appropriately for each of the client types.

- **Report**: Reports allow the display of data to the user in *hardcopy* format, either on screen (preview mode) or via a printer device. Report objects can also update data in processes with or without accompanying data display output.

- **Codeunit**: Codeunits are containers for code, which are always structured in code segments called functions.

- **Query**: Queries support extracting data from one or more tables, making calculations, and outputting in the form of a new data structure. Queries can output data directly to charts, Excel, XML, and OData.

- **XMLport**: XMLports allow the importing and exporting of data from/to external files. The external data structure can be in XML or other file formats.

- **MenuSuite**: MenuSuites contain menu entries which refer to other types of objects. MenuSuites are different from other objects, especially since they cannot contain any code or logic. MenuSuites are translated into the Departments menu entries in the Navigation Pane for presentation to the users.

C/SIDE

NAV 2013 includes an extensive set of software development tools. The NAV development tools are accessed through the **C/SIDE (Client/Server Integrated Development Environment)** which runs within the Development Environment client. This environment and its complement of tools are generally just referred to as C/SIDE. C/SIDE includes the C/AL compiler. All NAV programming uses C/AL. No NAV development can be done without using C/SIDE, but Visual Studio tools are required for the report layout work. Prior to NAV 2009, it was possible to do all NAV development within the embedded IDE.

According to Microsoft, NAV 2013 report layout design requires use of Visual Studio 2010, including the Visual Web Developer feature. Claus Lundstrum, in his blog at `http://mibuso.com/blogs/clausl/2012/05/31/free-visual-studio-designer-for-editing-reports-in-dynamics-nav-2013-and-other-options/` explains how to get the free Visual Web Developer 2010 Express to work for NAV 2013 report layout designing.

C/SIDE is referred to as the **Object Designer** within NAV. It is accessed through a separate shortcut which is installed as part of a typical full system installation. When we first open the **Object Designer** window, we will see the following screen:

Downloading the example code

You can download the example code files for all Packt books you have purchased from your account at `http://www.packtpub.com`. If you purchased this book elsewhere, you can visit `http://www.packtpub.com/support` and register to have the files e-mailed directly to you.

Object Designer tool icons

Whenever we open an object in the applicable Designer (Table Designer, Page Designer, and so on.) for that object, we will see a set of tool icons at the top of the screen. The following table lists those icons and the object types to which they apply. On occasion, an icon will appear even when it is of no use. Refer the following table:

	Find	Properties	Field Menu	Symbol Table	C/AL Code
Table	✓	✓		✓	✓
Page	✓	✓	✓	✓	✓
Report	✓	✓	✓	✓	✓
Codeunit	✓	✓	✓ but of no use	✓	
Query	✓	✓	✓	✓	✓
XMLport	✓	✓		✓	✓
MenuSuite	✓ but of no use	No icon – Alt+Enter			

C/AL programming language

The language in which NAV is coded is **C/AL** (an acronym for **Client Application Language**). A sample of some C/AL code within the C/AL Editor is shown in the following screenshot:

C/AL syntax has considerable similarity to Pascal. As with any programming language, readability is enhanced by careful programmer attention to structure, logical variable naming, process flow consistent with that of the code in the base product, and good documentation both inside and outside of the code

For several decades, one of the highest goals of software development has been to focus on design before coding and, wherever possible, to accomplish design goals with a minimum amount of code. More than most application software products, Dynamics NAV facilitates that approach. When working on enhancements of NAV, we can spend a majority of our NAV development time determining what to do and what existing capabilities support the task at hand. Then, much of our NAV development work is done by making entries in tables, defining properties of objects ranging from controls to functions to programs, and assembling references to previously defined objects. This approach allows us to minimize the number of lines of code required because we are reusing objects that already exist. As NAV's tools continue to mature, our development work continues to be more heavily weighted in favor of design. Hopefully, the end result is that we are more productive and cost effective on behalf of our customers.

NAV object and system elements

Following are some key terms as used in NAV:

- **Fields**: These are the individual data items, defined either in a table or in the working storage of an object.

- **Records**: These are groups of fields (data items) that are handled as a unit in most Input/Output operations. The table data consists of rows (records) with columns (fields).

- **Controls**: In MSDN, a control is defined as follows:

    a component that provides (or enables) user-interface (UI) capabilities

- **Properties**: These are the attributes of the element (for example, object, data field, or control) that define some aspect of its behavior or use. Example attributes include display caption, relationships, and if the elements are either editable or viewable.

- **Triggers**: The generic definition is a mechanism that initiates (fires) an action when an event occurs and is communicated to the application object. A trigger is either empty or contains code that is executed when the associated event fires the trigger. Each object type, data field, control, and so on, may have its own set of pre-defined triggers. The event trigger name begins with the word On such as OnInsert, OnOpenPage, and OnNextRecord. NAV triggers have similarities to those in SQL, but they are not the same (and may not even serve similar purposes). NAV triggers are locations within the various objects where a developer can place comments or C/AL code. When we look at the C/AL code of an object in its Designer, the following have a physical resemblance to the NAV event-based triggers:

    ◦ **Documentation** which can contain comments only, no executable code. Every object type except MenuSuite has a single Documentation section at the beginning of the C/AL code.

    ◦ **Functions** which can be defined by the developer. They represent callable routines that can be accessed from other C/AL code either inside or outside the object where the called function resides. Many functions are provided as part of the standard product. As a developer, we may add our own custom functions as needed.

- **Object numbers and field numbers**: All objects of the same object type are assigned a unique number. All fields within an object are assigned a unique number within the object (that is, the same field number may be repeated in many objects referring to similar or different data). The object numbers from 1 to 50,000 and in the 99,000,000 range are reserved for use by NAV as part of the base product. Objects in this number range can be modified or deleted, but not created with a developer's license. Field numbers are often assigned in ranges matching the related object numbers (that is starting with 1 for fields relating to objects numbered 1 to 49,999; starting with 99,000,000 for fields in objects in the 99,000,000 and above number range). Object and field numbers from 50,000 to 99,999 are generally available to the rest of us for assignment as part of customizations developed in the field using a normal development license. If feasible, object numbers from 90,000 to 99,999 should not be used for permanent objects as those numbers are sometimes used in training materials. Microsoft allocates other ranges of object and field numbers to **Independent Software Vendor (ISV)** developers for their add-on enhancements. Some of these (the 14,000,000 range in North America, other ranges for other geographic regions) can be accessed, modified, or deleted, but not created using a normal development license. Others (such as in the 37,000,000 range) can be executed, but not viewed or modified with a typical development license.

The following table summarizes object numbering practice:

Object Number range	Usage
1 – 9,999	Base-application objects
10,000 – 49,999	Country-specific objects
50,000 – 99,999	Customer-specific objects
100,000 – 98,999,999	Partner-created objects
Above 98,999,999	Microsoft territory

- **Work Date**: This is a user-controlled date which is used as the default date for many transaction entries. The System Date is the date recognized by Windows. The Work Date that can be adjusted at any time by the user, is specific to the workstation, and can be set to any point in the future or the past. This is very convenient for procedures such as ending a Sales Order entry for one calendar day at the end of the first shift, and then entering Sales Orders by the second shift dated to the next calendar day. There are settings to allow limiting the range of Work Dates allowed. We can set the Work Date by selecting **the Microsoft Dynamics icon dropdown and navigating to the Set Work Date...** option or clicking on the date in the Status Bar at the bottom of the RTC window, then entering a date in the **Set Work Date** screen seen here:

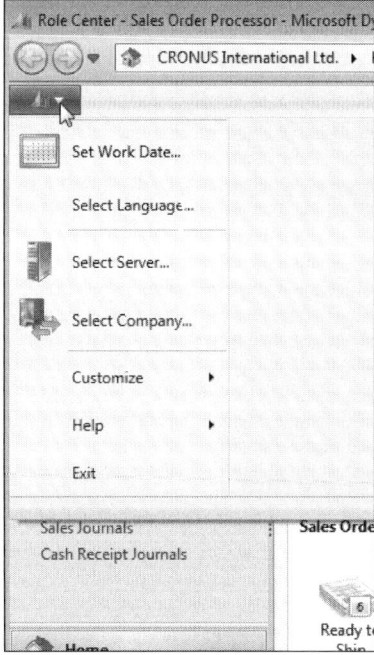

Clicking on **Set Work Date...** in the dropdown options displays the following **Set Work Date** screen:

- **License:** A data file supplied by Microsoft that allows a specific level of access to specific object number ranges. NAV licenses are very clever constructs which allow distribution of a complete system, all objects, modules, and features (including development) while constraining exactly what is accessible and how it can be accessed. Each license feature has its price. Microsoft Partners have access to "full development" licenses to provide support and customization services for their clients. End-user firms can also purchase licenses allowing them developer access to NAV. A Training License can also be generated which contains any desired set of features and expires after a specified period of time.

  - **License limits**: The NAV license limits access to the C/AL code within tables pages and codeunits differently than the C/AL code buried within reports or XMLports. The latter can be accessed with a "lower level" license (i.e. less expensive). If our customer has license rights to the Report Designer, which many do, they can access C/AL code within Report and XMLport objects. But access to C/AL code in a table, page or codeunit requires a more expensive license with Developer privileges. As a result, C/AL code within tables, pages and codeunits is more secure than that within report and XMLport objects.

NAV functional terminology

For various application functions, NAV uses terminology that is more akin to accounting than to traditional data processing terminology. Some examples are as follows:

- **Journal**: A table of unposted transaction entries, each of which represents an event, an entity, or an action to be processed. There are General Journals for general accounting entries, Item Journals for changes in inventory, and so on.

- **Ledger**: A detailed history of posted transaction entries that have been processed. For example, General Ledger, a Customer Ledger, a Vendor Ledger, an Item Ledger, and so on. Some Ledgers have subordinate detail ledgers, typically providing a greater level of quantity and/or value detail.

- **Posting**: The process by which entries in a Journal are validated, and then entered into one or more Ledgers.

- **Batch**: A group of one or more Journal entries that were posted in one group.

- **Register**: An audit trail showing a history, by Entry No. ranges, of the Journal Batches that have been posted.

- **Document**: A formatted page such as an Invoice, a Purchase Order, or a Payment Check, typically one page for each primary transaction.

User Interface

NAV 2013 user interface is intended to be role oriented (also called role tailored). The term *role oriented* means tailoring the options available to fit the user's specific job tasks and responsibilities. If user access is via the Windows Client or the Web Client, the Role Tailored Client will be employed. If the user access is via the SharePoint client or another client, the developer will have more responsibility to make sure that the user experience is role tailored.

The first page which a user will come in contact with is a **Role Center page**. The Role Center page provides the user with a view of work tasks to be done; it acts as the user's *home page*. The Role Center page should be tailored to the job duties of each user, so there will be a variety of Role Center page formats for any firm.

Someone whose role centers on Order Entry will see a different RTC home page than the user whose role centers around Invoicing, even though both are primarily focused in what we generally think of as Sales and Receivables. The RTC, as implemented in NAV 2013, allows a great deal of flexibility for implementers, system administrators, managers, and individual users to configure and reconfigure screen layouts and the set of functions that are visible from time to time.

The following screenshot is the out-of-the-box **Role Center** for **Sales Order Processor**:

The key to properly designing and implementing any system, but especially a role tailored system, is the quality of the User Profile Analysis done as the first step in requirements analysis. User Profiles identify the day-to-day needs of each user as those relate to accomplishing the businesses goals. The individual users' tasks must be mapped to individual NAV functions or elements, identifying how that task will be supported by the system. The **Microsoft Dynamics Sure Step Methodology** tools provide a very robust set of guidelines, document templates, and tools for the system implementation process. It is very important that the up-front work be done and done well. The best programming cannot compensate for a bad definition of what the goals are.

In our exercises, we will assume that the up-front work has been well done and we will concentrate on addressing the requirements defined by our project team.

Developing in NAV 2013 – hands-on

One of the best ways to learn a new set of tools, such as a programming environment and language, is to experiment with them. We're going to have some fun doing that throughout this book. We're going to experiment where the cost of errors (otherwise known as Learning) is small. Our development work will be a custom application of NAV 2013 for a relatively simple, but realistic, application.

We're going to do our work using the Cronus demo database that is available with all NAV 2013 distributions and is installed by default when we install the NAV 2013 demo system. The simplest way to install the NAV 2013 demo is to locate all the components on a single workstation. A 64-bit system running Windows 7 Professional will suffice. Additional requirements information is available in the MSDN library (www.msdn.com) under the heading *System Requirements for Microsoft Dynamics NAV 2013*. Other helpful information on installing NAV 2013 (the demo option is a good choice for our purposes) and addressing a variety of setup questions is available in the *NAV 2013* area of the MSDN library. In fact, all the *Help information for NAV 2013* is accessible in the MSDN library.

The Cronus database contains all of the NAV objects and a small, but reasonably complete, set of data populated in most of the system's functional applications areas. Our exercises will interface very slightly with the Cronus data, but do not depend on any specific data values.

To follow along with our exercises as a developer, you will need a developer license for the system with rights allowing the creation of objects in the 50,000 to 50,099 number range. This license should also allow at least read access to all of the objects numbered below 50,000. If you don't have such a license, check with your Partner or your Microsoft sales representatives to see if they will provide a training license for your use.

Our scenario for development exercises

Our company runs a small, for-profit radio station. The station is WDTU and it broadcasts at 91.5 FM. The radio station is free form, which means there are many different DJs all with their own style and music. Each DJ is given a three-hour slot of time, and is responsible for playing the government required **public service announcements (PSAs)**, sports, news and weather at the top of each hour, and a set amount of paid advertisements.

We have been moving our vast vinyl and compact disc collection to high-quality MP3s on our internal data store, but will still allow DJs to bring in their own music if we don't have it in our library. For the music already converted, we need to have a user-friendly interface to select the songs played and to preview them for entry into the playlist. We also need an easy way for the DJ to create a provisional item if the record cannot be found.

Our DJs must be able to preview all songs that have been converted to MP3s on the show page as well as on their home page. To succeed as a for-profit business, the radio station needs to track what, when, and how many advertisements are broadcast in order to invoice customers. In order to operate as a licensed radio station, there are two major requirements and reporting agencies. ASCAP needs a list of all songs (or other copyrighted material) that is played during the shows during specific time periods. The government requires that the radio station perform public service by broadcasting PSAs, reporting the date and time each was played and reporting the total number of times each was played during a period of time. Currently, both reporting agencies require one month reporting intervals, but this may change.

Getting started with the application design

Our design for our radio station will start with a **Radio Show** table, a **Radio Show Card** page, a **Radio Show List** page, and a simple Radio Show Schedule List Report. Along the way, we will review the basics of each NAV object type.

When we open the NAV Development Environment for the first time, or to work on a different database, we must define what database should be opened. Click on **File | Database | Open**, then choose a database, as shown in the following screenshot:

Application tables

Table objects are the foundation of every NAV application. Tables contain data structure definitions, as well as properties that describe the behavior of the data, including data validations and constraints.

More business logic is required in complex applications than simple data type validation, and NAV allows C/AL code to be put in the table to control insertion, modification, and deletion of records as well as logic on the field level. When the bulk of the business logic is coded at the table level, it is easier to develop, debug, support, modify, and even upgrade. A good design in NAV requires that as much of the business logic as possible should reside in the tables.

Designing a simple table

Our primary master data table will be the **Radio Show** table, as this is the link between what we get paid for (advertisements) and what we owe (song royalties), as well as meeting our civic duty requirement (PSAs).

First, we will open the NAV Development Environment, click on **Tools | Object Designer** and select **Table**. We can view the design of existing master tables in NAV by highlighting the table (for example, Table 18 - Customer, or Table 27 - Item) and clicking on **Design**.

Each master table has a standard field for the primary key (a **Code** data type field of 20 characters called **No.**) and has standard information regarding the entity the master record represents (for example, Name, Address, City, and so on for the **Customer** table, and Description, Base Unit of Measure, Unit Cost, and so on for the **Item** table).

The Radio Show table will have the following field definitions:

Field names	Definitions
No.	20 character text (code)
Type	10 character text (code)
Description	50 character text
Resource No.	20 character text (code)
Resource Name	50 character text
Run Time	Duration
Start Time	Time
End Time	Time
Monday	Boolean

Field names	Definitions
Tuesday	Boolean
Wednesday	Boolean
Thursday	Boolean
Friday	Boolean
Saturday	Boolean
Sunday	Boolean

In the preceding list, three of the fields are defined as Code fields, which are text fields that limit the alphanumeric characters to upper case values. Code fields are used throughout NAV for primary key values. Code fields are used to reference or be referenced by other tables (also known as foreign keys). The **No.** will be the unique identifier in our table. We will utilize a set of standard internal NAV functions to assign a user-defined **No. Series** range that will auto increment the value on table insertion and possibly allow for user entry (as long as it is unique in the table) based on a setup value. The **Resource No.** references the standard **Resource** table and the **Type** field will reference a custom table we will create to allow for flexible **Type** values.

We will need to design and define the reference properties at the field level in the **Table Designer** window, as well as compile them, before the validation will work. At this point, let's just get started with some field definitions and create the foundation for the **Radio Show** table.

Creating a simple table

To view the table designer, open the NAV 2013 Development Environment and the database in which we will be doing our development. In the **Object Designer** window, click on **Table** (in the left column of buttons) and click on **New** (in the bottom row of buttons). Enter the first field number as 10 (the default is 1), and increment each remaining field number by 10 (the default is 1). This will allow us to add additional fields in between existing fields later, when necessary.

 Once a table is referenced by other objects, or contains any data, the field numbers of previously-defined fields should not be changed.

In the **Description** field, we will put notes for the fields that will need properties set at a later time. The following screenshot shows our new table definition in the **Table Designer** window:

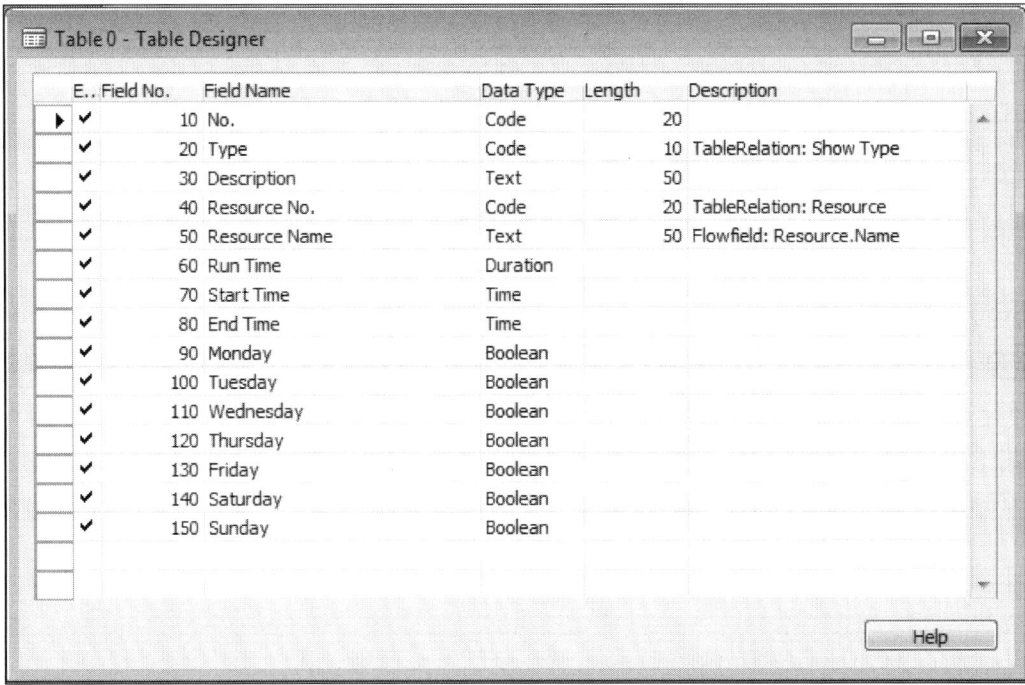

Now we can close the table definition. (Click on **File** | **Save** or *Ctrl + S* or press *ESC* or close the window. The first two options are the explicit methods of saving our work.) We will see a message reminding us to save our changes, as shown in the following screenshot:

Click on **Yes** to save the changes. We must now assign the object number (in this case use `50000`) and a unique name (it cannot duplicate the first 30 characters of another table object in the database). We will name our table `Radio Show` because that is the type of master record we will be storing in the table. The **Save As** window is shown in the following screenshot:

Note that the **Compiled** option is automatically checked, which is the default for NAV. Once we click on **OK** and the object is successfully compiled, it is immediately ready to be executed within the application. If the object we were working on was not ready to be compiled without error, we could unselect the **Compiled** option in the **Save As** window, as shown in the preceding screenshot.

Be careful, as uncompiled objects will not be considered by C/SIDE when changes are made to other objects. Until we have compiled an object, it is a work in progress, not an operable routine. There is a **Compiled** flag on every object that gives its compilation status. Even when we have compiled an object, we have not confirmed that all is well. We may have made changes that affect other objects which reference the modified object. As a matter of good work habit, we should recompile all objects before we end work for the day.

Pages

Pages provide views of data or processes designed for on-screen display (or exposure as web services) and also allow for user data entry into the system. Pages act as containers for action items (menu options).

There are several basic types of display/entry pages in NAV, they are given as follows:

- **List**
- **Card**
- **Document**
- **Journal/Worksheet**

There are also page parts (they look and program like a page, but aren't intended to stand alone) as well as user interfaces that appear as pages, but are not page objects. The latter user interfaces are generated by various dialog functions.

List pages

List pages display a simple list of any number of records in a single table. The **Customer List** page (with its associated FactBoxes) in the following screenshot shows a subset of the data for each customer displayed. List pages/forms often do not allow entry or editing of the data. Journal/Worksheet pages look like list pages, but are intended for data entry. Standard list pages are always displayed with the navigation pane on the left. The **Customer List** page is seen in the following screenshot:

Card pages

Card pages display one record at a time. These are generally used for the entry or display of individual table records. Examples of frequently accessed card pages include **Customer Card** for customer data, **Item Card** for inventory items, and **G/L Account Card** for General Ledger accounts.

Card pages often have FastTabs (one FastTab consisting of a group of controls with each tab focusing on a different set of related customer data). FastTabs can be expanded or collapsed dynamically, allowing the data visible at any time to be controlled by the user.

Card pages for master records display all the required data entry fields. Typically, they also display summary data about related activity so that the Card page can be used as the primary inquiry point for master records. The following screenshot is a sample of a standard **Customer Card**:

Document pages

Another page style within NAV consists of what looks like a Card page plus a List page. An example is the **Sales Order** page as shown in the following screenshot. In this example, the upper portion of the page is in Card page format with several tabs showing sales order data fields that have a single occurrence on the page (in other words, they do not occur in a repeating column). The lower portion of the Document page is in List page format (all fields are in repeating columns) showing the Sales Order line items.

Line items may include product to be shipped, special charges, comments, and other pertinent order details. The information to the right of the data entry is related data and computations (FactBoxes) that have been retrieved and formatted. At the top of the page is the information for the Ordering customer. The bottom right contains information for the item on the selected line. The following screenshot shows an example of the **Sales Order Document page**:

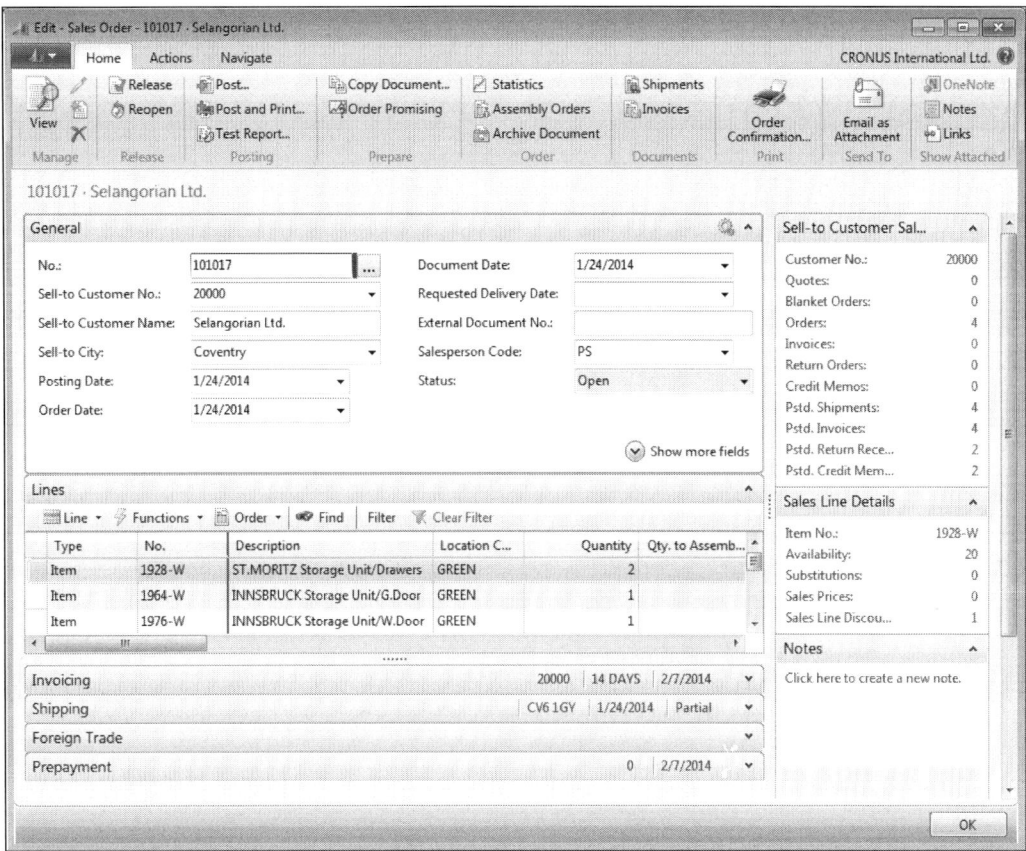

Journal/Worksheet pages

Journal and Worksheet pages look very much like List pages. They display a list of records in the body of the page. Many have a section at the bottom that shows details about the selected line and/or totals for the displayed data. These pages may also include a Filter pane and perhaps a FactBox. The biggest difference between Journal/ Worksheet pages and basic List pages is that Journal and Worksheet pages are designed to be used for data entry (though this may be a matter of personal or site preference). An example of the **Requisition Worksheet** page in **Purchasing** is shown in the following screenshot. The Req. Worksheet assists the user in determining and defining which purchases should be made. Refer the following screenshot:

Standard elements of pages

A page consists of page properties and triggers, controls, control properties, and triggers. Data controls generally are either labels displaying constant text or graphics, or containers that display data or other controls. Controls can also be buttons, action items, and page parts. While there are a few instances where we must include C/AL code within a page or page control triggers, it is good practice to minimize the amount of code embedded within pages. Any data-related C/AL code should be located in the table object rather than in the page object.

Creating a List page

Now we will create a List page for the table we created earlier. A List page is the initial page that is displayed when a user accesses any data table. The NAV Development Environment has wizards (object generation tools) to help create basic pages. Generally, we should expect to spend additional time in the Page Designer tool, after our wizard work, to make the layout ready to be presented to users.

Our first List page will be the basis for viewing our **Radio Show** master records. From the **Object Designer** window, click on **Page**, then click on **New**. The **New Page** screen will appear. Enter the name (`Radio Show`) or table object ID (`50000`) in the **Table** field. This is the table to which the page will be bound. We can add additional tables to the page object C/AL Global Variables after we close the wizard, as we are then working within the **Object Designer**. Choose the option **Create a page using a wizard:** , and select **List.** Click on **OK**, as shown in the following screenshot:

The next step in the wizard shows the fields available for the List page. We can add or remove any of the field columns using the >, <, >>, and << buttons. This is shown in the following screenshot:

Add all the fields using **>>** and click on **Next**, as shown in the following screenshot:

The next wizard step shows the available Subforms, System FactBoxes, and Charts that are available to add to our page. These can be seen in the following screenshot:

We can add these later in the **Page Designer** window as needed. Click on **Finish** to exit the **List Page Wizard** and enter the **Page Designer**, which is shown in the following screenshot:

Click on **Preview** to view the page with the default ribbon. Note that in the **Preview** mode we cannot insert, modify, or delete any data. The **Preview** page is not connected to the database data. We will need to compile the page and **Run** it to manipulate the data. The **Page Preview** window is shown in the following screenshot:

The availability of some capabilities and icons (such as **OneNote**) will depend on what software is installed on our development workstation. Close the preview of the **List** page and close the window or press *ESC* to save. Number the page 50000 and name the object Radio Show List, as shown in the following screenshot:

Creating a Card page

Next, let's create a **Card** page. The wizard process for a **Card** page is almost the same as for a **List** page, with an additional step. In **Object Designer**, with the **Page** option selected, click on **New** again. Enter the same table (`Radio Show`) and make sure the **Create a page using a wizard:** option is selected and that **Card** is highlighted, as shown in the following screenshot:

The next step in the wizard is specific to Card pages, which allows us to create FastTabs. These are the display tools that allow the user to expand or collapse window sections for ease of viewing. For our **Radio Show** we will divide our table fields into two **FastTab** sections as shown in the following screenshot. The **FastTabs** will be **General** (primary key, description, resource information, and duration) and **Schedule** (days of the week), as shown in the following screenshot:

After defining the FastTab names, we must assign the data fields to the tabs on which they are to appear. We will select the tabs based on the FastTab names we assigned. We can select the fields from the **Available Fields** list and assign the order as we did in **List Page Wizard**. Click on the **Next>** button to proceed.

For the **General** FastTab, select the following fields: **No.**, **Type**, **Description**, **Resource No.**, **Resource Name**, **Run Time**, **Start Time**, and **End Time**, as shown in the following screenshot:

Click on the **Schedule** tab to populate the **Schedule** FastTab. Select **Monday**, **Tuesday**, **Wednesday**, **Thursday**, **Friday**, **Saturday**, and **Sunday**, as shown in the following screenshot:

The last **Card Page Wizard** step is to add the available Subpages, System FactBoxes, and Charts. Again, if we decide later we want any of those, we will add them from within the **Page Designer** window. The last step is shown in the following screenshot:

Click on **Finish** to view the generated code in the **Page Designer** dialog. We will have the following screen:

Click on **Preview** to show a view-only display of the card page, which will display as follows:

Exit out of the **Preview** and **Page Designer** windows and save the page as **ID** 50001, and **Name** as Radio Show Card, as shown in the following screenshot:

Later on we can add an action to the **List** page which will link to the **Card** page for to insert and edit **Radio Show** records. We will also add the **List** page to the **Role Center** page for our radio station user.

Creating some sample data

Even though we haven't added all the bells and whistles to our **Radio Show** table and pages, we can still use them to enter sample data. The **Radio Show** list page will be the easiest to use for this.

In **Object Designer**, with pages selected, highlight page **50000**, **Radio Show** list, and click on **Run**. Then click the **New** icon on the ribbon. An empty line will open up where we can enter our sample data. Of course, since our table is very basic at this point, without any validation functionality, table references, function calls, and so on, we will need to be creative and enter all the individual data fields accurately and completely on our own. Examples are shown in the following screenshot:

Enter the data shown in the following table. Later on, after we add more capabilities to our table and pages, some of the fields will be either automatically entered or available on a lookup basis. But for now, simply key in each field value. If the data that we key in now conflicts with the validations we create later (such as data in referenced tables), we may need to delete this test data and enter new test data later. Consider this data temporary so that we can see what the page looks like with the data. The data is given in the following table:

No.	Type	Description	Resource No.	Resource Name	Run Time
RS00001	TALK	Marks Morning Talk Show	MARK	Mark Hanson	4 hours
RS00002	MUSIC	Local Show with Dave P	DAVE P	Dave Poulaski	2 hours
RS00003	CALL-IN	What's Up Metro City?	LINDA	Linda Martin	2 hours
RS00004	CALL-IN	I'm Listening Metro City	MATT S	Matt Saunders	2 hours
RS00005	MUSIC	Working It Out Afternoon Show	MATTR	Matt Richards	3 hours
RS00006	MUSIC	World News	PHIL	Phil Petersen	3 hours

Creating a List Report

Open the **Object Designer**, select **Report** and click on **New**. The **Report Dataset Designer** is empty when it displays, so we need to add the first **Data Source** (table) to the first blank row. Type 50000 or Radio Show into the **Data Source** column, as shown in the following screenshot:

To add multiple data fields from the table we can use the **Field Menu** option, which can be accessed via the icon on the toolbar or the **View | Field Menu**. The **Field Menu** option will show a list of all the fields in the **Radio Show** table. The toolbar is shown in the following screenshot:

Highlight the first six fields in the **Field Menu** dialog. Then click on the next blank line in **Report Dataset Designer**, as shown in the following screenshot:

A confirmation box will appear asking if we want to add the fields selected. Click on **Yes**, highlighted in the following screenshot:

The fields will appear in the **Report Dataset Designer** dialog without needing to type them in manually, as shown in the following screenshot:

Now we need to proceed to the report layout tool which is part of Visual Studio 2010 (or the free Visual Web Developer 2010 Express). Click on **View | Layout**, as shown in the following screenshot:

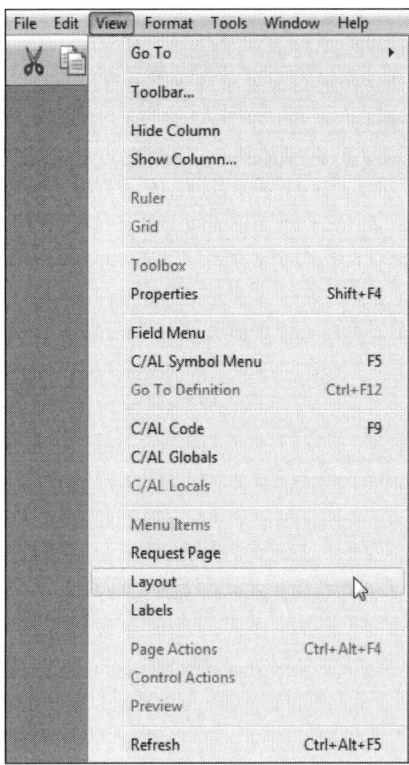

Visual Studio 2010 will open with a blank design surface and no dataset controls visible. Unlike the **Page Designer**, there is no report wizard to help with the layout of a new report. All the report layout design work must start from scratch with the blank design surface. The report design surface is shown in the following screenshot:

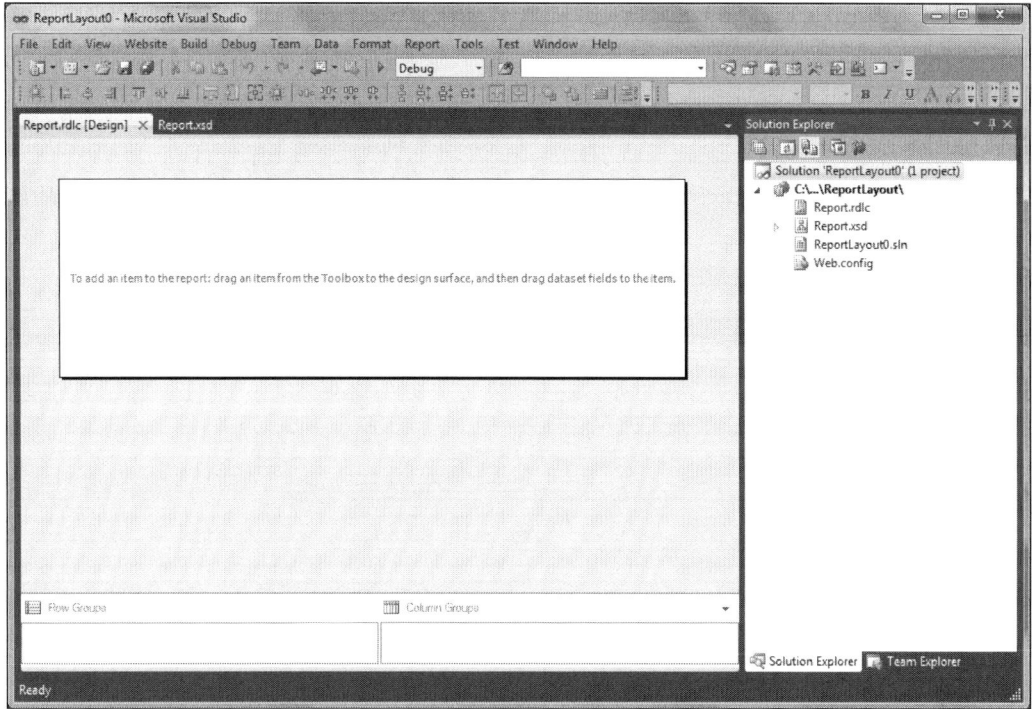

To show the dataset available from NAV, click on **View** and select **Report Data** (the last item on the list), as shown in the following screenshot:

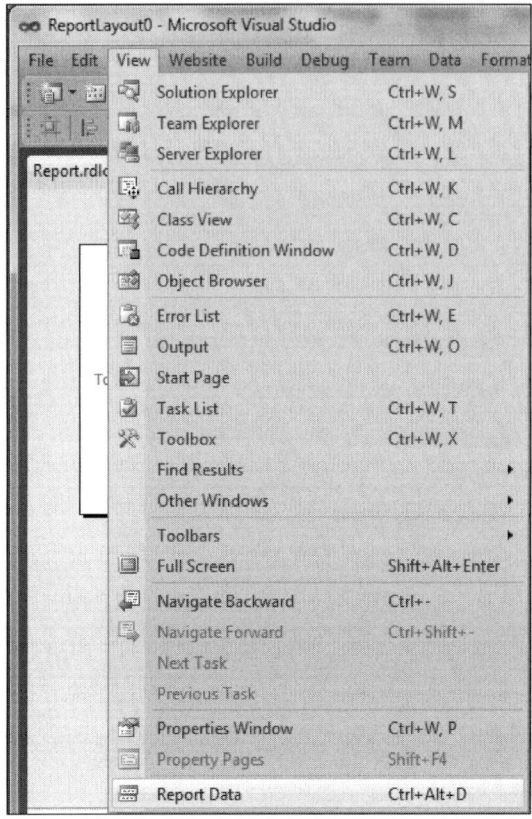

A new **Report Data** pane will show on the left of the Visual Studio layout window, as seen in the following screenshot:

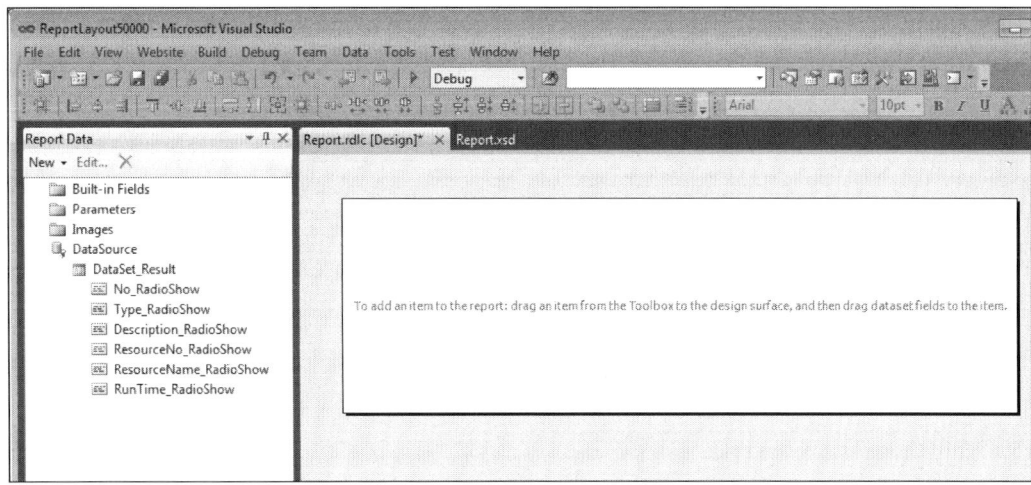

To create our simple list we will insert a simple table object (a data region with fixed number of columns but variable number of rows) to the design surface. Right-click anywhere on the design surface and expand the **Insert** sub-menu to view the tools available on the report. Click on the **Table** tool object, then we can use drag-and-drop to bring controls from the toolbox to the design surface. These steps are shown in the following screenshot:

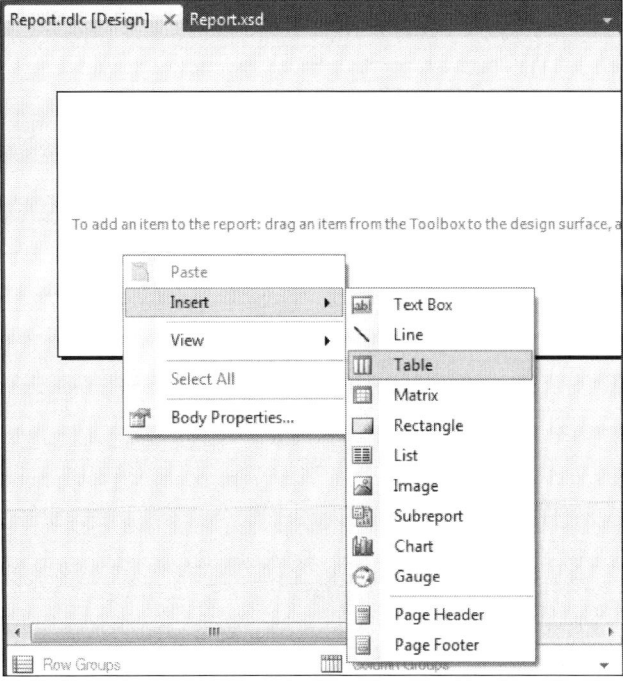

The table layout object defaults to three columns with a **Header** row (repeated once) and a **Data** row (repeated for each row of data retrieved from NAV). This is shown in the following screenshot:

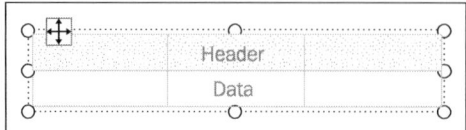

Drag-and-drop each of the six columns into the **Table** object. To add additional columns, right-click on the table object header and select **Add Columns** (we could also drag-and-drop a field from the dataset to the table). The caption with the basic format of *Field Name Table Name* will default into the header row (for example, the field name Type followed by the table name Radio Show), as shown in the following screenshot:

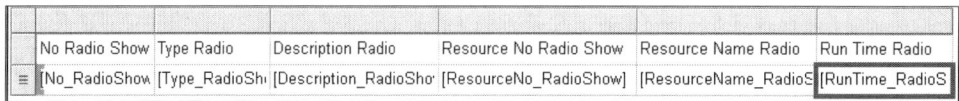

Let's do a little clean-up in the header row by making the captions look as they do in standard NAV reports by manually typing in the field names as headings, as shown in the following screenshot. (Later on, we will learn that this is not the optimum method and these headings should be defined in the C/SIDE RD before we get to the VS RD.)

We will save our work by clicking on **File | Save All** (or *Ctrl + Shift + S*) and then exit from Visual Studio (**File | Exit** or *Alt + F4*). Next, we will see the Save changes? to the RDLC (client report definition data) confirmation box. Click on **Yes**, as shown in the following screenshot:

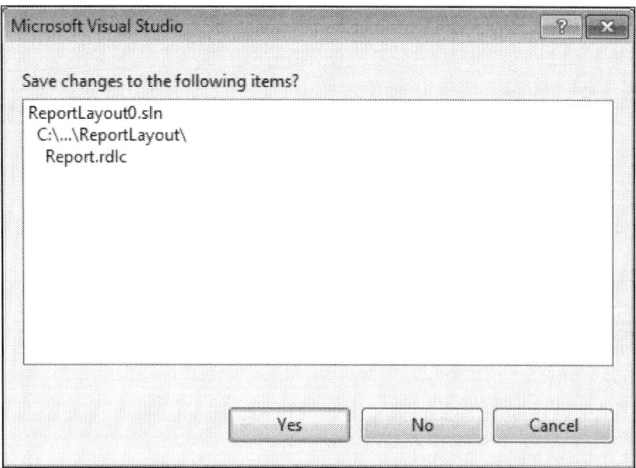

Back in NAV **Object Designer**, exit out of the report or click on **File | Save**, and we will need to respond to two confirmation boxes. The first asks if we want to save the report layout from Visual Studio. Click on **Yes**, as shown in the following screenshot:

The second confirmation appears when we change focus to the Report Designer. It allows us to load the RDLC report layout XML into the NAV database report object. Enter 50000 for the **ID**, and name the report Radio Show List. Click **OK** to save it, as shown in the following screenshot:

To view the report, make sure the new report object is selected, then click on **Run** in the **Object Designer** dialog, as shown in the following screenshot:

An instance of **RTC (Role Tailored Client)** will open with the Report Request Page showing. This is where the user can set filters, choose a sort sequence and choose print options. For our example, this page is shown in the following screenshot:

Click on **Preview** to display the report onscreen. The report will show our simple table layout with the fixed definition column captions showing exactly as we typed them. This is seen in the following screenshot:

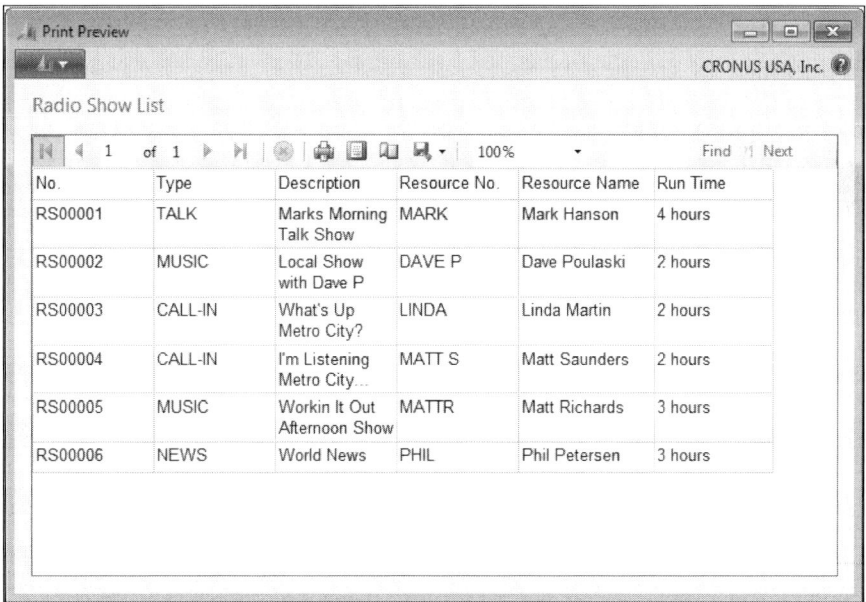

Much more to come

All we've done so far is scratch the surface. But if you're following along on your own system, especially if you've done a little experimenting along the way, you have a pretty good overview of the development process for NAV 2013.

Other NAV object types

We'll finish up our introductory review of NAV's object types.

Codeunits

A codeunit is a container for *chunks* of C/AL code to be called from other objects. These chunks of code are called *functions*. Functions can be called from any of the other NAV object types that can contain C/AL code. Codeunits can also be exposed (published) as web services. This allows the functions within a published codeunit to be invoked by external routines.

Codeunits are suited structurally to contain only functions. Even though functions could be placed in other object types, the other object types have superstructures that relate to their designed primary use as pages, reports, and so on.

Codeunits act only as a container for C/AL-coded functions. They have no auxiliary functions, no method of user interaction, and no pre-defined processing. If we are creating one or two functions that are closely related to the primary activity of a particular report, but these functions are needed from both within and outside of the report, then, by all means, include the functions in the report. Otherwise, use a Codeunit.

There are several codeunits delivered as part of the standard NAV product which are really function libraries. These codeunits consist totally of utility routines, generally organized on some functional basis (for example, associated with Dimensions or with some aspect of Manufacturing or some aspect of Warehouse management). Many of these can be found by filtering the Codeunit Names on the strings "Management" and "Mgt" (the same could be said for some of the tables with the string "Buffer" in their name). Some developers create their own libraries of favorite special functions and include such a *function library* codeunit in systems on which they work.

If a Codeunit is structured very simply, and can operate in a stand-alone mode, it is feasible to test it in the same way one would test a Report or a Page. Highlight the Codeunit and click on the **Run** button. The Codeunit will run for a single cycle. However, most codeunits are more complex and must be tested by a calling routine.

Queries

Queries are objects whose purpose is to very efficiently create extracted sets of data from the NAV database. NAV 2013 Queries translate directly into T-SQL query statements and run on the server side rather than on the service tier. A Query can extract data from a single table or multiple tables. In the process of extracting data, a Query can do different types of Joins (Inner Join, Outer Join, Cross Join), can filter, can calculate FlowFields (special NAV calculations which are discussed in detail in *Chapter 3, Data Types and Fields*), can sort, and can create sums and averages. Queries obey the NAV data structure business logic.

The output of a Query can be a CSV file (useful for Excel charts), an XML file (for charts or external applications) or an OData file (for a web service). Queries can be published for web service access similarly to Pages and Codeunits. Query results can also be viewed by Pages and Cues, but are especially powerful when output to charts.

MenuSuites

MenuSuites are the objects that are displayed in the Navigation Pane menus. They differ considerably from the other object types we have discussed earlier because they not only have a completely different structure, but they are also maintained differently. MenuSuite entries do not contain triggers. The only customization that can be done with MenuSuites is to add, delete, or edit menu entries which are made up of a small set of properties.

In the Role Tailored Client, the data in the MenuSuites object is presented in the Departments page.

XMLports

XMLports are a tool for importing and exporting data. XMLports handle both XML-structured data and other external text data formats. **XML** stands for **eXtensible Markup Language** and has become the de facto standard for exchanging data between dissimilar systems. For example, XMLports could be used to communicate between our NAV ERP system and our accounting firm's financial analysis and tax preparation system.

XML is designed to be extensible, which means that we can create or extend the definition as long as we communicate the revised XML format to our correspondents. There is a standard set of syntax rules to which XML formats must conform. XML is becoming more and more important because most new software uses XML. For example, the new versions of Microsoft Office are quite XML friendly. All web services communications are in the form of an exchange of XML-structured data.

The non-XML text data files handled by XMLports fall into two categories. One is known as comma separated value or comma delimited files (usually having a .csv file extension). Of course, the delimiters don't actually need to be commas. The other category is fixed format, in which the relative position and length of each field is pre-defined.

XMLports can contain C/AL logic for any type of appropriate data manipulation, either when importing or exporting. Functions such as editing, validating, combining, filtering, and so on, can be applied to the data as it passes through an XMLport.

Backups and documentation

As with any system where we can do development work, careful attention to documentation and backing up our work is very important. C/SIDE provides a variety of techniques for handling each of these tasks.

When we are working within the Object Designer, we can back up individual objects of any type or groups of objects by exporting them. These exported object files can be imported in total, selectively in groups, or individually, to recover the original version of one or more objects.

When objects are exported to text files, we can use a standard text editor to read or even change them. For example, if we wanted to change all of the instances of the field name Customer to Patient, we might export all of the objects to text and execute a mass *Find and Replace*. Making such code changes in a text copy of an object is subject to a high probability of error, as we won't have any of the many safety features of the C/SIDE environment to limit what we can do.

Internal documentation (that is, inside C/SIDE) of object changes can be done in three areas. First is the Object Version List, a field attached to every object, visible in the **Object Designer** screen. Whenever a change is made in an object, a notation should be added to the Version List.

The second area for documentation is the **Documentation** trigger that appears in every object type except **MenuSuites**. The **Documentation** trigger is at the top of the object and is the recommended location for noting a relatively complete description of any changes that have been made to the object. Such descriptions should include a brief description of the purpose of the change as well as technical information.

The third area we can place documentation is inline with modified C/AL code. Individual comment lines can be created by starting the line with double forward slashes //. Whole sections of comments (or commented out code) can be created by starting and ending the section with a pair of curly braces {   }. Depending on the type of object, and the nature of the specific changes, we should generally annotate each change inline everywhere it affects the code, so all the changes can be easily identified by the next developer looking at this object.

In short, everything that we learned earlier about good documentation practices applies when doing development in NAV C/SIDE. This holds true whether the development is new work or a modification of existing logic.

Summary

In this chapter, we covered some basic definitions of terms related to NAV and C/SIDE. We followed with the introduction of seven types of NAV objects (Tables, Pages, Reports, Codeunits, Queries, MenuSuites, and XMLports). We also introduced Page and Report Creation through review and hands-on use beginning with a NAV application for the WTDU Radio Show programming management. Finally, we looked briefly at the tools that we can use to integrate with external entities, and we discussed how different types of backups and documentation are handled in C/SIDE. Now that we have covered these basics in general terms, let's dive into the detail of the primary object types.

In the next chapter, we will focus on Tables, the foundation of an NAV system.

Review questions

1. An ERP system such as NAV 2013 includes a number of functional areas. Which of the following are part of NAV 2013? Choose four.

    a. Order Processing

    b. Human Resources

    c. Computer Aided Design (CAD)

    d. Inventory Control

    e. General Accounting

2. New functionality in NAV 2013 includes (choose three):

    a. Assembly Management

    b. Filtering

    c. Copy and Paste with Excel

    d. Enhanced charting

    e. SQL Server database

3. What are the seven NAV 2013 object types?

4. NAV 2013 includes support for publishing objects as Web Services.
   True or False?

5. NAV 2013 development is done in the C/SIDE IDE and Visual Studio 2010.
   True or False?

6. The C/AL programming language is similar to which other language?
   Choose one.

    a. COBOL

    b. Java

    c. PHP

    d. Pascal

7. The Work Date can only be changed by the System Administrator.
   True or False?

8. All NAV objects except XMLports can contain C/AL code. True or False?

9. Match the following table types and descriptions for NAV.

    a. Journals   1) Audit trail

    b. Ledgers   2) Validation process

    c. Register   3) Invoice

    d. Document   4) Transaction entries

    e. Posting   5) History

10. Which of the following describe NAV 2013? Choose two.
    a. Object based
    b. C# IDE
    c. Object oriented
    d. Customizable
    e. Includes a Storefront module

11. Field number increments in a Table design default to what? Choose one.
    a. 10
    b. 1
    c. 64
    d. 100
    e. 10000

12. The home page for a NAV 2013 User is called what? Choose one.
    a. Role Home
    b. Home Center
    c. Main Page
    d. Role Center

13. A List Page, not a Card Page, is the initial page that a user sees when the users access any data table. True or False?

14. Page Previews from the Development Environment can be used for data entry and maintenance. True or False?

15. Visual Studio 2010 is used in NAV 2013 for what work? Choose one.
    a. Report data definition
    b. Report layout
    c. Role Center design
    d. Query processing

16. Codeunits are the only NAV 2013 objects that can contain functions. True or False?

17. Query output can be used as a Data Item for Reports. True or False?

18. What object number range is available for assignment to customer-specific objects? Choose two.

    a. 20 – 500

    b. 50000 – 60000

    c. 150000 – 200000

    d. 50000 – 99999

    e. 10000 – 100000

19. XMLports can only process XML formatted data. True or False?

20. NAV 2013 Reports are often generated automatically through the use of a wizard. True or False?

2
Tables

When done well, software is invisible.   *– Bjarne Stroustrup*
Design and programming are human activities; forget that and all is lost.
       – Bjarne Stroustrup

The foundation of any system is the data structure definition. In NAV, the building blocks of this foundation are the tables and the individual data fields that the tables contain. Once the overall analysis and process definition has been completed, any new design work must begin with the data structure. For NAV, that means the tables and their contents.

A NAV table includes much more than just the data fields and keys. A NAV table definition also includes data validation rules, processing rules, business rules, and logic to ensure referential integrity. The rules are in the form of properties and C/AL code.

In this chapter, we will learn about the structure and creation of tables. Details about Fields, the components of tables, will be covered in the following chapter. Our topics in this chapter include:

- An overview of tables, including Properties, Triggers, Keys, SumIndexFields, and Field Groups
- Enhancing our sample application by creating and modifying tables
- Types of tables, that is, Fully Modifiable, Content Modifiable, and Read-Only tables

An overview of tables

There is a distinction between the table (data definition and data container) and the data (the contents of a table). The **table definition** describes the data structure, validation rules, storage, and retrieval of the data which is stored in the table (container). The definition is defined by the design and can only be changed by a developer. The data is the variable content that originates from the user activities. The place where we can see the data explicitly referenced independently of the table as a definition of structure is in the **Permissions** setup data. In the following screenshot, the data is formally referred to as **Table Data**:

The table is not the data, it is the definition of data contained in the table. Even so, we commonly refer to both the data and the table as if they were one and the same. That is what we will do in this book.

All permanent data must be stored in a table. All tables are defined by the developer working in the development environment. As much as possible, critical system design components should be embedded in the tables. Each table should include the code that controls what happens when new records are added, changed, or deleted, as well as how data is validated when added or changed. The table object should include the functions commonly used to manipulate the table and its data, whether for database maintenance or in support of business logic.

The table designer in C/SIDE provides the capabilities to define the table design, the definition of the data structure. We will explore these capabilities through examples and analysis of the structure of table objects. We find that the approach of embedding control and business logic within the table object has a number of advantages:

- Clarity of design
- Centralization of rules for data constraints
- More efficient development of logic
- Increased ease of debugging
- Easier upgrading

Components of a table

A table is made up of Fields, Properties, Triggers (some of which may contain C/AL code), and Keys. Fields also have Properties and Triggers; Keys also have properties.

A table definition which takes full advantage of these capabilities reduces the effort required to construct the other parts of the application. A good table design can significantly enhance the application's processing speed, efficiency, and flexibility.

A table can have:

- Up to 500 fields
- A defined record size of up to 8,000 bytes (with each field sized at its maximum)
- Up to 40 different keys

Naming a table

There are standardized naming conventions defined for NAV which we should follow. Names for tables and other objects should be as descriptive as possible, while keeping to a reasonable length. This helps to make our work more self-documenting.

Table names should always be singular. The table containing customers should not be named `Customers`, but `Customer`. The table we created for the WDTU Radio Station NAV enhancement was named `Radio Show`, even though it will contain data for all of WDTU's radio shows.

In general, we should always name a table so it is easy to identify the relationship between the table and the data it contains. For example, two tables containing the transactions on which a document page is based should normally be referred to as a **Header** table (for the main portion of the page) and a **Line** table (for the line detail portion of the page). As an example, the tables underlying a Sales Order page are the Sales Header and the Sales Line tables. The Sales Header table contains all the data that occurs only once for a sales order, while the Sales Line table contains all the lines for the order.

> Additional information on naming a table can be found in the old, but still useful, *Terminology Handbook for C/SIDE and C/AL Programming Guide*, which can be found on the Microsoft MSDN site (`http://social.msdn.microsoft.com/Search/ en-US?query=Terminology%20Handbook%20for%20 C%2FSIDE&ac=8` and `http://social.msdn.microsoft. com/Search/en-US?query=C%2FAL%20Programming%20 Guide%20&ac=8`). Of course, you should always refer to the **Developer and IT Pro Help** that is part of NAV and is accessible from the Development Environment.

Table numbering

There are no hard and fast rules for table numbering, except that we must only use the table object numbers that you are licensed to use. If all we have are the rights to the **Table Designer**, we are generally allowed to create tables numbered from 50000 to 50009 (unless your license was defined differently than the typical one). If we need more table objects, we can purchase licensing for table objects numbered up to 99999. **Independent Software Vendors** (**ISVs**) can purchase access to tables in other number ranges.

When creating several related tables, ideally we should assign them related numbers in sequential order. It requires considerable effort to renumber tables containing data, so we let common sense be our guide to assigning table numbers.

Table properties

The first step in studying the internal construction of a table is to open it in Design mode. This is done as follows:

1. Open the Development Environment.
2. Click on the **Table** button in the left-hand side column of buttons.
3. Highlight the table you want to work on (in this case, **Table 18 Customer**).
4. Click on the **Design** button at the bottom right of the screen.

At this point we have the **Customer** table open in the **Table Designer** in **Design** mode. In *Chapter 1, An Introduction to NAV 2013*, we reviewed the function of the icons across the top of the **Table Designer**, but they are labeled in the following screenshot as a memory aid:

We can access the properties of a table while viewing the table in the **Design** mode. Place the cursor on an empty field line (the line below all the fields as shown in the preceding screenshot), and click on the **Properties** icon or press *Shift + F4* or go to **View | Properties**. If we access properties while focus is on a field line, we will see the properties of that field.

This will take us to the **Table - Properties** display. The following screenshot is the **Table - Properties** display for the **Customer** table in the demonstration company database, **Cronus**, which is included in each distribution of NAV.

The contents of the screenshot are as follows:

- **ID**: This is the object number of the table.
- **Name**: This is used for internal identification of the table object and acts as the default caption when data from this table is displayed.
- **Caption**: This contains the caption defined for the currently selected language. The default language for NAV is US English (ENU).
- **CaptionML**: This defines the **MultiLanguage** caption for the table. For an extended discussion on the language capabilities of NAV, refer to the *MultiLanguage Functionality* section in the online **Developer and IT Pro Help**.
- **Description**: This property is for optional documentation usage.

- **DataPerCompany**: This lets us define whether or not the data in this table is segregated by company (the default), or whether it is common (shared) across all of the companies in the database. The generated names of tables within SQL Server (not within NAV) are affected by this choice.

- **Permissions**: This allows us to grant users of this table different levels of access (**r**=read, **i**=insert, **m**=modify, **d**=delete) to the table data in other table objects.

- **LookupPageID**: This allows us to define what page is the default for looking up data in this table

- **DrillDownPageID**: This allows us to define what page is the default for drilling down into the supporting detail for data that is summarized in this table.

- **DataCaptionFields**: This allows us to define specific fields whose contents will be displayed as part of the caption. For the **Customer** table, the **No.** and the **Name** fields will be displayed in the title bar at the top of a page showing a customer record.

- **PasteIsValid**: This determines if the users are allowed to paste data into the table.

- **LinkedObject**: This lets us link the table to a SQL Server object. This feature allows the connection, for data access or maintenance, to a non-NAV system or an independent NAV system. For example, a linked object could be an independently hosted and maintained special purpose database, and thus offload that processing from the main NAV system. When this property is set to Yes, the **LinkedInTransaction** property becomes available. The **LinkedInTransaction** property should be set to No for any linkage to a SQL Server object outside the current database. The object being linked must have a SQL Server table definition that is compatible with the Microsoft Dynamics NAV table definition.

As a developer, it is likely that you will regularly deal with the **ID**, **Name**, **LookupPageID**, **DrillDownPageID** properties, **Caption**, **CaptionML** (outside the United States), **DataCaption**, and **Permissions** properties. We rarely deal with the others.

Table triggers

To display the triggers with the table open in the **Table Designer**, click on the **C/AL Code** icon or *F9* or go to **View | C/AL Code**. The first (top) table trigger is the **Documentation** trigger. This trigger is somewhat misleadingly named as a "trigger" as it only serves as the location for needed documentation. No C/AL code in a **Documentation** trigger is executed. There are no syntax or format rules here, but you should follow a standard format of some type.

Every change to an object should be briefly documented in the **Documentation** trigger. The use of a standard format for such entries makes it easier to create them as well as to understand them two years later. Here is an example:

```
CDS.02 - 2014-03-16  Change to track when new customer added
  - Added field 50012 "Start Date"
```

The **Documentation** trigger has the same appearance as the four other triggers in a table definition, shown in the following screenshot, each of which can contain C/AL code:

The code contained in a trigger is executed prior to the event represented by the trigger. In other words, the code in the **OnInsert()** trigger is executed before the record is inserted into the table. This allows the developer a final opportunity to perform validations and to enforce data consistency such as referential integrity. We can even abort the intended action if data inconsistencies or conflicts are found.

These triggers are automatically invoked when record processing occurs as the result of user action. But when table data changes occur as the result of C/AL code instruction or data imports, the developer's code determines whether or not the triggers are invoked and the code within is executed.

- **OnInsert()**: This is executed when a new record is to be inserted in the table through the User Interface. (In general, new records are added when the last field of the primary key is completed and focus leaves that field. See the **DelayedInsert** property in *Chapter 4, Pages – the User's Interactive Interface*, for an exception).

- **OnModify()**: This is executed when a record is rewritten after the contents of any field other than a primary key field has been changed. The change is determined by comparing xRec (the image of the record prior to being changed) to Rec (the current record copy). During our development work, if we need to see what the "before" value of a record or field is, we can reference the contents of xRec and compare that to the equivalent portion of Rec. These variables (Rec and xRec) are system-defined variables.

- **OnDelete()**: This is executed before a record is to be deleted from the table.

- **OnRename()**: This is executed when some portion of the primary key of the record is about to be changed. Changing any part of the primary key is a rename action. This maintains a level of referential integrity. Unlike some systems, NAV allows the primary key of any master record to be changed and automatically maintains all the affected references in other records.

There is an inconsistency in the handling of data integrity by NAV. On one hand, the **OnRename()** trigger automatically maintains one level of referential integrity when any part of the primary key is changed (that is, the record is renamed). However, if we delete a record, NAV doesn't do anything to maintain referential integrity. For example, child records could be orphaned by a deletion, left without any parent record. Or if there are references in other records back to the deleted record, they are left with no target. As developers, we are responsible for ensuring this aspect of referential integrity on our own.

When we write C/AL code in one object that updates data in another (table) object, we can control whether or not the applicable table update trigger fires (executes). For example, if we were adding a record to our **Radio Show** table and used the following C/AL code, the **OnInsert()** trigger would fire.

```
"Radio Show".INSERT(TRUE);
```

However, if we use either of the following C/AL code options instead, the **OnInsert()** trigger would not fire and none of the attendant logic would be executed:

```
"Radio Show".INSERT(FALSE);
```
or

```
"Radio Show".INSERT;
```

It's always a good habit to write code explicitly so there is no doubt what the intended action is.

The default logic such as enforcing primary key uniqueness will happen whether or not the **OnInsert()** trigger is fired.

Keys

Table keys are used to identify records, and to speed up filtering and sorting. Having too few keys may result in painfully slow inquiries and reports. However, each key incurs a processing cost, because the index containing the key must be updated every time information in a key field changes. Key cost is measured primarily in terms of increased index maintenance processing. There is also additional cost in terms of disk storage space (usually not costly) and additional backup/recovery time (sometimes very important).

When a system is optimized for processing speed, it is critical to analyze the SQL Server indexes that are active because that is where the updating and retrieval time are determined. The determination of the proper number and design of keys and indices for a table requires a thorough understanding of the types and frequencies of inquiries, reports, and other processing for that table.

Every NAV table must have at least one key—the primary key. The primary key is always the first key in the key list. By default, the primary key is made up of the first field defined in the table. In many of the reference tables, there is only one field in the primary key and the only key is the primary key. An example is the **Payment Terms** table in the following screenshot:

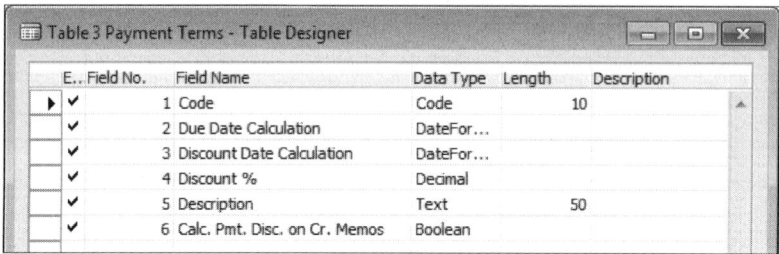

To see the **Keys** window, click on **View | Keys**.

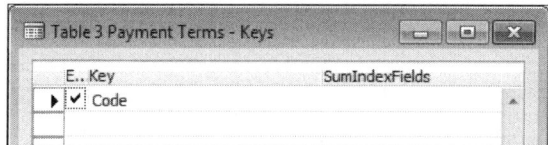

The primary key must have a unique value in each table record. We can change the primary key to be any field, or combination of fields up to 16 fields, but the uniqueness requirement must be met. It will automatically be enforced by NAV, because NAV will not allow us to add a record in a table with a duplicate primary key.

When we examine the primary keys in the supplied tables, we see that many of them consist only of or terminate in a **Line No.**, an **Entry No.**, or another data field whose contents serve to make the key unique. For example, the **Res. Ledger Entry** table in the following screenshot uses just the **Entry No.** as the primary Key. It is a NAV standard that **Entry No.** fields contain a value that is unique for each record.

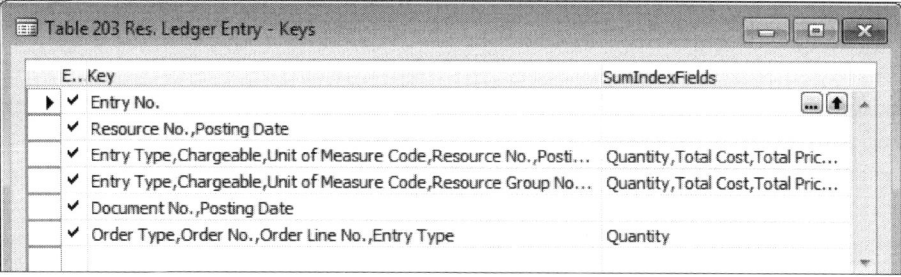

The primary key of the **Sales Line** table shown in the following screenshot is made up of several fields, with the **Line No.** field of each record as the terminating primary key field. In NAV, the **Line No.** fields are assigned a unique number within the associated document. The **Line No.** fields combined with the preceding fields in the primary key (usually including fields such as **Document Type** and **Document No.** which relate to the parent Header record) makes each primary key entry unique. The logic supporting the assignment of **Line No.** values is done within explicit C/AL code. It is not an automatic feature.

All keys except the primary key are secondary keys. There are no required uniqueness constraints on secondary keys. There is no requirement to have any secondary keys. If we want a secondary key not to have duplicate values, our C/AL code must check for duplication before completing the new entry.

The maximum number of fields that can be used in any one key is 16 with a maximum total length of 900 bytes. At the same time, the total number of different fields that can be used in all of the keys combined cannot exceed 16. If the primary key includes three fields (as in the preceding screenshot), then the secondary keys can utilize up to 13 other fields (16 minus 3) in various combinations, plus any or all of the fields in the primary key. If the primary key has 16 fields, then the secondary keys can only consist of different groupings and sequences of those 16 fields. Behind the scenes, each secondary key has the primary key appended to the backend.

Other significant key attributes include key groups and SQL Server-specific properties.

- **Key Groups** allow sets of keys to be disabled or enabled either manually or programmatically. Disabled keys are not automatically updated until they are enabled again. The manual disable/enable is done from the **Key Groups** button on the **Tables** screen accessed from the **File | Database | Information** option. Programmatic disable/enable is done using the `KeyGroupDisable`, `KeyGroupEnable`, and `KeyGroupEnabled` functions. A Key Group can be just one key. Key Groups are useful for managing keys that are only needed infrequently. For example, if a group of keys used only for monthly reports is disabled during the month, no index maintenance processing will be done day to day. At the end of month, the Key Group can be enabled and the necessary index recreation processing be done during off hours. Once the monthly reports are done, the Key Group can again be disabled.

- A number of SQL Server-specific key-related parameters have been added to NAV. These key properties can be accessed by highlighting a key in the **Keys** form, then clicking on the **Properties** icon or pressing *Shift + F4*. We can also have those properties display in the **Keys** screen by accessing **View | Show Column** and selecting the columns we want displayed. The following screenshot shows both the **Show Column** choice form and the resulting **Keys** form with all the available columns displayed:

SumIndexFields

Since the beginning of NAV (Navision), one of its unique capabilities has been the SIFT feature (**SIFT** stands for **SumIndexField Technology**). These fields serve as the basis for FlowFields (automatically accumulating totals) and are unique to NAV. This feature allows NAV to provide almost instantaneous responses to user inquiries for summed data, calculated on-the-fly at runtime, related to the SumIndexFields. The cost is primarily that of the time required to maintain the SIFT indices when a table is updated.

NAV 2013 maintains SIFT totals using **SQL Server Indexed Views**. An indexed view is a view that has been preprocessed and stored. NAV 2013 creates one indexed view for each enabled SIFT key. SIFT keys are enabled and disabled through the **MaintainSIFTIndex** property. SQL Server maintains the contents of the view when any changes are made to the base table unless the **MaintainSIFTIndex** property is set to No.

SumIndexFields are accumulated sums of individual fields (columns) in tables. When the totals are pre-calculated, they are easy to use and provide very high-speed access to inquiries. If users need to know the total of the Amount values in a ledger table, the `Amount` field can be attached as a SumIndexField to the appropriate keys. In another table such as `Customer`, FlowFields can be defined as display fields take the advantage of the SumIndexFields. This will give users very rapid response for calculating a total Balance amount inquiry based on detailed ledger amounts based to those keys. We will discuss the various data field types and FlowFields in more detail in a later chapter.

In a typical ERP system, tens of thousands, millions, or even hundreds of millions of records might have to be processed to give such results, taking considerable time. In NAV, only a few records need to be accessed to provide the requested results. The processing is fast and the programming is greatly simplified.

SQL Server SIFT values are maintained through the use of SQL Indexed Views. By use of the key property **MaintainSIFTIndex**, we can control whether or not the SIFT index is maintained dynamically (faster response) or only created when needed (less ongoing system performance load). The C/AL code is the same whether the SIFT is maintained dynamically or not.

Too many keys or SIFT fields can negatively affect system performance for two reasons. The first, which we already discussed, is the index maintenance processing load. The second is the table locking interference that can occur when multiple threads are requesting update access to a set of records that update SIFT values.

Having unnecessary date fields in a SIFT key creates many extra entries, affecting performance. Integer fields usually create an especially large number of unique SIFT index values and Option fields create a relatively small number of index values. Conversely, the lack of necessary keys or SIFT definitions can also cause performance problems.

The best design for a SIFT index has the fields which will be used most frequently in queries positioned on the left-hand side of the index in order of descending frequency of use. In a nutshell, you should be careful in your design of keys and SIFT fields. While a system is in production, applicable SQL Server statistics should be monitored regularly and appropriate maintenance actions taken.

Field Groups

When a user begins to enter a data element in a field where the choices are constrained to existing data (for example an Item No., a Salesperson Code, a Unit of Measure code, a Customer No., and so on), good design dictates that the system will help the user by displaying the universe of acceptable choices. Put simply, a lookup list of choices will be displayed.

In the Role Tailored Client, the lookup display (a drop-down control) is generated dynamically when its display is requested by the user's effort to enter data in a field that references a table through the **TableRelation** property (which will be discussed in more detail in the next chapter). The format of the drop-down is a basic list. The fields that are included in that list and their left-to-right display sequence are either defined by default, or by an entry in the **Field Groups** table.

The Field Groups table is part of the NAV table definition much like the Keys table is. In fact, the Field Groups table is accessed very similar to the Keys, via **View** | **Field Groups** as shown in the following screenshot:

If we look at the Field Groups for **Table 27 - Item**, we see the drop-down information defined in a Field Group, which must be named DropDown (without the hyphen):

The drop-down display created by this particular Field Group is shown in the following screenshot on the Sales Order page containing fields such as **No.** and **Description** in the same sequence as in the Field Group definition:

If no Field Group is defined for a table, the system defaults to using the Primary Key plus the **Description** field.

Since Field Groups can be modified, they provide another opportunity for tailoring the user interface. As you can see in the preceding screenshot, the standard structure for the fields in a Field Group is to have the Primary Key appear first. The user can choose any of the displayed fields to be the default filter column, the defacto lookup field.

As a system option, the drop-down control provides a **find-as-you-type** capability, where the set of displayed choices filters and re-displays dynamically as the user types, character by character. The filter applies to the default filter column. Whatever field is used for the lookup, the referential field defined in the page determines what data field contents are copied into the target table. In the preceding screenshot, the reference table/field is the Sales Line table/field "No." and the target table/field is the Item table/field "No."

As developers, we can change the order of appearance of the fields in the drop-down display. We can also add or delete fields for the display by changing the contents of the Field Group. For example, we could add a capability to our page that provides an "alternate search" capability (where if the match for an Item No. isn't found in the **No.** field, the system will look for a match based on another field). Fields in a field group must be in a key to work, though this is not enforced by C/SIDE.

Consider this situation: The customer has a system design where the Item No. contains a basic, hard to remember, sequentially assigned code to uniquely identify each item. But the **Search Description** field contains a product description that is relatively easy for the users to remember. When the user types, the find-as-you-type feature helps them focus and find the specific Item No. to be entered for the order. In order to support this, we simply need to add the **Search Description** field to the Field Group for the Item table as the first field in the sequence. The following screenshot shows that change in the **Item** Field Group table:

The effect of this change can be seen in the following screenshot which shows the revised drop-down control. The user has begun entry in the **No.** field, but the lookup is focused on the newly added **Search Description** field. Find-as-you-type filtered the displayed items down to just those that match the data string entered so far.

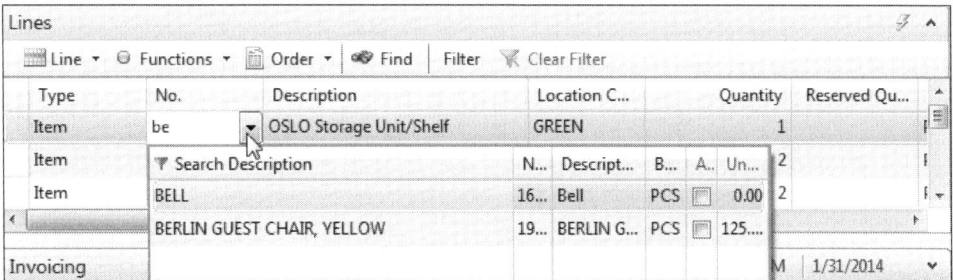

The result of our change is to allow the user to lookup items by their **Search Description**, rather than by the harder to remember **Item No.** Obviously, any field in the Item table which in a key could have been used, including custom fields added for this particular implementation.

Enhancing our sample application

Now we can take our knowledge of tables and expand our WDTU application. Our base Radio Station table needs to be added to and modified. We also need to create and reference additional tables.

While we want to have a realistic design in our sample application, we will make changes that illustrate the main (and what we feel are the most important) features in NAV table design. If there are capabilities or functionality that you feel is missing, then feel free to add them. Adjust the examples as much as you wish to make them more meaningful to you.

Creating and modifying tables

In *Chapter 1, An Introduction to NAV 2013*, we created the Radio Show table for the WDTU application. At that time we had the minimum fields that allowed us to usefully define a master record. Now let's set properties on existing data fields, add more data fields, and create an additional data table to which the Radio Show table can refer.

Our new data fields are shown in the following table:

Field No.	Field Name	Description
1000	Frequency	An Option data type (,Hourly,Daily,Weekly,Monthly) for the frequency of a show; to be used within a show (such as news, sports, or weather). A space/blank is used for the first option to allow a blank data field value to be valid.
1010	PSA Required Qty.	A number (stored as an integer) of Public Service Announcements that need to be played per show; will be used by playlist generation and posting logic.
1020	Advertisement Required Qty.	A number (stored as an integer) of advertisements that need to be played per show; will be used by playlist generation and posting logic.

Field No.	Field Name	Description
1030	**News Required**	Is news required to be broadcast during the show (a Boolean)?
1040	**News Duration**	The duration (stored as a duration) of the news program embedded within the show.
1050	**Sports Required**	Is sports news required to be broadcast during the show (a Boolean)?
1060	**Sports Duration**	The duration (stored as a duration) of the sports program embedded within the show.
1070	**Weather Required**	Is weather news required to be broadcast during the show (a Boolean)?
1080	**Weather Duration**	The duration (stored as a duration) of the weather program embedded within the show.
1090	**Avg. Listeners**	A decimal FlowField (stored as a Data Type decimal, Data Class FlowField) that averages the number of listeners as reported by the ratings agency. More on FlowFields in *Chapter 3, Data Types and Fields*.
1100	**Avg. Listener Share**	A decimal FlowField (stored as a Data Type decimal, Data Class FlowField) that averages the show's share of the total number of listeners as reported by the ratings agency.
1110	**Advertising Revenue**	A decimal flow field (stored as a Data Type decimal, Data Class FlowField) that sums the advertising revenue shown in the playlist ledger.
1120	**Royalty Cost**	A decimal flow field (stored as a Data Type decimal, Data Class FlowField) that sums the royalties due based on the playlist ledger.
1130	**Date Filter**	A date FlowFilter (stored as a Data Type date, Data Class FlowFilter) that will change the calculations of the flow fields based on the date filter applied. More on FlowFilters in *Chapter 3, Data Types and Fields*.

After we have completed our **Radio Show** table, it will look like this:

Next we need to fill the **OptionString** and **Caption** properties for the **Option** field **Frequency**. Highlight the **Frequency** field, then click on the **Properties** icon or press *Shift + F4*. Enter values for the **OptionString** property as shown in the next screenshot; don't forget the leading space followed by a comma to get a space/blank as the first option. Be sure to copy and paste the same information to the **OptionCaption** property. The **OptionCaptionML** property will fill in automatically with a copy of that information (since we do not have another language installed).

Next we want to define the reference table we are going to tie to the **Type** field. The table will contain a list of the available Radio Show Types such as Music, Talk, Sports, and so on. We will keep this table very simple, just containing **Code** as the unique key field and **Description** as the text field. Both fields will be of the default length as shown in the following layout. Create the new table and save it as Table 50001 with the name of **Radio Show Type**.

Field No.	Field Name	Description	Data Type	Length
10	Code	Primary Key of data type Code	Code	10
20	Description	A text field	Text	30

Before we can use this table as a reference from the Radio Station table, we need to create a list page that will be used both for data entry and data selection for the table. We will use **Page Designer**, and **Page Wizard** to create a **List** page. We should be able to do this pretty quickly. Click on **Pages**, click on the **New** button, enter 50001 in the **Table** field, then choose to use the wizard to create a page type of **List** (the table field will redisplay the table name).

Populate the page with both (all) the fields from the Radio Show Type table. Our designed page should look like the following screenshot:

Save the page as number 50002, with the name of Radio Show Types, then exit **Page Designer**, with the name of Radio Show Types. Test the page by highlighting it, then clicking on the **Object Designer** menu's **Run** button. The new page will be displayed. While the page is still open, go ahead and make some entries (by clicking on **New**), like the examples shown in the following screenshot:

Now we'll return to the Radio Show Type table and set the table's properties for **LookupPageID** and **DrillDownPageID** to point to the new page we have just created. As a reminder, we will use **Design** to open the table definition, then focus on the empty line below the description field, and either click on the **Properties** icon or press *Shift + F4*. In the values for each of the two **PageID** properties, we can either enter the page name (Radio Show Types) or the page number (50002). Either entry will work and give the result shown in the following screenshot:

Assigning a Table Relation property

Finally, we open the Radio Show table again by highlighting the table line and clicking on the **Design** button. This time highlight the **Type** field and access its **Properties** screen. Highlight the **TableRelation** property and click on the ellipsis button (the three dots). We see the **Table Relation** screen with four columns as shown in the following screenshot. The middle two columns are headed **Table** and **Field**. In the top line in the **Table** column, enter 50001 (the table number) or Radio Show Type (the table name). In the same line, the **Field** column, click on the ellipsis button (...) and choose **Code**.

We exit the **Table Relation** screen (by clicking on the **OK** button) and return to the **Type - Properties** page, which is shown in the following screenshot. Save and exit the modified table.

To check that the **TableRelation** property is working properly, run the Radio Show table (that is, highlight the table name and click on the **Run** button). Then highlight the **Radio Show Type** field and click on the drop-down arrow to view the list of available entries. We could also run the **Radio Show List** page and have almost exactly the same view of the data. This is because the **Run** of a table creates a temporary list page which includes all the fields in the table, thus it contains the same data fields as the page we created using the Page Wizard.

If all has gone according to plan, the **Radio Show Type** field will display a drop-down arrow (the downward pointing arrow button). Whether we click on that button or press *F4*, we will invoke the drop-down list for the Radio Show Type table.

Assigning an InitValue property

Another property we can define for several of the Radio Show fields is **InitValue**. WDTU has a standard policy that news, sports, and weather be broadcast for a few minutes each at the top of every hour in the day. We want the Boolean (Yes/No) fields **News Required**, **Sports Required**, and **Weather Required** to default to `Yes`. We also want the default time value of the **News Duration**, **Sports Duration**, and **Weather Duration** to be 2 minutes, 2 minutes, and 1 minute respectively. That way the first five minutes of every hour can be spent on keeping the listeners informed.

Setting the default for a field to a specific value simply requires setting the **InitValue** property to the desired value. In the case of the "Required" Boolean fields, that value is set to Yes. Now, using the Table Designer, we must Design the Radio Station table, access the **Properties** screen for the **News Required** field. Repeat this for the **Sports Required** and **Weather Required** fields. After we have filled in the values for the three fields, exit the **Properties** screen, exit the Table Designer, and save the changes.

In the case of the "Duration" fields, we will set the **InitValue** property to 2 minutes each for **News Duration** and **Sports Duration**, and 1 minute for **Weather Duration**.

Adding a few activity-tracking tables

Our WDTU organization is a profitable and productive radio station. We track historical information about our advertisers, royalties owed, and listenership. We track the music that is played, the rates we charge for advertisements based on the time of day, and we provide a public service by broadcasting a variety of government and other public service announcements.

We aren't going to cover all these features and functions in the following detailed exercises. However, it's always good to have a more complete view of the system on which we are working, even if we are only working on one or two components. In this case, the parts of the system not covered in detail in our exercises will be opportunities for you to extend your studies and practice on your own.

Of course any system development should start with a Design Document that completely spells out the goals and the functional design details. The *Microsoft Dynamics Sure Step* project methodology has been a very useful toolset to utilize for project management. However it is only available on PartnerSource, does not contain support for NAV 2013, and no update is currently planned. Neither system design nor project management will be covered in this book, but when we begin working on production projects, proper attention to both of these areas will be critical to success.

Based on these requirements, we need to expand our application design. So far we have defined a minimal Radio Show table, one reference table (Radio Show Type), and created pages for each of them. Ideally, you also entered some test data and then added a few additional fields to the Radio table (which we will not add to our pages).

Now we will add a supplemental table, document (header and line) tables, plus add a ledger (activity history) table relating to Playlist activities. Following that, we will also create some pages to utilize our new data structures.

Our WDTU application will now include the following tables:

- Radio Show: A master list of all programs broadcast by our station
- Radio Show Type: A reference list of possible types of radio shows
- Playlist Header: A single instance of a Radio Show with child data in the form of Playlist Lines
- Playlist Line: Each line represents one of a list of items and/or durations per Radio Show
- Playlist Item Rate: A list of rates for items played during a show as determined by our advertising sales staff or the royalty organization we use
- Radio Show Ledger: A detailed history of all the time spent and items played during the show with any related royalties owed or advertisement revenue expected
- Listenership Ledger: A detailed history of estimated listenership as provided by the ratings organization we subscribe to
- Record Label: A reference list of possible record labels

Remember, one purpose of this example system is for you to follow along in a hands-on basis in your own system. You may want to try different data structures and other object features. For example, you could add functionality to track volunteer activity, perhaps even detailing the type of support the volunteers provide.

For the best learning experience, you should be creating each of these objects in your development system to learn by experimenting. In the course of these exercises, it will be good if you make some mistakes and see some new error messages. That's part of the learning experience. A test system is the best place to learn from mistakes at the minimum cost.

New tables for our WDTU project

First, we create a **Playlist Header** table (table number **50002**), which will contain one record for each scheduled radio show.

Then we will create the associated Playlist Line table (table number 50003). This table will contain child records to the Playlist Header table. Each Playlist Line record represents one scheduled piece of music or advertisement or public service announcement or embedded show within the scheduled radio show defined in the Playlist Header table. The description for each of the **Option** fields shows the information that needs to be entered into the **OptionString** and **OptionStringML** properties for those fields.

Now we'll create our **Playlist Item Rate** table. These rates include both what we charge for ad time and what we must pay in royalties for material we broadcast.

A ledger table contains the detailed history of processed activity records. In this case, the data is a detailed history of all the Playlist Line records for previously broadcast shows.

Now we'll create one more ledger table to retain the data we received from the listenership rating service.

Finally, the last new table definition for now, our **Record Label** table (they're still called record labels even when what they distribute is totally electronic recordings).

New list pages for our WDTU project

Each of the new tables we have created should be supported with an appropriately named list page. As part of our WDTU project work, we should create the following pages:

- **50003 Playlist** (this is a Document page type)
- **50005 Playlist Item Rates**
- **50006 Radio Show Ledger**
- **50007 Listenership Ledger**
- **50008 Record Labels**

Keys, SumIndexFields, and table relations in our examples

What we've created so far are basic table definitions for the WDTU project. The next step is to flesh out those definitions with additional keys, SIFT field definitions, table relations, and so on. The purpose of these are to make our data easier and faster to access, to take advantage of the special features of NAV to create data totals and to facilitate relationships between various data elements.

Secondary keys and SumIndexFields

The Playlist Line table default primary key was the one field **Playlist No**. In order for the primary key to be unique for each record, another field is needed. In this case that is the **Line No.** field, which is incremented via C/AL code for each record. So we'll change the key for table 50003 accordingly.

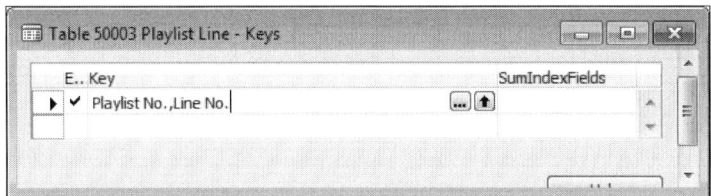

We know that a lot of reporting will be done based on the data in the Radio Show Ledger. We also know that we want to do reporting on data by Radio Show and by the type of entry (individual song, specific ad, and so on). So we add secondary keys for each of those, including the **Date** field so we can rapidly filter the data by date. The reporting that is financial in nature will undoubtedly need totals for the **Fee Amount** field, so we'll put that in the **SumIndexFields** column for our new keys.

We know that to do the necessary Listenership analysis, we will need an additional key combined with **SumIndexFields** for totaling listener statistics.

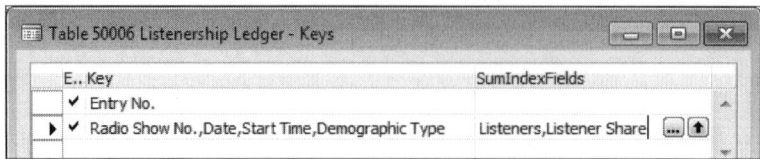

To utilize the **SumIndexFields** we have just defined, we will need to define the corresponding FlowFields in other tables. We will leave that part of the development effort for the next chapter where we are going to discuss fields in detail, including Flowfields and FlowFilters.

Table relations

For those tables where we defined fields that are intended to refer to data in other tables for lookups and validation, we must define the relationships in the referring tables. Sometimes those relationships are complicated, being dependent on other values within the record.

In Table 50003, Playlist Line, we have the **No.** field. If the **Type** field contains **Resource**, then the **No.** field should contain Resource No. If the **Type** field contains **Show**, then the **No.** field should contain a Show No. And, if the **Type** field contains **Item**, the **No.** field should contain an Item No. The pseudo-code (structured text approximating code syntax) for that logic can be written as:

```
IF Type = 'Resource' THEN No. := Resource.No.
    ELSE IF Type = 'Show' THEN No. := Radio Show.No.
    ELSE IF Type = 'Item' THEN No. := Item.No.
```

Fortunately, a tool built into the C/SIDE editor makes it easy for us to build that complex logic in the **TableRelation** property. When we click on the **TableRelation** property, then click on the ellipsis button (three dots), we get a **Table Relation** screen we can use to construct the necessary logic structure.

When we exit the **Table Relation** screen by clicking on the **OK** button, the **TableRelation** line looks like the following:

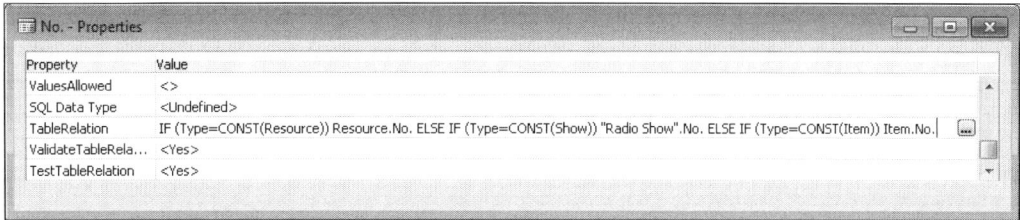

Table 50004, Playlist Item Rate, has a similar **TableRelation** requirement for the **No.** field in that table. In this case, the **No.** field will refer to the Vendor No. if **Type** = Vendor or to the Customer No. if **Type** = Customer.

When we exit the **Table Relation** screen this time (by clicking on the **OK** button), the **TableRelation** line looks like the following:

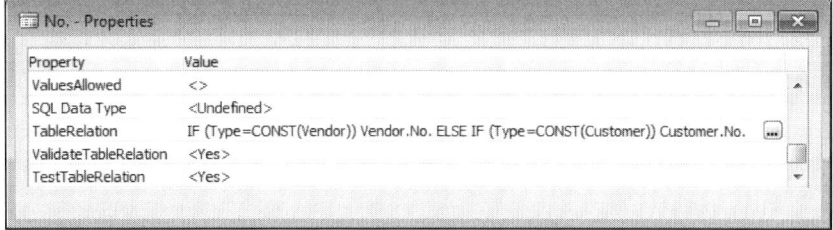

Modifying a standard table

One of the biggest advantages to the NAV system development environment is the fact that we are allowed to enhance the tables that are part of the standard product. Many package software products do not provide this flexibility. Nevertheless, with privilege comes responsibility. When we modify a standard NAV table, we must do so carefully.

In our system, we are going to use the standard **Item** table — **Table 27**, to store data about recordings such as music and advertisements and PSAs that we have available for broadcast. One of the new fields will be an **Option** field. Another will refer to the **Record Label** table we created earlier. When the modifications to the Item table design are completed, they will look like the following screenshot:

Note that we were careful not to touch any of the standard fields that were already defined in the Item table. Plus, we numbered all of our new fields in the range of 50000 to 99999 to make them easy to identify as belonging to a Partner modification.

Version list documentation

In *Chapter 1, An Introduction to NAV 2013*, we mentioned the importance of good documentation, one component being the assignment of version numbers to modifications and enhancements. Frequently, modifications are identified with a combination letter number code, the letters indicating who did the modification (such as the NAV Partner initials — or, in this case, the book authors' combined initials) and the numbers being a sequential number for this specific modification. Our Partner initials are CDS, so all our modifications will have a version number of CDSxx. We will use the chapter number of this book for the sequential number, such as:

- CDS01 – Chapter 01
- CDS02 – Chapter 02
- CDS01,02 – Chapter 01 and 02

When applied to the tables objects we have created so far, our Version List entries look like the following for the tables (**Table 27 Item** not shown):

Similar version numbers should be assigned to the pages and report that have been created thus far.

When working on a customer's system, a more general purposed versioning structure should be used in the same general format as the one used by Microsoft for the product. Such a structure would be in the format CDS7.00.01 (CDS company, NAV Version 7, minor version 00 (no Service Pack), build 01). The next release of objects would then be CDS7.00.02. In the **Documentation** trigger, there should be a sequential list of changes showing each incremental version followed by a list of all the features implemented for that version. This approach provides a standardized Version List externally and the full detail internally of changes. If done properly and combined with good external documentation, the result is a system that is much easier to maintain.

Types of tables

For this discussion, we will divide table types into three groups. As developers, we can change the definition and the contents of the first group (the Fully Modifiable tables). We cannot change the definition of the base fields of the second group, but we can change the contents (the Content Modifiable tables) and add new fields. The third group can be accessed for information, but neither the definition nor the data within is modifiable (the Read-Only tables).

Fully Modifiable tables

The following tables are included in the Fully Modifiable Tables group:

Master

The Master table type contains primary data (such as customers, vendors, items, employees, and so on). These are the tables that should be designed first because everything else will be based on these tables. When working on a modification, any necessary changes to Master tables should be defined first. Master tables always use card pages as their primary user input method. The Customer table is a Master table. A Customer record is shown in the following screenshot:

The preceding screenshot shows how the Card page segregates the data into categories on different FastTabs (for example, **General**, **Communication**, **Invoicing**, and so on) and includes primary data fields (for example, **No.**, **Name**, **Address**), reference fields (for example, **Salesperson Code**, **Responsibility Center**), and a FlowField (for example, **Balance (LCY)**).

Journal

The Journal table type contains unposted activity detail, data that other systems refer to as **transactions**. Journals are where most repetitive data entry occurs. In the standard system, all Journal tables are matched with corresponding Template tables (one Template table for each Journal table). The standard system includes journals for Sales, Cash Receipts, General Journal entries, Physical Inventory, Purchases, Fixed Assets, and Warehouse Activity, among others.

The transactions in a Journal can be segregated into batches for entry, edit review, and processing purposes. Journal tables always use **Worksheet** pages as their primary user input method. The following screenshots shows two Journal Entry screens. They both use the **General Journal** table, but each have quite a different appearance, and are based on different pages and different templates:

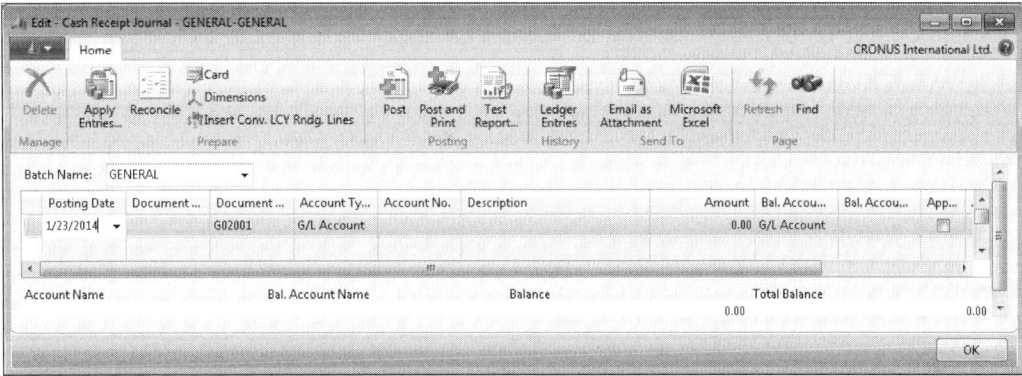

Comparing the preceding and following screenshots, the differences include not only which fields are visible, but also what logic applies to data entry defaults and validations:

Template

The Template table type operates behind the scenes, providing control information for a Journal, which operates in the foreground. By use of a Template, multiple instances of a Journal can be tailored for different purposes. Control information contained by a Template includes the following:

- The default type of accounts to be updated (for example, Customer, Vendor, Bank, General Ledger)

- The specific account numbers to be used as defaults, including balancing accounts

- What transaction numbering series will be used

- The default encoding to be applied to transactions for the Journal (for example, Source Code, Reason Code)

- Specific Pages and Reports to be used for data entry and processing of both edits and posting runs

As an example, **General Journal Templates** allow the General Journal table to be tailored in order to display fields and perform validations that are specific to the entry of particular transaction categories such as **Cash Receipts**, **Payments**, **Purchases**, **Sales**, and other transaction entry types. Template tables always use tabular pages for user input. The following screenshot shows a listing of the various General Journal Templates defined in the Cronus International Ltd. demonstration database:

In addition to the Templates, there are Batch tables that allow us to set up any number of batches of data under each journal template. The Batch, Template, Journal Line structure provides much flexibility in data organization and definition of required fields while utilizing a common underlying table definition (for example, the General Journal).

Ledger

The Ledger table type contains posted activity detail, the data other systems call history. NAV data flows from a Journal through a Posting routine into a Ledger. A significant advantage of NAV Ledger design is the fact it allows retaining all detail indefinitely. While there are routines supporting compression of the Ledger data, if at all feasible, you should retain the full historical detail of all activity. This allows users to have total flexibility for comparative or trend data analysis.

Ledger data is considered accounting data in NAV. We are not allowed to directly enter the data into a Ledger or change existing data in a Ledger (except for fields such as Due Date), but must "Post" to a Ledger. Posting is done by creating Journal Lines, validating the data as necessary, then posting those journal lines into the appropriate ledgers. Although we can physically force data into a Ledger with our Developer tools, we should not do so.

Because Ledger data is accounting data, we are not permitted to delete data from a Ledger table. We can compress or summarize Ledger data (very carefully), eliminating detail, but we should not change anything that would affect accounting totals for money or quantities.

User views of Ledger data are generally through use of List pages. The following screenshots show a **Customer Ledger Entries** list (financially oriented data) and an **Item Ledger Entries** list (quantity-oriented data). In each case, the data represents historical activity detail with accounting significance. There are other data fields in addition to those shown in the following screenshots. The fields shown here are representative. The users can utilize page-customization tools (which we will discuss in *Chapter 4, Pages – the User's Interactive Interface*) in order to change personalized page displays in a wide variety of ways.

The following is a screenshot of the **Item Ledger Entries** list:

The **Customer Ledger Entries** page displays critical information such as **Posting Date** (the effective accounting date), **Document Type** (the type of transaction), **Customer No.**, the **Original** and **Remaining Amount** of the transaction. The record also contains the **Entry No.** field, which uniquely identifies each record. The **Open** entries are those where the transaction amount has not been fully applied, such as an invoice amount not fully paid or a payment amount not fully consumed by invoices.

The **Item Ledger Entries** page displays similar information pertinent to inventory transactions. As previously described, **Posting Date**, **Entry Type**, and **Item No.**, as well as the assigned location for the item, control the meaning of each transaction. Item Ledger Entries are expressed both in **Quantity** and **Amount** (value). Open entries here are tied to the **Remaining Quantity**, such as material that has been received but is still available in stock. In other words, the **Open** entries represent current inventory.

Both the Customer Ledger Entry and Item Ledger Entry tables have underlying tables that provide additional details for entries affecting values.

Reference tables

The **Reference** (also called **Supplemental**) table type contains lists of codes, descriptions or other validation data. Reference table examples are postal zone codes, country codes, currency codes, exchange rates, and so on. Reference tables are often accessed by means of one of the **Setup** menu options because they must be set up prior to being used for reference purposes by other tables. In our WDTU example, tables 50001 Radio Show Type and 50007 Record Label are Reference tables

The following screenshots show some sample reference tables for **Locations**, **Countries**, and **Payment Terms**. Each table contains data elements that are appropriate for its use as a reference table, plus, in some cases, fields that control the effect of referencing a particular entry. These data elements are usually entered as a part of a setup process and then updated manually as appropriate.

The **Location List** in the preceding screenshot is a simple validation list of the Locations for this implementation. Usually, they represent physical sites, but depending on the implementation, they can also be used simply to segregate types of inventory. For example, locations could be **Refrigerated** versus **Unrefrigerated** or there could be locations for **Awaiting Inspection**, **Passed Inspection**, and **Failed Inspection**.

The **Countries/Regions** list in the preceding screenshot is used as validation data, defining the acceptable country codes. It also provides control information for the mailing **Address Format** (general organization address) and the **Contact Address Format** (for the individual contact's address).

The **Payment Terms** table shown in the following screenshot provides a list of payment terms codes along with a set of parameters that allows the system to calculate specific terms. In this set of data, for example, the **1M (8D)** code will yield payment terms of due in one month with a discount of **2%** applied for payments processed within eight days of the invoice date. In another instance, **14D** payment terms will calculate the payment as due in 14 days from the date of invoice with no discount available.

Register

The Register table type contains a record of the range of transaction ID numbers for each batch of posted Ledger entries. Register data provides an audit trail of the physical timing and sequence of postings. This, combined with the full detail retained in the Ledger, makes NAV a very auditable system, because we can see exactly what activity was done and when it was done.

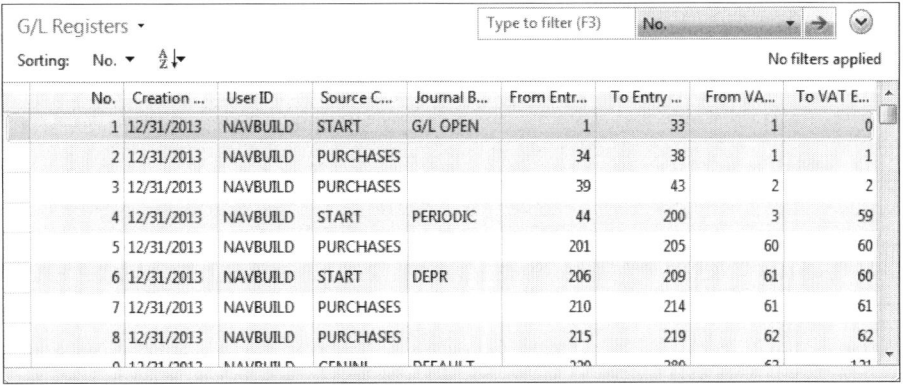

The user views the Register through a tabular page, as shown in the previous screenshot. We see that each Register entry has the **Creation Date**, **Source Code**, **Journal Batch Name**, and the identifying **Entry No.** range for all the entries in that batch.

Another NAV feature, the Navigate function, which we will discuss in detail in a later chapter, also provides a very useful auditing tool. The Navigate function allows the user (who may be a developer doing testing) to highlight a single Ledger entry and find all the other Ledger entries and related records that resulted from the posting that created that highlighted entry.

Posted Document

The Posted Document type contains the posted copies of the original documents for a variety of data types such as Sales Invoices, Purchase Invoices, Sales Shipments, and Purchase Receipts. Posted Documents are designed to provide an easy reference to the historical data in a format similar to what one would normally store in paper files. A Posted Document looks very similar to the original source document. For example, a Posted Invoice will look very similar to the original Sales Order or Sales Invoice. The Posted Documents are included in the **Navigate** function.

The following screenshots show **Sales Order** before Posting and the resulting **Posted Sales Invoice** document. Both documents are in a Header/Detail format, where the information in the Header applies to the whole order and the information in the Detail is specific to the individual Order Line. As part of the **Sales Order** page, there is information displayed to the right of the actual order. This is designed to make life easier for the user by giving information about related data which is available without requiring a separate lookup action.

First, we see the **Sales Order** document ready to be posted.

The following screenshot is that of the **Sales Invoice** document after the **Sales Order** has been posted:

Setup

The Setup table type contains system or functional application control information. There is one Setup table per functional application area, for example, one for **Sales & Receivables**, one for **Purchases & Payables**, one for **General Ledger**, one for **Inventory**, and so on. Setup tables contain only a single record. Since a Setup table has only one record, it can have a Primary Key field which has no value assigned (this is how all the standard NAV Setup tables are designed).

Inventory Setup is shown as follows:

Temporary

The Temporary table is used within objects to hold temporary data. A Temporary table does not exist outside the instance of the object where it is defined using a permanent table as the source of the table definition The Temporary table has exactly the same data structure as the permanent table after which it is modeled.

Temporary tables are created empty when the parent object execution initiates, and they disappear along with their data when the parent object execution terminates (that is, when the Temporary table variable goes out of scope).

Temporary tables are not generally accessible to users except on a display only basis. They cannot directly be the target of a report object, but can be the primary source table for pages. Temporary tables are intended to be work areas and as such, are containers of data. The definition of a Temporary table can only be changed by changing the definition of the permanent table on which it has been modeled.

Content Modifiable tables

There is only one table type included in the Content Modifiable Table group.

System

The System table type contains user-maintainable information that pertains to the management or administration of the NAV application system. System tables are created by NAV; we cannot create System tables. However, with full developer license rights, we can modify System tables to extend their usage. With full system permissions, we can also change the data in System tables.

An example is the User table, which contains user login information. This particular System table is often modified to define special user access routing or processing limitations. Other System tables contain data on report-to-printer routing assignments, transaction numbers to be assigned, batch job scheduling, and so on. The following are examples of System tables in which definition and content can be modified. The first three relate to system security functions:

- **User**: The table of identified users and their security information
- **Permission**: The table defining what individual Permission Sets are allowed to do, based on object permission assignments
- **Access Control**: The table of the Security roles that are assigned to each Windows Login

The following tables are used to track a variety of system data or control structures:

- **Company**: The companies in this database. Most NAV data is automatically segregated by Company.
- **Database Key Groups**: This defines all of the key groups that have been set up to allow enabling and disabling table keys.
- **Chart**: This defines all of the chart parts that have been set up for use in constructing pages.
- **Web Service**: This lists the pages, queries, and code units that have been published as web services.
- **Profile**: This contains a list of all the active profiles and their associated Role Center pages. A profile is a collection of NAV users who are assigned to the same Role Center.
- **User Personalization**: In spite of its name, this table does not contain information about user personalization that has occurred. Instead, this table contains the link between the user ID and the Profile ID, the language, company, and debugger controls. (A personalization is a change in the layout of a page by a user, such as adding or removing fields, page parts, restructuring menus, resizing columns, and so on. This information is in the User Metadata table).

The following tables contain information about various system internals. Their explanation is outside the scope of this book:

- **Send-to Program**
- **Style Sheet**
- **User Default Style Sheet**
- **Record Link**
- **Object Tracking**
- **Object Metadata**
- **Profile Metadata**
- **User Metadata**

Read-only tables

There is only one table type included in the read-only table group

Virtual

The Virtual table type is computed at runtime by the system. A Virtual table contains data and is accessed like other tables, but you cannot modify either the definition or the contents of a Virtual table. We can think of the Virtual tables as system data presented in the form of a table so it is readily available to C/AL code. Some of these tables (such as the Database File, File, and Drive tables) provide access to information about the computing environment. Other Virtual tables (such as Table Information, Field, and Session tables) provide information about the internal structure and operating activities of our database. A good way to learn more about any of these tables is to create a list or card page bound to the table of interest. We include all the fields in the page layout, **Save** the page and **Run** it. We can then view the field definition and data contents of the target virtual table.

Some virtual tables (such as Date and Integer) provide tools that can be used in our application routines. The Date table provides a list of calendar periods (such as days, weeks, months, quarters, and years) to make it much easier to manage various types of accounting and managerial data handling. The Integer table provides a list of integers from -2,147,483,647 to 2,147,483,647. As we explore standard NAV reports, we will frequently see the Integer table being used to supply a sequential count in order to facilitate a reporting sequence.

We cannot see these tables presented in the List of Table objects, but can only access them as targets for Pages, Reports, or Variables in C/AL code. The knowledge of the existence, contents, and usage of these Virtual tables is not useful to an end user. However, as developers, we will regularly use some of the Virtual tables. There is educational value in studying the structure and contents of these tables, as well as being able to create valuable tools with knowledge of and by accessing one or more Virtual tables.

The following screenshot shows a list of most of the Virtual and System tables:

Summary

In this chapter, we have focused on the foundation level of NAV data structure: tables and their internal structure. We worked our way through the hands-on creation of a number of tables and their data definitions in support of our WDTU application. We briefly discussed Field Groups and how they are used.

We identified the essential table structure elements including properties, object numbers, triggers, keys, and SumIndexFields. Finally, we reviewed the types of tables found in NAV 2013.

In the next chapter, we will dig deeper into the NAV data structure to better understand how fields and their attributes are assembled to make up the tables. We will also focus on what can be done with triggers. Then we will explore how other object types use tables, working towards developing a full kit of tools with which to perform NAV development.

Review questions

1. Which of the following is a correct description of a table in NAV 2013? Choose two.

    a. A NAV table is the definition of data structure

    b. A NAV table includes a built-in data entry page

    c. A NAV table can contain C/AL code but that should be avoided

    d. A NAV table should implement many of the business rules of a system

2. Tables can have up to 1000 data fields with a maximum total record size of 8 GB? True or False?

3. Table numbers intended to be used for customized table objects should only range between 5000 to 9999. True or False?

4. Which of the following are Table triggers? Choose two.

    a. OnInsert

    b. OnChange

    c. OnNewKey

    d. OnRename

5. All primary keys should contain only one data field. True or False?

6. NAV table design in the product always ensures referential integrity for all parent-child table relationships when a record is deleted. True or False?

7. Keys can be enabled or disabled in executable code. True or False?

8. SumIndexFields can be used to calculate totals. True or False?

9. The DropDown display on a field lookup in the RTC can be changed by modifying the table's Field Groups True or False?

10. Temporary tables can be saved in a special database storage area. True or False.

11. Table Permissions (for access to another table's data) include which of the following permissions. Choose three.

    a. read

    b. sort

    c. delete

    d. modify

12. Which of the following tables can be modified by Partner developers? Choose three.

    a. Customer

    b. Date

    c. User

    d. Item Ledger Entry

13. The TableRelation property allows a field in one table to reference data in another table. True or False?

14. Tables can be created or deleted dynamically. True or False?

15. SQL Server for NAV supports SIFT by which mechanism? Choose one.

    a. SQL SIFT indexes

    b. SQL Dynamic Indexes

    c. SQL Indexed Views

    d. SIFT not supported in SQL

16. Ledger data in NAV can be freely updated through either posting routines or direct data entry. True or False?

3
Data Types and Fields

Do little things now; so shall big things come to thee by and by asking to be done.
– Persian Proverb

Design must reflect the partial and aesthetic in business but above all…good design must primarily serve people. *– Thomas J. Watson, Sr.*

The design of an application should begin at the simplest level, with the design of the data elements. The type of data your development tool supports has a significant effect on your design. Because NAV is designed for financially-oriented business applications, NAV data types are financial and business oriented.

In this chapter, we will cover many of the data types you will use within NAV. For each data type, we will cover field properties and how particular properties, such as FieldClass, are used to support application functionality. FieldClass is a fundamental property that defines whether the contents of the field are data to be processed or control information to be interpreted. In particular, we will be covering:

- Basic definitions
- Fields
- Data types
- FieldClass properties
- Filtering

Basic definitions

First, let's review some basic NAV terminology:

- **Data type**: Defines the kind of data that can be held in a field, whether it be numeric (for example, integer or decimal), text, a table RecordID, time, date, Boolean, and so forth. The data type defines what constraints can be placed on the contents of a field, determines the functions in which the data element can be used (not all data types are supported by all functions), and defines what the results of certain functions will be.

- **Fundamental data type**: A simple, single component structure consisting of a single value at any point in time, for example, a number, a string, or a Boolean value.

- **Complex data type**: A structure made up of or relating to simple data types, for example, records, program objects such as Pages or Reports, BLOBs, DateFormulas, an external file, an indirect reference variable, and so on.

- **Data Element**: An instance of a data type that may be a Constant or a Variable.

- **Constant**: A data element explicitly specified in the code by a literal value. Constants are not modifiable during execution, but only by a developer using C/SIDE. All the simple data types can be represented by constants. Examples are "MAIN" (Code or Text), 12.34 (Decimal), and "+01-312-444-5555" (Text).

- **Variable**: A data element that can have a value assigned to it dynamically during execution. Except for special cases, a variable will be of a single, unchanging, specific data type

Fields

A field is the basic element of data definition in NAV—the "atom" in the structure of a system. The elemental definition of a field consists of its number, its description (name), its data type, and, of course, any properties required for its particular data type. A field is defined by the values of its properties and the C/AL code contained in its triggers.

Field properties

The specific properties that can be defined for a field depend on the data type. There are a minimum set of universal properties. We will review those first. Then we will review the rest of the more frequently used properties, both those that are data dependent and those that are not. You can check out the remaining properties by using **Developer and IT Pro Help** from within the **Table Designer**.

We can access the properties of a field while viewing the table in Design mode, highlighting the field, and then clicking on the **Properties** icon, or clicking on **View | Properties** or pressing *Shift + F4*. All of the property screenshots in this section were obtained this way for fields within the standard **Customer** table. As we review various field properties, you will learn more if you follow along in your NAV system using the **Object Designer**. Explore different properties and the values they can have. Use NAV 2013's Help functions liberally for additional information and examples.

The property value that is enclosed in **< >** (less than and greater than brackets) is the default value for that property. When we set a property to any other value, **<   >** should not be present unless they are supposed to be a part of the property value (for example, as part of a Text string value).

All of the fields, of any data type, have the following properties:

- **Field No.**: The identifier for the field within the containing table object.
- **Name**: The label by which C/AL code references the field. A name can consist of up to 30 characters, including special characters. The name can be changed at any time and NAV will automatically ripple that change throughout the system. The name is used as the default caption when data from this field is displayed and no caption has been defined. Changing names that are in use in C/AL code can cause problems with some functions such as web services and GETFILTERS where the reference is based on the field name rather than the field number.
- **Caption**: This contains the defined caption for the currently-selected language. It will always be one of the defined multi-language captions. The default language for a NAV installation is determined by the combination of a set of built-in rules and the languages available in the installation.
- **CaptionML**: This defines the MultiLanguage caption for the table. It also identifies the language in use, for example ENU for US English (as seen in the following screenshot).
- **Description**: This is an optional use property, for our internal documentation.
- **Data Type**: This defines what type of data format applies to this field (for example, Integer, Date, Code, Text, Decimal, Option, Boolean, and so on)
- **Enabled**: This determines whether or not the field is activated for user-generated events. The property defaults to **<Yes>** and is rarely changed.

The following screenshot shows the properties for the **Picture** field with the **Data Type** value of **BLOB** in the **Customer** table:

The set of properties shown for a **BLOB** data type field is the simplest set of field properties. After the properties that are shared by all of the data types, appear the BLOB-specific properties—**SubType**, **Owner**, and **Compressed**.

- **SubType**: Defines the type of data stored in the **BLOB** field and sets a filter in the import/export function for the field. The three sub-type choices are **Bitmap** (for bitmap graphics), **Memo** (for text data), and **User-Defined** (for anything else). User-Defined is the default value.

- **Owner**: Defines the NAV server user who owns the object in the **BLOB** field.

- **Compressed**: This defines whether the data stored in the **BLOB** field is stored in a compressed format. There is no documentation on how or when compression is meant to be used, but if you want to access **BLOB** data with an external tool (from outside of NAV), this property must be set to No.

The properties of **Code** and **Text** data type fields are quite similar to one another. This is logical since both represent types of textual data. These can be seen in the following screenshot:

The following are some common properties between the **Code** and **Text** data types:

- **DataLength**: Specifies the maximum number of characters the field can contain. This is 250 characters in a table but, if no maximum is specified, unlimited in a global variable stored only in memory.

- **InitValue**: The value that the system will supply as a default when the field is initialized.

- **AltSearchField**: Replaced by Field Groups (described in *Chapter 2, Tables*) in the Role Tailored Client; it was a feature implemented in the old Classic Client. Presumably this was left in place for some aspect of backward compatibility.

- **Caption Class**: Can be set up by the developer to allow users to dynamically change the caption for a text box or a check box. Caption Class defaults to empty. For more information, refer to **Developer and IT Pro Help**. Used in base NAV in the Dimensions fields.

- **Editable**: Set to No when we don't want to allow a field to be edited, such as if it is a computed or assigned value field that the user should not change. **Editable** defaults to Yes.

- **NotBlank**, **Numeric**, **CharAllowed**, **DateFormula**, and **ValuesAllowed**: Each of these allows us to place constraints on the data that can be entered into this field by a user. They do not affect data updates driven by application C/AL code.

- **SQL Data Type**: Applies to Code fields only. SQL Data Type allows you to define what data type will be allowed in this particular Code field and how it will be mapped to a SQL Server data type. This controls sorting and display. Options are **Varchar**, **Integer**, and **BigInteger**. **Varchar** is the default and causes all of the data to be treated as text. **Integer** and **BigInteger** allow only numeric data to be entered. In general, once set, this property should not be changed. These settings do not affect data handling done in SQL Server external to NAV.

- **TableRelation**: Used to specify that the data field is related to data in a specified table. The target table field must be in the Primary Key. The relationship can be conditional and/or filtered. The relationship can be used for validation, lookups, and data-change propagation.

- **ValidateTableRelation**: If a **TableRelation** is specified, set this to Yes in order to validate the relation when data is entered or changed (in other words, confirm that the entered data exists in the target table). If a **TableRelation** is defined and this property is set to No, the table referential integrity will not be maintained. Caution: Application code can be written that will bypass this validation.

- **TestTableRelation**: An infrequently used property that only controls whether or not the relationship should be tested during a database integrity test. If **ValidateTableRelation** is No, then **TestTableRelation** should be No. Setting this property to No will eliminate table referential integrity testing.

- **ExtendedDataType**: This property allows the optional designation of an extended data type that automatically receives special formatting and validation. Type options include an e-mail address, a URL, a phone number, report filter, progress bar ratio, or a masked entry (as dots). An action icon may also be displayed as shown in the following screenshot, where there are three fields with **ExtendedDataType** defined:

Let's take a look at the properties of two more data types, **Decimal** and **Integer**, especially those properties related to numeric content.

- **DecimalPlaces**: This sets the minimum and maximum number of decimal places (**min:max**) for storage and for display in a **Decimal** data item. Default is 2 (2:2), minimum is 0 and the maximum is 255.

- **BlankNumbers**, **BlankZero**, and **SignDisplacement**: Can be used to control the formatting and display of the data field on a Page.

- **MinValue** and **MaxValue**: When set, these constrain the range of data values allowed for user entry. The range available depends on the field data type.

- **AutoIncrement**: Allows defining one field in a table to automatically increment for each record entered. When used, which is not often, it is almost always to support the automatic updating of a field used as the last field in a Primary Key, enabling the creation of a unique key. Use of this feature does not ensure a contiguous number sequence. Under some circumstances, use of this feature can lead to table locking conflicts. When defined in the property, the automatic functionality should not be overridden in code.

These properties can be seen in the following screenshot:

The properties for an **Option** data type are similar to those of other numeric data types, logical since an **Option** is stored as an integer, but there are also **Option**-specific properties.

- **OptionString**: Details the text interpretations for each of the stored integer values contained in an **Option** field
- **OptionCaption** and **OptionCaptionML**: These serve the same captioning and multi-language purposes as caption properties for other data types

Internally, the options are stored as integers tied to each option's position in **OptionString** starting with position **0, 1, 2**, and so on. **OptionString** and **OptionCaption** are shown in the following screenshot:

Field triggers

To see what field triggers are, let us look at our **Table 50000 Radio Show**. Open the table in the Design mode, highlight the **No.** field, press *F9* and see the following:

Each field has two triggers, the **OnValidate()** trigger and the **OnLookup()**trigger, which function as follows:

- **OnValidate()**: The C/AL code in this trigger is executed whenever an entry is made by the user. The intended use is to validate that the entry conforms to the design parameters for the field. It can also be executed under program control through use of the VALIDATE function (which we will discuss later).

- **OnLookup()**: Lookup behavior can be triggered by pressing *F4* or *Shift + F4* from an ellipsis button or by clicking on the lookup arrow in a field as shown in the following screenshot:

- If the field's **TableRelation** property refers to a table, then the default behavior is to display a drop-down list to allow selection of an entry from that table to be stored in this field. The list will be based on the Field Groups defined for the table. We may choose to override that behavior by coding different behavior for a special case. We must be careful, because any entry whatsoever in the body of an **OnLookup()** trigger, even a comment line, and even a blank line with nothing on it, will eliminate the default behavior, even if it's simply a comment line.

Data structure examples

Some of the good examples of tables in the standard product to review for particular features are:

- Table 18 – Customer, for a variety of data types and Field Classes. This table contains some fairly complex examples of C/AL code in the table Triggers. A wide variety of field property variations can be seen in this table as well.

- Table 50 – Accounting Period and Table 167 – Job, both have good examples of OnValidate trigger C/AL code, as do all of the primary master tables such as Customer, Vendor, Item, and so on.

Field numbering

The number of each field within its parent table object is the unique identifier that NAV uses internally to identify that field. We can easily change a field number when we are initially defining a table layout. But after other objects such as pages, reports, or codeunits are referencing the fields in a table, it becomes difficult to change the numbers of referenced fields. Deleting a field and reusing its field number for a different purpose is not a good idea and can easily lead to programming confusion.

> We cannot re-number or delete a field that has data present in the database. We cannot reduce the defined size of a field to less than the largest size of data already present in that field. These limits are the compiler working to protect you and your database.

For the new fields that we add to tables that are a part of the standard NAV product, the new field numbers must be in the 50,000 to 99,999 number range, unless we have been explicitly licensed for another number range. Field numbers for fields in new tables that we create may be anything from 1 to 999,999,999 (in all cases without the commas).

When a field representing the same data element appears in related tables (for example, journal and ledger), the same field number should be assigned to that data element for each of the tables. Not only is this consistent approach easier for reference and maintenance, but it also supports the TRANSFERFIELDS function. TRANSFERFIELDS allows you to copy data from one table's record instance to another table's record instance by doing record to record mapping based on the field numbers.

If we plan ahead and number the fields logically and consistently from the beginning of our design work, we will create code that's easier to maintain. It's a good idea to leave frequent gaps in field number sequences within a table. This allows easier insertion of new fields numerically adjacent to related, previously defined fields.

See *Object Numbering Conventions* in the **Developer and IT Pro Help** in the Development Environment for additional information.

Field and Variable naming

In general, the rules for naming fields (data elements in a table) and variables (data elements within the working storage of an object) are the same and we will discuss them on that basis. The **Developer and IT Pro Help** section *Naming Conventions* describes many recommended best practices for naming within NAV.

Variables in NAV can either be global (with a scope across the breadth of an object) or local (with a scope only within a single function). Variable names should be unique within the sphere of their scope. There must not be any duplication between global and local names. Even though the same local name can be used in more than one function within the same object, doing this is not a good idea and will almost certainly confuse the developer that follows you. Therefore, we should make our working variable names unique within the object. In addition, performance can be impacted by declaring complex data types (such as records) locally as this will introduce overhead on each call.

Uniqueness includes not duplicating reserved words or system variables. Refer to the *C/AL Reserved Words* list in the **Developer and IT Pro Help**. Avoid using, as a variable name, any word that appears as an UPPER CASE word in either the **Developer and IT Pro Help** or any of the published NAV technical documentation. For example, we shouldn't use the word PAGE as a variable name.

Variable names in NAV are not case sensitive. There is a 30-character length limit on variable names (as well as field names in tables). Variable names can contain all ASCII characters except for control characters (ASCII values 0 to 31 and 255) and the double quote (ASCII value 34), as well as some Unicode characters used in languages other than English. Characters outside the standard ASCII set may display differently on different systems.

Note that the compiler won't tell us an asterisk (*, ASCII value 42) or question mark (?, ASCII value 63) cannot be used in a variable name. But, because both the asterisk and the question mark can be used as *wildcards* in many expressions, especially filtering, neither one should be used in a variable name.

Unless the variable name is enclosed in double quotes, the first character of a variable name must be a letter A to Z (upper or lower case) or an underscore (_, ASCII value 95). Alphabets other than the 26-character English alphabet may interpret the ASCII values to characters other than A to Z, and may include more than 26 characters. The variable name can be followed by any combination of the legal characters.

If we use any characters other than the alphabet, numerals, and underscore, we must surround our variable name with double quotes each time we use it in C/AL code (for example, *Cust List*, which contains an embedded space, or **No.**, which contains a period).

See *Naming Conventions* in the **Developer and IT Pro Help** for additional C/AL variable naming guidance.

Data types

We are going to segregate the data types into several groups. We will first look at Fundamental data types, then Complex data types.

Fundamental data types

Fundamental data types are the basic components from which the complex data types are formed. They are grouped into Numeric, String, and Date/Time data types.

Numeric data

Just like other systems, NAV supports several numeric data types. The specifications for each NAV data type are defined for NAV independent of the support SQL Server database rule. But some data types are stored and handled somewhat differently from a SQL Server technician point of view than how they appear to us as NAV developers and users. For more details on the SQL Server-specific representations of various data elements, you should refer to **Developer and IT Pro Help**. Our discussion will focus on the NAV representation and handling for each data type.

The various numeric data types are as follows:

- **Integer**: An integer number ranging from -2,147,483,648 to +2,147,483,647.

- **Decimal**: A decimal number in the range of +/- 999,999,999,999,999.99. Although it is possible to construct larger numbers, errors such as overflow, truncation, or loss of precision might occur. In addition, there is no facility to display or edit larger numbers.

- **Option**: A special instance of an integer, stored as an integer number ranging from 0 to +2,147,483,547. An option is normally represented in the body of your C/AL code as an option string. We can compare an option to an integer in C/AL rather than using the option string, but that's not a good practice because it eliminates the self-documenting aspect of an option field.

  An option string is a set of choices listed in a comma-separated string, one of which is chosen and stored as the current option. Since the maximum length of this string is 250 characters, the practical maximum number of choices for a single option is less than 125. The currently selected choice within the set of options is stored in the option field as the ordinal position of that option within the set. For example, selection of an entry from the option string of red, yellow, blue would result in the storing of 0 (red), 1 (yellow), and 2 (blue). If red were selected, 0 would be stored in the variable; and if blue were selected, 2 would be stored. Quite often, an option string starts with a blank to allow an effective choice of "none chosen". An example of this (blank, Hourly, Daily,…) follows:

| ✔ | 1000 | Frequency | Option | ,Hourly,Daily,Weekly,Monthly |

- **Boolean**: A Boolean variable is stored as 1 or 0, in C/AL code is programmatically referred to as True or False, but sometimes referred to in properties as Yes or No. Boolean variables may be displayed as Yes or No (language dependent), P or blank, True or False.

- **BigInteger**: 8-byte Integer as opposed to the 4 bytes of Integer. BigIntegers are for very big numbers (from -9,223,372,036,854,775,808 to 9,223,372,036,854,775,807).

- **Char**: A numeric code between 0 and 255 representing an ASCII character. Char variables can operate either as text or as numbers. Numeric operations can be done on Char variables. Char variables can also be defined with character values. Char variables cannot be defined as permanent variables in a table, but only as working storage variables within C/AL objects.

String data

The following are the data types included in String data:

- **Text**: This contains any string of alphanumeric characters. In a table, a Text field can be from 1 to 250 characters long. In working storage within an object, a Text variable can be any length if there is no length defined. If a maximum length is defined, it must not exceed 1024. NAV 2013 does not require a length to be specified, but if we define a maximum length, it will be enforced. When calculating the *length* of a record for design purposes (relative to the maximum record length of 8000 bytes), the full defined field length should be counted.

- **Code**: The length constraints for Code variables are the same as those for text variables. All of the letters are automatically converted to uppercase when data is entered into a Code variable; any leading or trailing spaces are removed.

Date/Time data

The following are the data types included in Date/Time data:

- **Date**: This contains an integer number, which is interpreted as a date ranging from January 1, 1754 to December 31, 9999. A 0D (numeral zero, letter D) represents an undefined date (stored as a SQL Server **DateTime** field) interpreted as January 1, 1753. According to the **Developer and IT Pro Help** that NAV 2013 supports a **DateTime** field value of 1/1/0000 as a special case for backward compatibility. There is also confusing mention in Help of a date range beginning 1/3/0001. This requires use of the SQL data type `DateTime2` and there is no documentation for how this can be accessed in NAV.

  A date constant can be written as a letter D preceded by either six digits in the format *MMDDYY* or eight digits as *MMDDYYYY* (where *M* = month, *D* = day and *Y* = year). For example, 011914D or 01192014D both represent January 19, 2014. Later, in **DateFormula**, we will find *D* interpreted as day, but here the trailing *D* is interpreted as the date (data type) constant. When the year is expressed as *YY* rather than *YYYY*, the century portion (in this case, 20) is 20 if the two digit year is from 00 to 29, or 19 if the year is from 30 through 99.

  NAV also defines a special date called a **Closing** date, which represents the point in time between one day and the next. The purpose of a closing date is to provide a point at the end of a day, after all of the real date- and time-sensitive activity is recorded — the point when accounting *closing* entries can be recorded.

Closing entries are recorded, in effect, at the stroke of midnight between two dates—this is the date of closing of accounting books, designed so that one can include or not include, at the user's option, closing entries in various reports. When sorted by date, the closing date entries will get sorted after all normal entries for a day. For example, the normal date entry for December 31, 2013 would display as 12/31/13 (depending on the date format masking), and the closing date entry would display as C12/31/13. All of the C12/31/13 ledger entries would appear after all normal 12/31/13 ledger entries. The following screenshot shows some 2013 closing date entries mixed with normal entries from December 2013 and January 2014:

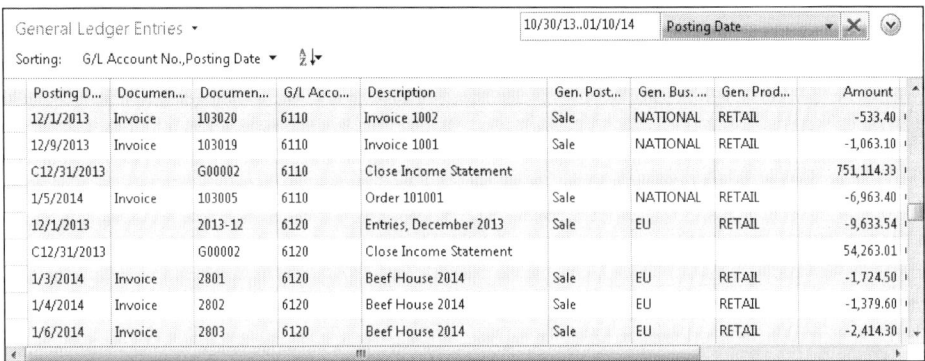

- **Time**: This contains an integer number, which is interpreted on a 24-hour clock, in milliseconds, from 00:00:00 to 23:59:59:999. A 0T value (numeral zero, letter T) represents an undefined time.

- **DateTime**: This represents a combined Date and Time, stored in **Coordinated Universal Time (UTC)** and always displays local time (that is, the local time on your system). DateTime fields do not support NAV Closing dates. DateTime is helpful for an application that must support multiple time zones simultaneously. DateTime values can range from January 1, 1753 00:00:00.000 to December 31, 9999 23:59:59.999, but dates earlier than January 1, 1754 cannot be entered (don't test with dates late in 9999 as an intended advance to the year 10000 won't work). Assigning a date of 0DT yields an undefined or blank DateTime.

- **Duration**: This represents the positive or negative difference between two DateTime values, in milliseconds, stored as a BigInteger. Durations are automatically output in the text format *DDD* days *HH* hours *MM* minutes *SS* seconds.

Complex data types

Each complex data type consists of multiple data elements. For ease of reference, we will categorize them into several groups of similar types.

Data structure

The following data types are in the data structure group:

- **File**: Refers to any standard Windows file outside the NAV database. There is a reasonably complete set of functions to allow creating, deleting, opening, closing, reading, writing, and copying (among other things) data files. For example, we could create our own NAV routines in C/AL to import or export data from a file that had been created by some other application.

 With the three-tier architecture of NAV 2013, business logic runs on the server, not the client. We need to keep this in mind anytime we are referring to local external files as they will be on the server by default.

- **Record**: Refers to a single data row within a NAV table. Quite often, multiple variable instances of a Record (table) are defined to support a validation process, allowing access to different records within the table at one time within the same function.

Objects

Page, Report, Codeunit, Query, and XMLPort each represent an object data type. Object data types are used when there is a need for reference to an object or a function in another object. Examples:

- Invoking a Report or an XMLPort from a Page or a Report
- Calling a function for data validation is coded as a function in a Table or a Codeunit

Automation

The following are Automation data types:

- **OCX**: Allows the definition of a variable that represents and allows access to an ActiveX or OCX custom control. Such a control is typically an external application object, which you can invoke from your NAV object.

- **Automation**: Allows the definition of a variable that we may access similarly to an OCX. The application must act as an Automation Server and must be registered with the NAV client or server calling it. For example, we can interface from NAV into the various Microsoft Office products (Word, Excel, and so on) by defining them in Automation variables.

- **DotNet**: Allows the definition of a variable for .NET Framework interface types within an assembly. This supports accessing .NET Framework type members including methods, properties, and constructors from C/AL. These can be members of the global assembly cache or custom assemblies.

Input/Output

The following are the Input/Output data types:

- **Dialog**: Supports the definition of a simple user interface window without the use of a Page object. Typically, Dialog windows are used to communicate processing progress or to allow a brief user response to a go/no-go question, though this latter use could result in bad performance due to locking. There are other user communication tools as well, but they do not use a Dialog type data item.

- **InStream** and **Outstream**: These allow reading from and writing to external files, BLOBS, and objects of the Automation and OCX data types.

DateFormula

DateFormula provides for the definition and storage of a simple, but clever, set of constructs to support the calculation of runtime-sensitive dates. A DateFormula is a combination of:

- Numeric multipliers (for example 1, 2, 3, 4, and so on)
- Alpha time units (all must be upper case)
    - D for a day
    - W for a week
    - WD for day of the week, that is day 1 through day 7 (either in the future or in the past, not today), Monday is day 1, Sunday is day 7
    - M for calendar month
    - Y for year
    - CM for current month, CY for current year, CW for current week

- Math symbols interpretation
  - + (plus) as in CM + 10D means the Current Month end plus 10 Days (in other words, the 10th of next month)
  - – (minus) as in (-WD3) means the date of the previous Wednesday
- Positional notation (D15 means the 15th day of the month and 15D means 15 days)

Payment Terms for Invoices supports full use of DateFormula. All DateFormula results are expressed as a date based on a reference date. The default reference date is the system date, not the Work Date.

Here are some sample DateFormulas and their interpretations (displayed dates are based on the US calendar) with a reference date of July 11, 2014, a Friday:

- CM: The last day of the Current Month, 07/31/14
- CM + 10D: The 10th of next month, 08/10/14
- WD6: The next sixth day of week, 07/12/14
- WD5: The next fifth day of week, 07/18/14
- CM – M + D: The end of the current month minus one month plus one day, 07/01/14
- CM – 5M: The end of the current month minus five months, 02/28/14

Let us take the opportunity to use the DateFormula data type to learn a few NAV development basics. We will do so by experimenting with some hands-on evaluations of several DateFormula values. We will create a table to calculate dates using DateFormula and Reference Dates.

First, we will create a table using the Table Designer as we did in earlier instances. Go to **Tools** | **Object Designer** | **Tables**. Click on the **New** button and define the fields as in the following screenshot. Save it as `Table 50099`, named `Date Formula Test`. After we are done with this test, we will save this table for some later testing. Our table will look like the following screenshot:

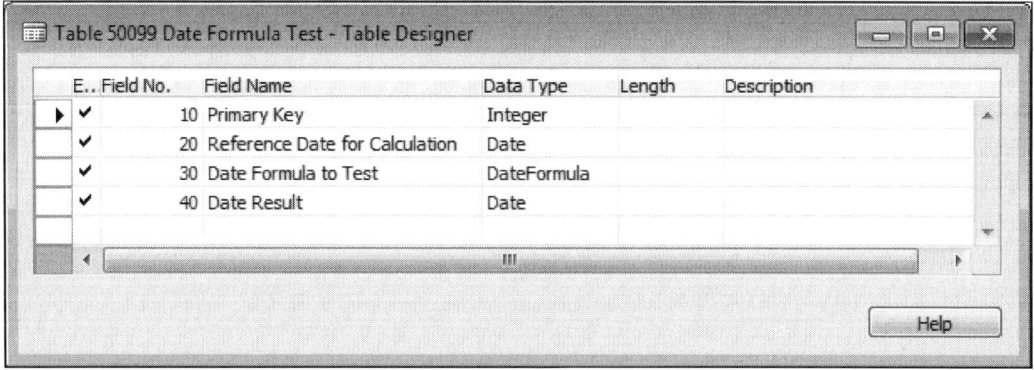

Now we will add some simple C/AL code to our table so that when we enter or change either the Reference Date or the DateFormula data, we can calculate a new result date.

First, access the new table via the **Design** button, then go to the global variables definition form through the **View** menu option, the sub-option **C/AL Globals**, and finally choose the **Functions** tab. Type in our new function name as `CalculateNewDate` on the first blank line as shown in the following screenshot and then exit (by means of *Esc* key) from this form back to the list of data fields:

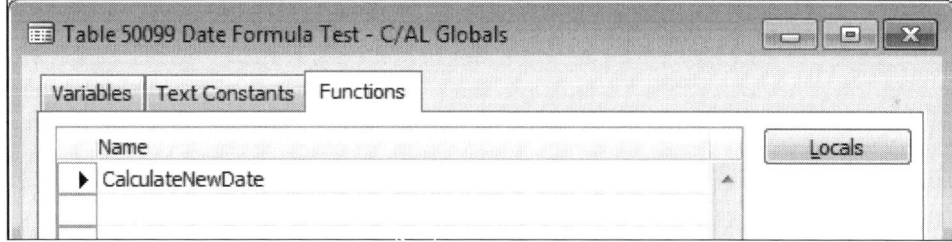

From the **Table Designer** form displaying the list of data fields, either press *F9* or click on the **C/AL Code** icon:

This will take us to the following screen, where we will see all of the field triggers, plus the trigger for the new function that we just defined. The table triggers are not visible, unless we scroll up to show them. These are shown in the following screenshot:

As our goal this time is to focus on experimenting with the DateFormula, we will not go into detail about the logic we are creating. The logic we're going to code is as follows:

When an entry is made (new or changed) in either the "Reference Date" field or in the "Date Formula" to Test field, invoke the "CalculateNewDate" function to calculate a new "Result Date" value based on the entered data.

First, we will create the logic within our new function, **CalculateNewDate()**, to evaluate and store a **Date Result** based on the DateFormula and Reference Date that we enter into the table.

Just copy the C/AL code exactly as shown in the following screenshot, exit, compile, and save the table:

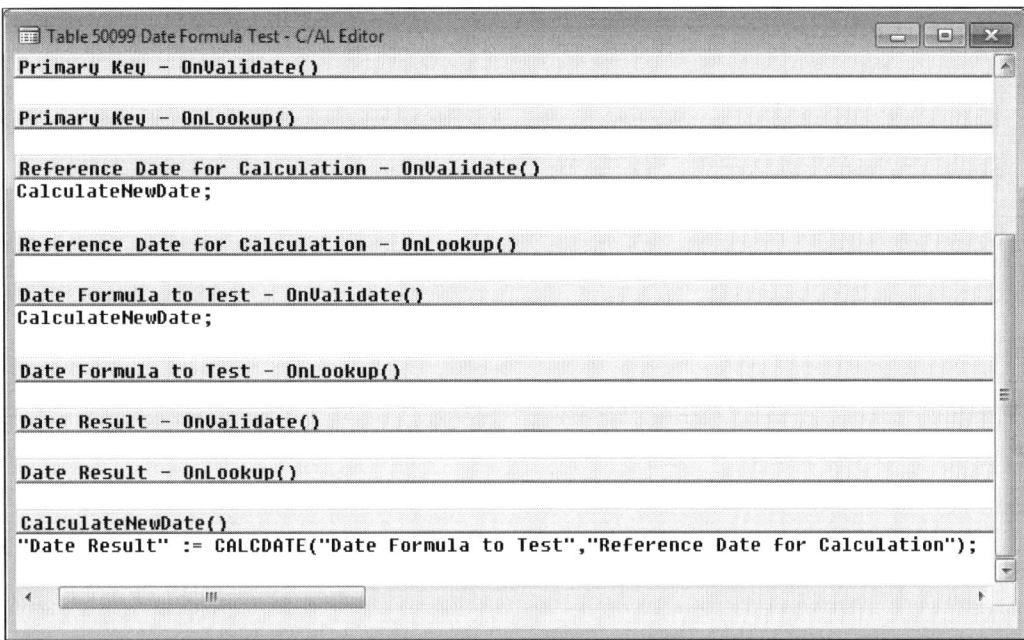

When you close and save the table, if you get an error message of any type, you probably have not copied the C/AL code exactly as it is shown in the screenshot (also the following is given for ease of copying).

```
CalculateNewDate;

"Date Result" := CALCDATE("Date Formula to Test","Reference Date for
Calculation");
```

This code will cause the function **CalculateNewDate()** to be called via the **OnValidate()** trigger when an entry is made in either the **Reference Date for Calculation** or the **Date Formula to Test** fields. The function will place the result in the **Date Result** field. The use of an integer value in the redundantly named **Primary Key** field allows you to enter several records into the table (by manually numbering them 1, 2, 3, and so on).

Let's experiment with several different date and date formula combinations. We will access the table via the **Run** button. This will cause NAV to generate a default format page and run it in the Role Tailored Client.

Enter a **Primary Key** value of 1 (one). In **Reference Date for Calculation**, enter either an upper or lower case T for Today, the system date. The same date will appear in the **Date Result** field, because at this point there is no Date Formula entered. Now enter 1D (numeral 1 followed by upper or lower case D, C/SIDE will take care of making it upper case) in the **Date Formula to Test** field. We will see the **Date Result** field contents are changed to be one day beyond the date in the **Reference Date for Calculation** field.

Now for another test entry. Start with a 2 in the **Primary Key** field. Again, enter the letter T (for Today) in the **Reference Date for Calculation** field and enter the letter W (for Work Date) in the **Date Formula to Test** field. We will get an error message telling us that our formulas should include a number. Make the system happy and enter 1W. We now will see a date in the **Date Result** field one week beyond our system date.

Set the system's Work Date to a date somewhere during a month (remember, we discussed setting the Work Date in *Chapter 1, An Introduction to NAV 2013*). Start another line with the number 3 as the **Primary Key** field, followed by a W (for Work Date) in the **Reference Date for Calculation** field. Enter cm (or CM or cM or Cm, it doesn't matter) in the **Date Formula to Test** field. Our result date will be the last day of our Work Date month. Now enter another line using the Work Date, but enter a formula of -cm (the same as before, but with a minus sign). This time our result date will be the first day of our Work Date month. Notice that the DateFormula logic handles month end dates correctly, even including Leap Year. The following screen shows the **Date Formula Test** window:

Enter another line with a new **Primary Key**. Skip over the **Reference Date for Calculation field** and just enter 1D in the **Date Formula to Test** field. What happens? We get an error message stating that **"You cannot base a date calculation on an undefined date."** In other words, NAV cannot make the requested calculation without a Reference Date. If we put this function into production, we might want our code to check for a Reference Date before calculating. We could default an empty date to the System Date or the Work Date and avoid this particular error.

The following screenshot shows different sample calculations. Build on these and experiment on your own. We can create a variety of different algebraic date formulae and get some very interesting results. One NAV user has due dates on Invoices of the 10th of the next month. Invoices are dated at various times during the month than they are actually printed. By using the DateFormula of CM + 10D, the due date is automatically calculated to be the 10th of the next month.

Primary Key	Reference Date for Calcul...	Date Formu...	Date Result
1	10/3/2013	1D	10/4/2013
2	10/3/2013	1W	10/10/2013
3	4/6/2014	CM	4/30/2014
4	4/6/2014	-CM	4/1/2014
5	10/3/2013	CM	10/31/2013
6	2/3/2012	CM	2/29/2012
7	2/3/2011	CM	2/28/2011
8	9/25/2013	1M	10/25/2013
9	9/25/2014	-1M	8/25/2014
10	10/3/2014	-1W-1D	9/25/2014
11	9/25/2014	1D+1W	10/3/2014
12	10/3/2014	-1W	9/26/2014
13	1/15/2014	-CM-1D	12/31/2013
14	1/15/2014	-1Y-CM	1/1/2013

Don't forget to test with WD (weekday), Q (quarter), and Y (year) as well as D (day), W (week), and M (month). For our code to be language independent, we should enter the date formulae with < > delimiters around them (example: <1D+1W>). NAV will translate the formula into the correct language codes using the installed language layer.

Although our basic focus for the work we just completed was the Date Formula data type, we've accomplished a lot more than simply learning about that one data type.

- We created a new table just for the purpose of experimenting with a C/AL feature that you might use. This is a technique that comes in handy when we are learning a new feature, trying to decide how it works or how we might use it.

- We put some critical OnValidate logic in the table. When data is entered in one area, the entry is validated and, if valid, the defined processing is done instantly.

- We created a common routine as a new function. That function is then called from all the places to which it applies.

- We did our entire test with a table object and a default tabular page that is automatically generated when you **Run** a table. We didn't have to create much of a supporting structure to do our testing. Of course, when we are designing a change to a complicated existing structure, we will likely have a more complicated testing scenario. One of our goals will always be to simplify our testing scenarios, both to minimize the setup effort and to keep our test narrowly focused on the specific issue.

- Finally, and most specifically, we saw how NAV tools make a variety of relative date calculations easy. These are very useful in business applications, many aspects of which are date centered.

References and other data types

The following data types are used for advanced functionality in NAV, sometimes supporting an interface with an external object.

- **RecordID**: Contains the object number and Primary Key of a table.

- **RecordRef**: Identifies a row in a table, a record. RecordRef can be used to obtain information about the table, the record, the fields in the record, and the currently active filters on the table.

- **FieldRef**: Identifies a field in a table, thus allows access to the contents of that field.

- **KeyRef**: Identifies a key in a table and the fields in that key.

Since the specific record, field and key references are assigned at run time, RecordRef, FieldRef, and KeyRef are used to support logic that can run on tables that are not specified at design time. This means that one routine built on these data types can be created that performs a common function for a variety of different tables and table formats.

- **Variant**: Defines variables typically used for interfacing with Automation and OCX objects. Variant variables can contain data of various C/AL data types for passing to an Automation or OCX object as well as external Automation data types that cannot be mapped to C/AL data types.

- **TableFilter**: For variables that only can be used for setting security filters from the Permissions table.

- **Transaction Type**: Has optional values of **UpdateNoLocks, Update, Snapshot, Browse**, and **Report**, which define SQL Server behavior for a NAV Report or XMLport transaction from the beginning of the transaction.

- **BLOB**: Can contain either a graphic in the form of a bitmap, specially formatted text, or other developer-defined binary data up to 2 GB in size. The term **BLOB** stands for **Binary Large Object**. BLOBs can only be included in tables, not used to define working storage Variables. See **Developer and IT Pro Help** for additional information.

- **BigText**: Can contain large chunks of text up to 2 GB in size. BigText variables can only be defined in the working storage within an object, but not included in tables. BigText variables cannot be directly displayed or seen in the debugger. There is a group of special functions that can be used to handle BigText data. See **Developer and IT Pro Help** for additional information.

> If you wish to handle text strings in a single data element greater than 250 characters in length, you can use a combination of BLOB and BigText variables.

- **GUID**: Used to assign a unique identifying number to any database object. **GUID** stands for **Globally Unique Identifier**, a 16-byte binary data type that is used for the unique global identification of records, objects, and so on. The GUID is generated by an algorithm developed by Microsoft.

- **TestPage**: Used to store a test page which is a logical representation of a page that does not display a user interface. Test pages are used when doing NAV application testing using the automated testing facility that is part of NAV.

- **ExecutionMode**: Appears to have two optional values ExecutionMode::Standard or ExecutionMode::Debug, indicating the state of the current session.

Data type usage

About half of the data types can be used to define the data either stored in tables or in working storage data definitions (that is, in a Global or Local data definition within an object). BLOB and TableFilter data types can only be used to define table stored data, but not working storage data. About half of the data types can only be used for working storage data definitions.

The following list shows which data types can be used for table (persisted) data and which ones can be used for working storage (variable) data:

Table Data Types	Working Storage Data Types
	Action
	Automation
BigInteger	BigInteger
	BigText
BLOB	
Boolean	Boolean
	Char
Code	Code
	Codeunit
Date	Date
DateFormula	DateFormula
DateTime	DateTime
Decimal	Decimal
	Dialog
	DotNet
Duration	Duration
	ExecutionMode
	FieldRef
	File
GUID	GUID
	Instream
Integer	Integer
	KeyRef
	OCX
Option	Option
	Outstream
	Page
	Record
RecordID	RecordID
	RecordRef
	Report
TableFilter	
	TestPage
Text	Text
Time	Time
	TransactionType
	Variant
	WideChar
	XMLport

FieldClass property options

Almost all data fields have a FieldClass property. FieldClass has as much effect on the content and usage of a data field as does the data type, in some instances maybe more. In the next chapter, we'll cover most field properties, but we'll discuss FieldClass property options now.

FieldClass – Normal

When the FieldClass is Normal, the field will contain the type of application data that's typically stored in a table, content we would expect based on the data type and various properties.

FieldClass – FlowField

FlowFields must be dynamically calculated. FlowFields are virtual fields; they do not contain data in the conventional sense. A FlowField contains the definition of how to calculate the data (at run time) that it represents. Depending on the **CalcFormula** Method, this could be a value, a reference lookup, or a **Boolean**. When the **CalcFormula** Method is **Sum**, the FieldClass connects a data field to a previously defined SumIndexField in the table defined in the CalcFormula. Any FlowField processing will be significantly affected by the key configuration of the table being processed. While we must be careful not to define extra keys, having the right keys defined will have a major effect on system performance and thus on user satisfaction. Most of the time, the **Editable** property for a FlowField is set to No.

A FlowField value is always 0, blank or false, unless it has been calculated. If a FlowField is displayed directly on a page, it is calculated automatically when the page is rendered. FlowFields are also automatically calculated when they are the subject of predefined filters as part of the properties of a data item in an object (this will be explained in more detail in the chapters covering Reports and XMLports). In all other cases, a FlowField must be forced to calculate using the C/AL RecordName.CALCFIELDS(FlowField1, [FlowField2],...) function or by use of the function SETAUTOCALCFIELDS. This is also true if the underlying data is changed after the initial display of a page (that is, the FlowField must be recalculated to take a data change into account).

 Because a FlowField does not contain actual data, it cannot be used as a field in a key, in other words, we cannot sort on a FlowField. Also, we cannot define a FlowField that is based on another FlowField.

When a field has its FieldClass set to `FlowField`, another directly associated property becomes available: **CalcFormula** (conversely, the **AltSearchField**, **AutoIncrement**, and **TestTableRelation** properties disappear from view when **FieldClass** is set to `FlowField`). The **CalcFormula** is the place where we can define the formula for calculating the **FlowField**. On the **CalcFormula** property line, there is an ellipsis button. Clicking on that button will bring up the following:

The following screenshot shows the seven FlowField methods:

The seven FlowFields are described in the following table:

FlowField Method	Field data type	Calculated Value as it applies to the specified set of data within a specific column (field) in a table
Sum	Decimal	The sum total
Average	Decimal	The average value (the sum divided by the row count)
Exist	Boolean	Yes or No / True or False - does an entry exist?

FlowField Method	Field data type	Calculated Value as it applies to the specified set of data within a specific column (field) in a table
Count	Integer	The number of entries that exist
Min	Any	The smallest value of any entry
Max	Any	The largest value of any entry
Lookup	Any	The value of the specified entry

The **Reverse Sign** control allows you to change the displayed sign of the result for FlowField types **Sum** and **Average** only; the underlying data is not changed. If a Reverse Sign is used with the FlowField type **Exists**, it changes the effective function to *does not Exist*.

Table and **Field** allows us to define the Table and the Field within that table to which our Calculation Formula will apply. When we make the entries in our **Calculation Formula** screen, there is no validation checking by the compiler that we have chosen an eligible table and field combination. That checking doesn't occur until run time. Therefore, when we are creating a new FlowField, we should test it as soon as we have defined it.

The last, but by no means the least significant, component of the FlowField calculation formula is the **Table Filter**. When we click on the ellipsis in the table filter field, the window shown in the following screen will appear:

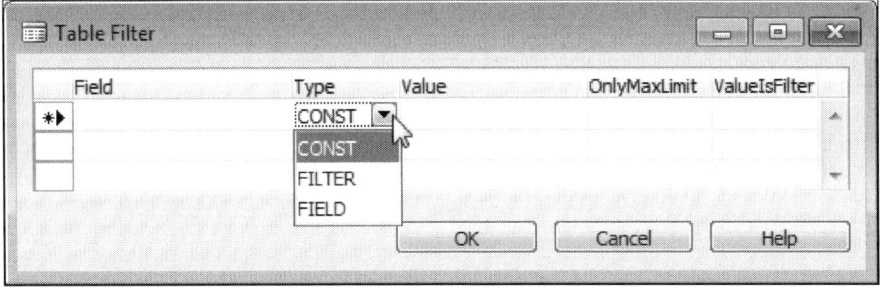

When we click on the **Field** column, we will be invited to select a field from the table that was entered into the **Table** field earlier. The **Type** field choice will determine the type of filter. The **Value** field will have the filter rules define on this line, which must be consistent with the **Type** choice. The explanation is given in the following table:

Filter type	Value	Filtering action	OnlyMax-Limit	Values-Filter
CONST	A constant that will be defined in the Value field	Uses the constant to filter for equally valued entries		
FILTER	A filter that will be spelled out as a literal in the Value field	Applies the filter expression from the Value field		
FIELD	A field from the table within which the FlowField exists	Uses the contents of the specified field to filter for equally valued entries	False	False
		If the specified field is a FlowFilter and the **OnlyMaxLimit** parameter is **True**, then the FlowFilter range will be applied on the basis of only having a MaxLimit, that is, having no bottom limit. This is useful for the date filters for Balance Sheet data. (See **Balance at Date** field in the **G/L Account** table for an example)	True	False
		Causes the contents of the specified field to be interpreted as a filter (See **Balance at Date** field in the **G/L Account** table for an example)	True or False	True

FieldClass – FlowFilter

FlowFilters control the calculation of FlowFields in the table (when the FlowFilters are included in the CalcFormula). FlowFilters do not contain permanent data, but instead contain filters on a per user basis, with the information stored in that user's instance of the code being executed. A FlowFilter field allows a filter to be entered at a parent record level by the user (for example, G/L Account) and applied (through the use of FlowField formulas, for example) to constrain what child data (for example, G/L Entry records) is selected.

A FlowFilter allows us to provide flexible data selection functions to the users. The user does not need to have a full understanding of the data structure to apply filtering in intuitive ways to both the primary data table and also to subordinate data. Based on our C/AL code design, FlowFilters can be used to apply filtering on multiple tables subordinate to a parent table. Of course, it is our responsibility as the developers to make good use of this tool. As with many C/AL capabilities, a good way to learn more is by studying standard code as designed by the Microsoft developers of NAV.

A number of good examples on the use of FlowFilters can be found in the **Customer** (Table 18) and **Item** (Table 27) tables. In the **Customer** table, some of the FlowFields using FlowFilters are **Balance**, **Balance (LCY)**, **Net Change**, **Net Change (LCY)**, **Sales (LCY)**, and **Profit (LCY)**. The **Sales (LCY)** FlowField FlowFilter usage is shown in the following screenshot:

Similarly constructed FlowFields using FlowFilters in the **Item** table include **Inventory**, **Net Invoiced Qty.**, **Net Change, Purchases (Qty.)**, and a number of other fields.

Throughout the standard code, there are FlowFilters in most of the master table definitions. There are the Date Filters and Global Dimension Filters (global dimensions are user-defined codes that facilitate the segregation of accounting data by groupings such as divisions, departments, projects, customer type, and so on). Other FlowFilters that are widely used in the standard code are those related to Inventory activity such as **Location Filter**, **Lot No. Filter**, **Serial No. Filter**, and **Bin Filter**.

The following screenshot shows two fields from the **Customer** table, both with a **Data Type** of **Date**. On the right side of the screenshot is the **Date Filter** field (**FieldClass** of `FlowFilter`); on the left side of the screenshot is the **Last Date Modified** field (**FieldClass** of `Normal`). It's easy to see that the properties of the two fields are very similar except for those that differ because one is a **Normal** field and the other is a **FlowFilter** field.

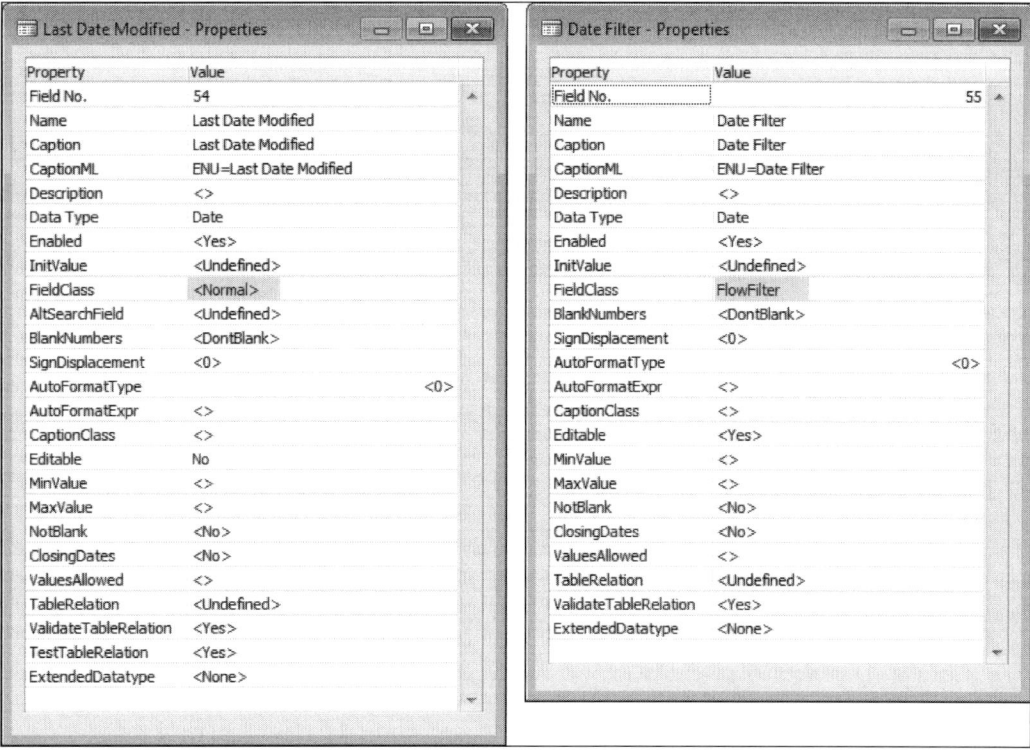

FlowFields and a FlowFilter for our application

In our application we have decided to have several FlowFields and a FlowFilter in Table 50000 – Radio Show. The reason for these fields is to provide instant analysis for individual shows based on the detailed data stored in subordinate tables. In *Chapter 2, Tables*, we showed Table 50000 with fields 1090 through 1130 but didn't provide any information how those fields should be constructed. Let's go through that construction process now. Here's how the fields 1090 through 1130 should look when we open Table 50000 in the Table Designer. If you didn't add these fields during the *Chapter 2* exercise, you can do that now.

✔	1090	Avg. Listeners	Decimal	FFld: Listenership Ledger
✔	1100	Avg. Listener Share	Decimal	FFld: Listenership Ledger
✔	1110	Advertising Revenue	Decimal	FFld: Radio Show Ledger
✔	1120	Royalty Cost	Decimal	FFld: Radio Show Leder
✔	1130	Date Filter	Date	Flow Filter for date datatype

These five fields will be used for statistical analysis for each Radio Show as follows:

- **Field 1090 – Avg. Listeners**: The average number of listeners as reported by the ratings agency
- **Field 1100 – Avg. Listener Share**: The percent of one station's total estimated listening audience per time slot
- **Field 1110 – Advertising Revenue**: A sum total of the advertising revenue generated by show
- **Field 1120 – Royalty Cost**: A sum total of the royalties incurred by the show by playing copyrighted material
- **Field 1130 – Date Filter**: A filter to restrict the data calculated for the above four fields.

To begin with we will set the calculation properties for the first FlowField, **Avg. Listeners**.

1. If you don't already have Table 50000 open in the Table Designer, then open it via **Tools | Object Designer**, select the **Table** button on the left as the object type. Find **Table 50000, Radio Show**, select it and click on **Design**.

2. Scroll down to field **1090**, select it and click on the **Properties** icon at the top of the screen or click on *Shift + F4*. Highlight the **FieldClass** property, click on the Dropdown arrow () and select **FlowField**. A new property will appear called **CalcFormula** directly underneath the **FieldClass** property. An **Assist Edit** button (⋯) will appear. Click on it and the Calculation Formula form will appear as follows:

3. Select **Average** from the **Method** dropdown, leave the **Reverse Sign** field unchecked, and type Listenership Ledger or 50006 into the **Table** field. You can either type Listeners or click on the **Lookup** button (⬆) to select the Listeners field from the table. Lastly, we want to define a filter to allow the Radio Show statistics to be reviewed based on a user definable date range. Click on the **Assist Edit** button on the **Table Filter** field. The following screen will appear:

4. Click on the Lookup arrow in the **Field** column and select **Date** from the **Listenership Ledger – Field List**.

5. In the **Type** column, click on the Dropdown arrow and you will see three choices for defining what type of filter to apply: **CONST, FILTER, FIELD**. In this case, we want to apply a field filter, so choose **FIELD**.

6. The last part of the **Table Filter** definition is the **Value** column. Click on the Lookup arrow in the **Value** column and choose **Date Filter** from the **Radio Show – Field List**. This will cause the **Date Filter** field value in the Radio Show record to be applied to the values in the **Date** field in the **Listenership Ledger**, controlling what data to use for the FlowField Average calculation.

7. Select **OK** and our **Calculation Formula** screen should look like this:

8. Click on **OK** and the **CalcFormula** property will fill in with the following text:

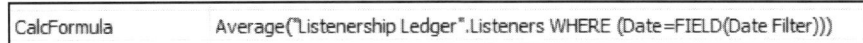

9. Since this is a text field, you could enter the syntax manually, but it's much easier and less error prone to use the **Calculation Formula** screen.

10. Set the **Editable** property to No.

11. For **Field 1100 – Avg. Listener Share**, repeat the procedure we just went through, but for **Field** select **Listener Share** from the **Listenership Ledger – Field List**. Your result should look like the following:

12. For Fields **1110 – Advertising Revenue** and **1120 – Royalty Cost**, the FlowField calculation is a sum with multiple fields having filters applied. For each field, the first step will be to set the **FieldClass** property to FlowField, then click on the **Assist Edit** button in the **CalcFormula** property to call up the **Calculation Formula** screen.

13. For **Advertising Revenue**, leave the **Method** to **Sum**, for **Table** enter Radio Show Ledger or the table number, 50005, and set **Field** to Fee Amount.

14. Click on the **Assist Edit** button for the table filter. Fill in the first row with the **Field** with **Date**, the **Type** with **FIELD**, and the **Value** with **Date Filter**. Fill in the second row set **Field** to **Format**, **Type** to **FILTER**, and enter Advertisement in the **Value** column (since we are filtering to a single value, we could also have used **CONST** for the **Type** value). The FlowField will now add up all the Fee Amount values that have a **Format** option selected as **Advertisement** for the date filter applied from the Radio Show table, shown as follows:

Advertisement is an available value of the field **Format** (Data Type Option) in the Radio Show Ledger, and if we typed a value that was not an Option value such as Commercial, an error would have displayed showing us what the available Option choices are. The error would be as follows:

We can use this feature as a development aid when we don't remember what the Option values are. We can enter a known incorrect value (such as xxx), press *F11* to compile and find out all the correct Option values.

15. Click on **OK** on the **Table Filter** form, and **OK** again on the **Calculation Formula** form.

16. Start **Royalty Cost** the same way all the way through the **Table** and **Field** choices in the **Calculation Formula** form. Click on the **Assist Edit** button for the table filter. Just as before, fill in the first row with the **Field Date**, the **Type** as FIELD, and the **Value** with **Date Filter**.

17. Fill in the second row set **Field** to **Format** and **Type** to FILTER. In the **Value** column, enter Vinyl|CD|MP3. This means we will filter for all records where the field **Format** contains a value equal to Vinyl or CD or MP3 (the Pipe symbol is translated to the Boolean "or"). As a result, this FlowField will sum up all the Fee Amount values that have a **Format** option selected as Vinyl, CD, or MP3, and a date satisfying the **Date Filter** specified in the **Radio Show** table.

18. The last field we will define in this exercise is the **Date Filter** field. We have already been referencing this Radio Show table field as a source of a user-defined date selection to help analyze the data from the listenership, payable, and revenue data, but we have not yet defined the field. This one is much easier than the FlowFields as no calculation formula is required.

19. Select the properties for the **Date Filter** field and set the **FieldClass** property to **FlowFilter** as shown here:

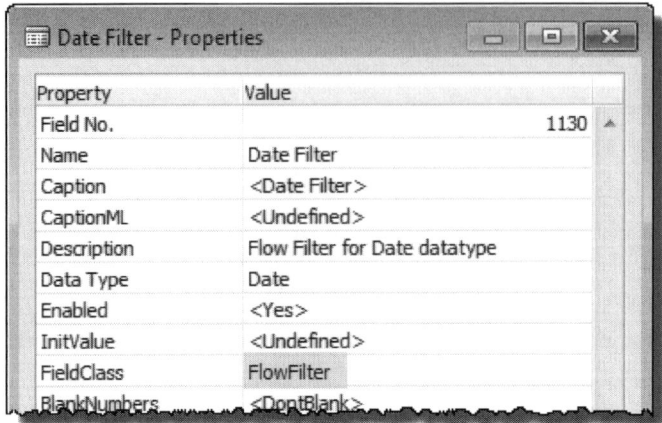

20. Close the **Date Filter - Properties** window and exit Table Designer, compiling the Radio Show table as you do so. Ideally you should also update the **Version List** field to indicate you've made additional changes to this table.

Filtering

Filtering is one of the most powerful tools within NAV. Filtering is the application of defined limits on the data that is to be considered in a process. When you apply a filter to a Normal data field, you will only view or process records where the filtered data field satisfies the limits defined by the filter. When you apply a filter to a FlowField, the calculated value for that field will only consider data satisfying the limits defined by the filter. Filter structures can be applied in at least three different ways, depending on the design of the process.

The first way is for the developer to fully define the filter structure and the value of the filter. This might be done in a report designed to show information on only a selected group of customers, such as those with an unpaid balance. The **Customer** table would be filtered to report only customers who have an outstanding balance greater than zero.

The second way is for the developer to define the filter structure, but allow the user to fill in the specific value to be applied. This approach would be appropriate in an accounting report that was to be tied to specific accounting periods. The user would be allowed to define what periods are to be considered for each report run.

The third way is the ad hoc definition of a filter structure and value by the user. This approach is often used for general analysis of ledger data where the developer wants to give the user total flexibility in how they slice and dice the available data.

It is common to use a combination of the different filtering types. For example, the report just mentioned that lists only customers with an open Balance (via a developer-defined filter) could also allow the user to define additional filter criteria. If the user wants to see only Euro currency customers, she would filter on the **Customer Currency Code** field.

Filters are an integral part of the implementation of both FlowFields and FlowFilters. These flexible, powerful tools allow the NAV designer to create pages, reports, and other processes that can be used under a wide variety of circumstances. In most competitive systems, user inquiries and processes need to be quite specific. The NAV C/AL toolset allows you to create relatively generic user inquiries and processes, and then allow the users to apply filtering to generate results that fit their specific needs.

The user sees FlowFilters filtering referred to as **Limit Totals** onscreen. Application of filters and ranges may give varying results depending on Windows settings or the SQL Server collation setup. A good set of examples of filtering options and syntax can be found in **Developer and IT Pro Help** in the section titled *Entering Criteria in Filters*.

Experimenting with filters

Now it's time for some experimenting with filters. We want to accomplish a couple of things through our experimentation. First, get more comfortable with how filters are entered. Second, see the effects of different types of filter structures and combinations. If we had a database with a large volume of data, we could also test the speed of filtering on fields in keys and on fields not in keys. But the amount of data in the basic Cronus database is small, so any speed differences will be difficult to see in these tests. An Extended (large data volume) Demo Database may be available for downloading from PartnerSource (it was available for NAV 2009 R2).

We could experiment on any report that allows filtering. A good report for this experimentation is the **Customer/Item List**. This reports which customer purchased what items. The **Customer/Item List** can be accessed on the Role Tailored Client Departments menu via **Sales & Marketing** | **Sales** | **Reports** | **Customer** | **Customer/Item Sales**.

When you initially run **Customer/Item Sales**, you will see just three data fields listed for entry of filters on the **Customer** table as shown in the following screenshot:

There are also two data fields listed for the entry of filters on the **Item Ledger Entry** table as shown in the following screenshot (which has the **Item Ledger Entry** FastTab expanded so you can see its predefined filter entry options):

For both the **Customer** and **Item Ledger Entry**, these are the fields that the developer determined should be emphasized. If you run the report without entering any filter constraints at all, using the standard Cronus data, the first page of the report will resemble the following:

Data Types and Fields

If we want to print information only for customers whose names begin with the letter **A**, our filter will be very simple, similar to the following screenshot:

The resulting report will be similar to the following screenshot, showing only the data for the two customers on file whose names begin with the letter **A**:

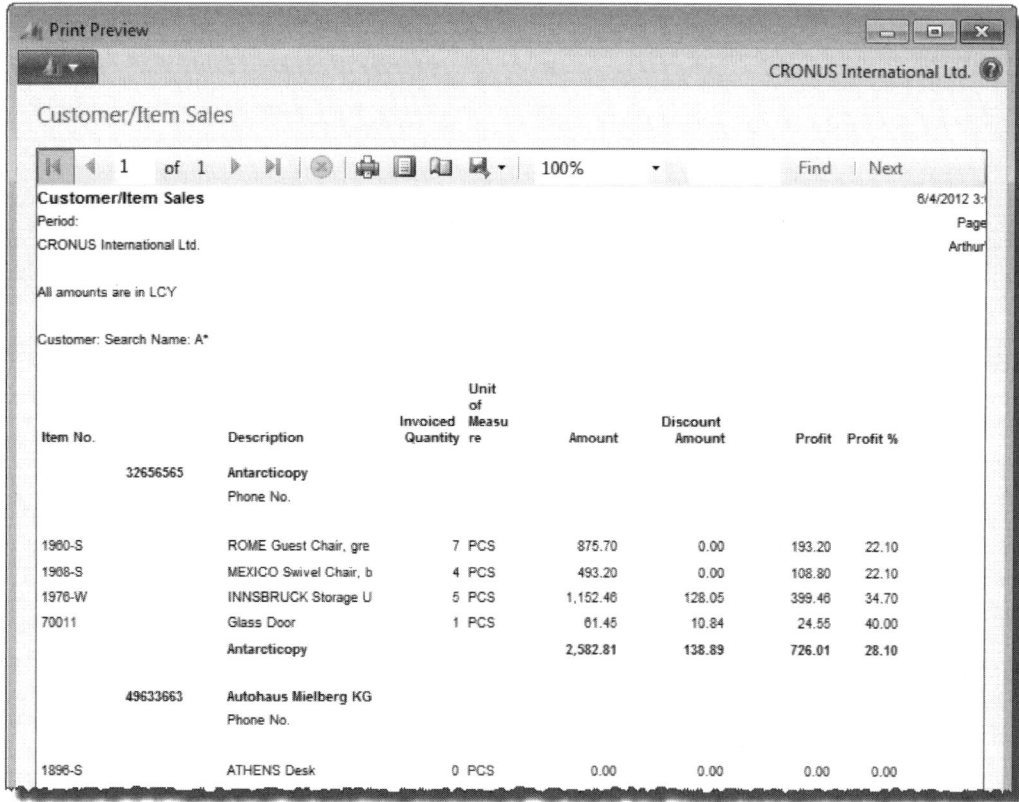

If we want to expand the customer fields to which we can apply filters, we can access the full list of other fields in the customer table. We can either click on the Dropdown symbol next to a filter field that is not already in use or click on the **Add Filter** button to add a new filter field with a Dropdown list access. If the number of fields available for filtering is longer than the initial list display allows, the bottom entry in the list is **Additional Columns**. If we click on that, we might end up with a display like the following. Notice that the lists are in alphabetical order, based on the field names:

From these lists we can choose one or more fields and then enter filters on those fields. If we chose **Territory Code**, for example, then the **Request Page** would look similar to the following screenshot. And if we clicked on the lookup arrow in the **Filter** column, a screen would pop-up, allowing us to choose from data items in the related table, in this case, **Territories**:

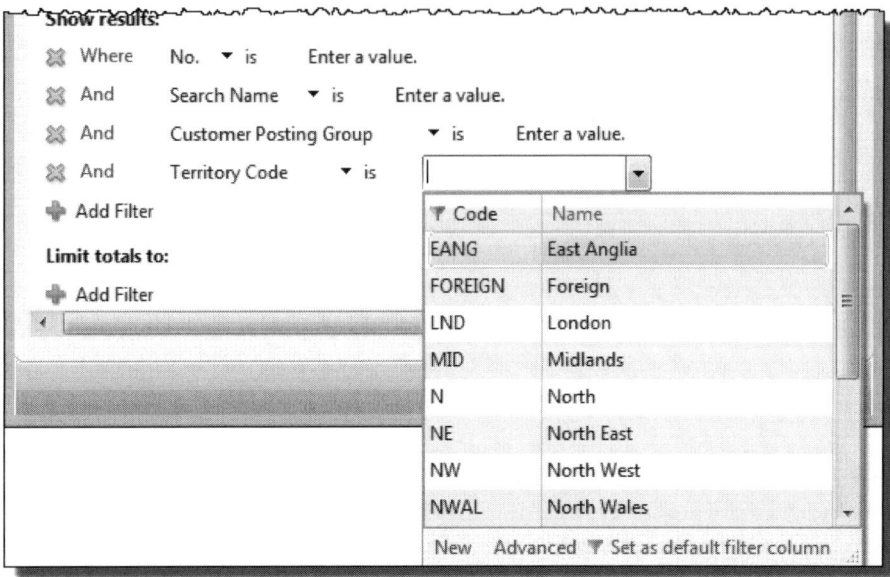

This particular **Request Page** has FastTabs for each of the two primary tables in the report. Click on the **Item Ledger Entry** FastTab to filter on the Item-related data. If we filter on the **Item No.** for Item Nos that contain the letter **W**, the report will be similar to the following screenshot:

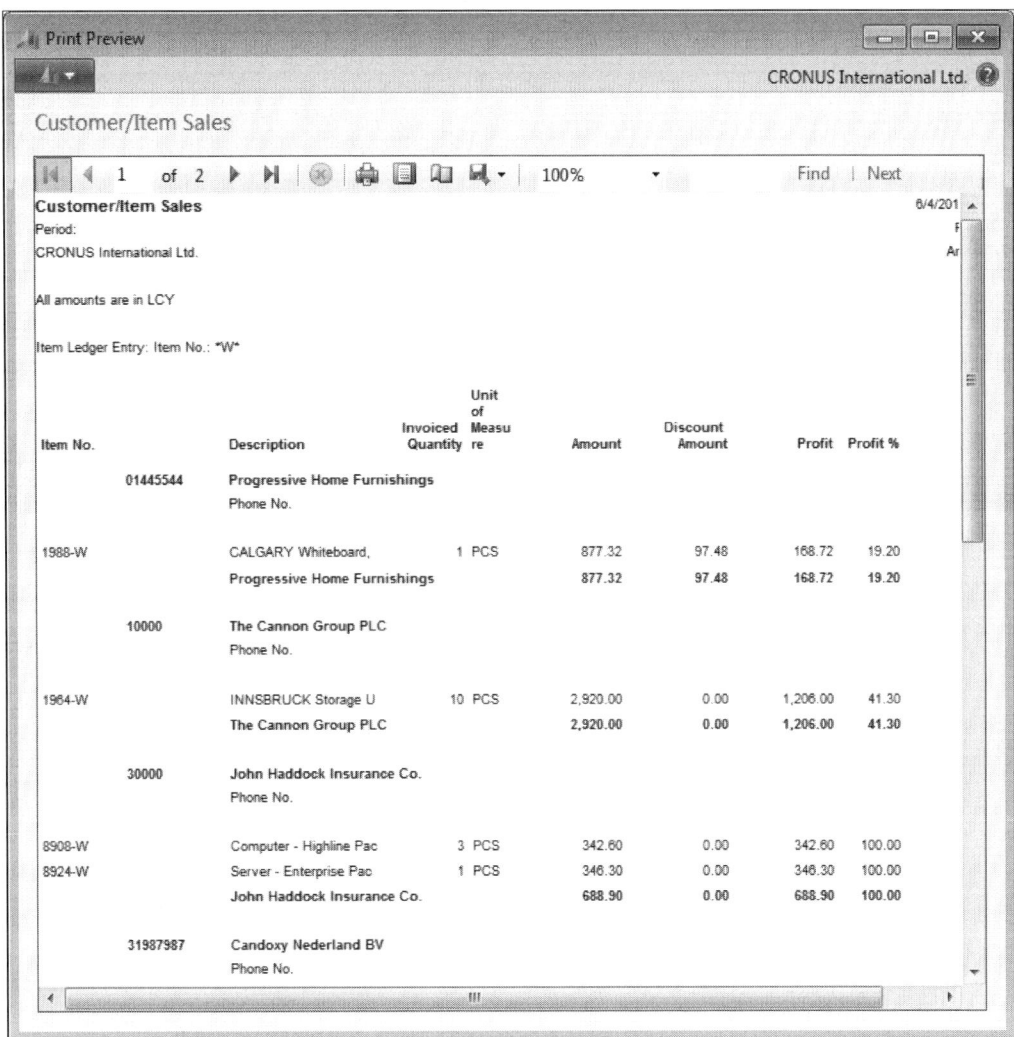

If we want to see all of the items containing either the letter **W** or the letter **S**, our filter would be *W* | *S*. If we made the filter **W** | **S**, then we would get only entries equal exactly to **W** or to **S** because we didn't use any wildcards.

You should go back over the various types of filters we discussed and try each one and try them in combination. Get creative! Try some things that you're not sure may work; see what happens. Explore a variety of reports or list pages in the system by applying filters to see the results of your experiments. A good page on which to apply filters is the **Customer List (Sales & Marketing | Sales | Customers)**. This filtering experimentation process is safe (you can't hurt anything or anyone) and a great learning experience.

Accessing filter controls

NAV 2013 has two very different approaches to setting up filtering; one for the Development Environment and the other for the Role Tailored Client. Because you will be developing in the former, we will briefly cover filtering there. Because you will be targeting your development for use in the Role Tailored Client, you need to be totally comfortable with filtering there.

Development Environment filter access

There are four buttons at the top of the screen that relate to filtering, plus one for choosing the active key. Depending on your system configuration (OS and setup), they will look like those in the following screenshot:

From left to right, they are:

- **Field Filter** *(F7)*: Highlight a field, press *F7* (or select **View | Field Filter**), and the data in that field will display ready for us to define a filter on that data field. We can freely edit the filter before clicking on **OK**.

- **Table Filter** *(Ctrl + F7)*: Press the *Ctrl* key and *F7* simultaneously (or select **View | Table Filter**). We will get a screen that allows us to choose fields in the left column and enter related filters in the right column. Each filter is the same as would have been created using the **Field Filter** option. The multiple filters for the individual fields are **ANDed** together (that is, they all apply simultaneously). If we invoke the **Table Filter** form when any **Field Filters** are already applied, they will be displayed in the form.

- **Flow Filter** *(Shift + F7)*: Since we cannot view any data containing FlowFields in the Development Environment, using the Flow Filter in the Development Environment is not useful.

- **Show All** *(Shift + Ctrl + F7)*: This will remove all Field Filters, but will not remove any Flow Filters.

- **Sort** *(Shift + F8)*: This allows us to choose which key is active on a displayed data list. When we are viewing a form and want to check if the filters are in effect, we should check the bottom of the screen for the word **FILTER**.

Role Tailored Client filter access

The method of accessing fields to use in filtering in the **Role Tailored Client** (**RTC**) is quite different from that in the Development Environment.

When a page such as the **Customer List** is opened, the filter section at the top of the page looks like the following screenshot. On the upper right corner is a place to enter single-field filters. This is the **Type to filter** (also known as **Quick**), essentially equivalent to the Field Filter in the Development Environment. The fields available for filtering are the same as the visible columns showing in the List. On the left is a **Sorting** field, which allows the choice of keys followed by a choice of Ascending or Descending.

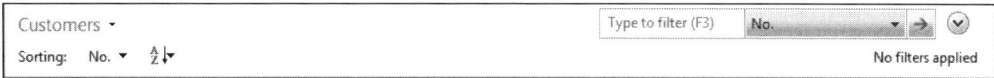

If we click on the chevron circle button in the upper right corner to expand the Filter Pane, the result will look similar to the following. This filter display includes an additional filtering capability, **Show Results**, allowing entry of **Limit totals to** filters.

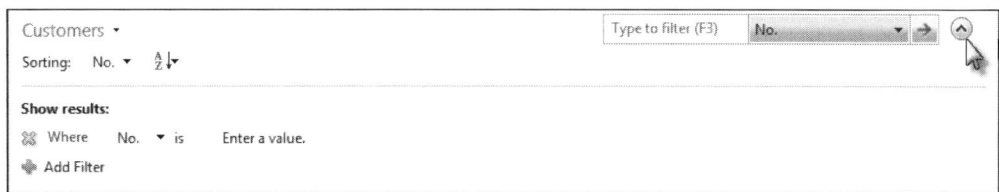

If we go to the Filter Pane header line (where the Page's Menu Caption is, **Customers** in this page) and click on the drop-down symbol, we will see a set of selection options (the filter menu) like that in the following screenshot. The **Advanced filter** provides for the entry of multiple Field Filters (essentially the same as the Development Environment Table Filter). The **Limit totals** filter provides for the entry of FlowFilter constraints.

This is one of two places we can clear filters of all types (we can also enter *Ctrl + Shift + A* as indicated in the filter menu). Choosing the **Change sorting** option simply puts focus on the key field in the **Sorting** part. The **Save View As...** option allows the user to save the filtered view, name it and add it to an **Activity Group** in the Navigation pane. The following screenshot shows a series of Saved Views on Sales Orders (most of them out-of-the-box). The **YELLOW Location** entry is a Saved View created by a user.

If we click on **Limit totals** (or click *Ctrl + Shift + F3*), the **Limit totals to:** portion of the Filter pane will display. When we click on the Dropdown arrow, we will get a list of all the FlowFields to which we can apply one or more **Limit totals** (FlowFilters).

Depending on the specific page and functional area, FlowField filtering can be used to segregate data on Dimension fields. For example, in the page shown in the preceding screenshot, we could filter for data regarding a single Department or Project or range of Departments or Projects or a range of Customer Ship-to locations.

Summary

In this chapter, we focused on the basic building blocks of NAV data structure, fields, and their attributes. We reviewed the types of data fields, properties, and trigger elements for each type of field. We walked through a number of examples to illustrate most of these elements, though we have postponed exploring triggers until later, when we have more knowledge of C/AL. We covered Data Type and FieldClass, properties that determine what kind of data can be stored in a field.

We reviewed and experimented with the date calculation tool that gives C/AL an edge in business applications. We discussed filtering, how filtering is considered as we design our database structure, and how the users will access data. Finally, more of our NAV Radio Show application was constructed.

In the next chapter, we will look at the many different types of Pages in more detail. We'll put some of that knowledge to use to further expand our example NAV application.

Review questions

1. The maximum length for a C/AL field or variable name is 250 characters long. True or False?

2. Which property is used to support the multi-language feature of NAV? (choose one)

    a. Name

    b. CaptionML

    c. Caption

    d. LanguageRef

3. The Table Relation property defines the reference of a data field to a table. The related table data field must be: (choose one)

    a. In any key in the related table

    b. Defined in the related table, but not in a key

    c. In the Primary Key in the related table

    d. The first field in the Primary Key in the related table

4. The ExtendedDataType property supports designation of all but one of the following data types, displaying an appropriate action icon. (choose the one not supported):

    a. Email address

    b. Website URL

    c. GPS location

    d. Telephone number

    e. Masked entry

5. Which of the following are Field Triggers (choose two)?

    a. OnEntry

    b. OnValidate

    c. OnDeletion

    d. OnLookup

6. It is important to have a consistent, well planned approach to field numbers, especially if you plan to use the TransferFields function. True or False?

7. Which of the following are complex data types? Choose three.

    a. Records

    b. Strings of text

    c. DateFormula

    d. DateTime data

    e. Objects

8. Every table must have a Primary Key. A Primary Key entry can be defined as unique or duplicates allowed, based on a table property. True or False?

9. FlowField data is not stored in the NAV table data. True or False?

10. The following two filters are equivalent. True or False?

    ○   (X* | ?K3* | 12??5)

    ○   (?K3*) OR (12??5) OR (X*)

11. Limit totals apply to FlowFilters. True or False?

12. Field Filters and Limit totals cannot both be used at the same time. True or False?

13. All Data Types can be used to define data both in tables or in working storage. True or False?

14. One of the following is not a FlowField Method (choose one).

  a. Count

  b. Max

  c. Median

  d. Exist

  e. Average

15. FlowFilter data is not stored in the database. True or False?

4
Pages – the User's Interactive Interface

Design is a plan for arranging elements in such a way as best to accomplish a particular purpose.
– Charles Eames

Always design your program as a member of a whole family of programs, including those that are likely to succeed it.
– Edsger Dijkstra

Pages are NAV 2013's object type for interactively presenting information. The page rendering routines that *paint* the page on the target display handle much of the data presentation detail. This allows a variety of clients to be created such as a SharePoint client, a Web browser resident client, the Windows RTC client, mobile clients, or even clients targeted to devices other than common video displays.

One of the benefits of Page technology is the focus on the user experience rather than the underlying data structure. As always, the designer/developer has the responsibility of using the tools to their best effect. Another advantage of NAV 2013 pages is the flexibility they provide the user for personalization, allowing the user to tailor what is displayed, and how it is organized.

In this chapter, we will explore the various types of pages offered by NAV 2013. We will review many options for formatting, data access, and tailoring your pages. We will also learn about the Page Designer tools and the inner structures of pages. Topics we will cover include:

- Page Design and Structure Overview
- Types of Pages
- Page Designer

- Page Components
- Page Controls
- Page Actions
- WDTU Page Enhancement exercises 1 and 2

Page Design and Structure Overview

Pages serve the purpose of input, output, and control. Pages are views of data or process information designed for on-screen display only. Pages are also user data entry vehicles.

Pages are made up of various combinations of Controls, Properties, Actions, Triggers, and C/AL Code.

- Controls provide the user with ways to view, type, and edit text, choose options or commands, initiate actions, and view status.
- Properties are attributes or characteristics of an object that define its state, appearance, or value.
- Actions are menu items (which may be icons).
- Triggers are predefined functions that are executed when certain actions or events occur.

The internal structure of a page maps to an XML structure, some of which is readily visible in the Page Designer display while the rest is in the background.

Page Design Guidelines

C/SIDE allows us to create pages with a number of different *look and feel* attributes. The standard NAV application only uses a few of the possibilities, and closely follows a set of **Graphical User Interface (GUI)** guidelines that provide consistency throughout the system. Those guidelines are described in an interactive document named **Microsoft Dynamics NAV 2013 User Experience Guidelines (UX Guide** for short). You should obtain a copy of this guide from the MSDN Library (`http://msdn.microsoft.com/en-us/library/jj128065(v=nav.70).aspx`) and study it.

Good design practice dictates that enhancements integrate seamlessly with the existing software unless there is an overwhelming justification for being different. When we add new pages or change existing pages, the changes should have the same look and feel as the original pages unless the new functionality requires significant differences. This consistency not only makes the user's life better, it makes support, maintenance, and training more efficient.

There will be instances where we will need to create a significantly different page layout in order to address a special requirement. Maybe we need to use industry specific symbols, or we need to create a screen layout for a special display device. Perhaps we are going to create a special *dashboard* display to report on status of work queues. Even when we are going to be different, we should continue to be guided by the environment and context in which our new work will operate.

NAV 2013 Page structure

Let's take a look at what makes up a typical page in the NAV 2013 Role Tailored Client. The page in the following screenshot includes a List page at its core (the Content Area):

The **Travel Buttons** serve the same purpose that they serve in the Explorers—to move backward or forward through previously displayed pages.

The **Title Bar** displays Page Caption and product identification.

The **Address Bar** (also referred to as the Address Box) displays the navigation path that led to the current display. It defaults to the following format, which is sometimes referred to as the *breadcrumb* path:

If we click on one of the right-facing arrowheads in the Address Bar, child menu options will be displayed in a drop-down list (as in the following screenshot). The same list of options subordinate to **Sales Orders** is displayed both in the drop-down menu from the Address Bar, and in the detailed list of options in the Navigation Pane.

If we click in the blank space in the Address Bar to the right of the breadcrumbs, the path display will change to a traditional path format, shown as follows:

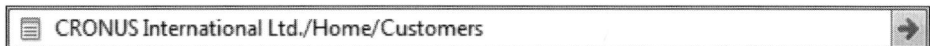

The **Global Command Bar** provides access to a general set of menu options, which varies slightly based on what is in the content area. The left-most menu in the Command Bar is accessed by clicking on the Microsoft Dynamics icon. It provides access (as shown in the next screenshot) to some basic application information and administration functions:

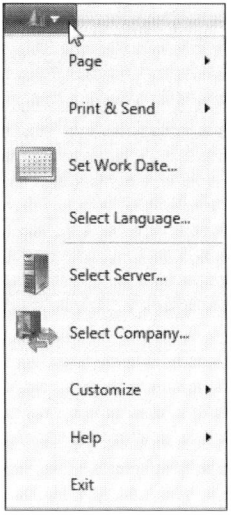

The **FilterPane** is where the user controls filtering and sorting to be applied to the page display.

The **Ribbon** contains shortcut icons to actions. These same commands will be duplicated in other menu locations, but are in the Ribbon for quick and easy access. The Ribbon can be collapsed (made not visible) or expanded (made visible) under user control.

The **Search Field** allows users to find pages and reports based on the object's name. Search finds only pages and reports that are accessible from the Navigation Pane.

The **Navigation Pane** contains menu options based on the active Role Center (tied to the user's login). It also contains activity buttons, at a minimum the **Home** and **Department** buttons. The **Departments** button and its menu items are generated based on the contents of the NAV MenuSuite.

The **Status Bar** shows the name of the active Company, the Work Date, and the current User ID. If you click on the company name, you can change companies. If you click on the Work Date, you can change it.

The **Content Area** is the focus of the page. It may be a Role Center, a List page or a Department menu list.

The **FactBox Pane** can appear on right side of certain page types (Card, List, ListPlus, Document, Navigate or Worksheet). This area can contain FactBoxes or SystemParts. (A FactBox can only display a CardPart or a ListPart. FactBoxes are intended to provide no-click and one-click access to related information about the data in focus in the Content Area.)

Types of pages

Let's review the types of pages available for use in an application. Then we will create several examples for our WDTU Radio Station system.

Each time we work on an application design, we need to carefully consider which page type is best to use for the functionality we are creating. Types of pages available include RoleCenter, List, Card, ListPart, CardPart, ListPlus, Document, Worksheet, Navigate, ConfirmationDialog, and StandardDialog. Pages can be created and modified by the developer and can be personalized by the administrator, super user, or user.

Role Center page

A user's assigned Role Center page is their home page in NAV, the page where they land when first logging into NAV 2013. The purpose of a Role Center page is to provide a task-oriented home base which focuses on the tasks that the user typically needs in order to do his/her job on a day-to-day basis. All the user's common tasks should be no more than one or two clicks away.

The standard NAV distribution includes 22 pre-defined Role Center pages, including generic roles such as Bookkeeper, Sales Manager, and Production Planner. Some of the provided Role Centers are richly featured and have been heavily tailored by Microsoft as illustrations of what is possible. On the other hand, some of the provided Role Centers are only skeletons, acting essentially as place holders.

 It is critical to understand that the provided Role Center pages are intended to be templates and examples, not final deliverables.

Role Centers that are specific to the customer's organization structure and user role profiles should be created for every NAV implementation. You should take advantage of the guidance for the design and creation of Role Center pages that is part of the *Microsoft Dynamics Sure Step Methodology* documentation and tools. Even if that material has not been updated for NAV 2013, it still provides much useful information.

Central to each Role Center page is the **Activities** area. The **Activities** area provides the user with a visual overview of their primary tasks. Central to the **Activities** part are the **Cues**. Each Cue icon represents a filtered list of documents in a particular status, thus indicating an amount of work to be handled by the user.

The following screenshot shows a **Role Center** page for the user role profile of **Sales Order Processor**:

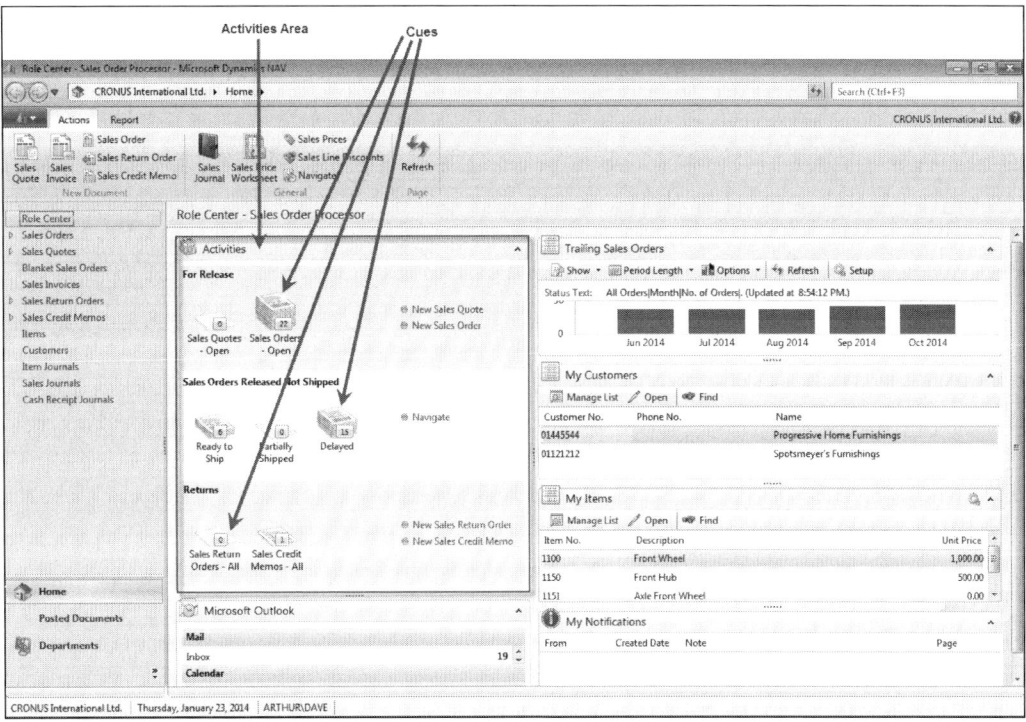

List page

List pages are the first pages accessed when choosing any menu option to access data. This includes all the entries under the Home Button on the Navigation Pane. A List page displays a list of records (rows), one line per record, with each displayed data field in a column.

When a List page is initially selected, it is not editable. When you double-click on an entry in a List, either an editable Card page is displayed or the List page entry becomes directly editable. Examples of this latter behavior are the Reference table pages such as Post Codes, Territories, and Languages. A List page can also be used to show a list of master records in order to allow the user to scan records, or to easily choose a record on which to focus.

List pages may optionally include FactBoxes. Some NAV 2013 List pages, such as Customer Ledger Entries (Page 25), allow editing of some fields (for example Invoice Due Dates) and not other fields.

The following screenshot shows a typical list page — the **Item** List – Page 31:

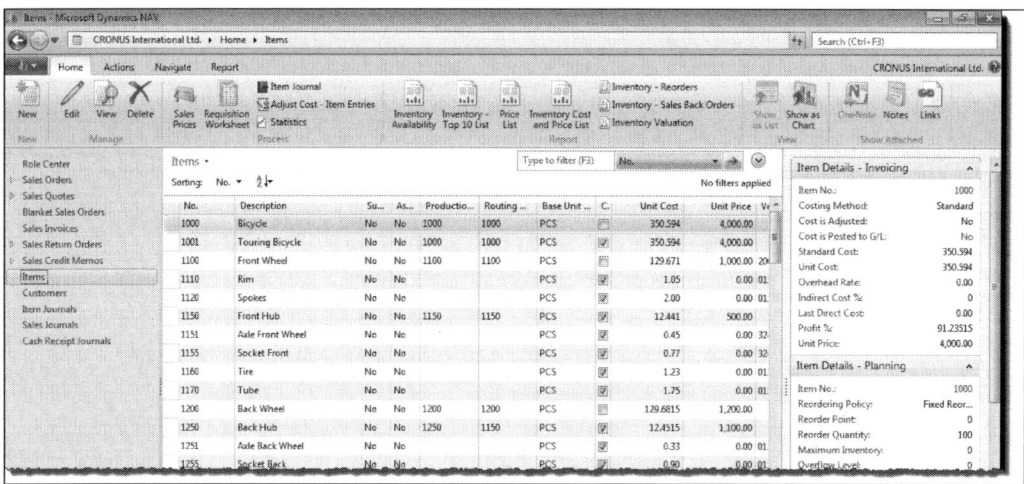

Card page

Card pages display and allow updating of a single record at a time. Card pages are used for master tables and setup data. Complex cards can contain multiple FastTabs and FactBoxes as well as display data from subordinate tables. An example Card page image for the **Customer Card** – Page 21, follows with the **General** FastTab expanded and the other FastTabs collapsed:

Document page

Document (task) pages have at least two FastTabs in a header/detail format. The FastTab at the top contains the header fields in a card style format, followed by a FastTab containing multiple records in a list style format (a ListPart page). Examples are Sales Orders and Invoices, Purchase Orders and Invoices, and Production Orders. The Document page type is appropriate whenever you have a parent record tied to subordinate child data in a one-to-many relationship. A Document page may have FactBoxes. An example Sales Order Document page follows (Sales Order – Page 42):

FastTab

FastTabs, as shown in the preceding **Customer Card** and **Sales Order** screenshots, are collapsible/expandable replacements for traditional left-to-right forms tabs. FastTabs are often used to segregate data by subject area on a Card page or a Document page. In this image the **General** and **Lines** FastTabs are expanded and the other FastTabs are collapsed. Individually important fields can be Promoted so they display on the FastTab header when the tab is collapsed, allowing the user to see this data with minimal effort. Examples appear on the Sales Order's Invoicing and Shipping FastTabs. Promoted field displays disappear from the FastTab header when the FastTab is expanded.

ListPlus page

A ListPlus page is similar in layout to a Document page, as it will have at least one FastTab with fields in a card type format and one FastTab at the bottom with a list page (grid) format. Unlike a Document page, a ListPlus page may have more than one FastTab with card format fields and one or more FastTabs with a list page format, while a Document page can only have a single list style page. The card format portion of a ListPlus page often contains control information determining what data is displayed in the associated list, such as in Page 113 – Budget, shown in the following image:

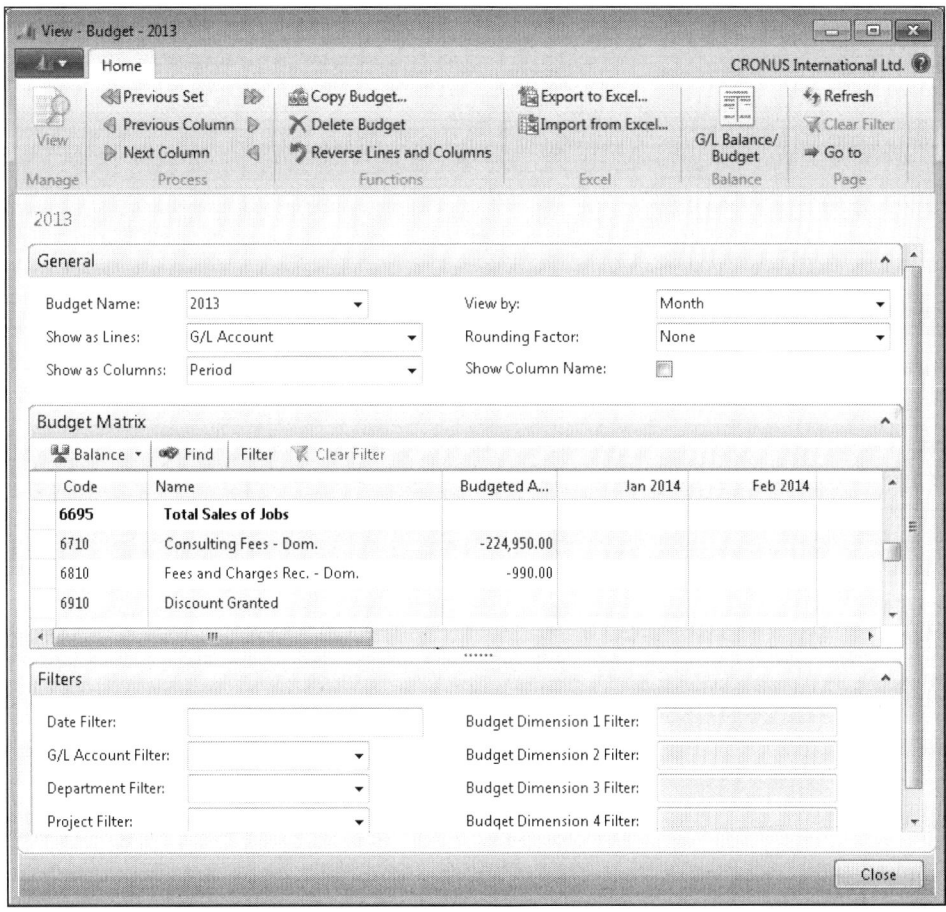

A ListPlus page may also have FactBoxes. Other examples of ListPlus pages are Page 155 – Customer Sales and Page 157 – Item Availability by Periods.

Worksheet (Journal) page

Worksheet pages are widely used in NAV to enter transactions. This page format consists of a list style section showing multiple records line by line in the content area, followed by a section containing either additional detail fields for the line in focus or containing totals. All of the Journals in NAV use Worksheet pages. Data is usually entered into a Journal/Worksheet by keyboard entry, but in some cases via a batch process.

The following screenshot shows a Worksheet page, **Sales Journal** – Page 253:

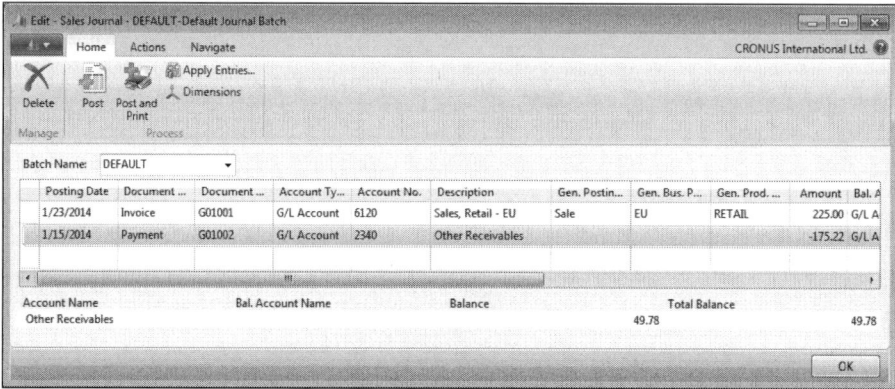

ConfirmationDialog page

This is a simple display page embedded in a process. It is used to allow a user to control the flow of a process. A sample ConfirmationDialog page is as follows:

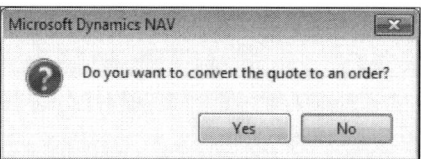

StandardDialog page

The StandardDialog page is also a simple page format to allow the user to control a process, such as **Copy Tax Setup** (Page 476). The StandardDialog page allows the entry of control data such as that shown in the following screenshot:

NavigatePage

The primary use of the NavigatePage page type in NAV 2013 is as the basis for Wizard pages. All the instances of Wizard pages in NAV 2013 are in the Marketing functionality area of the system. Some Wizard page examples are pages: 5077 – Create Interaction, 5097 – Create To-do, 5126 – Create Opportunity, 5129 – Update Opportunity, and 5146 – Assign Opportunity. A Wizard page consists of multiple user data entry screens linked together to provide a series of steps necessary to complete a task.

Two screens from a Wizard page (Page 5097 – **Create Interaction**) are as follows:

A special use of the NavigatePage in NAV is the redundantly named Navigate page (Page 344). The Navigate function has been a very powerful, unique feature of NAV since the 1990s. The Navigate function is implemented using the NavigatePage page type.

The Navigate page allows the user to view the summary of the number and type of posted entries having the same document number and posting date as a related entry or as a user-entered value. The user can drill down to examine the individual entries. Navigate is a terrific tool for tracking down related posted entries. It can be productively used by a user, an auditor, or even by a developer.

An unusual page feature of the Navigate page is the use of standard tabs at the bottom of the page display, rather than the normal NAV 2013 page FastTabs. A sample **Navigate** page is shown in the following screenshot:

Special pages

There are two special purpose page types. One is a component of other objects, the second is automatically generated.

Request page

A Request page is a simple page which allows the user to enter information to control the execution of a Report or XMLport object. Request pages can have multiple FastTabs, but can only be created as part of a Report object. All Request page designs will be similar to the following screenshot for the Item **Price List** (Report 715) Request page:

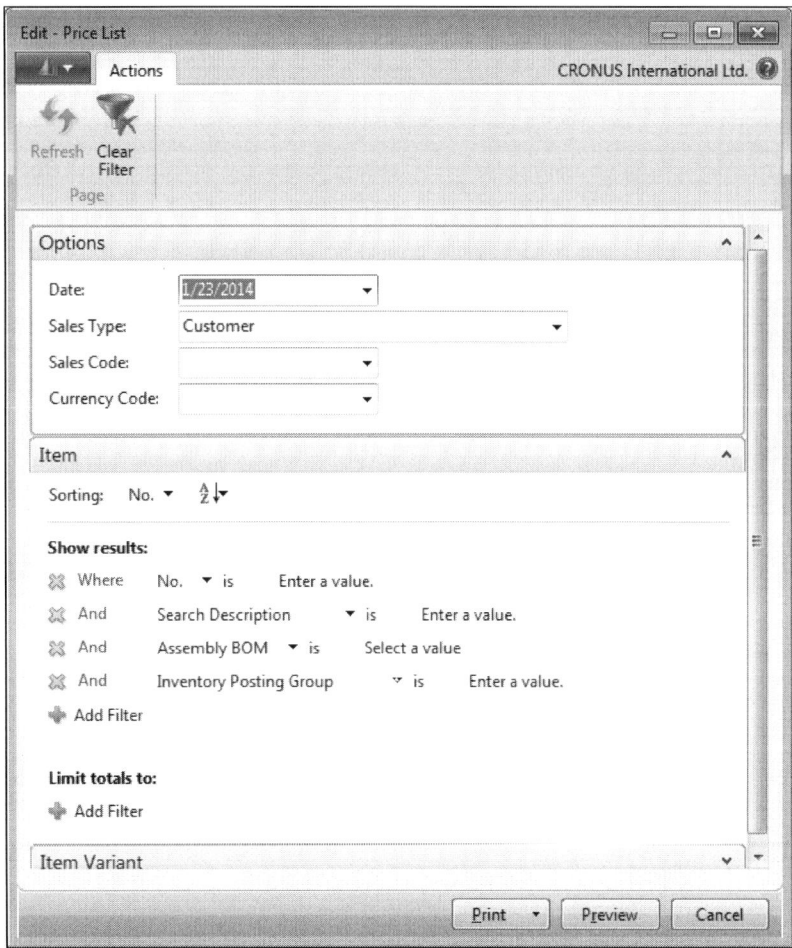

Departments page

The Departments page is a one-of-a-kind, system-generated page. We never directly create a Departments page as it is generated from the entries in the MenuSuite object. As we create new objects and add those to the MenuSuite, we will be providing the material needed to update the Departments menu/page. The look and feel of the Departments page cannot be changed (though individual entries can be added, changed, deleted, or made invisible).

The Departments page acts as a *site map* to the NAV system for the user. When we add new objects to the MenuSuite (thus to the Departments menu), NAV UX design guidelines encourage the entry of duplicate links within whichever sections the user might consider looking for that page. An example **Departments** page is shown in the following screenshot:

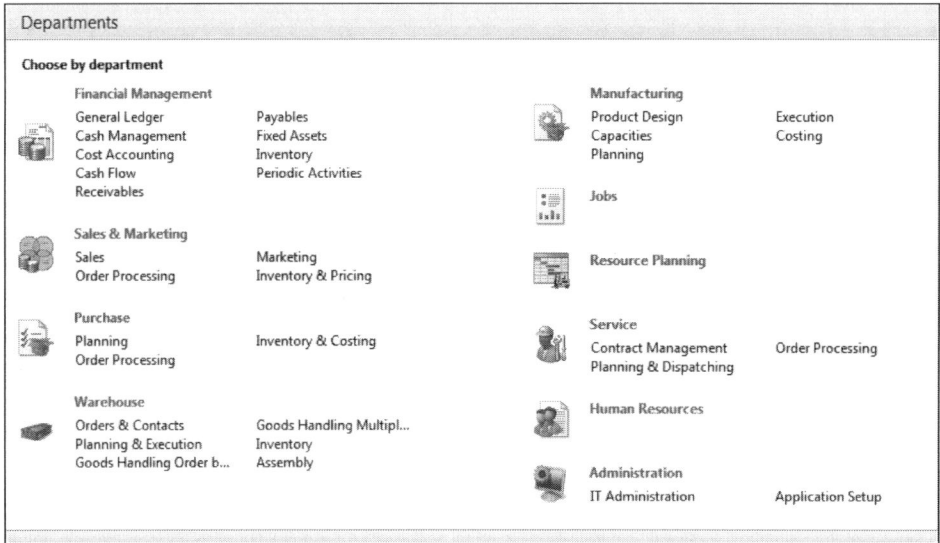

Page parts

Several of the page types we have reviewed thus far contain multiple panes with each pane including special purpose parts. Let's look at some of the available component page parts.

Some page parts compute the displayed data on the fly, taking advantage of flow fields which can be resource intensive. As a developer, you need to be careful about causing performance problems through overuse of such displays.

FactBox Area

The FactBox Area can be defined on the right side of certain page types including Card, List, List Plus, Document, Worksheet, and Navigate (though a FactBox Area doesn't seem to be useful on a NavigatePage, nor is it used in any in the standard system). A FactBox Area can contain Page parts (CardPart or ListPart), Chart parts, and System parts (Outlook, Notes, MyNotes or Record Links). A variety of standard CardParts, ListParts, and ChartParts are available which can be used in FactBoxes. System parts cannot be modified. All the others can be enhanced from the standard instances, or new ones may be created from scratch.

CardParts and ListParts

CardParts are used for FactBoxes that don't require a list. CardParts display fields or perhaps a picture control. An example of the **Customer Statistics** FactBox (Page 9080 – Sales Hist. Sell-to FactBox) is shown in the following screenshot:

ListParts are used for FactBoxes that require a list. A list is defined as columns of repeated data. No more than two or three columns should appear in a FactBox list. A screenshot of the three-column **My Customers** FactBox list part (Page 9150) is as follows:

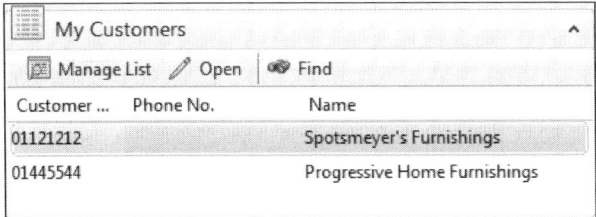

Charts

In NAV 2013 there are two standard ways of including charts in your pages. The first one, Chart parts, is a carryover from NAV 2009. The second one, the Chart Control Add-in, is new in NAV 2013.

Chart part

A Chart part displays list data in graphic form. A Chart part is a default optional component of all FactBox Areas. If a FactBox exists, it has a Chart part option available. Chart parts are populated by choosing one of the available charts stored in the Chart table (Table 2000000078). Some Charts require range parameters, others do not (they default to a defined data range). Most of the supplied charts are two-dimensional, but a sampling of three-dimensional, dynamic charts is included. A MSDN NAV Team blog provides an extensive description of chart construction and a utility for creating new charts (`http://blogs.msdn.com/b/nav/archive/2011/06/03/chart-generator-tool-for-rtc-cgtrtc.aspx`). A sample standard chart is shown in the following screenshot.

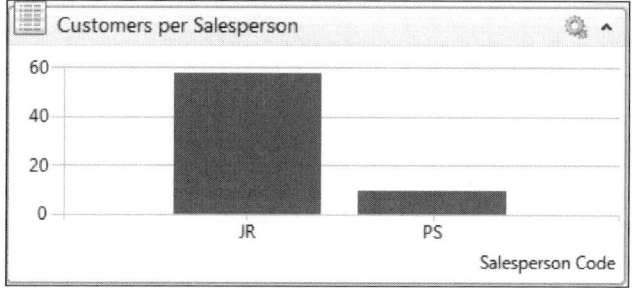

Chart Control Add-in

The NAV 2013 distribution includes a charting capability that is based on a Control Add-In (created with .NET code written outside of C/SIDE and integrated into NAV). An example is the Trailing Sales Orders chart in a FactBox Page part (Page 760) that appears in the Sales Order Processor Role Center (Page 9006). A screenshot of that chart is as follows:

The *Cash Flow Chart Example* in the NAV 2013 **Developer and IT Pro Help** describes how to create charts using the Chart Control Add-In.

Page names

Card pages are named in a similar manner as the table with which they are associated, plus the word *Card*. Examples include Customer table and Customer Card, Item table and Item Card, Vendor table and Vendor Card, and so on.

List pages are named similarly to the table with which they are associated. List pages which are simple non-editable lists have the word *List* associated with the table name. Examples are Customer List, Item List, and Vendor List. For each of these, the table also has an associated card page. Where the table has no associated card page, the list pages are named after the tables, but in the plural format. Examples include Customer Ledger Entry table and Customer Ledger Entries, Check Ledger Entry table and Check Ledger Entries, Country/Region table and Countries/Regions page, Production Forecast Name table and Production Forecast Names page.

The single-record Setup tables that are used for application control information throughout NAV are named after their functional area plus the word *Setup*. The associated Card page should also be (and generally is) named similarly to the table. For example, General Ledger Setup table and General Ledger Setup page, Manufacturing Setup table and Manufacturing Setup page, and so on.

Journal entry (worksheet) pages are given names tied to their purpose, plus the word *Journal*. In the standard product, several Journal pages for different purposes are associated with the same table. For example, the Sales Journal, Cash Receipts Journal, Purchases Journal and Payments Journal all use the General Journal Line table as their SourceTable (they are different pages all tied to the same table).

If there is a Header and Line table associated with a data category such as Sales Orders, the related page and subpage ideally should be named to describe the relationship between the tables and the pages. However, in some cases, it's better to tie the page names directly to the function they perform rather than the underlying tables. An example is the two pages making up the display called by the Sales Order menu entry—the Sales Order page is tied to the Sales Header table, and the Sales Order Subform page is tied to the Sales Line table. The same tables are involved for the Sales Invoice page and Sales Invoice Subform page. The use of the word *Subform* rather than *Subpage*, as in Sales Invoice Subform, is a leftover from previous versions of NAV which had forms rather than pages.

Sometimes, while naming pages, you will have a conflict between naming pages based on the associated tables and naming them based on the use of the data. For example, the menu entry Contacts invokes a Main page/Subpage named Contact Card and Contact Card Subform. The respective tables are the Contact table and the Contact Profile Answer table. The context usage should take precedence in the page naming as done here.

Page Designer

The **Page Designer** is accessed from within the Development Environment through **Tools | Object Designer | Page**. The **Page Designer** can be opened either for creation of a new page using the **New** button or for editing an existing page using the **Design** button.

New Page Wizard

When you click on the **New** button or press *F3* or navigate to **Edit | New**, you will bring up the **New Page** Wizard, seen as follows:

You can proceed to the Page Designer with the PageType property set to Card and no SourceTable defined by clicking on **OK** with **Create blank page** selected and without entering a Table Name or Number. Or you could enter a Table Name or Number, select **Create a page using a wizard**, and select a PageType. That will take you directly to the Page Designer with the PageType property set to your choice and the SourceTable assigned to the table you entered. But it's almost always more efficient to use the Wizard to create at least a rough version of your page design, then modify the generated object structure and code to get your ultimate desired result.

To use the Page Wizard, first you enter the name or number of the table to which you want your page to be bound. Then you choose what PageType you want to create – Card, List, RoleCenter, CardPart, ListPart, Document, Worksheet, ListPlus, ConfirmationDialog, StandardDialog, or NavigatePage. The subsequent steps the Page Wizard will take you through depend on the PageType chosen. The following chart shows which options are available through the Wizard for each Page Type.

Page Type	FastTabs	Fields to Display	FactBoxes	Page Designer
RoleCenter	-	-	-	✓
Card	✓	✓	✓	✓
List	-	✓	✓	✓
Document	✓	✓	✓	✓
ListPlus	✓	✓	✓	✓
Worksheet	-	✓	✓	✓
ConfirmationDialog	✓	✓	-	✓
StandardDialog	-	-	-	✓
NavigatePage	✓	✓	✓	✓
CardPart	-	✓	-	✓
ListPart	-	✓	-	✓

Just to see what the Page Wizard looks like, we'll step through an example definition of a Card page based on our Table 50000 – Radio Show (this example is just to illustrate the Page Wizard process – we aren't creating a page that we'll keep for our Radio Show application).

We will invoke the Page Designer Wizard by clicking on the **New** button with the **Page** button highlighted. Enter 50000 in the **Table** field, select the **Create a page using a wizard:** option, select **Card** and click on the **OK** button. The next screen allows us to define FastTabs. It displays with a default first FastTab titled **General**. For our example, we'll add two more FastTabs, **Tab 1** and **Tab 2**:

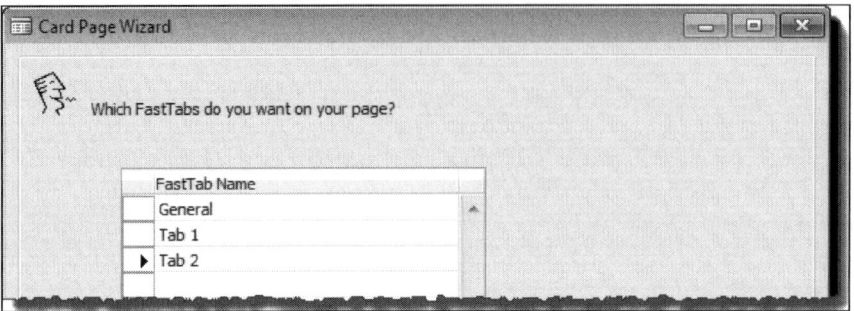

We click on **Next** and proceed to the screen to assign fields from our bound table to each of the individual tabs. The single arrow buttons move one field either onto or off of the selected tab. The double arrow buttons move all the fields in the chosen direction. In the following screenshot, five fields have been selected and assigned to the **General** tab:

If we realize that we should have defined our tabs differently, we could click on the **Back** button and return to the FastTab definition screen.

After all the desired fields have been assigned to the appropriate tab, we will click on **Next** and move on to the screen that allows us to assign FactBoxes to the Page. A considerable number of page components are made available by the Wizard for assignment as FactBoxes.

As we see in the following screenshot, many of the choices are not appropriate for use in most pages. We can only select previously created page parts for FactBoxes. This leads to an important concept.

> We need to plan our page design development ahead of time and construct the component parts first.

If we had not yet defined the FactBoxes for our current page design, we could pick other similar page components and then make the appropriate code replacement later in the Page Designer.

Once we have done all the assignment work that is feasible within the Page Wizard, we will click on **Finish**. The Page Wizard will generate the object structure and C/AL code for our defined page and present the results to us in the **Page Designer** as shown in the following screenshot:

Had this example been the real thing, we should have planned ahead and created our custom FactBox page parts before we used the Wizard to create our card page. The alternative was to simply add a couple of FactBox page parts as place holders which we can replace later. That gives us the structure we want and compensates for our lack of planning. We could wait and just add the FactBoxes later, but we wouldn't be taking advantage of the help the Wizard can provide.

Page Components

All pages are made up of certain common components. The basic elements of a page object are the page triggers, page properties, controls, control triggers, and control properties.

Page Triggers

The following screenshot shows the page triggers. The **Help** section **Page and Action Triggers** provide good general guidance to the event which causes each page trigger to fire. Note that the **OnQueryClosePage** trigger isn't related to any Query object action.

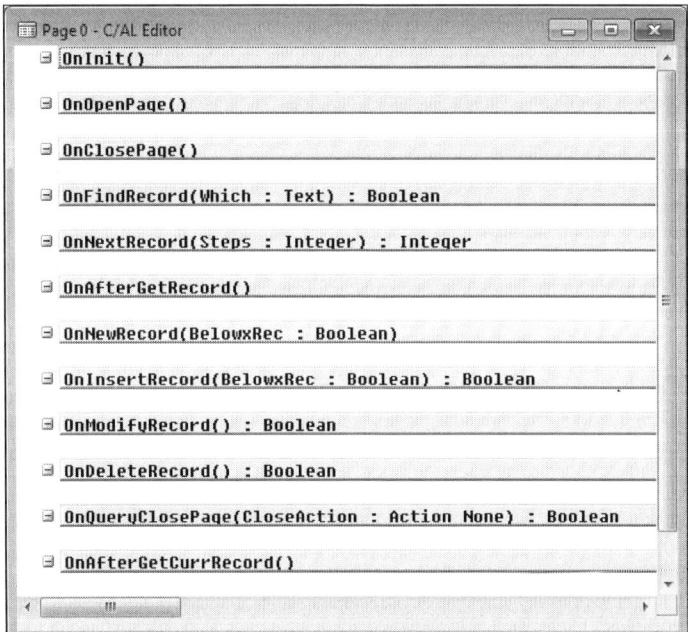

In general, according to best practices, we should minimize the C/AL code placed in Page triggers, putting it in a Table or Field trigger or calling a Codeunit function instead. However, many standard pages include a modest amount of code supporting page specific filter or display functions. When we develop a new page, it's always a good idea to look for similar pages in the standard product and be guided by how that page operates internally. Sometimes special display requirements result in complex code being required within a page. It is important that the code be only for display purposes not for data modification.

Page properties

We will now look at the properties of the **Radio Show List** page we created earlier. The list of available page properties is the same for all page types. The setting of those properties varies considerably from page to page. The following screenshot shows the **Page - Properties** screen of our Radio Show List page (Page 50000). This screen is accessed by opening Page 50000 in the Page Designer, highlighting the first empty line in the **Controls** list and clicking on the **Properties** icon (or *Shift + F4* or **View | Properties**).

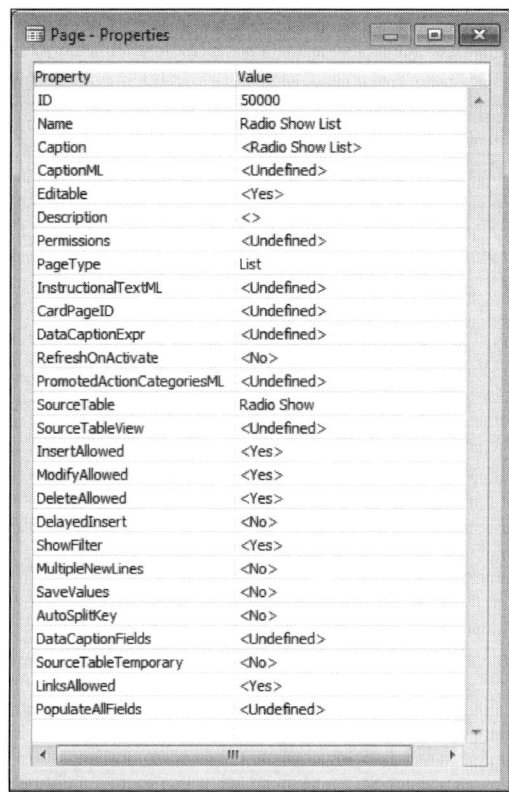

Many of these properties are still in their default condition. The following are the properties with which we are most likely to be concerned:

- **ID**: The unique object number of the page.

- **Name**: The unique name by which this page is referenced in C/AL code.

- **Caption** and **CaptionML**: The page name to be displayed, depending on the language option in use.

- **Editable**: This determines whether or not the controls in the page can be edited (assuming the table's **Editable** properties are also set to Yes). If this property is set to Yes, the control passes the **Editable** property on to the individual controls.

- **Description**: For internal documentation only.

- **Permissions**: This is used to instruct the system to allow the users of this page to have certain levels of access (r=read, i=insert, m=modify, d=delete) to the TableData in the specified table objects. For example, users of Page 499 (Available - Sales Lines) are allowed to only read or modify (Permissions for Sales Line = rm) the data in the Sales Line table.

 Whenever defining special permissions, be sure to test with an end-user license. In fact, it's always important to test with an end-user license.

- **PageType**: Specifies how this page will be displayed, using one of the available nine page types (RoleCenter, Card, List, ListPlus, Worksheet, ConfirmationDialog, StandardDialog, NavigatePage, CardPart, ListPart).

- **CardPageID**: The ID of the Card page that should be launched when the user double-clicks on an entry in the list. This is only used on List pages.

- **RefreshOnActivate**: When set to **Yes** causes the page to refresh when the page is activated.

- **PromotedActionCategoriesML**: Allows changing the language for Promoted Action Categories from the default English (ENU) to another language or to extend the number of Promoted Action Categories from the standard three options (New, Process, Reports) to add up to seven more categories. See the **Help** section *How to: Define Promoted Action Categories Captions for the Ribbon*.

- **SourceTable**: The name of the table to which the page is bound.

- **SourceTableView**: This can be utilized to automatically apply defined filters and/or open the page with a key other than the Primary Key.

- **ShowFilter**: Set to No to have the Filter pane default to not visible. The user can still make the Filter pane visible.

- **DelayedInsert**: This delays the insertion of a new record until the user moves focus away from the new line being entered. If this value is no, then a new record will automatically be inserted into the table as soon as the primary key fields have been completed. This property is generally set to Yes when **AutoSplitKey** (see below) is set to Yes. It allows complex new data records to be entered with all the necessary fields completed.

- **MultipleNewLines**: When set to Yes, it allows the insertion of multiple new lines between existing records. However, it defaults to No, which prevents users from inserting new lines between records.

- **SaveValues**: If set to Yes, causes user-specific entered control values to be retained and redisplayed when the page is invoked another time.

- **AutoSplitKey**: This allows for the automatic assignment of a primary key, provided the last field in the primary key is an integer (there are exceptions to this, but we won't worry about them in this book). This feature enables each new entry to be assigned a key so it will remain sequenced in the table following the record appearing above it. Note that AutoSplitKey and DelayedInsert are generally used jointly. On a new entry at the end of a list of entries, the trailing integer portion of the primary key, often named Line No., is automatically incremented by 10,000 (the increment value cannot be changed). When a new entry is inserted between two previously existing entries, their current key-terminating integer values are summed and divided by two (hence the term AutoSplitKey) with the resultant value being used for the new entry key terminating integer value. Since 10,000 (the automatic increment) can only be divided by two and rounded to a non-zero integer result 13 times, only 13 new automatically numbered entries can be inserted between two previously recorded entries by the AutoSplitKey function.

- **SourceTableTemporary**: Allows use of a temporary table as the SourceTable for the page. This can be very useful where there is a need to display data based on the structure of a table, but not using the data as it persists in the database. Examples of such an application are Page 634 – Chart of Accounts Overview and Page 6510 – Item Tracking Lines. Note that the temporary instance of the source table is empty when the page opens up, so our code must populate it.

Page Preview tool

The Page Designer in NAV 2013 has a new Page Preview tool which is very helpful in defining our control placement and action menu layout. It is pointed out in the following screenshot:

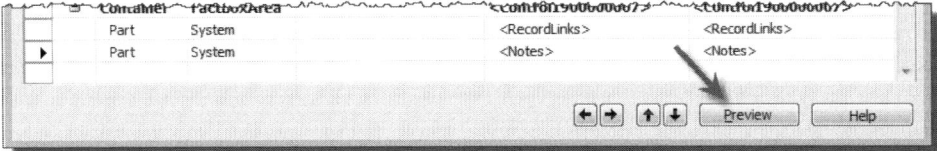

If we click on the **Preview** button while we have a page open in the **Page Designer**, a preview of that page's layout will display. The controls and actions are not active in the preview (this is display only), but we can display all the ribbon tabs and their controls.

The **Preview** screen is interactively linked to the **Page Designer** and its subordinate **Action Designer**. When we click on a control line in the **Page Designer** or an Action line in the **Action Designer**, the **Page Preview** highlights the generated object. Or when we click on a control or action displayed in the previewed page, the corresponding line in the **Page Designer** or **Action Designer** is highlighted. An example of a highlighted control shows in the following partial screenshot.

In the following screenshot, an action is highlighted in the **Preview** page:

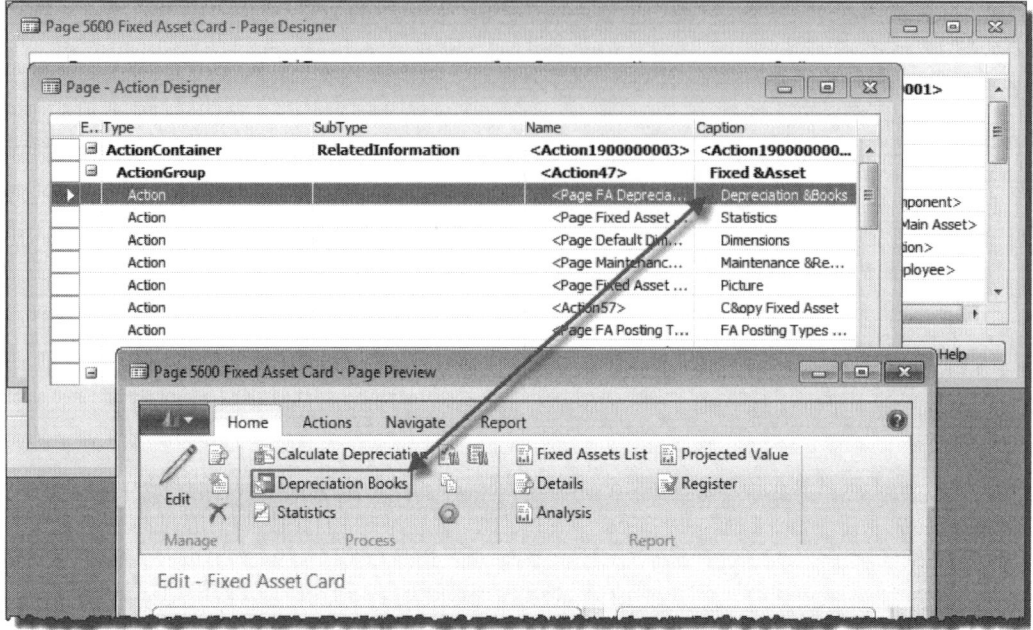

Inheritance

One of the attributes of an object oriented system is the inheritance of properties. While NAV is more properly described as object based rather than object oriented, the properties that affect data validation are inherited. Properties such as decimal formatting are also inherited. If the property is explicitly defined in the table, it cannot be less restrictively defined elsewhere.

Controls that are bound to a table field will inherit the settings of the properties that are common to both the field definition and the control definition. This basic concept applies on inheritance of data properties – beginning from fields in tables to pages and reports, and then from pages and reports to controls within pages and reports. Inherited property settings that involve data validation cannot be overridden, but all of the others can be changed. This is another example of why it is generally best to define the properties in the table, for consistency and ease of maintenance, rather than defining them for each instance of use in a page or a report.

WDTU Page Enhancement – part 1

Before we move on to learn about controls and actions, let's do some basic enhancement work on our WDTU Radio Show application. Back in *Chapter 1, An Introduction to NAV 2013*, we created some minimal pages, then later added new fields to our Radio Show master table (Table 50000). We'll now enhance the Radio Show List and Card to include those added fields.

Because our previous page development work resulted in simple pages, we have the opportunity to decide whether we want to start with the New Page Wizard and replace our original pages or use the Page Designer to modify the original pages. If we had done any significant work on these pages previously in the Page Designer, the choice to go right to the Page Designer would be easy. Let's do a quick evaluation to help us make our decision. First, let's take a look at the existing **Radio Show List** page in the following screenshot:

We want to compare the list of fields that exist in the source table (Radio Show – 50000) to what we see is already in the page. If there are only a couple of fields missing, it will be more efficient to do our work in the Page Designer. The quickest way to inspect the fields of the source table is to use the **About This Page** Help information available from the Dynamics logo dropdown at the upper left corner of the page ribbon seen in the following screenshot:

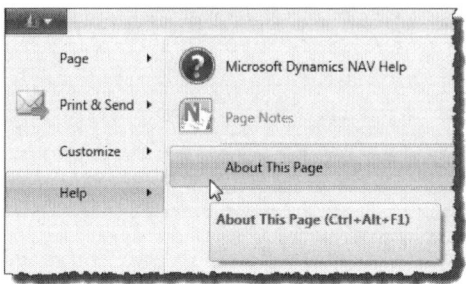

When we click on **About This Page** (or *Ctrl* + *Alt* + *F1*), the following screen displays:

When we scroll down the list of fields in Table 50000 (which are displayed alphabetically, not by field number or in order of placement in the page), we see that there are quite a few fields in the table that aren't in our page. This makes it easy to conclude that we should use the Page Wizard to create a new version of our Page 50000 – Radio Show List.

When the Wizard allows us to choose and sequence fields in our new list form, for the sake of simplicity, we will just insert all the fields at once in the order they appear in the table. In other words, we will choose the **>>** button to include all fields. Then, because we know that the **Date Filter** field is only for filter control of related tables and will not contain visible data, we will remove that field. Our Wizard screen will look like the following:

Finish the Page, Saving it as `Page 50000, Radio Show List`, overwriting the old version. If we want to be very safe, you would Export a copy of the original version of Page 50000 as a `.fob` file before starting (using **File | Export**).

Next we want to do essentially the same thing with the Radio Show Card. We'll make the same choice for the same reasons, to use the Page Wizard to create a new version of the card page. When we review the data fields, we decide that we should have four FastTabs: **General**, **Schedule**, **Requirements**, and **Statistics**. As before, the **Date Filter** field should not be on the page. After we have generated, compiled and saved our new Radio Show Card, it looks like the next screenshot:

Our final step at this point is to connect the Radio Show Card to the **Radio Show List** page so that when the user double-clicks on a list entry, the Card page will be invoked. This is a simple matter of opening our new Page 50000 in the Page Designer, highlighting the first empty line in the Controls list and clicking on the **Properties** icon (or *Shift + F4* or **View | Properties**). In the list of page properties display, we will find CardPageID. Fill in that property with either the name (Radio Show Card) or Object ID number (50000) of the target card, save and compile and run. We should see a ribbon like the following with both **Edit** and **Edit List** showing:

Clicking on **Edit** will bring up the Radio Show Card. Clicking on **Edit List** will make the line in the list editable in place. If we don't want the user to be able to edit within the list, we could change the List page property **Editable** to No and the **Edit List** option would not be available.

Page Controls

Controls on pages serve a variety of purposes. Some controls display information on pages. This can be data from the database, static material, pictures, or the results of a C/AL expression. Container controls can contain other controls. Group controls make it easy for the developer to handle a set of contained controls as a group. A FastTabs control also makes it easy for the user to consider a set of controls as a group. The user can make all the controls on a FastTab visible or invisible by expanding or collapsing the FastTab. The user also has the option to show or not to show a particular FastTab as a part of the page customizing capability. The **Help** sections *Pages Overview* and *How to: Create a Page* provide good background guidance on the organization of controls within page types for NAV 2013.

The following screenshot from the **Page Designer** shows all the data controls on the **Fixed Asset Card** (Page 5600). Expanded is a **+** or **−** indicating if the section is expanded or not. **Type** and **SubType** define how this control is interpreted by the Role-Tailored Client. **SourceExpr** defines the value of the control. **Name** is the internal reference name of the control. The **Caption** is what will appear on screen. The default values for **Name** and **Caption** are what are defined in the table.

The page's control structure can be seen in the indented format shown in this image. The **Container** controls define the primary parts of the page structure. The next level of structure is the Group control level. In this page, those are the **General**, **Communication**, and **Maintenance** groups (each of which represents a FastTab). Indented under each Group control are Field controls.

The **Fixed Asset Card** page, complete with the action ribbon, displays as follows:

The Group – FastTab correlation here is obvious. The **Lines** FastTab connection is less obvious. It comes from the line **Type** equals **Part**, **SubType** equals **Page**, **Name** equals **DepreciationBook**. The Part Page line has the same indentation level as do the Group entries, thus it is displayed at the same level as the Groups.

Control Types

There are four primary types of page controls `Container`, `Group`, `Field`, and `Part`. `Container`, `Group`, and `Field` controls are used to define the content area of pages. Part controls are used to define FactBoxes.

Container controls

Container controls can be one of three subtypes: `ContentArea`, `FactBoxArea`, or `RoleCenterArea`. Container controls define the root-level primary structures within a page. All page types start with a Container control. The `RoleCenterArea` Container control can only be used on a RoleCenter page type. A page can only have one instance of each Container subtype.

Group controls

Group controls provide the second level of structure within a page. Group controls are the home for fields. Almost every page has at least one Group control. The screenshot following, from **Page 5600 Fixed Asset Card**, shows two `Container` controls and three `Group` controls. All of these except the `ControlArea` Container control are collapsed in this image. Also showing is a page `Part` control which displays a `PagePart` as a FastTab.

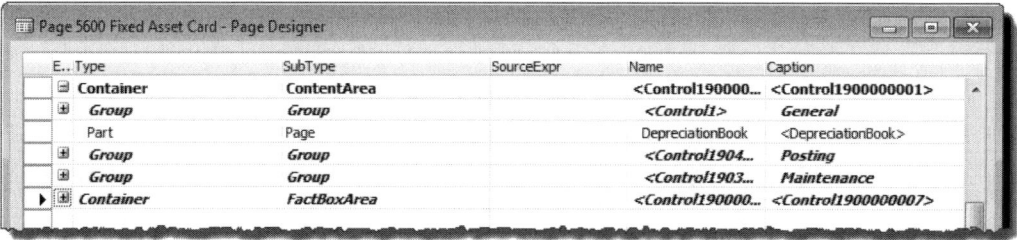

The **Properties** of the **Group** control are shown in the following image:

Several of the **Group** control properties are particularly significant because of their effect on all the fields within the group.

- **Visible**: TRUE or FALSE, defaulting to TRUE. The **Visible** property can be assigned a Boolean expression, which can be evaluated during processing. This allows for dynamically changing the visibility of a group of fields during processing based on some variable condition (the processing must occur in either the **OnInit** or **OnOpenPage** trigger and the variable must have its **IncludeInDataSet** property set to Yes).

- **Enabled**: TRUE or FALSE, defaulting to TRUE. The **Enabled** property can be assigned a Boolean expression to dynamically change the enabling of a group of fields.

- **Editable**: TRUE or FALSE, defaulting to TRUE. The **Editable** property can be assigned a Boolean expression to dynamically change the editability of a group of fields.

- **GroupType**: It will be one of the five choices—**Group**, **Repeater**, **CueGroup**, **FixedLayout**, or **GridLayout**. The **GroupType** property is visible on the Page Designer screen in the column headed SubType (see the earlier **Page Designer** screenshot).

    ° **Group** is used in Card type pages as the general structure for fields, which are then displayed in the sequence they appear in the Page Designer group.

    ° **Repeater** is used in List type pages as the structure for fields, which are displayed as repeated rows of those fields.

    ° **CueGroup** is used for Role Center pages as the structure for the actions that are the primary focus of a user's work day. CueGroups are found in page parts, typically having the word *Activities* in their name. The page parts are included in RoleCenter page definitions. The following screenshot shows a **CueGroup** defined in the **Page Designer**:

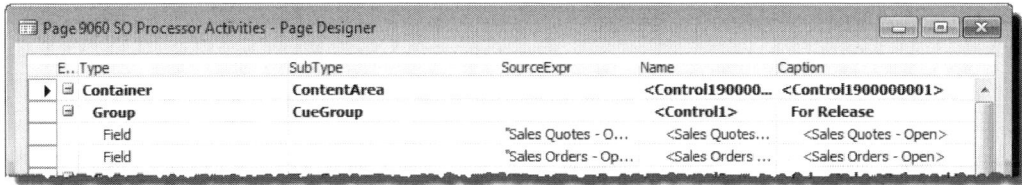

° The above cue group is displayed in the RTC as follows:

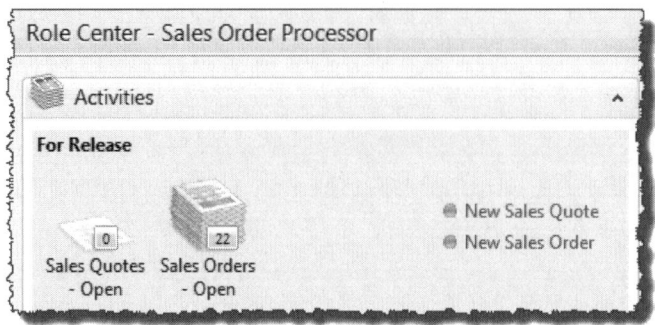

° **FixedLayout** is used at the bottom of List pages, following a Repeater group. The FixedLayout group typically contains totals or additional line-related detail fields. Many Journal pages, such as **Page 39 – General Journal**, **Page 40 – Item Journal**, and **Page 201 – Job Journal** have FixedLayout groups. The Item Journal FixedLayout group only shows the Item Description, (which is also available in a Repeater column) but could easily display other fields as well. A FixedLayout group can also display a lookup or calculated value like many of the Statistics pages (for example, **Page 151 – Customer Statistics**, **Page 152 – Vendor Statistics**).

° **GridLayout** provides additional formatting capabilities to layout fields row by row, column by column, spanning rows or columns, and hiding or showing captions. Page 970 is one example of GridLayout use. To learn more about GridLayout use, search Help for *Gridlayout*.

• **IndentationColumnName** and **IndentationControls**: These allow a group to be defined in the fields which will be indented, as shown in the following screenshot of the chart of the Accounts page. Examples of pages that utilize the indentation properties include **Page 16 – Chart of Accounts** and **Page 18 – G/L Account List**.

- **FreezeColumnID**: It freezes the identified column and all of the columns to the left, so they remain in a fixed position while the columns to the right can scroll horizontally. This is like freezing a pane in an Excel worksheet. Users can also do this as part of personalizing their display.

- **ShowAsTree**: It works together with the indentation property. **ShowAsTree** allows an indentation to be expanded or collapsed dynamically by the user for easier viewing. Examples are **Page 583 – XBRL Taxonomy Lines**, **Page 634 – Chart of Accounts Overview**, and **Page 5522 – Order Planning**.

Field controls

All field controls appear in the same format in the Page Designer. The **SubType** column is empty and the **SourceExpr** column contains the data expression that will be displayed.

All the field control properties are listed for each field, but individual properties only apply to the data type for which they make sense. For example, the **DecimalPlaces** property only applies to fields where the data type is decimal. Following is a screenshot of the properties for a field control:

We'll review some of the field control properties which are more frequently used or are more significant in terms of effect.

- **Visible**, **Enabled**, and **Editable**: They have the same functionality as the identically named group controls, but only apply to individual fields. If the group control is set to FALSE, either statically (in the control definition within the page) or dynamically by an expression evaluated during processing, the Group control's FALSE condition will take precedence over the equivalent Field control setting. Precedence applies in the same way at the next, higher levels of identically named properties at the Page level, and then at the table level. For example, if a data field is set to **Non-Editable** in the table, that setting will take precedence (overrides) over other settings in a page, control group, or control.

- **HideValue**: It allows the value of a field to be optionally displayed or hidden, based on an expression that evaluates to TRUE or FALSE.

- **MultiLine**: This should be set to TRUE in order to allow the field to display multiple lines of text.

- **OptionCaption** and **OptionCaptionML**: These set the text string options that are displayed to the user. The captions that are set as page field properties will override those defined in the equivalent table field property. The default captions are those defined in the table.

- **ShowCaption**: This should be set to Yes or No in order to determine whether or not the caption is displayed.

- **DecimalPlaces**: Applies to decimal fields only. If the number of decimal places defined in the page is smaller than that defined in the table, the display is rounded accordingly. If the field definition is the smaller number, it controls the display.

- **Width**: Allows setting a specific field display width – number of characters. Useful in association with Control SubType of GridLayout.

- **QuickEntry**: It allows the field to optionally receive focus or be skipped, based on an expression that evaluates to TRUE or FALSE.

- **Importance**: This controls the display of a field. This property only applies to individual (non-repeating) fields located within a FastTab. Importance can be set to Standard (the default), Promoted, or Additional:

  ○ **Standard**: Is the normal display. Implementations of the rendering routines for different targets may utilize this differently.

  ○ **Promoted**: If the property is set to **Promoted** and the page is on a collapsed FastTab, then the field contents will be displayed on the FastTab line. If the page is expanded, the field will display normally.

  ○ **Additional**: If the property is set to **Additional** and the FastTab is collapsed, there is no effect on the display. If the FastTab is expanded, then the user can determine whether or not the field is displayed by clicking on the **Show More Fields** or **Show Fewer Fields** display control in the lower-right corner of the FastTab

- **RowSpan** and **ColumnSpan**: Are used in conjunction with GridLayout controls as layout parameters.

- **ControlAddIn**: When the field represents a control add-in, this contains The name and public token key of the control add-in.

- **ExtendedDatatype**: It allows a text field to be categorized as a special data type. The default value is None. If **ExtendedDatatype** is selected, it can be any one of the following:

  ○ **Phone No.**

  ○ **URL**

- ◦ **E-Mail**
- ◦ **Filter**: Used on reports
- ◦ **Ratio**: For a processing progress bar display
- ◦ **Masked**: Fills the field with bold dots in order to mask the actual entry. The number of masking characters displayed is independent of the actual field contents. The contents of a masked field cannot be copied. If **ExtendedDatatype** is **Phone No.**, **URL**, or **E-Mail**, an active icon is displayed on the page following the text field providing access to call the phone number, access the URL in a browser, or invoke the e-mail client. Setting **ExtendedDatatype** will also define the validation that will automatically be applied to the field.

Page Part controls

Page Parts are used for FactBoxes and SubPages. Many of the properties of Page Parts are similar to other NAV components and operate essentially the same way in a Page Part as they operate elsewhere. Those properties include **ID**, **Name**, **Visible**, **Enabled**, **Editable**, **Caption**, **CaptionML**, **ToolTip**, **ToolTipML**, and **Description**.

Other properties are specific to Page Part controls are as follows:

- **SubPageView**: Defines the table view that applies to the named subpage (see WhseMovLines Part in **Page 7315 – Warehouse Movement**).

- **SubPageLink**: Defines the field(s) that links to the subpage and the link (based on a constant, a filter, or another field).

- **ProviderID**: It contains the ID of another Page Part control within the current page. This enables you to link a subordinate part to a controlling parent part. For example, **Page 42 – Sales Order** uses this property to update the Sales Line FactBox by defining a ProviderID link from the FactBox to the SalesLines FastTab. Other pages with similar links include **Page 41 – Sales Quote** and Pages 43, 44, 50, 507, and 5768.

- **PartType**: It defines the type of part to be displayed in a FactBox. There are three options. Each option also requires another related property to be defined:

PartType Option	Required property
Page	PagePartID
System	SystemPartID
Chart	ChartPartID

- **PagePartID**: It must contain the page object ID of a FactBox part, if the **PartTypeOption** is set to **Page**.

- **SystemPartID**: This must contain the name of a predefined system part if the **PartTypeOption** is set to **System**. Available choices are **Outlook, Notes, MyNotes**, and **RecordLinks**.

- **ChartPartID**: It must contain a chart ID if the **PartTypeOption** is set to **Chart**. The Chart ID is a link to the selected entry in the Chart table (table number 2000000078).

 NAV 2013 has a new Chart Control Add-in which provides significant additional charting capability. Information can be found in the **Help** section *Displaying Charts Using the Chart Control Add-in.*

Page Control triggers

The following screenshot shows Page Control triggers. There are five triggers for each Field control. Container, Group, and Part controls do not have associated triggers.

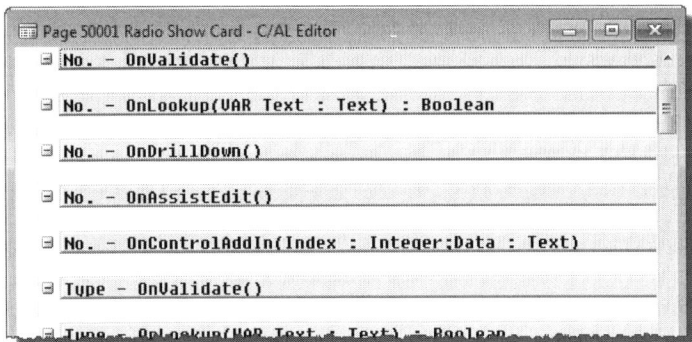

The guideline for the use of these triggers is the same as the one for Page triggers—if there is a choice, don't put C/AL code in a Control trigger. Not only will this make your code easier to upgrade in the future, but it will also make it easier to debug and easier for the developer following you to decipher your changes.

Bound and Unbound Pages

Pages can be created as **bound** (associated with a specific table), or **unbound** (not associated with a table). Typically, a Card or List page will be bound, but Role Center pages will be unbound. Other instances of unbound pages are rare. Unbound pages may be used for communicating status information or initiating a process. Examples of unbound pages are **Page 476 – Copy Tax Setup** and **Page 1040 – Copy Job** (both of which have a **PageType** property of **StandardDialog**).

WDTU Page Enhancement – part 2

Now that we have additional understanding of page structures, let's do a little more enhancing of our WDTU application pages. We've decided that it would be useful to keep track of specific listener contacts, a *fan* list. First we need to create a table of Fan information which we will save as Table 50010 – Radio Show Fan which should look like the following:

We want to be able to review the Fan list as we scan the Radio Show List. This requires adding a FactBox area to Page 50000 which, in turn, requires a Page Part for populating that FactBox. The logical sequence is to create the Page Part first, then add the FactBox to Page 50000. Since we just want a simple **ListPart** with three columns, we can use the Page Wizard to create our Page Part which we will save as Page 50080 – Radio Show Fan **ListPart**, including just the Name, E-mail, and the Last Contacted fields:

Next we will use the Page Designer to add a FactBox area to Page 50000, populate the FactBox area with our PagePart – Page 50080 and finally set the properties for the Page Part to link to the highlighted record in the Radio Show List page:

If we **Run** Table 50010 and insert a few test records first, we should see something like:

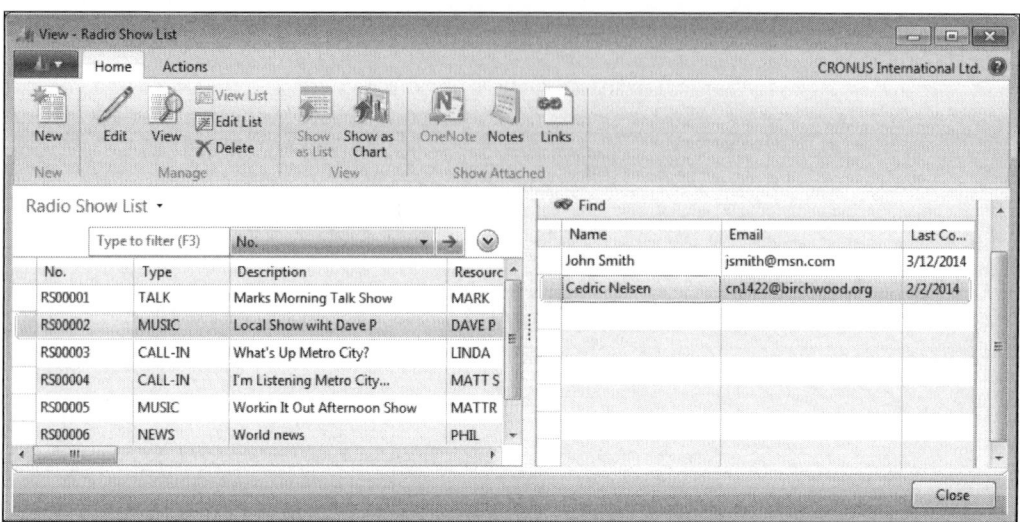

Before finishing this part of our enhancement work, we should create a List page that we can use to view and maintain the data in the table in the future (assign it as Page 50009 – Radio Fan List).

One other enhancement that we can do now, is promote some fields in the Radio Show Card so they can be seen when the FastTab is collapsed. All we have to do is choose the fields we want to promote, then change the page control property of **Importance** to **Promoted**. If we chose the fields **No.**, **Type**, **Description**, and **Avg. Listener Share** and promoted those, our card with collapsed FastTabs would look like the following (we don't currently have any Listener Share test data):

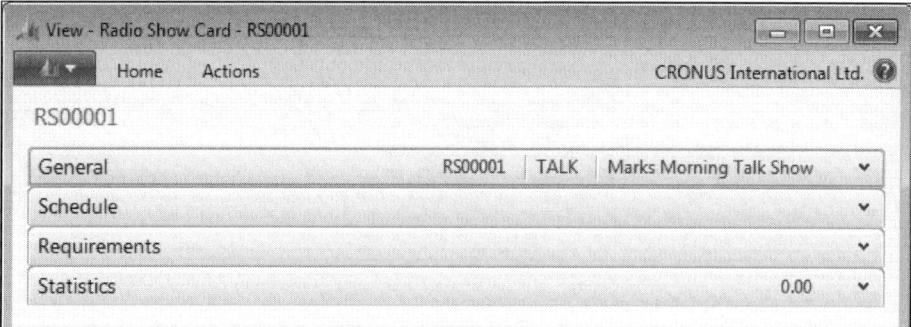

Page Actions

Actions are the menu items of NAV 2013. Action menus can be found in several locations. The primary location is the Ribbon appearing at the top of most pages. Other locations for actions are the Navigation Pane, Role Center Cue Groups, and the Action menu on FactBox page parts.

The **Action Designer**, where actions are defined, is accessed from the Page Designer form, by clicking on **View** and selecting **Page Actions** or **Control Actions** (Control Actions can only be used for Role Center Cue Group actions and for NavigatePage wizard actions). When we click on **Page Actions** (or *Ctrl + Alt + F4*) for the Fixed Asset page (Page 5600), we will see a list of Ribbon actions in the following screenshot as they appear in the **Action Designer**:

The associated Ribbon tabs for the preceding Page Action list are shown in the following images. First, the **Home** tab:

Second, the **Actions** tab:

Third, the **Navigate** tab:

Finally, the **Reports** tab.

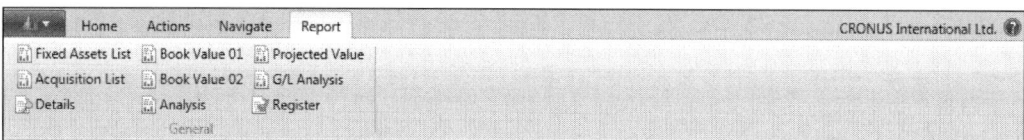

There are two default Ribbon tabs created for every Ribbon: **Home** and **Actions**. What actions appear by default is dependent on the PageType.

Actions defined by the developer appear on a Ribbon tab and tab submenu section based on a combination of the location of the action in the Page Actions structure and on the property settings of the individual action. There are a lot of possibilities, so it is important to follow some basic guidelines.

- Maintain the look and feel of the standard product wherever feasible and appropriate
- Put the actions on the **Home** tab that are expected to be used most

- Be consistent in organizing actions from tab to tab and page to page
- Provide the user with a complete set of action tools, but don't provide so many options that it's hard to figure out which one to use

Page Action Types and Subtypes

Page Action entries can have one of four types: ActionContainer, ActionGroup, Action, or Separator. At the time of the Beta, Separators don't seem to have any effect in the rendered pages. The Page Action Types use an indented hierarchical structure like this:

Action Types	Description
ActionContainer	Primary Action grouping
ActionGroup	Secondary Action grouping
Action	Action
Action Group	Secondary groups can be set up within and Action list for dropdown menus of Actions (a tertiary level)
Action	The indentation indicates this is part of a dropdown menu
Separator	A visual Separator marker
Action	Action
Separator	A visual Separator marker
Action Group	Back to the Secondary grouping level
ActionContainer	Back to the Primary grouping level

An ActionContainer action line type can have one of six **SubType** values as shown in the following screenshot. The SubTypes of HomeItems and ActivityButtons only apply to RoleCenter pages.

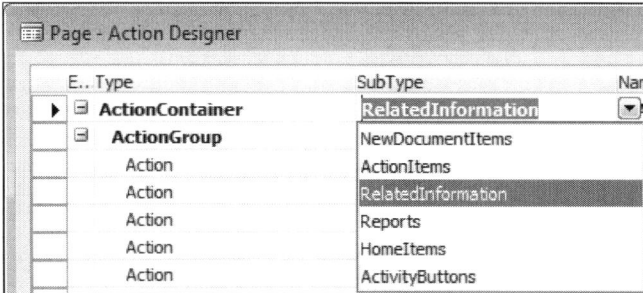

- Actions in a **Reports** SubType will appear on the Ribbon **Report** tab.
- Actions in a **RelatedInformation** SubType will appear on the Ribbon **Navigate** tab.

- Actions in an **ActionItems** SubType will appear on the Ribbon **Actions** tab.
- Actions in a **NewDocumentItems** SubType will appear on the Ribbon in a **New Documents** submenu section on the **Actions** tab.

Action Groups

Action Groups provide a submenu grouping of actions within the assigned tab. In the following screenshot, the **Page Preview** screen is highlighting the submenu **Main Asset** which is the Caption for the associated ActionGroup. In the **RelatedInformation** ActionContainer, you can see the other **ActionGroups**, **Fixed Asset**, **Insurance**, and **History**, matching the submenu groups on the ribbon's **Navigate** tab.

Action Properties

ActionContainer properties are as follows:

- **ID**: The automatically assigned unique object number of the action.
- **Name** and **Caption**: Displayed in the Action Designer.
- **CaptionML**: The action name displayed, depending on the language option in use.
- **Description**: For internal documentation.

ActionGroup properties are as follows:

- **ID**: The automatically assigned unique object number of the action.
- **Name** and **Caption**: Displayed in the Action Designer.
- **Visible** and **Enabled**: TRUE or FALSE, defaulting to **TRUE**. The **Visible** property can be assigned a Boolean expression, which can be evaluated during processing.
- **CaptionML**: The action name displayed, depending on the language option in use.
- **Description**: For internal documentation.
- **Image**: Can be used to assign an icon to be displayed. The icon source is the Activity Button Icon Library, which can be viewed in detail in the **Developer and IT Pro Help**.

Here is a screenshot of the **Properties** screen for an action from Page 5600 – Fixed Asset Card followed by explanations of those properties:

Action properties are as follows:

- **ID**: The automatically assigned unique object number of the action.
- **Name** and **Caption**: Displayed in the Action Designer.
- **Visible** and **Enabled**: TRUE or FALSE, defaulting to TRUE. The **Visible** property can be assigned a Boolean expression, which can be evaluated during processing.

- **RunPageMode**: Can be **View** (no modification), **Edit** (the default), or **Create** (New).

- **CaptionML**: The action name displayed, depending on the language option in use.

- **ToolTip** and **ToolTipML**: For helpful display to the user.

- **Description**: For internal documentation.

- **Image**: Can be used to assign an icon to be displayed. The icon source is the Action Icon Library, which can be viewed in detail in the **Developer and IT Pro Help**.

- **Promoted**: If **Yes**, show this action on the ribbon **Home** tab.

- **PromotedCategory**: If **Promoted** is Yes, defines the Category on the **Home** tab in which to display this action.

- **PromotedIsBig**: If **Promoted** is Yes, indicates if the icon is to be large (Yes) or small (No – the default).

- **Ellipsis**: If Yes, displays an ellipsis after the Caption.

- **ShortCutKey**: Provides a shortcut key combination for this action.

- **RunObject**: Defines what object to run to accomplish the action.

- **RunPageView**: Sets the table view for the page being run.

- **RunPageLink**: Defines the field link for the object being run.

- **RunPageOnRec**: Defines a linkage for the run object to the current record.

- **InFooterBar**: Documented as placing the action icon in the page footer bar.

To summarize a common design choice, individual Ribbon actions can be promoted to the **Home** ribbon tab based on two settings. First, set the **Promoted** property to Yes. Second, set the **PromotedCategory** property to define the category on the **Home** tab where the action is to be displayed. This promotion results in the action appearing twice in the ribbon, once where defined in the action structure hierarchy and once on the **Home** tab. See the preceding screenshot for example settings assigning that **Depreciation Books** action to the Process category.

Navigation Pane Button actions

In the Navigation Pane on the left side of the Role Tailored Client display, there is a Home Button where actions can be assigned as part of the Role Center page definition. The Navigation Pane definition is part of the Role Center. When defining the actions in a Role Center page, you can include a group of actions in an **ActionContainer** group with the **SubType** of **HomeItems**. These actions will be displayed in the Home Button menu on the Navigation Pane.

Additional Navigation Pane buttons can also easily be defined in a Role Center page action list. First, define an **ActionContainer** with the **SubType** of **ActivityButtons**. Each **ActionGroup** defined within this **ActionContainer** will define a new Navigation Pane Activity button. The screenshot following is a combination showing:

- The RTC for the Sales Order Processor Role Center on the left, focused on the Navigation Pane
- The Action Designer contents that define the Home and Posted Documents buttons showing on the right

The actions that are shown on the right, which aren't visible in the Navigation Pane on the left, are in submenus indicated by the small outline arrowheads to the right of several entries including **Sales Orders** and **Sales Quotes**. NAV will automatically do some of this grouping for us based on the pages referenced by the actions, including Cue Group Actions.

Actions Summary

The primary location for each user's job role based actions to appear is in the Navigation Pane. The Role Center action list provides detailed action menus for the Home button and any appropriate additional Navigation Pane button. Detailed page/task specific actions should be located in the Ribbon at the top of each page.

As mentioned earlier, a key design criterion for the NAV Role Tailored Client was to make it easy for a user to have access to the actions they need to get their job done, that is to role tailor the system to the individual users. Our job as developers is to take full advantage of all of these options, to make life easier for the user. In general, it's better to go overboard in providing access to useful capabilities, than to make the user search for the right tool or use several steps in order to get to it. The challenge is to not clutter up the first-level display with too many things, but still have the important user tools just one click away.

Learning more

Descriptions in this section include several excellent ways to learn more about pages.

UX (User Experience) Guidelines

The **User Experience (UX)** Guidelines documents developed by Microsoft are available for download from various Internet locations. Search MSDN for **Microsoft Dynamics NAV 2013 User Experience Guidelines**. These UX Guidelines serve both as a summary tutorial to the construction of pages and as recommendations for good design practices.

Creative plagiarism

When we want to create new functionality that you haven't developed recently (or at all), it's good to start with an existing object that has that capability and study it. In many lines of work, the term plagiarism is a nasty term. But when it comes to modifying a system such as NAV, plagiarism is a very effective research and design tool. When designing modifications for NAV, studying how the existing objects work and interact is often the fastest way to create new working models. You should allocate some time for exploring the NAV Cronus demonstration system.

Define what you want to do. Search through the Cronus demonstration system (or an available production system) in order to find one or more pages that have the feature you want to emulate (or a similar feature). If there are both complex and simple instances of pages that contain this feature, concentrate your research on the simple one first. Make a test copy of the page. Read the code. Use the Page Preview feature. Run the page. Make a minor modification. Preview again; run it again. Continue this until your ability to predict the results of changes eliminates surprises or confusion.

Experimenting on your own

If you have followed along with the exercises so far in this book, it's time for you to do some experimenting on your own. No matter how much information someone else describes, there is no substitute for a personal, hands-on experience. You will combine things in a new way from what was described here. You will either discover a new capability that you would not have learned otherwise, or you will have an interesting problem to solve. Either way, the result will be significantly more knowledge about pages in NAV 2013.

Don't forget to make liberal use of the **Help** information while you are experimenting. Almost all of the available NAV documentation is in the help files that are built into the product. Some of the help material is a bit sparse, but it is being updated on a frequent basis. In fact, if you find something missing or something that you think is incorrect, please use the **Documentation Feedback** function that is built into the NAV help system. The product team responsible for help pay close attention to the feedback they receive and use it to improve the product. Thus, we all benefit from your feedback.

Experimentation

Let's start with the blank slate approach, because that allows us to focus on specific features and functions. Since we've already gone through the mechanical procedures of creating a new page of the card and list types using the Page Designer to add controls and modify control properties, we won't detail those steps here. But as you move the focus of your experimentation from one feature to another, you may want to review what we covered in that area in this chapter.

Let's walk through some examples of experiments you might do now, then you can build on them as you get more adventuresome. Each of the objects you create at this point should be assigned into an object number range that you are reserving for testing.

1. Create a new Table 50050 (try using 50009 if your license won't allow 50050). Do this by opening Table 50004 in the Table Designer, then saving it as 50050 with the name Playlist Item Rate Test.

2. Enter a few test records into Table 50050, Playlist Item Rate. You can do this by highlighting the table, then click on **Run**.

3. Create a list page for Table 50050 with at least three or four fields.

4. Change the **Visible** property of a field, by setting it to **False**.

5. Save and run the page.

6. Confirm that the page looks as what you expected. Go into **Edit** mode on the page. See if the field is still invisible.

7. Use the page Customization feature (from the Microsoft Dynamics icon on the upper-left corner of the page) in order to add the invisible field, also remove a field that was previously visible. Exit Customization. View the page in various modes (such as **View**, **Edit**, **New**).

8. Go back into the **Page Designer** and design the page again.

9. One or two at a time, experiment with setting the **Editable**, **Caption**, **ToolTip**, and other control properties.

10. Don't just focus on text fields. Experiment with other data types as well. Create a text field that's 200 characters long. Try out the **MultiLine** property.

11. After you get comfortable with the effect of changing individual properties, you may want to change multiple properties at a time in order to see how they interact.

When you feel that you have thoroughly explored individual field properties in a list, try similar tests in a card page. You will find that some of the properties have one effect in a list, while they may have a different (or no) effect in the context of a card (or vice-versa). Test enough to find out. If you have some "Aha!" experiences, it means that you are really learning.

The next logical step is to begin experimenting with the group-level controls. Add one or two to your page, then begin setting the properties for that control, again experimenting with only one or two at a time, in order to understand very specifically what each one does. Do some experimenting to find out which properties at the group level override the properties at the field level, and which do not.

Once you've done group controls, do part controls. Build some FactBoxes using a variety of the different components that are available. Use the System components and some ChartParts as well. There is a wealth of pre-built parts that come with the system. Even if the parts that are supplied aren't exactly right for your application, they can often be used as a model for the construction of custom parts. Remember that using a model can significantly reduce both the design and the debugging work when doing custom development.

After you feel you have a grasp of the different types of controls in the context of cards and lists, maybe it's time to check out some of the other page types. Some of those won't require too much in the way of new concepts. Examples of these are the ListPlus, List Parts, Card Parts, and, to a lesser extent, even Document pages.

It may be at this point that you decide to learn by studying samples of the page objects that are part of the standard product. You could start by copying an object, such as Page 22 – Customer List to another object number in your testing range, then begin to analyze how it is put together and how it operates. Again, you should tweak various controls and control properties in order to see how that affects the page. Remember, you should be working on a copy, not the original! Plus, it's a good idea to back up your work one way or another before making additional changes. An easy way to backup individual objects is to highlight the object, then Export it into a .fob file (**File** | **Export**). The restore is the reverse, importing the .fob file.

Summary

At this point, you should be relatively comfortable in the navigation of NAV and with the use of the Object Designer. You should be able to use the Page Wizard as an advanced beginner. If you have taken full advantage of the various opportunities to create tables and pages, both with our guidance and experimentally on your own, you are beginning to become a NAV Developer.

We have reviewed different types of pages and worked with some of them. We have reviewed all of the controls that can be used in pages and have worked with several of them. We also lightly reviewed page and control triggers. We've had a good introduction to the Page Designer and significant insight into the structure of some types of pages. With the knowledge gained, we have expanded our WDTU application system, enhancing our pages for data maintenance and inquiry.

In the next chapter, we will learn our way around the NAV Query and Report Designers. We will dig into the various triggers and controls that make up reports. We will also do some Query and Report creation work to better understand what makes them tick and what we can do within the constraints of the Query and Report Designer tools.

Review questions

1. Once a Page has been developed using the Page Wizard, the developer has very little flexibility in the layout of the Page. True or False?

2. The Address Bar in the Role Tailored Client is display only and cannot be used for navigation. True or False?

3. Actions appear on the Role Center screen in several places. Choose two:

    a. Address Bar

    b. Ribbon

    c. Filter Pane

    d. Navigation Pane

    e. Command Bar

4. The Filter Pane includes **Show results – Where** and **Limit totals to** options. True or False?

5. RTC Navigation Pane entries always invoke which one of the following page types?

    a. Card

    b. Document

    c. List

    d. Journal/Worksheet

6. All page design and development is done within the C/SIDE Page Designer. True or False?

7. Two Activity Buttons are always present in the Navigation Pane. Which two?

    a. Posted Documents

    b. Departments

    c. Financial Management

    d. Home

8. Inheritance is the passing of property definition defaults from one level of object to another. If a field property is explicitly defined in a table, it cannot be less restrictively defined for that field displayed on a page. True or False?

9. Which of the following are true about the control property Importance? Choose two.

    a. Applies only to Card and CardPart pages

    b. Cannot affect FastTab displays

    c. Has three possible values: Standard, Promoted, and Additional

    d. Applies to Decimal fields only

10. Generally, all of the development work for a Card or List page can be done using the appropriate Wizard. True or False?

11. FactBoxes are delivered as part of the standard product. They cannot be modified nor can new FactBoxes be created. True or False?

12. The Page Preview tool can be used as a drag and drop page layout design tool. True or False?

13. Some field control properties can be changed dynamically (as the object executes). Which ones? Choose three.

    a. Visible

    b. Multiline

    c. Editable

    d. DecimalPlaces

    e. HideValue

14. GridLayout Group Type is designed to support Excel interfacing. True or False?

15. Ribbon tabs and menu sections are predefined in NAV and cannot be changed by the developer. True or False?

5
Queries and Reports

Programming without an overall architecture or design in mind is like exploring
a cave with only a flashlight: You don't know where you've been, you don't know
where you're going, and you don't know quite where you are.

– Danny Thorpe

However beautiful the strategy, you should occasionally look at the results.

– Winston Churchill

In NAV 2013, **Reports** and **Queries** are two ways to output data (and in the case of
Reports, also to manipulate data) for the purpose of presentation to a user. Each of
these objects uses tools and processes that are NAV based for the data extraction
(XMLports, which also can extract and manipulate data, will be covered in a later
chapter). In this chapter, we will focus on understanding the strengths of each of
these tools, when and how they might be used. We will cover the NAV side of both
Queries and Reports in detail to describe how to get the data we need to present to
our users. We will cover the output formatting and consumption of that data in less
detail. There are currently no wizards available for either Query building or Report
building, therefore all the work must be done the old-fashioned, one-step-at-a-time
way. The topics we will cover include are:

- Queries and Reports
- Report components – overview
- Report data flow
- Report components – detail
- Creating a Report in NAV 2013

Queries

Reports have always been available in NAV as a tool to retrieve data from multiple areas within NAV, and to process and/or manipulate the data (through Insert, Modify, or Delete) with the option of presenting the data in a formatted, printable format. But formerly data selection was done in C/AL by defining filtered individual tables as datasets (retrieved from the database with simple T-SQL statements), and performing loops to find the data required for the purpose.

The new NAV 2013 Query object is created with performance in mind. Instead of multiple calls to SQL to retrieve multiple datasets to be manipulated in C/AL, Queries allow the developer to utilize familiar NAV tools to create advanced T-SQL queries.

A NAV developer can utilize the new Query object as a source of data both in NAV and externally. Some external uses include:

- As a web service, which is Cloud-compatible
- As a web service that can generate XML or OData (different from XML as it contains the field definitions and styles along with the data)
- Feeding data to external reporting tools such as Excel, SharePoint, and SSRS

Internally, NAV Queries can be used as:

- A direct data source for Charts
- To provide data which Cues (displayed in Role Centers) are bound
- As a dataset variable in C/AL to be accessed by other object types (Reports, Pages, Codeunits, and so on). See `http://msdn.microsoft.com/en-us/library/hh167210(v=nav.70).aspx` for more information

Query objects are more limited than SQL stored procedures. Some compromises in the design of Query functionality were made in the name of performance. Data manipulation is not supported in Queries. Variables, sub-queries, and dynamic elements (such as building a query based on selective criteria) are not allowed within the Query object.

The closest SQL Server objects that Queries resemble are SQL Views. One of the new features that allows for NAV to generate advanced T-SQL statements is the use of SQL Joins. These include the following Join methods:

- **Inner**: This query compares each row of table A with each row of table B to find all the pairs of rows which satisfy the Join criteria
- **Outer**: Does not require each record in the two Joined tables to have a matching record

- **Left Join**: Every record from A will appear at least once even if matching B not found

- **Right Join**: Every record from B will appear at least once even if matching A not found

- **Cross Join**: Returns the Cartesian product of the sets of rows from A and B

 Union (joins all records from A and B without a Join criteria) is not available at this time.

Building a simple Query

Sometimes it is necessary to quickly retrieve detail information from one or more ledgers that may contain thousands to millions of records. The Query is the perfect tool for this data selection as it is perfectly scalable and can retrieve selected fields from multiple tables at once. The following example (using Cronus data) will show the aggregated quantity per bin of lot-tracked items in stock. This query might be presented to a user either via a report or a page display.

First, it is necessary to know what inventory is in stock and contains a lot number. This is accomplished using the **Item Ledger Entry** table. But the **Item Ledger Entry** record does not contain any bin information. That information is stored in the **Warehouse Ledger Entry** table. The **Location Code, Item No.**, and **Lot No.** are used to match **Item Ledger Entry** and **Warehouse Ledger Entry** records to make sure the correct Items are selected. In order to determine which bins are designated as pick bins, the **Bin Type** records that are marked as **Pick** = True need to be matched with the bins in the **Warehouse Ledger Entry**. Lastly, the **Quantity** on each **Warehouse Entry** need to be summed per **Location Code, Zone Code, Bin Code, Item No.**, and **Lot No.** to show the amount available in each bin.

The first step is to define the primary DataItem in the Data Source column. The first DataItem is the Item Ledger Entry table. We can either type in the table name or the table number (32). The Query may select from multiple tables (as we do in this example), but all except the first table must be indentted. Each successively indented DataItem must have a link defined to a lesser-indented DataItem (because Union joins are not supported).

After defining the `DataItem`, we move focus to the first blank line, and the **Type** will default to `Column`. Column is a field from the `DataItem` table that will be output as an available field from the Query dataset. The other option is `Filter`, which allows us to use a source column as a filter, and does not output this column in the dataset. Use the lookup arrow or the Field Menu to add the following fields under `Item Ledger Entry`: Item No. and Lot No.

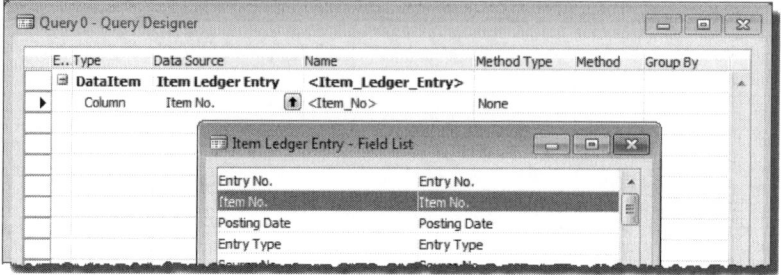

The next `DataItem` we need is the `Warehouse Entry` table. We need to join it to `Item Ledger Entry` by filling in the **DataItemLink** property. Link the **Location Code**, **Item No.**, and **Lot No.** fields between the two tables, as shown in the following screenshot:

The following steps will define the rest of the `DataItems`, `Columns`, and `Filters` for this query:

1. Select `Entry No.`, `Location Code`, `Zone Code`, `Bin Code`, and `Quantity` as `Columns` under the `Warehouse Entry DataItem`.

2. Add the `Bin` table as the next `DataItem`.

3. Set the DataItem Link between the Bin and Warehouse Entry as the Bin table `Code` field to the `Bin Code` field on the Warehouse Entry.

4. Add the `Bin Type` record as the last `DataItem` for this query. This has a `DataItem` Link between the `Bin Type` table `Code` field and the `Bin` table `Bin Type Code` field.

5. Set the DataItem Filter as `Pick = CONST(Yes)` to only show the quantities for bins that are enabled for picking.

6. For the dataset returned, only the total quantity per combination of **Location**, **Zone**, **Bin**, **Item**, and **Lot** is desired. For the `Column Quantity` in the `Warehouse Entry DataItem`, set the **Method Type** column to `Totals`. The **Method** will default to `Sum` and the columns above `Quantity` will be marked with **Group By** checked. This shows the grouping criteria for aggregation of the `Quantity` field.

Once the DataItems and Columns have been selected, the Query can be compiled and saved in the same manner as Tables and Pages. Number and name the Query object as shown in the following screenshot:

This query can be utilized internally in NAV 2013 through a Page or a Report object as an indirect data source. Currently, Page and Report objects can only select database tables, but you can define a Query as a variable, then use the dataset result to populate a table used as a source. Commonly this is done by defining the table utilized for a Page with the **SourceTableTemporary** property set to Yes, or by utilizing a virtual table, such as the Integer table, in a report.

In this example, we use the **Warehouse Entry** table because it contains all the fields in the Query dataset. In the **Page Properties**, we set **SourceTableTemporary** to Yes. In the **OnOpenPage** trigger, the temporary table is first cleared of any pre-existing values. Then the Query object (LotAvail) is filtered and opened. As long as the Query object has a dataset line available for output, the Query column values can be placed in the temporary record variable and be available for display, as in the following example:

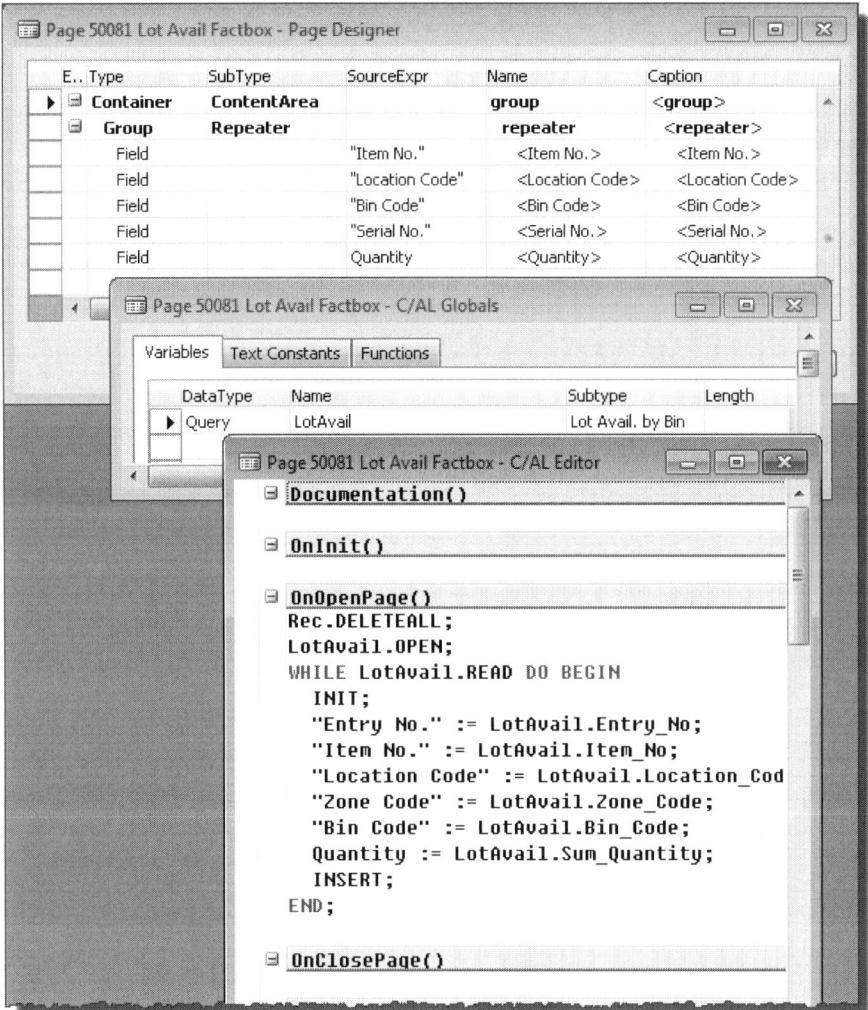

As the Query dataset is read, the temporary record dataset will be displayed on the page.

When a Query is used to supply data to a Report, an `Integer DataItem` is defined to control stepping through the Query results. Before the report read loop begins, the Query is filtered and invoked so that it begins processing. So long as the Query object continues to deliver records, the `Integer DataItem` will continue looping. At the end of the Query output, the report will proceed to its **OnPostDataItem** trigger processing, just as though it had completed processing a table rather than a Query created dataset.

Query and Query component properties

There are a number of Query properties that we want to review.

Query properties

The properties of the Query object can be accessed by highlighting the first empty line and clicking on the **Properties** icon (or clicking *Shift + F4* or **View | Properties**). The properties of the Query we created earlier look like the following screenshot:

We'll review three of these properties:

- **OrderBy**: Provides the capability to define a sort, data column by column, ascending or descending, giving the same result as if a key had been defined for the Query result, but without the requirement for a key.

- **TopNumberOfRows**: Allows specification of the number of data rows that will be presented by the Query. An undefined value defaults to the first 1000 rows, a 0 value shows all rows. Specifying a limit can make the Query complete much faster. This property can set dynamically from C/AL code.

- **ReadState**: Controls the state (committed or not) of data that is included and the type of lock that is placed on the data read.

The DataItem properties

A Query Line can be one of three types: DataItem, Column and Filter. Each has its own property set. Query DataItem properties can be accessed by highlighting a DataItem line and clicking on the **Properties** icon (or clicking *Shift + F4* or **View | Properties**).

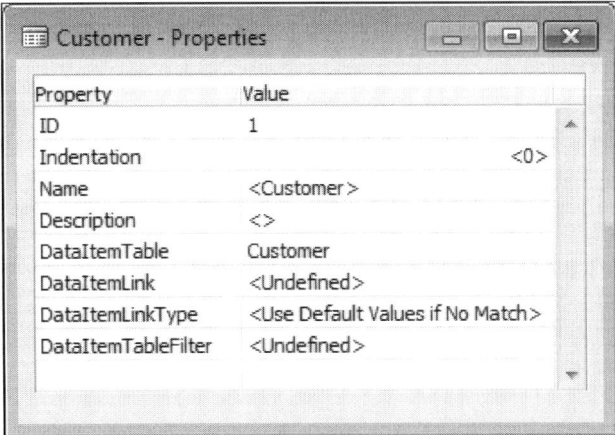

Again, we'll review a selected subset of these properties:

- **Indentation**: Indicates the relative position of this line within the Query's data hierarchy. The position in the hierarchy combined with the purpose of the line (data, lookup, or total) determine the sequence of processing within the Query.

- **DataItemLinkType**: Only can be used for the subordinate DataItem relative to its parent DataItem, in other words only applies in a multiple DataItem Query. There are three value options:

  ◦ **Use Default Values if No Match**: Includes the parent DataItem row even when there is no matching row in the subordinate DataItem

  ◦ **Exclude Row if No Match**: Skips the parent DataItem row if there is no matching row in the subordinate DataItem

  ◦ **SQL Advanced Options**: Enables another property, the **SQLJoinType** property

- **SQLJoinType**: Allows the specification of one of five different SQL Join Types (Inner, Left Outer, Right Outer, Full Outer, or Cross Join). More information is available in the Help sections *SQLJoinType Property* and *SQL Advanced Options for Data Item Link Types*.

- **DataItemTableFilter**: Provides the ability to define filters to be applied to the DataItem.

Column properties

The following is a Column property screen showing the **Sales_LCY** Column for our simple Query (the ColumnFilter property is in use):

Properties specific to Query Column controls:

- **MethodType**: Controls the interpretation of the following **Method** property. This can be Undefined/None, Date, or Totals.

- **Method**: Is dependent on the value of the **MethodType** property.
    - If **MethodType** = Date, then **Method** assumes that Column accesses a date value. The value of **Method** can be Day, Month or Year and the Query result for the Column will be the extracted day, month or year from the source date data.
    - If **MethodType** = **Totals**, then **Method** can be Sum, Count, Avg, Min, or Max. The result in the Column will be based on the appropriate computation. See the Help for *Method Property* for more information.

- **ReverseSign**: Reverses the sign of the Column value for numeric data.

Filter properties

Properties for Query Filter controls are shown in the following screenshot. This is the **Sales_LCY** control defined as a filter/non-visible result column.

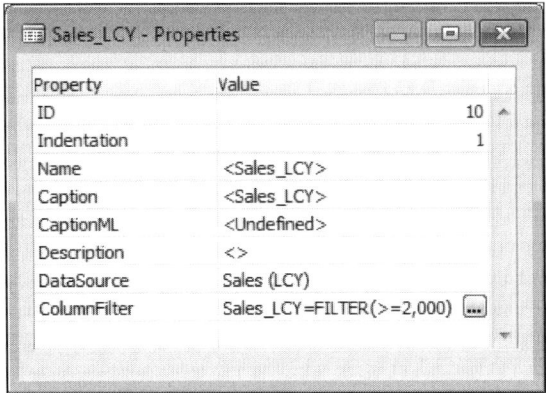

Reports

Some consider the library of reports provided as part of the standard NAV product distribution from Microsoft, to be relatively simple in design and limited in its features. Others feel that the provided reports satisfy most needs because they are simple. Their basic structure is easy to use. They are made much more powerful and flexible by taking advantage of of NAV's native filtering and SIFT capabilities. Some say that the simplicity of the standard product provides more opportunities for creative enhancement by users and professional NAV developers.

The fact remains that NAV's standard reports are basic. In order to obtain more complex or more sophisticated reports, we must use the features that are part of the product or feed processed data to external reporting tools. Through creative use of these features, many different types of complex report logic may be implemented.

First, we will review different types of reports and the components that make up reports. We'll look in detail at the triggers, properties, and controls that make up NAV report data processing. We will then study the Visual Studio Report Designer that is tightly integrated into NAV 2013. We'll create some reports with these Report Designer tools. We'll also modify a report or two using the Report Designer. We'll examine the data flow of a standard report and the concept of reports used for processing only (with no printed or displayed output).

What is a report?

A report is a vehicle for organizing, processing, and displaying data in a format suitable for outputting to the user. Reports may be displayed on-screen in the Preview mode, output to a file in CSV, XML, or PDF format, or printed to hardcopy in the old-fashioned way. All of the report screenshots in this book were taken from Preview mode reports.

Once generated, the data contents of a report are static. When a NAV 2013 Report is output in the Preview mode, the report can have interactive capabilities. Those capabilities only affect the presentation of the data; they do not change the actual data included in the report dataset. Interactive capabilities include dynamic sorting and detail/summary expand/collapse functions. All specification of the data selection criteria for a report must be done at the beginning, before the report view is generated. NAV 2013 also allows dynamic functionality for drilling down into the underlying data, drilling through to a page, and even drilling through into another report.

In NAV, report objects can also be classified as **Processing Only** (such as Report 795 Adjust Cost - Item Entries) by setting the correct report property (that is, by setting the **ProcessingOnly** property to **Yes**). A **ProcessingOnly** report will not display data to the user, but will simply process and update data in the tables. Report objects are convenient to use for processing in cases where the report's automatic read-process-write loop or the built-in Request page reduce coding that would otherwise be required. A report can add, change, or delete data in tables, whether the report is **ProcessingOnly** or a normal report generating output for viewing.

In general, reports are associated with one or more tables. A report can be created without being externally associated with any table, but that is an exception. Even if a report is associated with a particular table, it can freely access and display data from other referenced tables.

Two NAV report designers

NAV 2013 report design uses a pair of Report Designer tools. The first is the **Report Designer** that is part of the C/SIDE development environment. The second is the **Visual Studio Report Designer**. For simplicity, we will refer to these as C/SIDE RD and VS RD in this chapter

The typical report development process for a NAV 2013 report begins by doing foundation work in the C/SIDE RD. That's where all the data structure, working data elements, data flow, and C/AL logic are defined. The only way to create or modify report objects is to start in the C/SIDE RD. Once all of the elements of the dataset definition and Request page are in place, the development work proceeds to the VS RD where the layout and presentation work is done (including any desired dynamic options).

When a report is developed, VS RD builds a definition of the report layout in the XML-structured **Report Definition Language Client-side (RDLC)**. When we exit VS RD, the latest copy of the RDLC code is stored in the current C/SIDE Report object. When we exit the Report Designer and save our Report object, the C/SIDE RD saves the combined set of report definition information, C/SIDE and RDLC, in the database.

Because C/SIDE RD exports RDLC 2008 format for RTC, Visual Studio 2010 is required. We must either install the fully licensed version of Visual Studio 2010, or install both the Visual Web Developer 2010 Express and Microsoft Visual Studio 2010 Shell (Integrated) Redistributable Package. Visual Studio 2008 and Visual Studio 2012 both only support different formats of RDLC (2005 and 2010 respectively) and are not compatible with NAV 2013.

If we export a report object in text format, we will be able to see the two separate sets of report definition. The XML-structured RDLC is quite obvious (beginning with the heading RDLDATA).

```
CODE
{
  VAR
    LastFieldNo@1000 : Integer;
    ServItemFilter@1002 : Text[250];
    ServiceItemsCaptionLbl@9579 : TextConst 'ENU=Service Items';
    CurrReportPageNoCaptionLbl@2595 : TextConst 'ENU=Page';

  BEGIN
  END.
}
RDLDATA
{
    <?xml version="1.0" encoding="utf-8"?>
<Report xmlns:rd="http://schemas.microsoft.com/SQLServer/reporting/reportdesigner" x
  <DataSources>
    <DataSource Name="DataSource">
      <ConnectionProperties>
        <DataProvider>SQL</DataProvider>
        <ConnectString />
      </ConnectionProperties>
      <rd:DataSourceID>ea6fb201-8e76-4eca-99d0-00a7cefbc61f</rd:DataSourceID>
    </DataSource>
  </DataSources>
  <DataSets>
```

For the experienced NAV Classic Client report developer who is moving to Role Tailored Client projects, it will be a challenge to learn exactly which tasks are done using which report development tool, and learning the intricacies of the Visual Studio Report Designer layout tools. The biggest challenge for developers from many backgrounds will be the fact that there are no wizards to help with NAV 2013 report layout. All NAV 2013 report development must be done the hard way, manually, one field or format at a time. We should let Microsoft know that we would like them to invest in report layout wizards for future releases. You can submit suggestions through Microsoft Connect at `http://connect.microsoft.com/directory/`.

NAV allows us to create reports of many types with different "look and feel" attributes. The consistency of report look and feel does not have the same level of design importance as it has for pages. The standard NAV application only uses a few of the possible report styles, most of which are in a relatively basic format.

Good design practice dictates that enhancements should integrate seamlessly unless there is an overwhelming justification for being different. There are still many opportunities for reporting creativity. The tools available within NAV for accessing and manipulating data for reports are very powerful. Of course, there is always the option to output report results to other processing/presentation tools such as Excel or third-party products.

NAV report types

The following are the types of reports included in NAV 2013:

- **List**: A formatted list of data. A standard list is the **Inventory - List** report (Report 701).

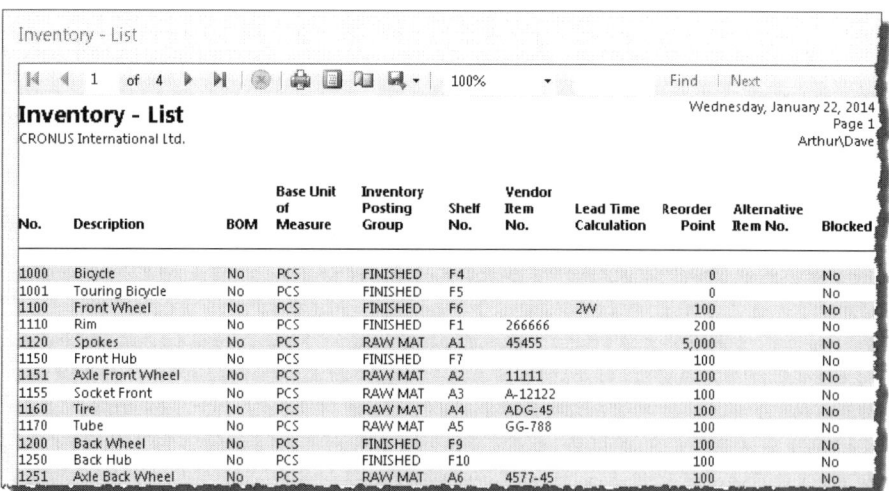

- **Document**: Is formatted along the lines of a pre-printed form, where a page (or several pages) contains a header, detail, and footer section with dynamic content. Examples are Customer Invoice, Packing List (even though it's called a list, it's a document report), Purchase Order, and Accounts Payable check

The following screenshot is of a Customer **Sales-Invoice** document report:

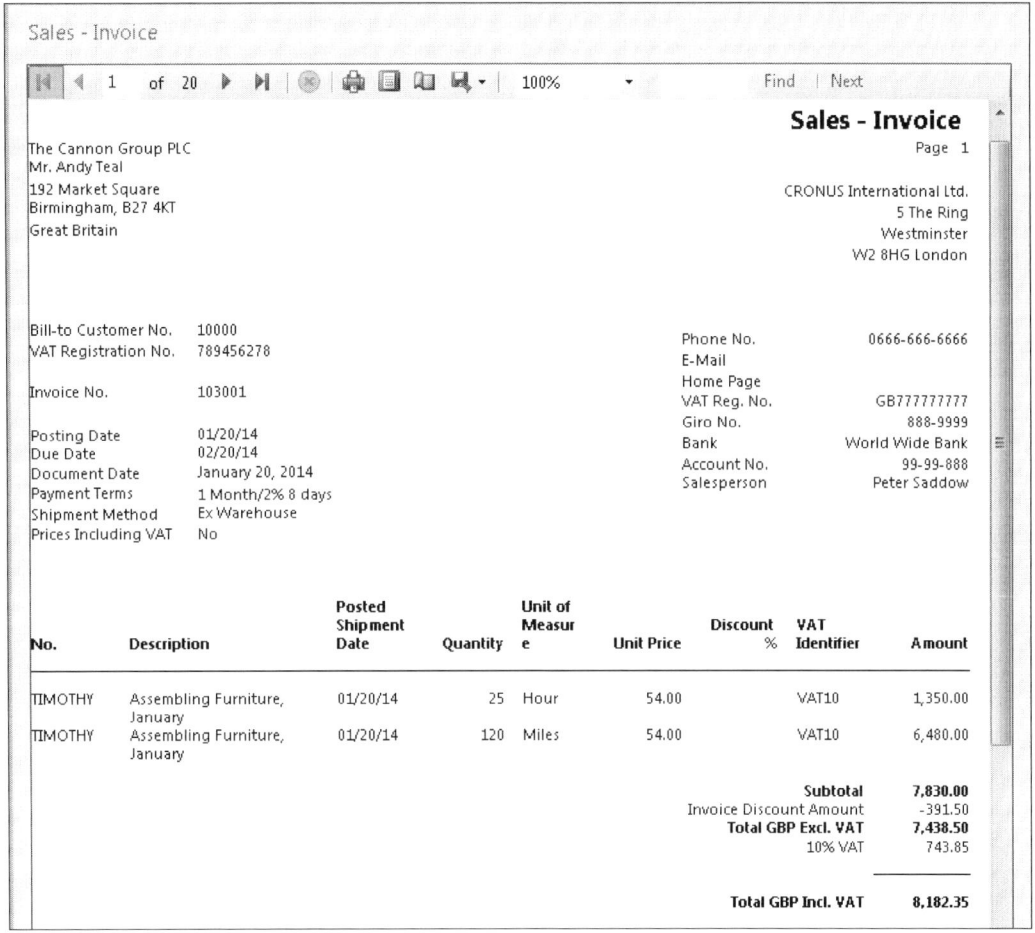

List and Document report types are defined based on their layouts. The next three report types are defined based on their usage rather than their layout:

- **Transaction**: Provides a list of ledger entries for a particular Master table. For example, a Transaction list of Item Ledger entries for all of the items matching a particular criteria, or a list of General Ledger entries for some specific accounts, as shown in the following screenshot:

- **Test**: These reports are printed from Journal tables prior to posting the transactions. Test reports are used to pre-validate data before posting. The following is a Test report for a **General Journal – Sales** batch with only one transaction, but with multiple problems and warning messages:

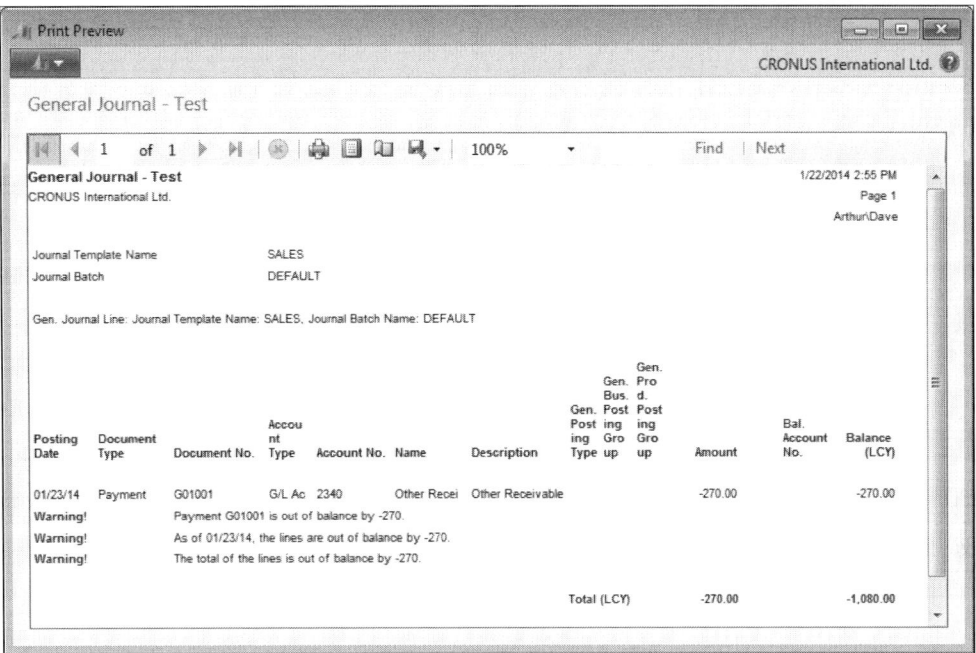

- **Posting**: Reports are printed as an audit trail as part of a "Post and Print" process. Posting report printing is controlled by the user's choice of either a **Posting Only** option or a **Post and Print** option. The Posting portions of both options work in a similar manner. Post and Print runs a report that is selected in the application setup. The default setup uses the same report that one would use as a transaction history report (like the one in the following screenshot). This type of posting audit trail report, which is often needed by accountants, can be regenerated completely and accurately at any time.

Posting Date	Docu ment Type	Document No.	G/L Account No.	Name	Description	VAT Amount	Gen. Posting Type	Gen. Bus. Postin g Group	Gen. Prod. Postin g Group	Amount	Entry No.
G/L Register											Thursday, January 23, 2014
CRONUS International Ltd.											Page 1
											Arthur\Dave
G/L Register: No.: 111											
Register No.	111										
01/22/14		G00001	1220	Increases during the	Packing Machine 201	22.19	Purchas	NATIO	MSC	88.78	2766
01/22/14		G00001	5630	Purchase VAT 25 %	Packing Machine 201	0.00				22.19	2767
01/22/14		G00001	8210	Office Supplies	Boxes for Packing M	4.92	Purchas	NATIO	MSC	19.70	2768
01/22/14		G00001	5630	Purchase VAT 25 %	Boxes for Packing M	0.00				4.92	2769
01/22/14		G00001	8210	Office Supplies	Glue for Packing Mac	5.55	Purchas	NATIO	MSC	22.20	2770
01/22/14		G00001	5630	Purchase VAT 25 %	Glue for Packing Mac	0.00				5.55	2771
01/22/14		G00001	5310	Revolving Credit	Materials for Packing	0.00				-163.34	2772

Report types summarized

The following list describes the different, basic types of reports available in NAV 2013:

Type	Description
List	Used to list volumes of like data in a tabular format, such as Sales Order Lines, a list of Customers, or a list of General Ledger Entries.
Document	Used in "record-per-page header" + "line item detail" situations, such as a Sales Invoice, a Purchase Order, a Manufacturing Work Order, or a Customer Statement
Transaction	Generally presents a list of transactions in a nested list format, such as a list of General Ledger Entries grouped by GL Account, Physical Inventory Journal Entries grouped by Item, or Salesperson To-Do List by Salesperson.
Test	Prints in a list format as a pre-validation test and data review, prior to a Journal Posting run. A Test Report option can be found on any Journal page such as General Journal, Item Journal, or the Jobs Journal. Test reports show errors that must be corrected prior to posting.
Posting	Prints in a list format as a record of which data transactions were posted into permanent status (that is, moved from a journal to a ledger). A posting report can be archived at the time of original generation or regenerated as an audit trail of posting activity.

There are other standard reports that don't fit within any of the preceding categories. Of course, many custom reports are also variations on or combinations of standard report structures.

Report naming

Simple reports are often named the same as the table with which they are primarily associated, plus a word or two describing the basic purpose of the report. Common key report purpose names include the words Journal, Register, List, Test, and Statistics. Some examples: **General Journal–Test**, **G/L Register**, and **Customer Order–Detail**.

When there are conflicts between naming based on the associated tables and naming based on the use of the data, the usage context should take precedence in naming reports, just as it does with pages. One requirement for names is that they must be unique; no duplicate names are allowed for a single object type.

Report components – overview

What we generally refer to as the report or report object is technically referred to as an **RDLC Report**. The RDLC Report is the information describing the logic to be followed when processing the data (the data model), as well as the output layout designed with Visual Studio Report Designer. RDLC Reports are stored in the NAV database.

We will use the term "report" whether we mean the output, the description, or the object. Reports share some attributes with pages including aspects of the designer, features of various controls, some triggers, and even some of the properties. Where those parallels exist, we should take notice of them. The consistency of any toolset, including NAV, makes it easier to learn and to use.

Report structure

The overall structure of an NAV RDLC Report consists of the following elements:

- Report Properties
- Report Triggers
- Request Page
    - Request Page Properties
    - Request Page Triggers
    - Request Page Controls
- Request Page Control Triggers
- Data Items
    - Data Item Properties
    - Data Item Triggers
    - Data Columns
- Data Column Properties
- Visual Studio Layout
    - VS Controls
- VS Control Properties

Report data overview

Report components Report Properties and Triggers, Request Page Properties and Triggers, and Data Items and their Properties and Triggers define the data flow and overall logic for processing the data. Another set of components, Data Fields and Working Storage, are defined subordinate to the Data Items (or Request Page). These are all designed in the **C/SIDE Report Dataset Designer (C/SIDE RD)**.

> **Data Fields** are defined in this book as the fields contained in the DataItems (application tables). **Working Storage** (also referred to as Working Data) fields are defined in this book as the data elements that are created within a report (or other object) for use in that object. The contents of Working Storage data elements are not permanently stored in the database. All of these are collectively referred to in the NAV Help as columns.

These components define the data elements that are made available to the Visual Studio Report Designer (VS RD) as a Dataset to be used in the layout and delivery of results to the user. In addition, Labels (text literals) can also be defined separately from any DataItem, but still included in the Dataset passed to the VS RD. Labels must be Common Language Specification (CLS)-compliant names (that means labels can contain only alpha and decimal and underscore characters and must not begin with an underscore).

> The VS RD cannot access any data elements that have not been defined within the C/SIDE RD. Each data element passed to the VS RD in the Dataset, whether a Data Field or Working Data, must be associated with a DataItem

The Report Request Page displays when a report is invoked. Its purpose is to allow users to enter information to control the report. Control information entered through a Request Page may include filters, control dates, other control parameters, and specifications as well as defining which available formatting or processing options to use for this instance of the report (that is, for this run). The Request Page appears once at the beginning of a report at run time. The following is a sample Request Page, the one associated with the **Customer - List** (Report 101):

Report Layout overview

The Report Layout is designed in the VS RD using data elements defined in Dataset DataItems by the C/SIDE RD, then made available to the VS RD. The Report Layout includes the Page Header, Body, and Page Footer.

In most cases, the Body of the report is based on a VS Table layout control. The VS RD table control is a data grid used for layout purposes and is not the same as a table of data stored in the NAV database. This terminology can be confusing. When the NAV Help files regarding reports refer to a table, we have to read very carefully to determine which meaning for "table" is intended.

Within the Report Body, there can be none, one, or more Detail rows. There can also be Header and Footer rows. The Detail rows are the definition of the primary, repeating data display. A report layout may also include one or more Group rows, used to group and total data that is displayed in the Detail row(s).

All of the report formatting is controlled in the Report Layout. The Font, field positioning, visibility options (including expand/collapse sections), dynamic sorting, and graphics are all defined as part of the Report Layout. The same is true for pagination control, headings and footers, some totaling, column-width control, and many other display details.

Of course, if the display target changes dramatically, for example, from a desktop workstation display to a browser on a phone, the appearance of the Report Layout will change dramatically as well. One of the advantages of SSRS is to support the required flexibility. Since we must expect significant variability in our users' output devices, we have to design accordingly.

Report data flow

One of the principal advantages of the NAV report is its built-in data flow structure. At the beginning of any report, you define the data items (the tables) that the report will process. We can create a processing only report that has no data items (if no looping though datasets is required), but that situation often calls for a codeunit to be used. In a report, NAV automatically creates a data flow process for each DataItem, or table reference. This automatically created data flow provides specific triggers and processing events for each of data item:

- Preceding the data item
- After reading each record of the data item
- Following the end of the data item

The underlying "black-box" report logic (the part we can't see or affect) automatically loops through the named tables, reading and processing one record at a time. Therefore, any time we need a process that steps through a set of data one record at a time, it is usually easier to use a report object.

The reference to a database table in a report is referred to as a **Data Item** or as a DataItem in the code (it can be referenced either way in descriptive text). The report data flow structure allows us to nest data items (create a hierarchical grandparent, parent, child structure). If Data Item 2 is nested within Data Item 1 and related to Data Item 1, then for each record in Data Item 1, all of the related records in Data Item 2 will be processed.

The following example uses tables from our WDTU system. The design is for a report to list all the scheduled instances of a Radio Show grouped by Radio Show for each Show Type. Thus **Radio Show Type** is the primary table (**DataItem1**). For each **Radio Show Type**, we want to list all the Radio Shows of that type (**DataItem2**). And for each **Radio Show,** we want to list all the scheduled instances of that show recorded in the **Playlist Header** (**DataItem3**).

Open Object Designer, select the **Report** object type, and click on the **New** button. On the **Report Dataset Designer** screen, we first enter the table name `Radio Show Type` (or table number 50001), as we can see in the following screenshot. The Data Item name, to which the C/AL code will refer, is **DataItem1** in our example here. Then we enter the second table, `Radio Show`, which is automatically indented relative to the data item above (the "superior" data item). That indicates the nesting of the processing of the indented data item within the processing of the superior data item.

For our example, we have renamed the Data Items to better illustrate report data flow. The normal behavior would be for the name in the right column to default to the table name shown in the left column (for example, the name for **Radio Show** would be **<Radio Show>** by default). This default Data Item name would only need to be changed if the same table appeared twice within the Data Item list. For the second instance of **Radio Show**, for example, we could simply give it the name `RadioShow2`.

For each record in the parent data item, the indented data item will be fully processed dependent on the filters, and the defined relationships between the superior and indented tables. In other words, the visible indentation is only part of the necessary definition.

For our example, we enter a third table, **Playlist Header**, and enter our example name of **DataItem3**:

The following chart shows the data flow for this Data Item structure. The chart boxes are intended to show the nesting that results from the indenting of the Data Items in the preceding screenshot. The **Radio Show** Data Item is indented under the **Radio Show Type** Data Item. That means for every processed Radio Show Type record, all of the selected Radio Show records will be processed. That same logic applies to the **Radio Show** records and **Playlist Header** records (that is, for each Radio Show record processed, all selected Playlist records are processed).

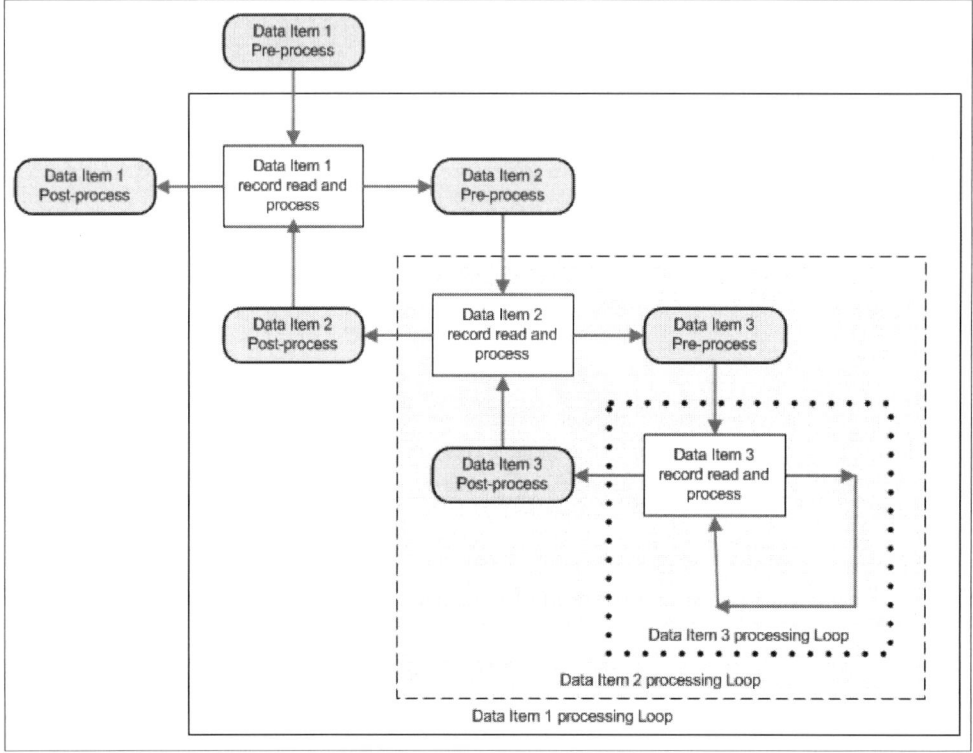

The blocks visually illustrate how the data item nesting controls the data flow. As we can see, the full range of processing for **DataItem2** occurs for each **DataItem1** record. In turn, the full range of processing for **DataItem3** occurs for each **DataItem2** record.

In the NAV 2013 Role Tailored Client, report processing occurs in two separate steps, the first tied primarily to what has been designed in the C/SIDE RD, the second tied to what has been designed in the VS RD. The processing of data represented in the preceding diagram occurs in the first step, yielding a complete dataset containing all the data that is to be rendered for output.

Once the dataset is processed for display by the RDLC code created by the VS RD, if the output is to be displayed in the NAV Client for Windows, the results are handed off to the Microsoft Report Viewer. The Microsoft Report Viewer provides the NAV 2013 reporting capabilities such as various types of graphics, interactive sorting and expand/collapse sections, output to PDF and Excel, and other advanced features.

Report components – detail

Earlier we reviewed a list of the components of a Report object. Now we're going to review detailed information for each of those components. Our goal here is to understand how the pieces of the report puzzle fit together.

C/SIDE Report properties

The C/SIDE RD Report properties are shown in the following screenshot. Some of these properties have essentially the same purpose as those in pages and other objects.

- **ID**: The unique report object number.
- **Name**: The name by which this report is referred to within C/AL code.

- **Caption**: The name that is displayed for this report; **Caption** defaults to Name.

- **CaptionML**: The **Caption** translation for a defined alternative language.

- **Description**: For internal documentation.

- **UseRequestPage**: Yes or No, controlling whether or not the report will begin with a Request Page for user parameters to be entered.

- **UseSystemPrinter**: Determines if the default printer for the report should be the defined system printer, or if NAV should check for a setup-defined User/Report printer definition. More on User/Report printer setup can be found in the NAV application help.

- **EnableExternalImages**: If Yes, allows links to external (non-embedded) images on the report. Such images can be outside the NAV database.

- **EnableHyperLinks**: If Yes, allows links to other URLs including other reports or to pages.

- **EnableExternalAssemblies**: If Yes, allows the use of external custom functions as part of the report.

- **ProcessingOnly**: Set to Yes when the report object is being used only to process data and no reporting output is to be generated. If this property is set to **Yes**, then that overrides any other property selections that would apply in a report-generating situation.

- **ShowPrintStatus**: If this property is set to Yes and the **ProcessingOnly** property is set to No, then a **Report Progress** window, including a **Cancel** button, is displayed. When **ProcessingOnly** is set to Yes, if we want a **Report Progress** Window, we must create our own dialog box.

- **TransactionType**: This can be in one of four basic options: Browse, Snapshot, UpdateNoLocks, and Update. These control the record locking behavior to be applied in this report. The default is UpdateNoLocks. This property is generally only used by advanced developers.

- **Permissions**: This provides report-specific setting of permissions, which are the rights to access data, subdivided into Read, Insert, Modify, and Delete. This allows the developer to define report and processing permissions that override the user-by-user permissions security setup.

- **PaperSourceFirstPage**, **PaperSourceDefaultPage**, and **PaperSourceLastPage**: All allow choice of paper source tray based on information in the fin.stx file (**fin.stx** is an installation file that contains the active language messages and reserved words in addition to some system control parameters that are defined by Microsoft and are not modifiable by anyone else).

Visual Studio Report properties

The Visual Studio RD **Properties** Window is docked by default on the right side of the screen (as with most VS RD windows, it can be redocked, hidden, or float as in the following screenshot):

By clicking on the drop-down arrow (at the head of the cursor arrow), we can choose which set of properties we want to access, those of the whole **Report**, the **Report Body**, the **Tablix**, or individual **Text Boxes**. Once we have chosen the set of properties, we can access those properties in one of two ways. The obvious way is through the window that opens up when you choose which control properties to display.

The following screenshot shows the properties of a **Text Box** with the **Font** properties highlighted and expanded. **Font** properties are the properties most often accessed to change the appearance of a report layout, although a variety of other field formatting properties are also utilized.

The other way to access property detail is by clicking on the **Property Pages** icon near the top of the **Properties** window:

This opens up a control-specific **Properties** window, which includes a menu of choices of property categories to access. In the following screenshot, **Text Box Properties** was opened and the **Font** properties accessed for display:

Many developers feel this view of report component properties is easier to use because it's easier to find and change all the properties options here. This applies to Report level properties controlling macro elements such as **Paper Orientation** as well as control level properties controlling micro elements such as font size. Report level properties also include the facility to include code defining functions which can be referenced by the controls. The code shown in the following screenshot is generated by NAV to support C/SIDE field formatting properties such as Blank When Zero:

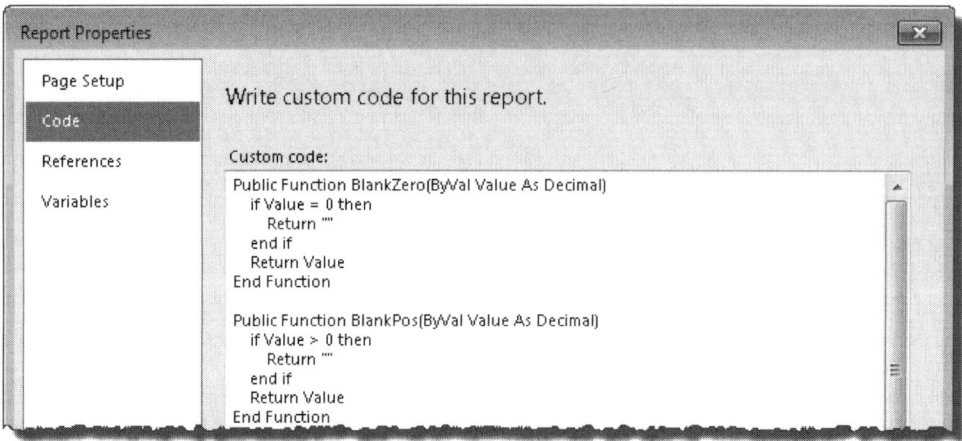

Report triggers

The following screenshot shows the Report triggers available in a report:

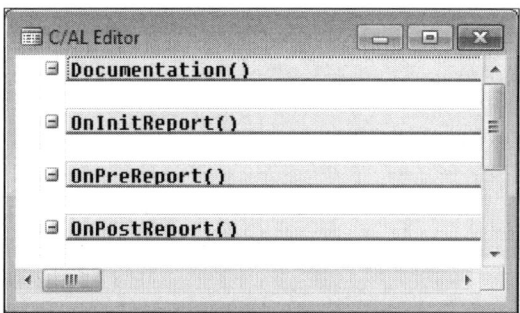

- **Documentation()**: Documentation is technically not a trigger since it can hold no executable code. It will contain whatever documentation we care to put there. There are no format restrictions.

- **OnInitReport()**: Executes once when the report is opened.

- **OnPreReport()**: Executes once after the Request Page completes. All the Data Item processing follows this trigger.

- **OnPostReport()**: If the report is completed normally, this trigger executes once at the end of all of the other report processing. All the Data Item processing precedes this trigger.

Request Page properties

The Request Page properties are a subset of Page properties covered in detail in *Chapter 4, Pages – the User's Interactive Interface*. Usually most of these properties are now changed simply because the extra capability is not needed. An exception is the **SaveValues** property which, when set to `Yes`, causes entered values to be retained and redisplayed when the page is invoked another time. A screenshot of the Request Page properties follows:

Request Page triggers

Request Pages have a full complement of triggers, thus allowing for complex pre-report processing logic. Because of their comparatively simplistic nature, most Request Pages do not need to take advantage of these trigger capabilities.

Data item properties

The following screenshot shows the properties of a Data Item:

These are descriptions of properties that are special to Data Items:

- **Indentation**: This shows the position of the referenced Data Item in the hierarchical structure of the report. A value of **0** (zero) indicates that this Data Item is at the top of the hierarchy. Any other value indicates the subject Data Item is subordinate to (that is nested within) the preceding Data Item.

- **DataItemTable**: This is the name of the NAV table assigned to this Data Item.

- **DataItemTableView**: This is the definition of the fixed limits to be applied to the Data Item (the key, ascending or descending sequence, and what filters to apply to this field).

> If we don't define a key, then the users can choose a key to control the data sequence to be used during processing. If we do define a key in the Data Item properties and, in the **ReqFilterFields** property, we do not specify any Filter Field names to be displayed, this Data Item will not have a FastTab displayed as part of the Request Page. That will stop the user from filtering this Data Item, unless we provide the capability in C/AL code.

- **DataItemLinkReference**: This names the Data Item in the hierarchy above the Data Item to which this one is linked. The linked Data Item can also be referred to as the parent Data Item.

- **DataItemLink**: This identifies the field-to-field linkage between this Data Item and its parent Data Item. That linkage acts as a filter because only those records in this table will be processed that have a value that matches with the linked field in the parent data item. If no field linkage filter is defined, all the records in the table will be processed for each record processed in its parent table.

- **ReqFilterFields**: This property allows us to choose certain fields to be named in the Report Request Page, to make it easier for the user to access them as filter fields. So long as the Report Request Page is activated for a Data Item, the user can choose any available field in the table for filtering, regardless of what is specified here.

- **CalcFields**: This names the FlowFields that are to be calculated for each record processed. Because FlowFields do not contain data, they have to be calculated to be used. When a FlowField is displayed on a page, NAV automatically does the calculation. When a FlowField is to be used in a report, we must instigate the calculation. That can either be done here in this property or explicitly within C/AL code.

- **MaxIteration**: This can be used to limit the number of iterations the report will make through this Data Item. For example, we would set this to **7** for processing with the virtual **Date** table to process one week's data.

- **PrintOnlyIfDetail**: This should only be used if this Data Item has a child Data Item, that is one indented/nested below it. If **PrintOnlyIfDetail** is **Yes**, then controls associated with this Data Item will only print when data is processed for the child Data Item.

Data Item triggers

Each Data Item has the following triggers available:

The data item triggers are where most of the flow logic is placed for a report. Developer-defined functions may be freely added, but generally they will be called from within these three triggers:

- **OnPreDataItem()**: Is the logical place for any preprocessing to take place that can't be handled in report or data item properties or in the two report preprocessing triggers.

- **OnAfterGetRecord()**: Is the data "read + process loop". Code placed here has full access to the data of each record, one record at a time. This trigger is repetitively processed until the logical end of table is reached for this data item. This is where we would typically access data in related tables. This trigger is represented on our report Data Flow diagram as any one of the boxes labeled **Data item processing Loop**.

- **OnPostDataItem()**: Executes after all the records in this data item are processed—unless the report is terminated by means of a User **Cancel** or by execution of a C/AL BREAK or QUIT function, or by an error.

Creating a Report in NAV 2013

Because NAV report layouts are all developed in Visual Studio, our familiarity with NAV C/SIDE will only get us part way to having NAV report development expertise. We've covered most of the basics for the C/SIDE part of NAV report development. Now we need to dig into the Visual Studio part. If you are already a Visual Studio reporting expert, you will not spend much time on this part of the book. If you know little or nothing about Visual Studio, you will need to experiment and practice.

Learn by experimentation

One of the most important learning tools available is experimentation. Report development is one area where experimentation will be extremely valuable. We need to know which report layouts, control settings and field formats work well and which do not. The best way to find out is by experimentation.

We should create a variety of test reports, beginning with the very simple and getting progressively more complex. If we document our discoveries as we go, we will end up with our own personal Help documentation, tailored to issues with which we are familiar. Once we've created a number of reports from scratch, we should modify test copies of some of the standard reports that are part of the NAV system.

We must make sure we are working on test copies, not the originals!

Some reports will be relatively easy to understand and others that are very complex, difficult to understand. The more we test, the better we will be able to determine which standard NAV report designs can be borrowed for our work and where we are better off starting from scratch.

Report building – phase 1

Our goal is to create a report for our WDTU data that will give us a list of all the scheduled radio show instances organized within **Radio Show** organized by **Radio Show Type**, as shown in the following screenshot:

The easy way to create the preceding is to simply type D in the **Data Type** column, enter our target table number (in this case 50001, then 50000, then 50002) in the **Data Source** column, drop to the next line and do it again. Then save our new report skeleton as Report **50001**, **Shows by Type**.

Before we go any further, let's make sure we've got some test data in our tables. To enter data, we can either use the pages we built earlier or, if those aren't done yet, we can just **Run** the tables and enter some sample data. The specifics of our test data aren't critical. We simply need a reasonable distribution of data so our report test will be meaningful. The following is an example minimal set of data:

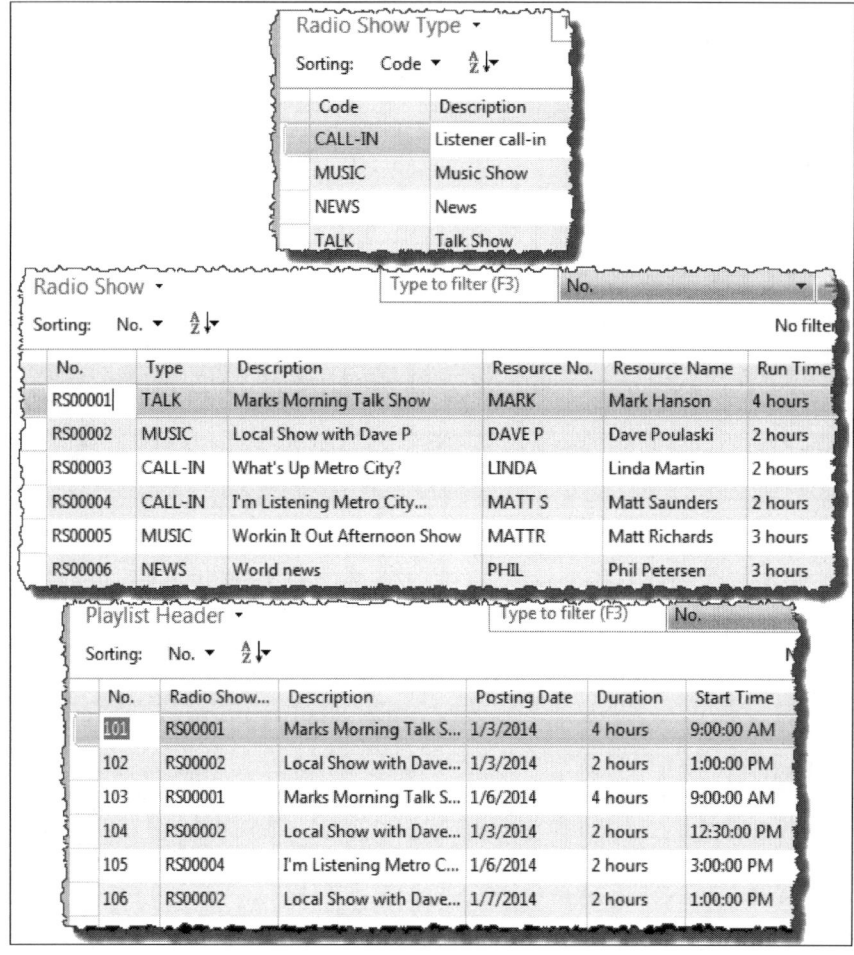

Since the C/SIDE part of our report design is relatively simple, we can do it as part of our phase 1 effort. It's simple because we aren't building any processing logic; we don't have any complex relationships to address. We just want to create a nice, neat nested list of data.

Our next step is to define the data fields we want to be available for processing and outputting by the VS RD. By clicking on the **Include Caption** column, we can cause the **Caption** value for each field to be available for use in the VS RD. At this point, we should do that for all the data fields. If some are not needed in our layout design, we can later return to this screen and remove the check marks where unneeded. Please note that the **Name** column value will end up as the VS dataset field name, to make sure it is easy to understand, describes what the data is and its source.

Each of the subordinate, nested DataItems must be properly linked to its parent DataItem. The **Playlist Header** DataItem is joined to the **Radio Show** DataItem by the Playlist Header "Radio Show No." field and Radio Show "No." field. The Radio Show DataItem is joined to the Radio Show Type DataItem by the Radio Show "Type" field and the Radio Show Type "Code" field. The Radio Show portion of the dataset returned is limited by setting the **PrintOnlyIfDetail** to Yes. This will skip the Radio Show record from being sent to VS RD if no Playlist Header records are associated with that Radio Show.

The other data that we can pass from the C/SIDE RD to the VS RD are the labels. Labels will be used later as captions in the report, and are enabled for multi-language support. Let's create a title label to hand over the fence to Visual Studio. Go to the **View** menu, and choose **Labels** to open the **Report Label Designer**.

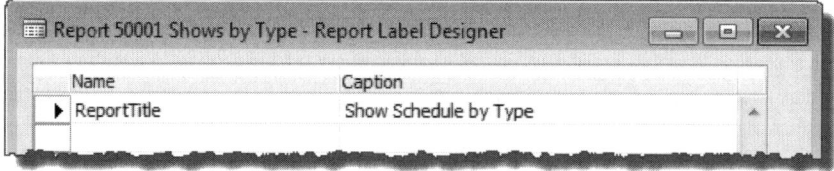

Now that we have our C/SIDE dataset definition completed, we should save and compile our work before doing anything else. Then, before we begin our VS RD work, it's a good idea to check that we don't have some hidden error that will get in our way later. The easiest way to do that is just to **Run** what we have now. What we expect to see is a basic Request Page display allowing us to run an empty report.

Report building – phase 2

To begin our report development work in Visual Studio, we must have our C/SIDE dataset definition open in **Design** mode. Then, go to **View | Layout** to open up Visual Studio Report Designer. If we have previously done VS development work on this report and saved it, that work will be displayed in the VS RD ready for our next effort. In this case, since we are just starting, we will see the following (assuming we haven't previously reorganized the layout of the various windows):

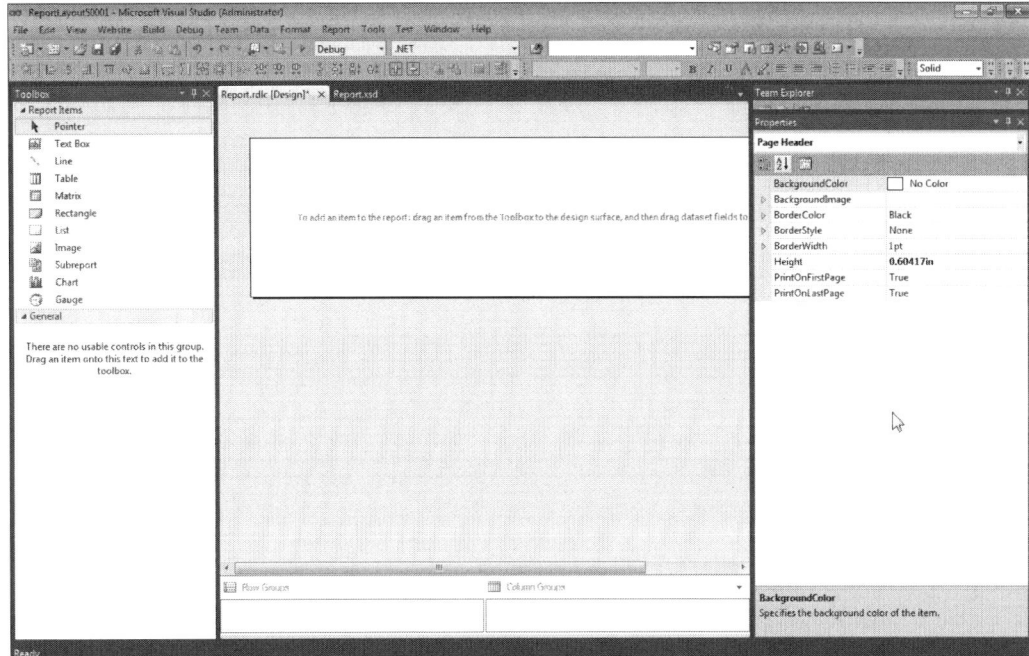

On the left-hand side is **Toolbox**, in the center is the layout work area (shaded with the report design surface rectangle in white in the center) and on the right is displayed the **Properties** of whatever has focus.

Before we start on our sample report VS RD work here, you should study some of the information on report design in NAV **Developer and IT Pro** Help. In particular, you should review *Walkthrough: Designing a Customer List Report* and *Walkthrough: Designing a Report from Multiple Tables*. These scripts will provide additional information that you will find helpful.

Since we're going to have a page header, let's start by adding that to our layout. Right-click on the shaded part of the layout work area and select **Add Page Header**.

Next we will add some fields to the Page Header. First, we will add the report title that we defined as a label earlier in the C/SIDE RD.

To access the DataSet Result definition that was passed from the C/SIDE RD to the VS RD, click on **View | Report Data** (or *Ctrl + Alt + D*).

This will display the DataSet Result. If we click on **Parameters** to expand that section, we will also see the **Labels** that we defined as well as the **Captions** we asked to be included.

As we can see, the DataSet Result display does not indicate which fields are associated with which NAV DataItems, emphasizing the importance of our names being well done as mentioned earlier. We will have to keep in mind what we have defined in our DataSet and with which DataItems they are associated. Good naming conventions that tie fields to their parent DataItems will address this. This will be especially important when we have multiple fields with the same name from different DataItems (such as Code, Description, or Amount).

The DataSet represents a record format in which all fields are present for all records. This is a classic "flat file" format where the hierarchical data structure has been "flattened" out to make it easier to pass from one environment, NAV, to another, Visual Studio.

We will drag the **Report Title** field over to the Page Header workspace and position it as feels appropriate. Now expand the **Built-in Fields Section** under Report Data. We will add some other fields, such as **User ID**, **Execution Time**, and **Page Number** to our Page Header. We will position these fields wherever we think appropriate.

At this point, it's a good time to save our work and test to see what we have so far:

1. Click on **File | Save Report.rdlc** (or *Ctrl + S*) to save the design as RDLC.
2. Click on **File | Exit** (or *Alt + F4*) to return to the C/SIDE RD.
3. Save and compile the report.
4. Respond **Yes** to the **The layout of report id 50001 has changed…Do you want to load the changes?** question.

This will bring the revised RDLC code into our C/SIDE object for the final compile and storage in the database.

Now **Run** the report. Our **Preview** output should look something like the following:

Not especially impressive, but not bad if this is our first try at creating a NAV 2013 report. The wrapped report title shows us that we need to make that textbox wider. By the way, the username is due to running tests on a computer named **Arthur**.

This would be a good point to do some experimenting with positioning or adding other heading information such as "Page" in front of the page number. When we highlight a field, the properties of that field are displayed, and are available for modification, in the **Properties** window. We could even experiment with various properties of the heading fields, choosing different fonts, bolding, colors, and so on. Because we only have a small number of simple fields showing, this is a good time to learn more about some of the report appearance capabilities that VS RD provides.

Report building – phase 3

Finally, we are ready to layout the data display portion of our Radio Shows by Type report. The first step of this phase is to layout the fields of our controlling DataItem data in such a way that we can properly group the subordinate DataItems' data.

Once again, **Design** the report and click **View** | **Layout** so that the Visual Studio report layout screen is displayed with the **Toolbox** window visible. We are now done with the Page Heading and from here on, all our work will be done in the Body of the VS report design surface.

From the toolbox, grab and drag a **List** control over to the body of the report design surface. Position the control at the top left of the body. Since we're going to define six layout lines to hold the necessary data and header controls, we may want to expand the List control and work area (though this can be done later, as needed).

1. Right-click in the List control so that a shaded area appears to the top and left of the control.

2. Right-click in the shaded area and select **Tablix Properties**.

3. Set the **Dataset name** value to **DataSet_Result** to make sure the List control is referencing our incoming NAV data.

4. Right-click again in the List control's shaded area and select **Row Group**, then **Group Properties**.

In the **Group Properties** screen, select the **General** tab, in the **Group expressions** area click on **Add**, then in **Group on**: select **[Type]**, because we want our data output grouped by the **Type** of Radio Show.

Return to the report layout design surface and drag a Table control from the Toolbox over to rest in the List control. This will be the container for our Radio Show Type DataItem fields so we want to position this control at the top left of the design area.

The empty control will start with two rows and three columns. Since we're only going to display two data fields (**Type** and **Description**), we only need two columns. So highlight the rightmost column (click in the body so that a shaded area appears on the left and top of the control, then click in the shaded area above the column), right click (in the shaded area at the top of the column) and delete it.

Because this section of our report acts as a heading to subordinate sections, we will delete the Data row from the Table control and replace it with a second Header row. Once again, click in the shaded area to highlight the Data row, select the **Delete Rows** option, respond **OK** to the confirmation message, highlight the Header row and insert a second Header row. We now have two rows and two columns of textboxes (cells) ready for data.

Right-click in the top-left cell, choose **Expression** and the Expression screen will be displayed. In that screen (shown following) click on **Parameters** and double-click on **TypeCaption**. In the **Expression** work area, the expression **=Parameters!TypeCaption.Value** will display:

Our next step is to place some data fields in the Table control. There are multiple ways to do this. We will use a simple approach because this is our first experience at this. Once the the basics have been mastered, other approaches should be explored.

Click in the lower left cell of the Table control. A field list icon will display. Click on the icon and we will see all the fields in the **Dataset_Result**.

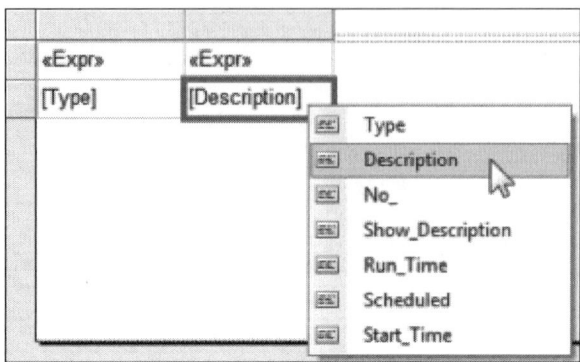

Select **Type** for the bottom-left cell and **Description** for the bottom-right cell.

We are at another good point to save and check our work. If you are one of those people who like to do as much as possible from the keyboard, *Ctrl + S* (to save the RDLC), *Alt + F4* (to exit the VS RD), *Esc* (to exit the C/SIDE RD), *Enter* (to load the changed RDLC), *Enter* (to save and compile), then *Alt + R* to **Run** the report. Now you'll likely have to use your mouse to respond to the Request Page.

Don't worry about the vertical spacing of our output. We can fix that later. We should get as many instances of the Radio Show type printed as we have Types of entries selected from the Playlist Header table.

Assuming our output looks pretty much like expected (a simple list of Show Types with column headings), we can move on to the next layer of layer definition. This time we will be defining how the Radio Show data fields will be shown, including the fact this set of data is grouped subordinate to the Type field.

Drag another Table control to the report design surface in the list control. Position this control below the last Table control in a position that will show its relation to the Type data records. Usually this will involve an indented positioning.

Click in the control to cause the shaded outer area to be displayed. Highlight the Header row and delete it. Highlight the Data row, right-click on it and choose **Insert Row – Inside Group** (**Above** or **Below** doesn't matter this time).

Right-click on one of the data rows and select **Row Group**, then **Group Properties**.

When the **Group Properties** screen displays, we want to do the same thing we did for the List control earlier. Select the **General** tab, in the **Group expressions** area click on **Add**, then in **Group on:** select **[Type]**. We could accomplish the same thing by selecting **Add Group** (as in the previous screenshot). But that would add a column on the left end of the table (grouping information) to be edited out.

In the bottom row of our second Table control, cause the field list icon to display, then choose a field for each of the three cells (**No., Show_Description**, and **Run_Time**). Because both our rows are defined as Data rows, we have to fill in the headings ourselves.

We could define expressions as we did earlier, but we want captions that are different than those that came across from C/SIDE RD. We could have used Labels here if we had defined them in C/SIDE RD. Or we can just do the simple thing, type in the column headings we want (**Show No., Description, Run Time**), overwriting the default headings. Highlight the middle column (**Description**) and stretch it out so a long description will display on one line rather than wrapping.

Now, once again, it's time to save and test. If we want to check if our VS RD work will compile, we can do that by clicking **Build | Build Solution** or *F6*. Note that a clean Visual Studio compile doesn't mean our report will work correctly or even run at all. NAV 2013 reports are complicated mechanisms with many parts and all the parts must work together for the final result to match our hopes and expectations.

Our third (and final) Table control for this report will hold data from the **Playlist Header DataItem**. The process for this table is almost exactly the same as for the second table. We will drag the table into place. Since we only need two columns for our data fields (**Scheduled** and **Start Time**), delete the default third column.

We will define our table as two **Data** rows. Delete the **Header** row, right-click on the **Data** row, **Insert Row – Inside Group** (**Above** or **Below**). This time we want to define a **Parent Group**, so right-click on the top row, choose **Add Group**, then choose **Parent Group**. When the **Tablix group** screen displays, fill in **Group by:** and choose **[No_]**.

We're almost done with this phase. Highlight the two bottom row cells and fill them with the desired data fields. If we want to change the heading names from the defaults, now is a good time to do that. Finally we save our RDLC code (*Ctrl + S*), exit VS (*Alt + F4*), exit CSIDE RD (*Esc, Enter*), save and compile (*Enter*). Let's **Run** our report and see what we've got.

While this report is not beautiful, it is serviceable, especially for a first try. One thing that we should improve before we show it to very many people is the formatting of the fields that are defined in NAV as a Date field and a Time field, but here are showing as DateTime field. The solution to this is to use the Visual Studio Format function, specifically the Predefined Date/Time Formats. You should look these up in MSDN at `http://msdn.microsoft.com/en-us/library/vstudio/az4se3k1 (v=vs.90).aspx`.

Modifying an existing report

The basic process we must follow to modify an existing report is the same whether the report is one of the standard reports that comes with NAV 2013 or a custom report that we are enhancing in some way. An important discipline to follow in all cases where we are modifying a report that has been in production is NOT to work on the original, but on a copy. In fact, if this is a standard report we are customizing, we should leave the original copy alone and do all our work on a copy. Not only is this safer because we will eliminate the possibility of creating problems in the original version, but it will make upgrading easier later on.

Now let's get back to modifying our **Shows by Type** report.

The way we can attach a format to the data value is through an Expression. We return to the VS RD by opening our report layout, right-click the **Scheduled** data Text Box and select **Expression**.

Figuring out the right formula for the format controls might take a little bit of trial and error, but that's OK, that's how we learn. In this case, the authors have done that part. The formulas to make the DateTime fields display as a Date and as a Time, and are shown in the following screenshots. First we'll work on the formula to make the date display in the desired format:

Then the formula to format the time field:

The result of applying these formats can be seen in this report screenshot:

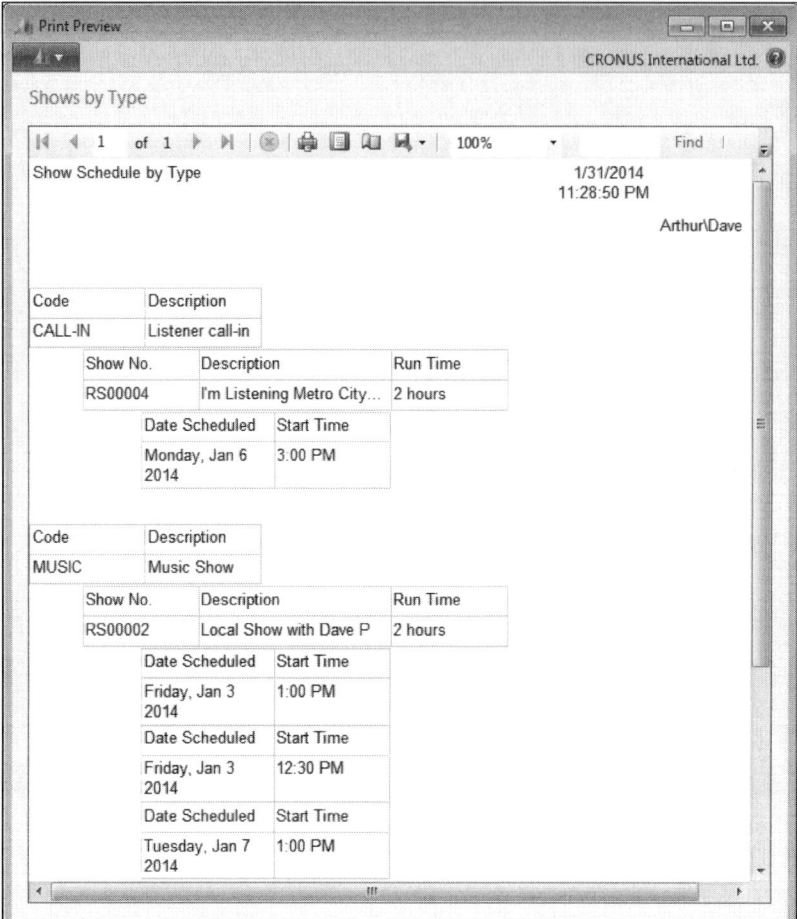

Runtime rendering

When NAV outputs a report (to screen, to hardcopy, or to PDF), NAV will render using the printer driver for the currently assigned printer. If we change the target printer for a report, the output results may change depending on the attributes of the drivers.

When we preview a report, by default it will be displayed in an interactive preview mode. This mode will allow us to access all of the dynamic functions designed into the report, functions such as sorting, toggling for expand/collapse display, and drilling into the report. However, it may not look like the hardcopy we get if we print it. If we click on the **Print Layout** button (pointed to by the arrow) in the following screenshot), then the printer layout version of the report will be displayed.

In most cases, the display on screen in **Preview – Print Layout** mode will accurately represent how the report will appear when actually printed. In some cases though, NAV's output generation on screen differs considerably from the hardcopy version. This appears to most likely occur when the selected printer is either an impact printer or a special-purpose printer (for example, a barcode label printer).

Inheritance

Inheritance operates for data displayed through report controls just as it does for page controls, but is obviously limited to print-applicable properties. Properties, such as decimal formatting, are inherited, but as we saw with our date and time fields, not all formatting is inherited. Remember, if the property is explicitly defined in the table, it cannot be less restrictively defined elsewhere. This is one of the reasons why it's so important to focus on table design as the foundation of the system.

Interactive report capabilities

NAV 2013 reports can have interactive features enabled. Of course, these features are only available when the report is displayed in preview mode; once the report is "printed" whether to a PDF, Excel, or an output device, the interactive capabilities are no longer present.

Interactive sorting

Among the useful interactive reporting features are interactive sorting and data expand/collapse. Two standard reports that are examples of the interactive sort feature are the **Customer - Top 10 List** (Report 111) and the **Customer - Summary Aging** (Report 105). We'll take a look at Report 111 to see how NAV does it.

Since we're going to open the Report in the Designer, the possibility exists that, through an unlucky combination of keystrokes, we could accidentally change this production report, the first thing we want to do is make a copy for our inspection. Open Report 111 in the C/Side Report Designer, then do a **Save As** to Report object 50111 with a different name, such as **Customer – Top 10 List Test**. Once that is done, we can safely do almost anything we want to Report 50111 because we can simply delete the object when we are done with it.

First, let's **Run** Report 50111 (or 111, they will look the same). At the top of four of the report columns we will see an up/down arrow icon representing an interactive sort control, as shown in the following screenshot:

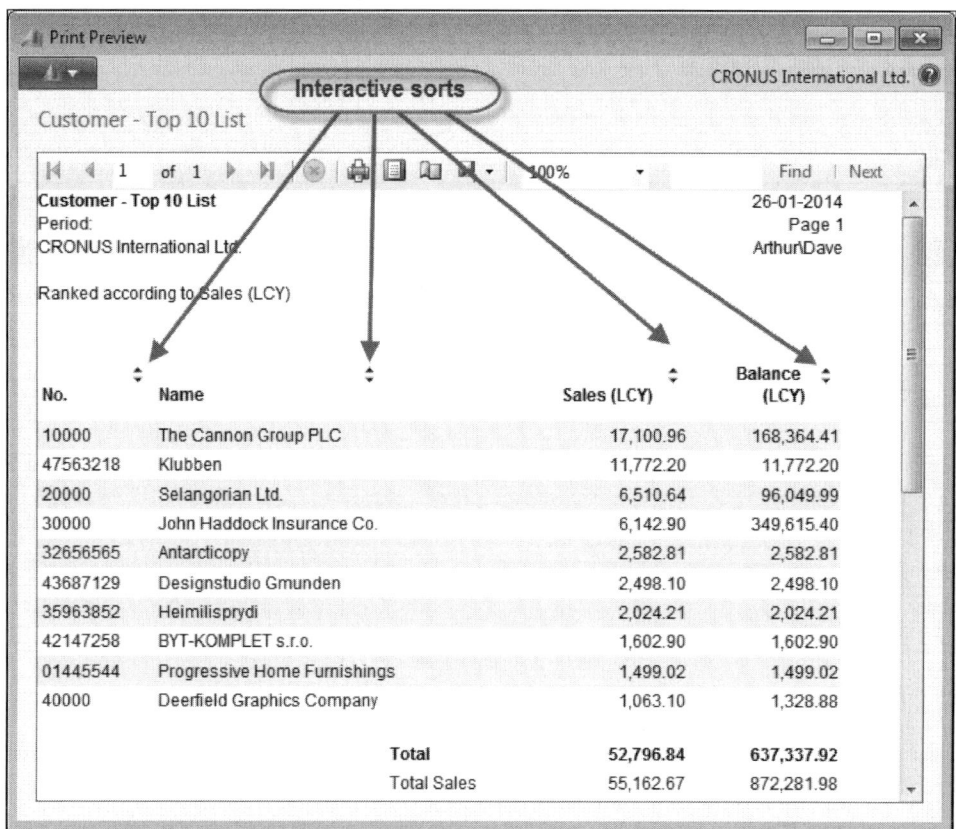

Now open test report 50111 in the C/SIDE RD, then **View | Layout** for VS RD review. Highlight the **SalesLCY_CustomerCaption** textbox as shown in the following screenshot. Right-click and show the properties; choose the **Interactive Sorting** tab. As we can see here, interactive sort options are set for this column, to sort the detail by the value of SalesLCY_Customer. If we look at the properties of the other three columns that have interactive sorting enabled, we see similar setups.

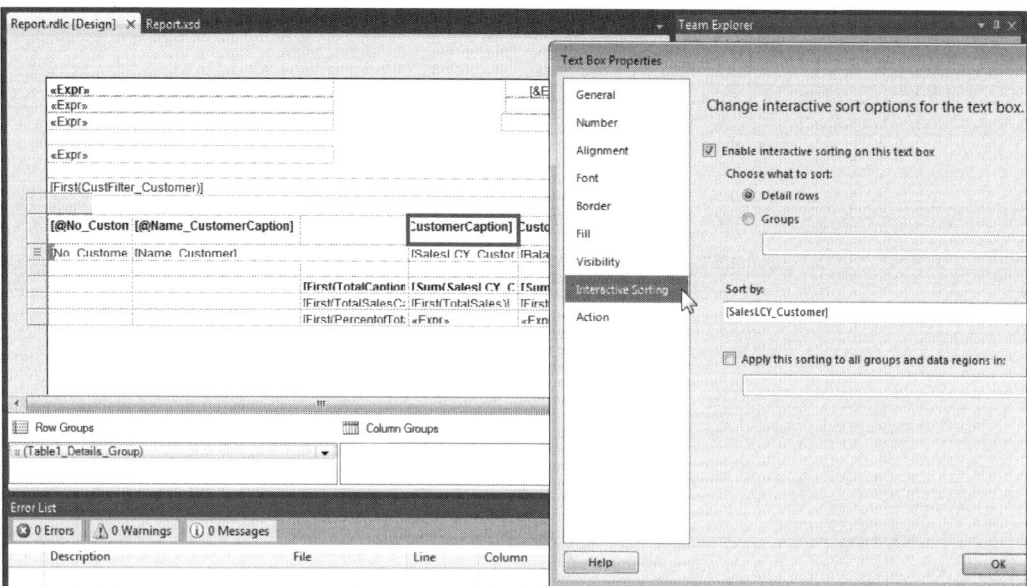

Interactive visible/not visible

As an experiment, we'll add a toggle to the rightmost column of our test report 50111 to make it visible or not visible at the user's option. In most cases, this feature would not be controlled by the user, but by a parameter such as one tied to the user's login.

First we add a textbox on the report where it seems appropriate to place an icon for visibility control of the rightmost column. That textbox will be **Textbox3** on this layout. Highlight the rightmost column by clicking in the shaded area above the column, then right-click on the highlighted column to see the following:

Choose the **Column Visibility** option:

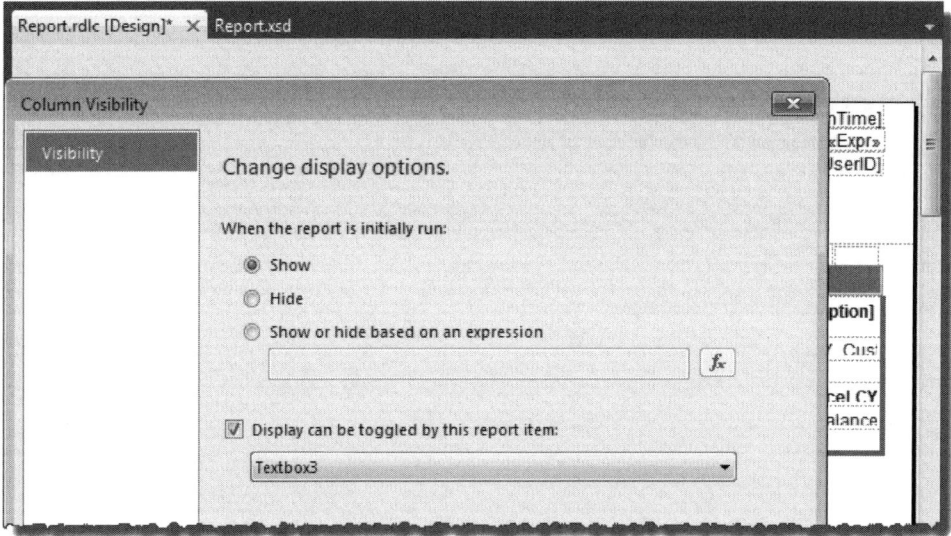

We can see that one of the options we have here, is to show or hide based on an expression. Of course the value of expression would likely be set under the control of program logic. Set the **Show** option, check the toggle control, then define on which field the toggling will be based. Save the RDLC, exit the VS RD, exit the C/SIDE RD, save, compile, and **Run** the modified report. We will see an image like that on the left. If we click on the plus sign icon, the plus will change to a minus, and the rightmost column is hidden, like in the partial screenshot on the right:

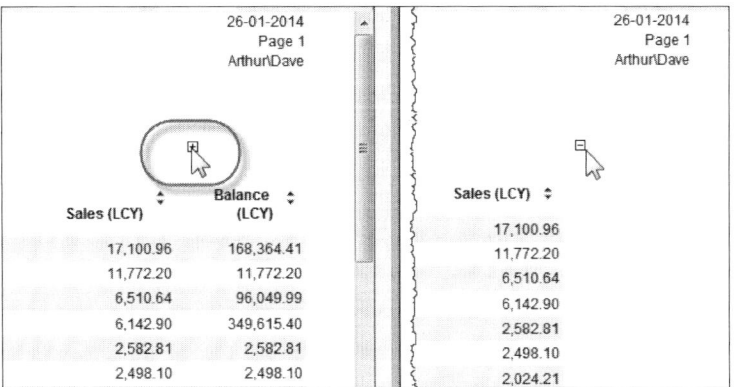

Request Page

A Request Page is a page that is executed at the beginning of a report. Its presence or absence is under developer control. A Request Page looks similar to the following screenshot based on one of the standard system reports, the **Customer – Order Detail** report, Report 108:

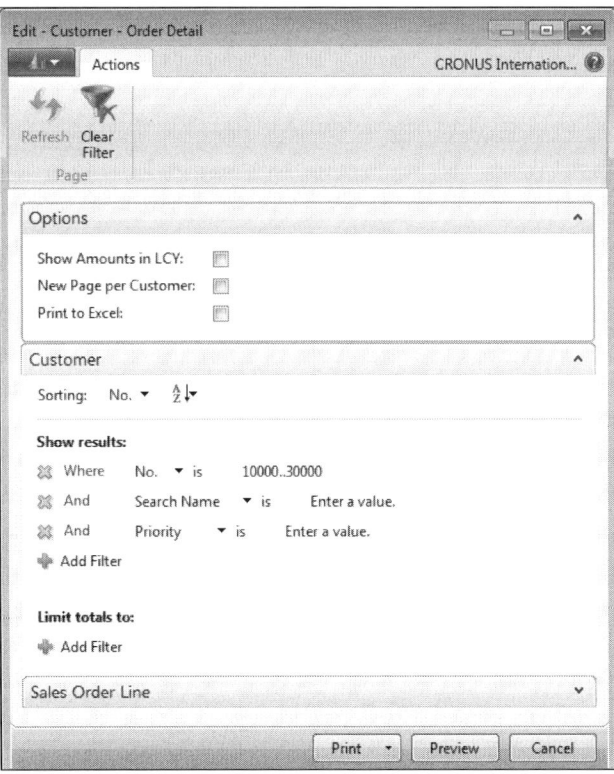

There are three FastTabs in this page. The **Customer** and **Sales Order Line** FastTab are tied to the data tables associated with this report. These FastTabs allow the user to define both data filters and Flow Filters to control the report processing. The **Options** FastTab exists because the software developer wanted to allow some additional user options for this report.

Add a Request Page option

Because we have defined the default sort sequences (**DataItemTableView**), except for the first DataItem, and we have not defined any Requested Filters (**ReqFilterFields**), the default Request Page for our report has only one DataItem FastTab. Because we have not defined any processing options that would require user input before the report is generated, we have no **Options** FastTab.

Our goal now is to allow the user to optionally input text to be printed at the top of the report. This could be a secondary report heading, instructions on interpreting the report or some other communications to the report reader.

1. Open Report 50001 in the C/SIDE Report Designer.

2. Access the **C/AL Globals** screen via **View | C/AL Globals**.

3. Add a global variable named **UserComment** with a **DataType** of **Text**. We will not define a **Length**; this will allow the user to enter a comment of any length.

4. Add this variable as a data Column to be passed to the VS RD. The Column must be subordinate to a DataItem. We do not need a caption as we will not label this field in the report layout.

5. Access the **Request Options Page Designer** via **View | Request Page**.

6. Enter three lines – a **Container**, **Group** and **Field** with the **SourceExpr** of **UserComment**.

7. Exit the Page Designer.

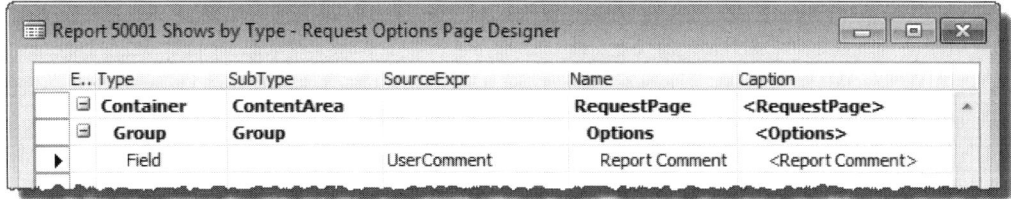

8. Access the Visual Studio Report Designer via **View | Layout**.

9. Add a Text Box to the Layout design surface just below the Report Title, stretching the box out as far as the report layout allows.

10. Right click in the Text Box and choose **Expression**.

11. In the **Expression** screen, click on **Datasets**, then double-click on the **UserComment** field.

12. Save the RDLC, exit VS RD, save, compile and exit the C/SIDE RD.
13. **Run** Report 50001.

Because we did not specify a maximum length on our **UserComment** field, we can type in as much information as we want. Try it, type in a whole paragraph for a test.

Processing-Only reports

One of the report properties we reviewed earlier was **Processing-Only**. If that property is set to Yes, then the report object will not output a dataset for display or printing, but will simply do the processing of the data we program it to do. The beauty of this capability is that we can use the built-in processing loop of the NAV report object along with its sorting and filtering capabilities to create a variety of data updating routines with a minimum of programming. Use of report objects also gives us access to the Request Page to allow user input and guidance for the run. We could create the same functionality using codeunit objects and programming all of the loops, the filtering, the user-interface Request Page, and so on ourselves. But with a Processing-Only Report, NAV gives us a lot of help, and makes it possible to create some powerful routines with minimal effort.

At the beginning of the run of a Processing-Only report, the user sees very little difference compared to a "normal" printing report. The Processing-Only Request Page looks very much as it would for a printing report, except that the **Print** and **Preview** choices are not available. Everything else looks the same. Of course we have the big difference of no visible output at the end of processing.

Creative report plagiarism

Just as we discussed in *Chapter 4, Pages – the User's Interactive Interface*, when we want to create a new report of a type that we haven't done recently (or at all), it's a good idea to find another report that is similar in an important way and study it. At the minimum, we will learn how the NAV developers solved a data flow, totaling or filtering challenge. In the best case, we will find a model that we can follow closely, respectfully plagiarizing a working solution, thus saving ourselves much time and effort.

Often, it is useful to look at two or three of the standard NAV reports for similar functions to see how they are constructed. There is no sense in re-inventing the design for a report of a particular type, when someone else has already invented a version of it. Not only that, but they have provided us with the plans and given us the ability to examine the C/AL code as well as the complete structure of the existing report object.

When it comes to modifying a system such as NAV, plagiarism is a very effective research and design tool. In the case of reports, our search for a model may be based on any of the several key elements. We might be looking for a particular data flow approach and find that the NAV developers used the Integer table for some Data Items (as many reports do).

We may need a way to provide some creative filtering similar to what is done in an area of the standard product. We might want to provide user options to print either detail or a couple of different levels of totaling, with a layout that looks good no matter which choice the user makes. We might be dealing with all three of these design needs in the same report. In such a case, it is likely that we are using multiple NAV reports as our models, one for this feature, another for that feature, and so forth.

If we have a complicated, application-specific report to create, we may not be able to directly model our report on a model that already exists. But, often we can still find ideas in standard reports that we can apply to our new design. We will almost always be better off using a model rather than inventing a totally new approach.

If our design concept is too big a leap from what has been done previously, we should consider what we might change so that we can build on the strengths of C/AL and existing NAV routines. Creating entirely new approaches may be very satisfying (when it works), but too often the extra costs exceed the incremental benefits.

Summary

In this chapter, we focused on the structural and layout aspects of NAV Report objects. We studied the primary structural components, data and format, along with the Request Page. We also experimented with some of the tools and modestly expanded our WDTU application.

In the next chapter, we are going to begin exploring the key tools that pull the pieces together of the C/SIDE development environment, and the C/AL programming language.

Review questions

1. Reports are fixed displays of data extracted from the system, designed only for hardcopy output. True or False?

2. Queries can be designed to directly feed the Visual Studio Report Designer. True or False?

3. Within the Visual Studio Report Designer, we can define calculations on table data or can define literals for display on a report. True or False?

4. NAV Report data flow includes a structure that provides for "child" DataItems to be fully processed for each record processed in the "parent" DataItem. What is the visible indication that this structure exists in a report Dataset Designer form? Choose one.

   a. Nesting

   b. Indentation

   c. Linking

5. NAV 2013 Queries can generate OData, CSV files and are Cloud compatible. True or False?

6. A report that only does processing and generates no printed output can be defined. True or False?

7. Report DataItem and Query DataItem structures are similar but Reports have more structure options. True or False?

8. The following are properties of Queries. Choose two.

   a. TopNumberOfRows

   b. FormatAs

   c. OrderBy

   d. FilterReq

9. NAV 2013 has two Report Designers. Reports can be created using either one by itself. True or False?

10. Which of the following are NAV 2013 Report Types? Choose three.

    a. List

    b. Document

    c. Invoice

    d. Posting

11. Queries cannot have multiple DataItems on the same indentation level. True or False?

12. Reports can be set to ProcessingOnly status dynamically by C/AL code. True or False?

13. Which of the following are defined in the C/SIDE Report Designer. Choose three.

    a. DataItems

    b. Field display editing

    c. Request Page

    d. Database updating

14. NAV 2013 reports can be run for testing directly from the Visual Studio Report Designer with an *Alt + R*. True or False?

15. Group properties are used to control the display of data in a Parent – Child relationship in Visual Studio Report Designer layouts. True or False?

16. Queries are used to support which items? Choose two.

    a. Charts

    b. Pages

    c. Cues

    d. Data Sorting

17. Most reports can be initially created using the Report Wizard. True or False?

18. Interactive capabilities available after a report display include what? Choose two.

    a. Font definition

    b. Data Show/Hide

    c. Sorting by columns

    d. Data filtering

6
Introduction to C/SIDE and C/AL

When I use a word, 'Humpty Dumpty said in rather a scornful tone, it means just what I choose it to mean — neither more nor less.' — Lewis Carroll

When the meaning is unclear there is no meaning. — Marty Rubin

So far we have reviewed the basic objects of NAV 2013: tables, data fields, pages, queries and reports. For each of these, we reviewed triggers in various areas, triggers whose purpose is to be containers for C/AL code. When triggers are "fired" (invoked), the C/AL code within is executed.

In this chapter, we're going to start learning the C/AL programming language. Many things you already know from your experience programming in other languages. Some of the basic C/AL syntax and function definitions can be found in the embedded NAV 2013 Help (as well as in the MSDN Library sections for Microsoft Dynamics NAV).

As with most of the programming languages, we have considerable flexibility for defining our own model for our code structure. However, when we are inserting new code within existing code, it's always a good idea to utilize the model and follow the structure that exists in the original code. When we feel compelled to improve on the model of the existing code, we should do so in small increments and we must take into account the effect of our changes on upgradability.

The goal of this chapter is to help us to productively use the C/SIDE development environment and to be comfortable in C/AL. We'll focus on the tools and processes that we will use most often. We will also review concepts that we can apply in more complex tasks down the road. This chapter's topics include:

- C/SIDE Object Designers and their navigation
- C/AL syntax, operators and built-in functions
- C/AL naming conventions
- Input/Output functions
- Creating custom functions
- Basic Process Flow structures

Understanding C/SIDE

With a few exceptions, all of the development for NAV 2013 applications takes place within the C/SIDE environment. Exceptions include use of Visual Studio for reporting as we saw in *Chapter 5*, *Queries and Reports*, plus work you might do in a .NET language to create compatible add-ins. While it is possible to do development in Text mode using a text editor, that approach is only appropriate for special cases of modifications to existing objects.

As an Integrated Development Environment, C/SIDE provides us with a reasonably full set of tools for our C/AL development work. While C/SIDE is not nearly as fully featured as Microsoft's Visual Studio, it is not intended to be a general purpose "one size fits all" development toolkit. Most importantly, C/SIDE and C/AL are designed for business application software development with a lot of features and functions specifically designed for business applications work.

C/SIDE includes a smart editor (it knows C/AL, though sometimes not as much as you would like), the one and only C/AL compiler, integration with the application database, and tools to export and import objects both in compiled format and as formatted text files.

We'll explore each of these C/SIDE areas in turn, starting with the Object Designer.

Object Designer

All the NAV object development work starts from within the Microsoft Dynamics Development Environment in the C/SIDE **Object Designer**. After you have invoked the Development Environment and connected to a NAV database, the **Object Designer** is accessed by selecting **Tools | Object Designer** or by pressing *Shift + F12* keys, as shown in the following screenshot:

The type of object on which we're going to work is chosen by clicking on one of the buttons on the left side of the **Object Designer** screen (shown in the following screenshot):

The choices match the seven object types **Table**, **Page**, **Report**, **Codeunit**, **Query**, **XMLport**, and **MenuSuite**. When we click on one of these, the **Object Designer** screen display is filtered to show only that object type. There is also an **All** button, which allows objects of all types to be displayed on screen.

No matter which object type has been chosen, the same four buttons appear at the bottom of the screen: **New**, **Design**, **Run**, and **Help**. But, depending on which object type is chosen, the effect of selecting one of these options changes. When we select **Design**, we open the object that is currently highlighted, in a Designer specifically tailored to work on that object type. When we select **Run**, we are requesting the execution of the currently highlighted object. The results, of course, will depend on the internal design of that particular object. When we select **Help**, the **C/SIDE Help** screen will display, positioned at the general **Object Designer** Help.

Starting a new object

When we select **New**, the screen we see will depend on what type of object has focus at the time we make the **New** selection. In each case, we will have the opportunity to begin creating a new object in the Designer used for that object type.

Accessing the Table Designer

The **Table Designer** screen for starting a new table is shown in the following screenshot:

The **Table Designer** invites us to begin defining data fields. All the associated C/AL code will be embedded in the underlying triggers and developer-defined functions.

Accessing the Page Designer

For the **Page Designer**, the first screen for a new page allows us to choose between the Wizard or the Designer.

If we use the Wizard, it will walk us through defining FastTabs (collapsible/ expandable groups of fields) and assigning fields to those tabs, as we saw in *Chapter 4, Pages – the User's Interactive Interface*. When we finish with the Wizard, we will be dropped into the **Page Designer** screen with our page well on the way to completion.

If we choose not to use the Wizard and want to begin designing our page from scratch, we will select the **Create blank page** option. The empty **Page Designer** screen will display. C/AL code that we create will be placed in triggers for the Page or its controls.

Accessing the Report Dataset Designer

For a **New Report**, the following screen is displayed:

Since NAV 2013 does not have a Report Wizard, we begin Report development by defining the primary **DataItem** for our report and continuing from there as we did in *Chapter 5, Queries and Reports*. Remember, all C/AL code in a Report is tied to the Report triggers and controls.

Accessing the Codeunit Designer

When we access the Codeunit Designer using the **New** button, a Codeunit structure is opened with the **C/AL Editor** active, as shown in the following screenshot:

Codeunits have no superstructure or surrounding framework around the single code **OnRun** trigger. Codeunits are primarily a shell in which we can place our own functions and code so that it can be called from other objects.

Query Designer

For a **New Query**, the following screen is displayed:

Much like a new Report, we begin Query development by defining the primary DataItem for our query and continuing from there as we did in *Chapter 5, Queries and Reports*. All C/AL code in a query is tied to the **OnBeforeOpen** trigger of the query (this code is often used to apply filters to the Query **DataItems** using the SETFILTER function).

XMLport Designer

XMLports are used for the tasks of importing and exporting both XML-formatted files and text files, particularly variations of the .csv format (but can handle many other text file formats, including both delimited and fixed formats). The **XMLport Designer** looks like the following screenshot:

There is no Wizard for XMLports. When we click on **New**, we proceed directly to the **XMLport Designer** screen.

XMLports are objects for defining and processing text-based data structures, including those which are defined in XML format. XML is a set of somewhat standardized data formatting rules for dissimilar applications to exchange data. XML-structured files have become an essential component of business data systems.

Once you become comfortable using C/SIDE and C/AL, we will learn more about XMLports for XML formatted data and as well as other text file formats. XMLports can be run directly from menu entries as well as from other objects. XMLport objects can also be passed as parameters to web services in a **Codeunit** function, thus supporting the easy passing of information such as a list of customers or inventory items.

MenuSuite Designer

MenuSuites are used to define the menus that are available from the **Departments** button in the **Navigation** pane and also appear on the **Departments** page in the NAV Windows client. The initial **MenuSuite Designer** screen that comes up when we ask for a new MenuSuite, asks what MenuSuite Design Level we are preparing to create. The following screenshot shows all 15 available **Design Level** values:

When one of those design levels has been used (created as a MenuSuite option), that design level will not appear in this list the next time **New** is selected for the **MenuSuite Designer**. MenuSuites can only exist at the 15 levels shown and only one instance of each level is supported. Once we have chosen a level to create, NAV shifts to the **MenuSuite Designer** mode. The following screenshot shows the navigation pane in Designer mode after selection of **Create | Dept - Company**:

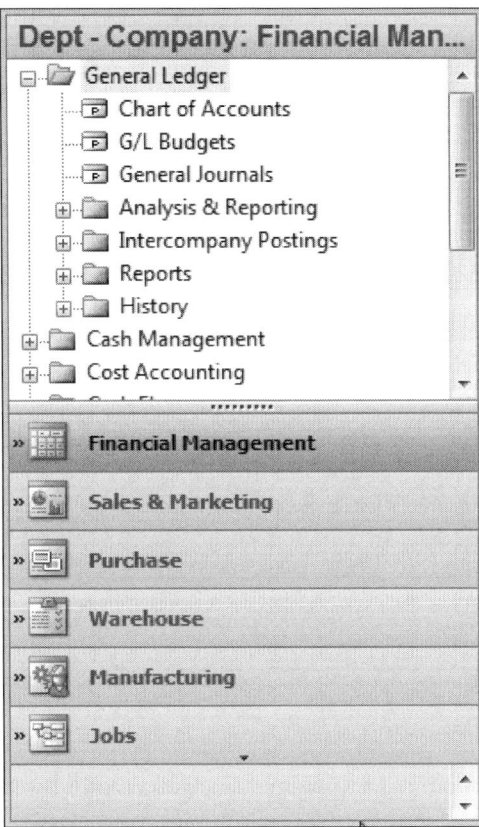

To add, change, or delete menu entries in the Navigation Pane Designer, highlight and right click an entry. That will display the following window. The action options visible in this **MenuSuite Designer** window are dependent on the entry which is highlighted and, sometimes, on the immediate previous action taken.

- **Create Item...** (*Insert*): Allows the creation of a new menu action entry (Item), utilizing the same window format for creation that is displayed when the entry **Properties** option is chosen.

- **Insert Items...**(*Shift + Insert*): Allows the insertion of a new instance of a menu action entry, choosing from a list of all the existing entries.

- **Create Group** (*Ctrl + Insert*): Allows the creation of a new group under which menu action entries can be organized.

- **Delete** (*Delete*): For deleting either an individual entry or a whole group.

- **Rename** (*F2*): To rename either an entry or a group.

- **Move Up** (*Ctrl + Shift + Up*) and **Move Down** (*Ctrl + Shift + Down*): Allows moving an entry or group up or down one position in the menu structure.

- **Cut** (*Ctrl + X*), **Copy** (*Ctrl + C*), and **Paste** (*Ctrl + V*): Provide the normal cut, copy, and paste functions for either entries or groups.

- **Properties** (*Alt + Enter*): Displays the applicable property screen.

A **Group Properties** screen only contains the **Caption** and **CaptionML** along with the **Department Page** checkmark field. The **Item Properties** screen looks like the following:

The **Object Type** field can be any of `Report`, `Codeunit`, `XMLport`, `Page`, or `Query`. The **Department** field can be `Lists`, `Tasks`, `Reports and Analysis`, `Documents`, `History`, or `Administration`, all groupings in the **Departments** menu.

To exit the Navigation Pane Designer, press the *Esc* key with focus on the navigation pane or right-click on the Navigation Pane Designer heading and selecting the **Close Navigation Pane Designer** option, as shown in the following screenshot:

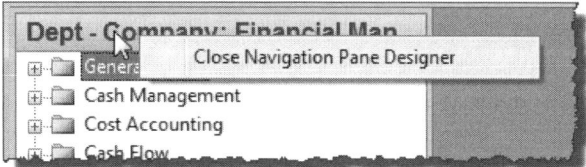

There are a number of basic differences between the MenuSuite Designer and the other object designers. Most are inherent in how MenuSuites differ from other NAV objects. One difference is the fact that no C/AL code can be embedded within a MenuSuite entry.

Object Designer navigation

In many places in the various designers within the **Object Designer**, standard NAV data entry keyboard shortcuts apply. For example:

- *F3* to create a new empty entry.
- *F4* to delete the highlighted entry.
- *F8* to copy the entry from the same column on the preceding record.

- *F5* to access the **C/AL Symbol Menu**, which shows us a symbol table for the object on which we are working. This isn't just any old symbol table; this is a programmer's assistant. More on this later in this chapter.

- *F9* to access the underlying C/AL code.

- *F11* to do an on-the-fly compile (very useful for error checking as you go).

- *Shift + F4* to access properties.

- *Ctrl + X, Ctrl + C,* and *Ctrl + V* in normal Windows mode for deletion (or cut), copy, and paste, respectively.

  We can cut, copy, and paste C/AL code, even functions, relatively freely within an object, from object to object, or to a text-friendly tool (for example, Word, or Excel text editor) much as if we were using a text editor. The source and target objects don't need to be of the same type.

When we are in a list of items that cannot be modified, for example, the **C/AL Symbol Menu**, we can focus on a column, key a letter, and jump to the next field in the column starting with that letter. This works in a number of places where search is not supported, so it acts as a very limited search substitute, applying only to an entry's first letter.

The easiest way to copy a complete object to create a new version is to:

1. Open the object in Design mode.

2. Click on **File | Save As** object, assign a new object number, and change the object name (no duplicate object names are allowed). A quick (mouseless) way to do a **Save As** is pressing *Alt + F*, then the *A* key—continuously holding down the *Alt* key while pressing first *F* and then *A*.

If we must use an object or field number for a different purpose other than the standard system assignment (not a good idea), we should make the change in place. Don't try a delete followed by add; it won't work.

Don't ever delete an object or a field numbered in a range where the license doesn't allow creation of an object. If there isn't a compiled (. fob) backup copy of what has been deleted available for import, the ability to replace the deleted item will be lost.

Exporting objects

Object Export from the Object Designer can be accessed for backup or distribution purposes via **File | Export**. Choosing this option, after highlighting the objects to be exported, brings up a standard Windows file-dialog screen with the file type options of . fob (NAV object) or . txt, as shown in the following screenshot:

The safer, more general-purpose format for exporting is as a compiled object, created with a file extension of .fob. But someone with a developer's license can export an object as a text file with a file extension of .txt. An exported text file is the only way to use a tool such as a text editor to do before and after comparisons of objects or to search objects for the occurrences of strings (such as variable names). An object text file can be used with a source-control tool such as Microsoft Visual SourceSafe, Microsoft Team Foundation, or ifacto ReVision for NAV (http://www.ifacto.be/en/revision).

A compiled object can be shipped to another system as a patch to install with little fear that it will be corrupted midstream. The system administrator at the other system simply has to import the new object with some directions from the developer. Exported compiled objects also make excellent backups. Before changing or importing any working production objects, it's always a good idea to export a copy of the "before" object images into a .fob file. These should be labeled so they can easily be retrieved. If we want to check what objects are included in a fob, we can open the file in a text editor, the objects contained will be listed at the beginning. Any number of objects can be exported into a single .fob file. We can later selectively import any one or several of the individual objects from that group .fob.

Importing objects

Object Import is accessed through **File | Import** in the **Object Designer**. The import process is more complicated than the export process because there are more decisions to be made. When we import a compiled version of an object, the **Object Designer** allows decisions about importing and provides some information to help us make them.

When we import a text version of an object, the new version is brought in immediately regardless of what it overwrites and regardless of whether or not the incoming object can actually be compiled. The object imported from a text file is not compiled until we do so in a separate action. By importing a text-formatted object, we could actually replace a perfectly good production object with something useless.

 Never import a text object until there is a current backup of all the objects that might be replaced.

Never send text objects to an end user for installation in their system.

When we import a compiled object from a `.fob` file, we will get one of two decision message screens, depending on what the Object Designer Import finds when it checks for existing objects. If there are no existing objects that the import logic identifies as matching and modified, then we will see the following dialog:

The safest thing to do is always open the **Import Worksheet**, in this case by clicking on the **No** button. Examine the information displayed before proceeding with the import.

If the `.fob` file we are importing is found to have objects that could be in conflict with existing objects that have been previously modified, then we will see the following:

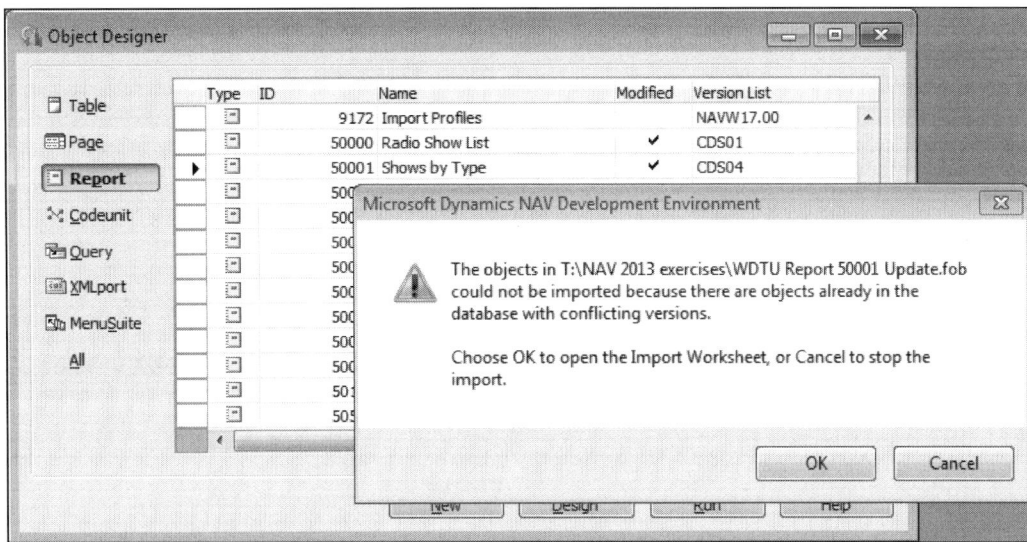

Of course we can always click on **Cancel** and simply exit the operation. Normally, we will click on **OK** to open the **Import Worksheet** and examine the contents.

While all of the information presented is useful at one time or another, usually we can focus on just a few fields. The basic question, on an object-by-object basis, is "Do I want to replace the old version of this object with this new one?"

At the bottom of the preceding screenshot, we can see the comparison of the **Existing** object and the **New** object information. Use this information to decide whether or not to take an action of **Create** or **Replace** or action of **Skip**. More information on using the Import Worksheet and the meaning of various warnings and actions can be found in the NAV **Developer and IT Pro Help** under **Import Worksheet**.

Although Import also allows us to merge the incoming and existing table versions, only very sophisticated developers should attempt to use this feature. The rest of us should always choose the Import Action **Replace** or **Skip** (or **Create**, if it is a new object).

Text objects

A text version of an object is especially useful for just a few specific development tasks. C/AL code or expressions can be placed in a number of different nooks and crannies of objects. In addition, sometimes object behavior is controlled by properties. As a result, it's not always easy to figure out just how an existing object is accomplishing its tasks.

An object exported to text has all its code and properties flattened out where we can use our favorite text editor to search and view. Text copies of two versions of an object can easily be compared in a text editor. Text objects can be stored and managed in a source code library. In addition, a few tasks, such as re-numbering an object, can be done more easily in the text copy than within C/SIDE.

Some useful practices

We should liberally make backups of objects on which we are working. Always make a backup of the object before changing it. Make backups regularly during development.

If our project involves several developers, we may want to utilize a source control system that tracks versioning and has a check-out, check-in facility for objects.

Compile frequently. We will find errors more easily this way. Not all errors will be discovered just by compiling. Thorough testing is always a requirement.

When we are developing pages or reports, we should do test runs (or previews) of the objects relatively frequently. Whenever we reach a stage where we have made a number of changes and again have a working copy, we should save it.

Never design a modification that places data directly in or changes data directly in a `Ledger` table without going through the standard Posting routines. It's tempting to do so, but that's a sure path to unhappiness. If we are creating a new ledger for our application, design the process with a Journal table and a Posting process consistent with the NAV standard flow.

 Follow the NAV standard approach for handling Registers, Posted Document tables, and other tables normally updated during Posting.

If at all possible, try to avoid importing modifications into a production system when there are users logged-in to the system. If a logged-in user has an object active that is being modified, they may continue working with the old version until they exit and re-enter. Production use of the obsolete object version may possibly cause confusion or even more serious problems.

Always test modifications in a reasonably current copy of the production system. Do the final testing by using real data (or at least realistic data) and a copy of the customer's production license. As a rule, we should never develop or test in the live production system. Always work in a copy. Otherwise, the price of a mistake, even a simple typo, can be enormous.

If we wish to check that changes to a production system are compatible with the rest of the system, we should import the changes into our test copy of the system and then recompile all of the objects in the system. We may uncover serious problems left by a previous developer with bad habits, so be prepared.

Changing data definitions

The integration of the development environment with the application database is particularly handy when we are making changes to an application that is already in production use. C/SIDE is good about not letting us make changes that are inconsistent with existing data. For example, let's presume we have a text field that is defined as 30 characters long and there is already data in that field in the database, one instance of which is longer than 20 characters. If we attempt to change the definition of that field to 20 characters long, we will get an error message when we try to save and compile the table object. We will not be able to force the change until we adjust either the data in the database or we adjust the change so that it is compatible with all of the existing data.

Saving and compiling

Whenever we exit the Designer for an object in which we have made a change, NAV wants to save and compile the object on which we were working. We will see a dialog similar to the following:

We have to be careful not to be working on two copies of the same object at once as we will lose the first set of changes when the second copy is saved. If we want to save the changed material under a new object number while retaining the original object, we must **Cancel** this option and exit the Designer by using the **File | Save As** option to rename and renumber the new copy.

If our object under development is at one of those in-between stages where it won't compile, we can deselect the **Compiled** checkbox and just save it by clicking on the **Save** button without compiling it.

> We should not complete a development session without getting an error-free compilation. Even if making big changes, make them in small increments.

On occasion, we may make changes that we think will affect other objects. In that case, from the **Object Designer** screen, we can select a group of objects to be compiled by marking them. Marking an object is done by putting focus on the object and pressing the *Ctrl + F1* keys. The marked object is then identified with a bullet in the left screen column for that object's row. After marking each of the objects to be compiled, use the **View | Marked Only** function to select just the marked objects.

We can then compile them as a group. Select all the entries (using *Ctrl + A* keys is one way to do this), press *F11*, and respond **Yes** to the question, **Do you want to compile the selected objects?** Once the compilation of all the selected objects is completed, we will get an **Error List** window indicating which objects had compilation errors of what error types.

After we respond to that message, only the objects with errors will remain marked. As the **Marked Only** filter will be on, so that just those objects that need attention will be shown on the screen. In fact, anytime we do a group compilation of object, those with errors will be marked so that we can use the **Marked Only** filter to select the ones needing attention.

Some C/AL naming conventions

In previous chapters, we discussed naming conventions for tables, pages, and reports. In general, the naming guidelines for NAV objects and C/AL encourage consistency, common sense, and readability. Use meaningful names. These make the system more intuitive to the users and more self-documenting.

When we name variables, we must try to keep the names as self-documenting as possible. We should differentiate between similar, but different, variable meanings such as **Cost** (cost from the vendor) and **Amount** (selling price to the customer). Embedded spaces, periods, or other special characters should be avoided (even though we find some violations of this in the base product). If we want to use special characters for the benefit of the user, we put them in the caption, not in the name. If possible, we will stick to letters and numbers in our variable names.

There are a number of reasons to keep variable names simple. Other software products with which we may interface may have limitations on variable names. Some special characters have special meaning to other software or in another human language. In NAV, ? and * are wildcards and must be avoided in variable names. $ has special meaning in other software. SQL Server adds its own special characters to NAV names and the resultant combinations can get quite confusing (not just to us but to the software). The same can be said for the names constructed by the internal RDLC generator, which replaces spaces and periods with underscores.

When we are defining multiple instances of a table, we should either differentiate clearly by name (for example, **Item** and **NewItem**) or by a suffix number (for example, **Item1**, **Item2**, **Item3**). In the very common situation where a name is a compound combination of words, begin each abbreviated word with a capital letter (for example, **NewCustBalDue**).

Avoid creating variable names that are common words that might be reserved words (for example, Page, Column, Number, and Integer). C/SIDE will sometimes not warn us that we have done so and we may find our logic and the automatic logic working at very mysterious cross purposes.

Do not start variables with a prefix "x", which is used in some automatically created variables (such as xRec). We should make sure that we clearly differentiate between working storage variable names and the field names originating in tables. Sometimes C/SIDE will allow us to have a global name, local name, and/or record variable name, all with the same literal name. If we do this, we are practically guaranteeing a variable misidentification bug where the compiler uses a different variable than what we intended to be referenced.

When defining a temporary table, preface the name logically, for example with Temp. In general, use meaningful names that help in identifying the type and purpose of the item being named. When naming a new function, we should be reasonably descriptive. Don't name two functions located in different objects with the same name. It will be too easy to get confused later.

In short, be careful, be consistent, be clear, and use common sense.

Variables

As we've gone through examples showing various aspects of C/SIDE and C/AL, we've seen and referred to variables in a number of situations. Some of the following is obvious, but for clarity's sake we'll summarize here.

In *Chapter 3, Data Types and Fields*, we reviewed various data types for variables defined within objects (referred to in *Chapter 3, Data Types and Fields*, as working storage data). Working Storage consists of all the variables that are defined for use within an object, but whose contents disappear when the object closes. Working Storage data types discussed in *Chapter 3, Data Types and Fields*, are those that can be defined in either the **C/AL Global Variables** or **C/AL Local Variables** tabs. Variables can also be defined several other places in an NAV object.

C/AL Globals

Global variables are defined on the **C/AL Globals** form, in the **Variables** tab.

Global Text Constants are defined on the **Text Constants** tab section of the **C/AL Globals** form. The primary purpose of the Text Constants area is to allow easier translation of messages from one language to another. By putting all message text in this one place in each object, a standardized process can be defined for language translation. There is a good explanation in the **NAV Developer and IT Pro Help** on *How to: Add a Text Constant to a Codeunit*. The information applies generally.

Global Functions are defined on the **Functions** tab of the **C/AL Globals** form. The following screenshot shows the **C/AL Globals** form:

C/AL Locals

Local identifiers only exist defined within the range of a trigger. This is true whether the trigger is a developer-defined function or one of the default system triggers or standard application-supplied functions.

Function local identifiers

Function local identifiers are defined on one or another of the tabs on the **C/AL Locals** form that we use for defining a function.

Parameters and **Return Value** are defined on their respective tabs.

The **Variables** and **Text Constants** tabs for **C/AL Locals** are exactly similar in use to the **C/AL Globals** tabs of the same names. The **C/AL Locals** form can be seen in the following screenshot:

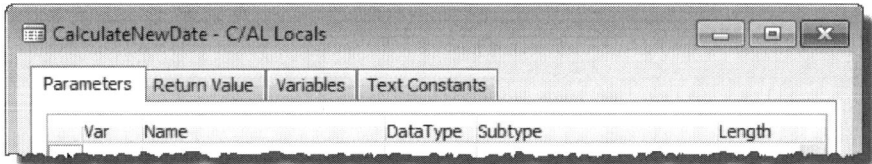

Other local identifiers

Trigger local variables are also defined on one or another of the tabs on the **C/AL Locals** form. The difference between trigger Local Variables and those for a function is that the only the **Variables** and **Text Constants** tabs exist for trigger Local Variables. The use of the **Variables** and **Text Constants** tabs are exactly the same for triggers as for functions. Whether we are working within a trigger or a defined function, we can access the local variables through the menu option **View | C/AL Locals**.

Special working storage variables

Some working storage variables have additional attributes to be considered.

Temporary tables

Temporary tables were discussed in *Chapter 2, Tables*. Let's take a quick look at how one is defined. Defining a Global Temporary table begins just like any other Global Variable definition of the Record data type. With an object open in the Designer:

1. Select **View | C/AL Globals**.

2. Enter a variable name, data type of `Record`.

3. Choose the table whose definition is to be replicated for this temporary table as the Subtype.

4. With focus on the new Record variable, click on the **Properties** icon (or press the *Shift + F4* keys).

5. Set the **Temporary** property to **Yes**.

That's it. We've defined a temporary table like the one in the following screenshot:

We can use the temporary table just as though it were a permanent table with some specific differences:

- The table contains only the data we add to it during this instance of the object in which it resides.

- We cannot change any aspect of the definition of the table, except by changing the permanent table (which was its template) using the Table Designer, then recompiling the object containing the associated temporary table.

- Processing for a temporary table is done wholly in the client system in a user specific instance of the business logic. It is, therefore, inherently single user.

- A properly utilized temporary table reduces network traffic and eliminates any locking issues for that table. It is often much faster than processing the same data in a permanent, database-resident table because both data transmission and physical storage I/O are significantly reduced.

> In some cases it's a good idea to copy database table data into a temporary table for repetitive processing within an object. This can give us a significant speed advantage for a particular task by updating data in the temporary table, then copying it back out to the database table at the end of processing.
>
> When using temporary tables, we need to be careful that references from C/AL code in the temporary table (such as data validations) don't inappropriately modify permanent data elsewhere in the database.

Arrays

Arrays of up to 10 dimensions containing up to a total of 1,000,000 elements in a single variable can be created in an NAV object. Defining an array is done simply by setting the **Dimensions** property of a variable to something other than the default **<Undefined>**. An example is shown in the following screenshot:

The semicolon separates the dimensions of the array. The numbers indicate the maximum number of elements of each of the dimensions. This example is a two-dimensional array which has three rows of 99 elements each. An array variable like **TotalArray** is referred to in C/AL as follows:

- The 15th entry in the first row is `TotalArray[1,15]`
- The last entry in the last row is `TotalArray[3,99]`

An array of a complex data type such as a record may behave differently than a single instance of the data type, especially when passed as a parameter to a function. In such a case, we must make sure the code is especially thoroughly tested so that we aren't surprised by unexpected results. NAV 2013 adds the capability to also use arrays from the .NET Framework. See the Help titled *Using Arrays* for more information.

Initialization

When an object is initiated, the variables in that object are automatically initialized. Booleans are set to False. Numeric variables are set to zero. Text and code data types are set to the empty string. Dates are set to 0D (the undefined date) and Times are set to 0T (the undefined time). The individual components of complex variables are appropriately initialized. The system also automatically initializes all system-defined variables.

Of course, once the object is active, through our code and property settings we can do whatever additional initialization we wish. If we wish to initialize variables at intermediate points during processing, we can use any of several approaches. First we reset a Record variable (for example, the **TempRadioShowLedger** temporary table defined in the preceding example) with the RESET function then initialize with the INIT function in statements in the form:

```
TempRadioShowLedger.RESET;
TempRadioShowLedger.INIT;
```

The RESET makes sure all previously set filters on this table are cleared. The INIT makes sure all the fields, except those in the Primary Key, are set either to their **InitValue** property value or to their data type default value. Primary Key fields must be explicitly set by C/AL code.

For all types of data, including complex data types, we can initialize fields with the CLEAR or CLEARALL function in a statement in the following form:

```
CLEAR(TotalArray[1,1]);
CLEAR(TotalArray);
CLEAR("Shipment Code");
```

The first example would clear a single element of the array, the first element in the first row. Because this variable is a Decimal data type, the element would be set to 0.0 when cleared. The second example would clear the entire array. In the third example, a variable defined as a Code data type would simply be set to an empty string.

System-defined variables

NAV also provides us with some variables automatically such as Rec, xRec, CurrPage, CurrReport, CurrXMLport. Which variables are provided is dependent on the object in which we are operating. Descriptions of some of these can be found in the **Help** titled *System-Defined Variables*.

C/SIDE programming

Many of the things that we do during development in C/SIDE might not be called programming by some people because they don't involve writing C/AL code statements. But so long as these activities contribute to the definition of the object and affect the processing that occurs, we'll include them in our broad definition of C/SIDE programming.

These activities include setting properties at the object and Data Item levels, creating Request pages in Reports, defining Controls and their properties, defining Report data structures and their properties, creating Source Expressions, defining Functions, and, of course, writing C/AL statements in all the places that you can put C/AL. We are going to focus on C/SIDE programming primarily as it relates to tables, reports, and codeunits.

We will touch on C/SIDE programming for pages and XMLports. In the case of RTC reports, C/AL statements can reside only in the components that are developed within the C/SIDE RD and not within the RDLC created by the VS RD.

 Because no coding can be done within MenuSuites, we will omit those objects from the programming part of our discussions.

NAV objects are generally consistent in structure. Most have some properties and triggers. Pages and reports have controls, though the tools that define the controls in each are specific to the individual object type. Reports have a built-in data item looping logic. XMLports also have data item looping logic but structured differently from reports (for example Report can have multiple DataItems at the 0 level and XMLports can only have one Node at the 0 level). All the object types that we are considering can contain C/AL code in one or more places. All of these can contain function definitions which can be called either internally or externally. Remember, good design practice says any functions designed as "library" or re-usable functions that are called from a variety of objects should be placed in a Codeunit. (or occasionally in the primary table).

> Don't forget that our fundamental coding work should focus on tables as much as possible, as tables are the foundation of the NAV system.

Non-modifiable functions

A function is a defined set of logic that performs a specific task. Similar to many other programming languages, C/AL includes a set of pre-written functions that are available to us to perform a wide variety of different tasks. The underlying logic for some of these functions is hidden, invisible, and not modifiable. These non-modifiable functions are supplied as part of the C/AL programming language. Some simple examples are:

- DATE2DMY: Supply a date and, depending on a calling parameter, it will return the integer value of the day, the month, or the year of that date.

- STRPOS: Supply a string variable and a string constant; the function will return the position of the first instance of that constant within the variable, or a zero if the constant is not present in the string contained in the variable.

- GET: Supply a value and a table, and the function will read the record in the table with a Primary Key equal to the supplied value, if a matching record exists.

- INSERT: Add a record to a table.

- MESSAGE: Supply a string and optional variables; this function will display a message to the operator.

Such functions are the heart of the C/SIDE-C/AL tools. There are over 100 of them. On the whole, they are designed around the essential purpose of an NAV system: business and financial applications data processing. These functions are not modifiable; they operate according to their predefined rules. For development purposes, they act as basic language components.

Modifiable functions

In addition to the pre-written "language component" functions, there are a large number of pre-written "application component" functions. The difference between the two types is that the code implementing the latter is visible and modifiable, though we should be extremely cautious about making such modifications.

An example of an application component function might be one to handle the task of processing a Customer Shipping Address to eliminate empty lines and standardize the layout based on user-defined setup parameters. This function would logically be placed in a Codeunit and thus made available to any routine that needs this capability.

In fact, this function exists. It is called `SalesHeaderShipTo` and is located in the **Format Address** Codeunit. You can explore the following Codeunits for some functions you might find useful to use or from which to borrow logic. This is not an all-inclusive list, as there are many functions in other Codeunits which you may find useful in a future development project, either to be used directly or as templates for designing your own similar function. Many have the words **Management** or **Mgt.** in their name.

Object number	Name
1	ApplicationManagement
356	DateComprMgt
358	DateFilter-Calc
359	PeriodFormManagement
365	Format Address
397	Mail
5052	AttachmentManagement
5054	WordManagement
6224	XML DOM Management

The pre-written application functions generally have been provided to address the needs of the NAV developers working at Microsoft. But we can use them too. Our challenge will be to find out that they exist and to understand how they work. There is very little documentation of these "application component" functions.

One significant aspect of these application functions is the fact that they are written in C/AL and their construction is totally exposed. In theory, they can be modified, though that is not advisable. If we decide to change one of these functions, we should make sure our change is compatible with all existing uses of that function.

A useful "trick" to find all the calls of a function is to add a dummy calling parameter to the function (temporarily) and then compile all objects in the system. You will get errors in all objects that call the changed function (don't forget to remove the dummy calling parameter and recompile when you're done with testing). This technique not only works for Microsoft-created functions, but also for functions created as part of a customization or add-on.

Custom functions

We can also create our own custom functions to meet any need. The most common reason to create a new function is to provide a single, standardized instance of logic to perform a specific task. When we need to use the same logic in more than one place, we should consider creating a callable function. If we need to create a customized variation on one of NAV's existing functions, we could copy the original to a new function name in the original Codeunit or copy it into our own Codeunit and modify it there.

We should also create a new function when we're modifying standard NAV processes. Whenever more than three or four lines of code are needed for the modification, we should consider creating the modification as a function. If we do that, the modification to the standard process can be limited to a call to the new function. It's usually not a good idea to embed a new function into an existing standard function. It's better to clone the existing function and make the modifications in-line.

Although using a function for inserting new code into the flow is a great concept, occasionally it may be difficult to implement in practice. For example, if we want to revise the way existing logic works, sometimes it's confusing to implement the change through just a call and an external (to the mainline process) function. In such a case, we may just settle for creating an in-line modification and doing a good job of commenting the modification. This is most reasonable when this code is only required in one place and does not also need to be referenced elsewhere.

If a new function will be used in several objects, then, unless it is specific to a single table, it should be housed in an (that is, modification-specific) codeunit. If it is only for use in a single object, then the new function can be resident in that object. This latter option also has the advantage of enabling direct access to the global variables within the object being modified, when necessary.

Creating a function

Let's take a quick look at how a function can be created. We're going to add a new codeunit to our C/AL application, **Codeunit 50000**. Since this is where we will put any callable functions that we need for our WDTU application, we will simply call it **Radio Show Management**. In that Codeunit, we're going to create a function to calculate a new date based on a given date. If that seems familiar, it's the same thing we did in *Chapter 3, Data Types and Fields*, to illustrate how a DateFormula data type works. This time, our focus is going to be on the creation of a function.

Our first step is to copy **Table 50099**, which we created for testing, and then save it as table **50098**. As a reminder, we do that by opening **Table 50099** in the Table Designer, then selecting **File | Save As**, changing the object number to **50098** and the **Name** to **Date Formula Test-2** (see the following screenshot), and then exiting and compiling.

Once that's done, change the Version List to show that this table has been modified. We used CDS and 03 for the original *Chapter 3, Data Types and Fields* table Version. Now we'll add ,06 to make the new table Version read CDS 03,06.

We will create our new Codeunit by simply clicking on the **Codeunit** button at the left of the **Object Designer** screen, then click on the **New** button and choosing **File | Save As**, and entering the **Object ID** of 50000 and Name as Radio Show Management.

Now comes the important part—designing and coding our new function. When we had the function operating as a local function inside the table where it was called, we didn't worry about passing data back and forth. We simply used the data fields that were already present in the table and treated them as global variables (which, in effect, they were). Now that our function will be external to the object from which it's called, we have to pass data values back and forth. Here's the basic calling structure of our function:

```
Output := Function (Input Parameter1, Input Parameter2)
```

In other words, we need to feed two values into our new callable function and accept a return value back on completion of the function's processing.

Our first step is to click on **View | C/AL Globals**, then the **Functions** tab. Enter the name of the new function following the guidelines for good names, (such as CalculateNewDate), and then click on the **Locals** button. This will allow us to define all the variables that will be local to the new function. The first tab on the **Locals** screen is **Parameters**, our input variables.

In keeping with good naming practices, we will define two input parameters, as shown in the following screenshot:

The Var column in the leftmost column of the Parameters tab form

If we checkmark the **Var** column, then the parameter is **passed by reference** to the original calling routine's copy of that variable. That means, when the called function (in this case, the function in the Codeunit) changes the value of an input parameter, the original variable value in the calling object gets changed. Since we've specified the input parameter passing here with the **Var** column unchecked, changes in the value of that input parameter will be **passed by value**. That makes the parameter local to this function and changes to its value will not affect the calling routine. Checking the **Var** column on one or more parameters is a way to effectively have multiple results passed back to the calling routine. Parameter passing with the **Var** column checked (by reference) is also faster than passing by value, especially when passing complex data types (for example, records).

Select the **Return Value** tab and define our output variable as shown in the following screenshot:

A **Name** is not required for the **Return Value** if the routine terminates processing with an EXIT([ReturnValue]). Once we complete the definition of our function and its local variables, we can exit by using the *Esc* key and the results will be saved. One way to view the effect of what we have just defined is to view the **C/AL Symbol Menu**. From the **Codeunit Designer** screen, with our new Codeunit 50000 in view and our cursor placed in the code area for our new function, we click on **View | C/AL Symbol Menu** (or just press *F5*) and see the following:

We see in the **C/AL Editor** that our CalculateNewDate function has been defined with two parameters and a result. Now press *Esc* or select **OK**, move the cursor to the OnRun trigger code area and again press *F5* to view the **C/AL Symbol Menu**. We don't see the two parameters and result variables.

Why? Because the **Parameters** and **Return Value** are local variables, which only exist in the context of the function and are not visible outside the function. We'll make more use of the **C/AL Symbol Menu** a little later, because it is a very valuable C/AL development tool. But right now we need to finish our new function and integrate it with our test Table **50098**.

Move the cursor back to the code area for our new function. Click on the menu item **Window | Object Designer | Table** button, then on Table **50098 | Design**, and press *F9*. That will take us to the **C/AL Code** screen for Table **50098**. Highlight and cut the code line from the local `CalculateNewDate` function. Admittedly, this will not be a particularly efficient process this time, but hopefully it will make the connection between the two instances of functions easier to envision. Using the **Window** menu, move back to our Codeunit function and paste the line of code we just cut from Table **50098**. We should see the following:

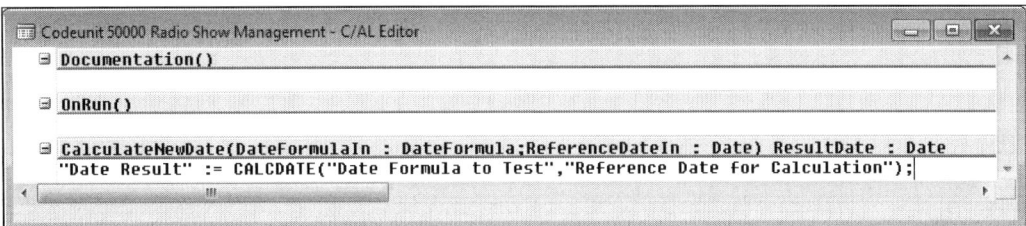

Edit the line of code just pasted into the codeunit so the variable names match those shown in our function trigger above. This will result in the following:

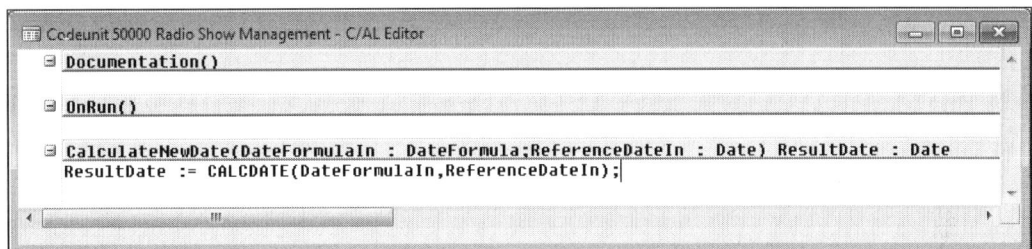

Press *F11* to check to see if we have a clean compile. If we get an error, we must do the traditional programmer thing. Find it, fix it, recompile. Repeat until we get a clean compile. Then exit and **Save** our modified **Codeunit 50000**.

Finally, we will return to our test Table 50098 to complete the changes necessary to use the external function rather than the internal function. We have two obvious choices for doing this. One is to replace the internal formula in our existing function with a call to our external function. This approach results in fewer object changes.

The other choice is to replace each of our internal function calls with a call to the external function. This approach may be more efficient at runtime because when we need the external function, we invoke it in one step rather than two. We will walk through the first option here and then you should try the second option on your own.

Which is best? It depends on our criteria. Such a decision comes down to a matter of identifying the best criteria on which to judge the design options, then applying those criteria. Remember, simple is good.

For the first approach (calling our new Codeunit resident function), we must add our new Radio Show Management codeunit 50000 to table 50098 as a variable. After Designing the table, **View | Globals**, click on the **Functions** tab, highlight the `CalculateNewDate` function, click on the **Locals** button, and click on the **Variables** tab. Add the Local variable as shown in the following screenshot (it's good practice to define variables as local unless global access is required):

The two lines of code that called the internal function `CalculateNewDate` must be changed to call the external function. The syntax for that call is:

```
Global/LocalVariable := Local/GlobalObjectName.FunctionName(Parameter1
,Parameter2,…);
```

Based on that, the new line of code should be:

```
"Date Result" := RadioShowMgt.CalculateNewDate("Date Formula to
Test","Reference Date for Calculation");
```

If all has gone well, we should be able to save and compile this modified table. When that step works successfully, we can **Run** the table and experiment with different Reference Dates and Date Formulas, just as we did back in *Chapter 3, Data Types and Fields*. We should get the same results for the same entries.

When you try out the other approach of replacing each of the calls to the internal function by directly calling the external function, you will want to:

- Either define the Radio Show Management codeunit as a Global variable or as a Local variable for each of the triggers where you are calling the external function
- Go to the **View | Globals | Functions** tab and delete the now unused internal `CalculateNewDate` function

You should now have a good feeling for the basics of constructing both internal and external functions and some of the optional design features available to you for building functions.

C/AL syntax

C/AL syntax is relatively simple and straightforward. The basic structure of most C/AL statements is essentially similar to what you learned with other programming languages. C/AL is modeled on Pascal and tends to use many of the same special characters and syntax practices as does Pascal.

Assignment and punctuation

Assignment is represented with a colon followed by an equal sign, the combination being treated as a single symbol. The evaluated value of the expression, to the right of the assignment symbol, is assigned to the variable on the left side.

```
ClientRec."Phone No." := '312-555-1212';
```

All statements are terminated with a semicolon. Multiple statements can be placed on a single program line, but that makes your code hard for the rest of us to read.

Fully qualified data fields are prefaced with the name of the record variable of which they are a part (see the preceding code line as an example where the record variable is named `ClientRec`). The same structure applies to fully qualified function references; the function name is prefaced with the name of the object in which they are defined.

Single quotes are used to surround string literals (see the phone number string in the preceding code line).

Double quotes are used to surround an identifier (for example, a variable or a function name) that contains any character other than numerals or upper and lower case letters. For example, the `Phone No.` field name in the preceding code line is constructed as "Phone No." because it contains a space and a period). Other examples would be "Post Code"(contains a space), "E-Mail" (contains a dash), and "No." (contains a period).

Parentheses are used much the same as in other languages, to indicate sets of expressions to be interpreted according to their parenthetical groupings. The expressions are interpreted in sequence, first the innermost parenthetical group, then the next level and so forth. The expression (A / (B + (C * (D + E)))) would be evaluated as follows:

- Summing D + E into Result1
- Multiplying Result1 times C yielding Result2
- Adding Result2 to B yielding Result3
- Dividing A by Result3

Brackets [ ] are used to indicate the presence of subscripts for indexing of array variables. A text string can be treated as an array of characters and you can use subscripts with the string name to access individual character positions within the string (but not beyond the terminating character of the string). For example, `Address[1]` represents the leftmost character in the Address text variable contents.

Brackets are also used for `IN` (In range) expressions, such as:

```
Boolean := SearchValue IN[SearchTarget]
```

Where `SearchValue` and `SearchTarget` are text variables.

Statements can be continued on multiple lines without any special punctuation. Since the C/AL code editor limits lines to 132 characters long, this capability is often used. The following example shows two instances that are interpreted exactly in the same manner by the compiler:

```
ClientRec."Phone No." := '312' + '-' + '555' + '-' + '1212';
ClientRec."Phone No." := '312' +
   '-' + '555' +
   '-' + '1212';
```

Expressions

Expressions in C/AL are made up of four elements: **constants**, **variables**, **operators**, and **functions**. We could include a fifth element, **expressions**, because an expression may include a subordinate expression within it. As we become more experienced in coding C/AL, we find that the capability of nesting expressions can be both a blessing and a curse, depending on the specific use and "readability" of the result.

We can create complex statements that will conditionally perform important control actions and operate in much the way that a person would think about the task. We can also create complex statements that are very difficult for a person to understand. These are tough to debug and sometimes almost impossible to deal with in a modification.

One of our responsibilities is to learn to tell the difference so we can write code that makes sense in operation, but is also easy to read and understand.

According to the **NAV Developer and IT Pro Help**, a C/AL Expression is a group of characters (data values, variables, arrays, operators, and functions) that can be evaluated with the result having an associated data type. Following are two code statements that accomplish the same result in slightly different ways. They each assign a literal string to a text data field. In the first one, the right side is a literal data value. In the second, the right side of the : = assignment symbol is an expression.

```
ClientRec."Phone No." := '312-555-1212';
ClientRec."Phone No." := '312' + '-' + '555' + '-' + '1212';
```

Operators

Now we'll review C/AL operators grouped by category. Depending on the data types we are using with a particular operator, we may need to know the type conversion rules defining the allowed combinations of operator and data types for an expression. The **NAV Developer and IT Pro Help** provides good information on type conversion rules. Search for the phrase *Type Conversion*.

Before we review the operators that can be categorized, let's discuss some operators that don't fit well in any of the categories. These include the following:

<table>
<tr><th colspan="2">Other Operators</th></tr>
<tr><th>Symbol</th><th>Evaluation</th></tr>
<tr><td>.</td><td>Member of:
Fields in Records
Controls in Forms
Controls in Reports
Functions in Objects</td></tr>
<tr><td>( )</td><td>Grouping of elements</td></tr>
<tr><td>[ ]</td><td>Indexing</td></tr>
<tr><td>::</td><td>Scope</td></tr>
<tr><td>..</td><td>Range</td></tr>
</table>

Explanations regarding uses of this set of symbols follow:

- The symbol represented by a single dot or period doesn't have a given name in the NAV documentation, so we'll call it the Member symbol or Dot operator (as it is referred to in the MSDN Visual Basic Developer documentation). It indicates that a field is a member of a table (`TableName.FieldName`) or that a control is a member of a page (`PageName.ControlName`) or report (`ReportName.ControlName`) or that a function is a member of an object (`Objectname.FunctionName`).

- Parentheses ( ) and Brackets [ ] could be considered operators based on the effect their use has on the results of an expression. We discussed their use in the context of parenthetical grouping and indexing using brackets, as well as with the `IN` function, earlier. Parentheses are also used to enclose the parameters in a function call:

```
Objectname.FunctionName(Param1,Param2,Param3);
```

- The Scope operator is a two-character sequence consisting of two colons in a row (::). The Scope operator is used to allow C/AL code to refer to a specific Option value using the text descriptive value rather than the integer value that is actually stored in the database. For example, in our C/AL database **Radio Show** table, we have an Option field defined that is called `Frequency` with Option string values of (blank), **Hourly**, **Daily**, **Weekly**, and **Monthly**. Those values would be stored as integers 0, 1, 2, 3, or 4, but we can use the strings to refer to them in code, which makes our code more self-documenting. The Scope operator allows us to refer to `Frequency::Hourly` (rather than 1) and `Frequency::Monthly` (rather than 4). These constructs are translated by the compiler to 1 and 4, respectively. If you want to type fewer characters when entering code, just enter enough of the Option string value to be unique, letting the compiler automatically fill in the rest when you next save, compile, close, and reopen the object. In similar fashion, we can refer to objects in the format `[Object Type::"Object Name"]` to be translated to the object number, for example, `PAGE.RUN(PAGE::"Session List");` is equivalent to `PAGE.RUN(9506);`

- The Range operator is a two character sequence (..), two dots in a row. This operator is very widely used in NAV, not only in C/AL code (including `CASE` statements and `IN` expressions), but also in filters entered by users. The English lowercase alphabet can be represented by the range `a..z`; the set of single digit numbers by the range `-9..9` (that is, minus 9 dot dot 9); all the entries starting with the letter a (lowercase) by `a..a*`. Don't underestimate the power of the range operator. For more information on filtering syntax, refer to the **NAV Developer and IT Pro Help** section *Entering Criteria in Filters*.

Arithmetic operators and functions

The Arithmetic operators include the following:

Arithmetic Operators		
Symbol	**Action**	**Data Types**
+	Addition	Numeric, String (concatenation), Date, Time
-	Subtraction	Numeric, Date, Time
*	Multiplication	Numeric
/	Division	Numeric
DIV	Integer Division (provides only the integer portion of the quotient of a division calculation)	Numeric
MOD	Modulus (provides only the integer remainder of a division calculation)	Numeric

As we can see in the **Data Types** column, these operators can be used on various data types. Numeric includes Integer, Decimal, Boolean, and Character data types. Text and Code are both String data.

Sample statements using DIV and MOD follow where BigNumber is an integer containing 200:

```
DIVIntegerValue := BigNumber DIV 60;
```

The contents of DIVIntegerValue after executing the preceding statement would be 3.

```
MODIntegerValue := BigNumber MOD 60;
```

The contents of MODIntegerValue after executing the preceding statement would be 20.

The syntax for these DIV and MOD statements is:

```
IntegerQuotient := IntegerDividend DIV IntegerDivisor;
IntegerModulus := IntegerDividend MOD IntegerDivisor;
```

Boolean operators

Boolean operators only operate on expressions that can be evaluated as Boolean. They are as follows:

Boolean Operators	
Symbol	Evaluation
NOT	Logical NOT
AND	Logical AND
OR	Logical OR
XOR	Exclusive Logical OR

The result of an expression based on a Boolean operator will also be Boolean.

Relational operators and functions

The Relational operators are listed in the following screenshot. Each of these is used in an expression of the format:

```
Expression RelationalOperator Expression
```

For example: (Variable1 + 97) > ((Variable2 * 14.5) / 57.332)

Relational Operators	
Symbol	Evaluation
<	Less than
>	Greater than
<=	Less than or Equal to
>=	Greater than or Equal to
=	Equal to
<>	Not equal to
IN	IN Valueset

We will spend a little extra time on the IN operator, because this can be very handy and is not documented elsewhere. The term **Valueset** in the **Evaluation** column for **IN** refers to a list of defined values. It would be reasonable to define a Valueset as a container of a defined set of individual values, or expressions, or other Valuesets. Some examples of IN as used in the standard NAV product code are as follows:

```
GLEntry."Posting Date" IN [0D,WORKDATE]

Description[I+2] IN ['0'..'9']

"Gen. Posting Type" IN ["Gen. Posting Type"::Purchase,
                        "Gen. Posting Type"::Sale]
```

```
SearchString IN ['','=><']

No[i] IN ['0'..'9']

"FA Posting Date" IN [01010001D..12319998D]
```

Here is another example of what IN used in an expression might look like:

```
TestString IN ['a'..'d','j','q','l'..'p'];
```

If the value of TestString were a or m, then this expression would evaluate to TRUE. If the value of TestString were z, then this expression would evaluate to FALSE. Note that the Data Type of the search value must be the same as the Data Type of the Valueset.

Precedence of operators

When expressions are evaluated by the C/AL compiler, the parsing routines use a predefined precedence hierarchy to determine what operators to evaluate first, what to evaluate second, and so forth. That precedence hierarchy is provided in the **NAV Developer and IT Pro Help** section *C/AL Operators – Operator Hierarchy*, but for convenience, the information is repeated here:

C/AL Operator Precedence Hierarchy		
Sequence	**Symbols**	
1	.	Member (Fields in Records, etc)
	[]	Indexing
	()	Parenthetical Grouping
	::	Scope
2		Unary instances of:
	NOT	Logical Not
	+	Positive value
	-	Negating value
3	*	Multiplication
	/	Division
	DIV	Integer division
	MOD	Modulus
	AND	Logical AND
	XOR	Logical Exclusive OR
4	+	Addition or Concatenation
	-	Subtraction
	OR	Logical OR
5	>	Greater than
	<	Less than
	>=	Greater than or equal to
	<=	Less than or equal to
	<>	Not equal to
	IN	IN Valueset
6	..	Range

For complex expressions, we should always freely use parentheses to make sure the expressions are evaluated the way we intend.

Frequently used C/AL functions

It's time to learn some more of the standard functions provided by C/SIDE.

There is a group of functions in C/AL called **Dialog** functions. We will focus on the most frequently used MESSAGE, ERROR, CONFIRM, and STRMENU functions. The purpose of these functions is to allow for communications (that is, dialog) between the system and the user. In addition, the **Dialog** functions can be useful for testing/debugging. In order to make it easier for us to proceed with our next level of C/AL development work, we're going to take time now to learn about those three dialog functions. None of these functions will operate if the C/AL code is running on the NAV Application Server as no GUI is available. To handle that situation, the Dialog function statements should be conditioned with the GUIALLOWED function to check whether or not the code is running in a GUI allowed environment. If the code is being used in a Web Service, it would not be GUIALLOWED.

In each of these functions, data values can be inserted through use of a substitution string. The substitution string is the % (percent sign) character followed by the number 1 through 10, located within a message text string. That could look like the following:

```
MESSAGE('A message + a data element to display = %1', "OrderAmount");
```

If the OrderAmount value was $100.53, the output from the preceding would be:

```
A message + a data element to display = $100.53
```

You can have up to ten substitution strings in one dialog function. The use of substitution strings and their associated display values is optional. You can use any one of the dialog functions simply to display a completely predefined text message with nothing variable. Use of a Text Constant (accessed through **View | C/AL Globals** in the **Text Constants** tab) is recommended as it makes maintenance and multilanguage enabling easier.

The MESSAGE function

MESSAGE is the most commonly used dialog function. It is easy to use for the display of transient data and can be placed almost anywhere in your C/AL code. All it requires of the user is acknowledgement that the message has been read. The disadvantage of messages is that they are not displayed until either the object completes its run or pauses for some other external action. Plus, if you should inadvertently create a situation that generates hundreds or thousands of messages, there is no graceful way to terminate their display once they begin displaying.

It's common to use MESSAGE as an elementary trace tool. You can program the display of messages to occur only under particular circumstances and use them to view either the flow of processing (by outputting simple unique codes from different points in your logic) or to view the contents of particular data elements through multiple processing cycles.

MESSAGE has the following syntax: MESSAGE (String [, Value1] , ...]), where there are as many ValueX entries as there are %X substitution strings (up to ten).

Here is a sample debugging message:

```
MESSAGE('Loop %1, Item No. %2',LoopCounter,"Item No.");
```

The display would look like the following (when the counter was 12 and the Item No. was I0123):

One challenge of using MESSAGE for debugging is making sure that all messages are removed before releasing the object to production.

The ERROR function

When an ERROR function is invoked, the execution of the current process terminates, the message is immediately displayed and the database returns to the status following the last COMMIT function as though the process calling the ERROR function had not run at all.

You can use the ERROR function in combination with the MESSAGE function to assist in repetitive testing. MESSAGE functions can be placed in code to show what is happening with an ERROR function placed just prior to where the process would normally complete. Because the ERROR function rolls back all database changes, this technique allows you to run through multiple tests against the same data without any time-consuming backup and restoration of your test data. The enhanced Testing functionality built into NAV 2013 can accomplish the same things in a much more sophisticated fashion, but sometimes there's room for a temporary, simple approach.

An ERROR function call is formatted almost exactly like a MESSAGE call. ERROR has the syntax ERROR (String [, Value1] ,...]), where there are as many ValueX entries as there are %X substitution strings (up to ten). If the preceding MESSAGE was an ERROR function instead, the code line would be:

```
ERROR('Loop %1, Item No. %2',LoopCounter,"Item No.");
```

The display would look like the following screenshot:

The big X in a bold red circle tells us this was an ERROR message, but some users might not immediately realize that. We can increase the ease of ERROR message recognition by including the word **ERROR** in your message, like the following:

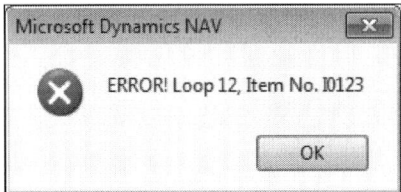

Even in the best of circumstances, it is difficult for the system to communicate clearly with the users. Sometimes our tools, in their effort to be flexible, make it too easy for developers to take the easy way out and communicate poorly or not at all. For example, an ERROR statement of the form ERROR('') will terminate the run and roll back all data processing without even displaying any message at all. An important part of your job, as a developer, is to ensure that your system communicates clearly and completely.

The CONFIRM function

A third dialog function is the CONFIRM function. A CONFIRM function call causes processing to stop while the user responds to the dialog. In a CONFIRM, you would include a question in your text because the function provides **Yes** and **No** button options. The application logic can then be conditioned on the user's response.

You can also use CONFIRM as a simple debugging tool to control the path the processing will take. Display the status of data or processing flow and then allow the operator to make a choice (**Yes** or **No**) that will influence what happens next. Execution of a CONFIRM function will also cause any pending MESSAGE outputs to be displayed before the CONFIRM function displays. Combined with MESSAGE and ERROR, creative use of CONFIRM can add to your debugging/diagnostic toolkit.

CONFIRM has the following syntax:

```
BooleanValue :=  CONFIRM(String [, Default]  [, Value1]  ,...)
```

When we do not specify a value for Default, the system will choose FALSE (which displays as **No**). We should almost always choose as a Default the option that will do no damage if accepted inadvertently by an inattentive user. Where the Default choice is FALSE, which is often the safest choice (but TRUE may be specified by the programmer) and there are as many ValueX entries as there are %X substitution strings (up to ten).

If you just code OK := CONFIRM(String), the Default choice will be False. Note that True and False appear onscreen as the active language equivalent of **Yes** and **No** (a feature that is consistent throughout NAV for C/AL Boolean values displayed from NAV code but not for RDLC report controls displayed by the report viewer, see the **NAV Developer and IT Pro Help** section's *How to: Change the Printed Values of Boolean Variables*).

A CONFIRM function call with a similar content to the preceding examples might look like this for the code and the display:

```
Answer := CONFIRM('Loop %1, Item No. %2\OK to continue?',TRUE,LoopCoun
ter,"Item No.");
```

In typical usage, the CONFIRM function is part of, or is referred to, by a conditional statement that uses the Boolean value returned by the CONFIRM function.

An additional feature is the use of the backslash (\), which forces a new line in the displayed message. This works throughout NAV screen display functions. Following are examples in **Text Constants Text063** and **Text064**:

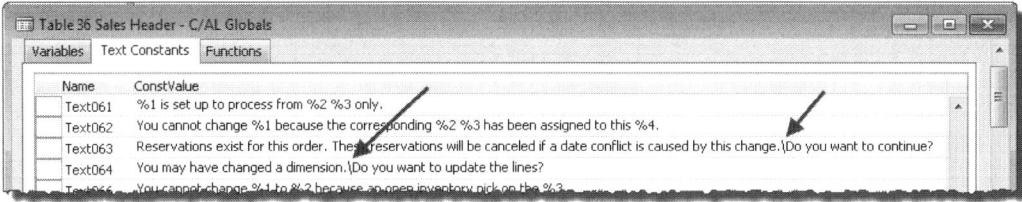

To display a backslash, we must put two of them in our message text string, \\.

The STRMENU function

A fourth dialog function is the STRMENU function. A STRMENU function call also causes processing to pause while the user responds to the dialog. The advantage of the STRMENU function is the ability to provide several choices, rather than just two (**Yes** or **No**). A common use is to provide an option menu in response to the user pressing a command button.

STRMENU has the following syntax:

```
IntegerValue := STRMENU(StringVariable of Options separated by commas
[, OptionDefault] [, Instruction])
```

Where IntegerValue will contain the user's selection and OptionDefault is an integer representing which option will be selected by default when the menu displays. If you do not provide an OptionDefault, the first option listed will be used as the default. Instruction is a text string which will display above the list of options. If the user responds **Cancel** or presses the *Esc* key, the value returned by the function is 0.

Use of the STRMENU function eliminates the need to use a Page object when asking the user to select from a limited set of options. The STRMENU can also be utilized from within a report or Codeunit when calling a Page would restrict processing choices.

If you phrase your instruction as a question rather than simply an explanation, then you can use STRMENU as a multiple choice inquiry to the user.

Here is an example of STRMENU with the instruction phrased as a question:

```
OptionNo := STRMENU('Red,Yellow,Stripes,Green,Blue,Unknown',6,
                    'Which of these is not like the others?');
```

Setting the default to 6 caused the sixth option (**Unknown**) to be the active selection when the menu is displayed.

Record functions

Now we will review some of the functions that we commonly use in Record processing.

The SETCURRENTKEY function

The syntax for SETCURRENTKEY is:

```
[BooleanValue :=] Record.SETCURRENTKEY(FieldName1,[FieldName2], ... )
```

The BooleanValue is optional. If you do not specify it and no matching key is found, a runtime error will occur.

Because NAV 2013 is based on the SQL Server database, SETCURRENTKEY simply determines the order in which the data will be presented to the processing. The actual choice of the index to be used for the query is made by the SQL Server Query Analyzer. For this reason, it is very important the data and resources used by the SQL Server Query Analyzer are well maintained. This includes maintaining the statistics that are used by the Query Analyzer, as well as making sure efficient index options have been defined.

The indexes that are defined in SQL Server do not have to be the same as those defined in the C/AL table definition (for example, you can add additional indices in SQL Server and not in the C/AL, you can disable indices in SQL Server but leave the matching keys enabled in C/AL, and so on). Any maintenance of the SQL Server indices should be done through the NAV Table Designer using the NAV keys and properties, not directly in SQL Server. Even though the system may operate without problem, any mismatch between the application system and the underlying database system makes maintenance and upgrades more difficult and error prone.

The SETRANGE function

The SETRANGE function provides the ability to set a simple range filter on a field. SETRANGE syntax is as follows:

```
Record.SETRANGE(FieldName [,From-Value] [,To-Value]);
```

Prior to applying its range filter, the SETRANGE function removes any filters that were previously set for the defined field (filtering functions are defined in more detail in the next chapter). If SETRANGE is executed with only one value, that one value will act as both the From and To values. If SETRANGE is executed without any From or To values, it will clear the filters on the field. This is a common use of SETRANGE. Some examples of the SETRANGE function in code are as follows:

- Clear the filters on Item.No.:

  ```
  Item.SETRANGE("No.");
  ```

- Filter to get only Items with a No. from 1300 through 1400:

  ```
  Item.SETRANGE("No.",'1300','1400');
  ```

- Or with the variable values from LowVal through HiVal:

  ```
  Item.SETRANGE("No.",LowVal,HiVal);
  ```

The SETFILTER function

SETFILTER is similar to, but much more flexible than, the SETRANGE function because it supports the application of any of the supported NAV filter functions to table fields. SETFILTER syntax is as follows:

```
Record.SETFILTER(FieldName, FilterExpression [Value],...);
```

The `FilterExpression` consists of a string (Text or Code) in standard NAV filter format including any of the operators < > * & | = in any legal combination. Replacement fields (%1, %2, …, %9) are used to represent the Values that will be inserted into the `FilterExpression` by the compiler to create an operating filter formatted as though it were entered from the keyboard. Just as with SETRANGE, prior to applying its filter, the SETFILTER function clears any filters that were previously set for the defined field.

- Filter to get only Items with a No. from 1300 through 1400:

    ```
    Item.SETFILTER("No.",'%1..%2','1300','1400');
    ```

- Or with any of the variable values of LowVal or MedVal or HiVal:

    ```
    Item.SETRANGE("No.",'%1|%2|%3',LowVal,MedVal,HiVal);
    ```

The GET function

GET is the basic data retrieval function in C/AL. GET retrieves a single record, based on the Primary Key only. GET has the following syntax:

```
[BooleanValue :=] Record.GET ( [KeyFieldValue1] [,KeyFieldValue2]
,...)
```

The parameter for the GET function is the Primary Key value (or all the values, if the Primary Key consists of more than one field).

Assigning the GET function result to a `BooleanValue` is optional. If the GET function is not successful with no record found and the statement is part of an IF statement, the process will terminate with a runtime error. Typically, therefore, the GET function is encased in an IF statement structured like the following:

```
IF Customer.GET(NewCustNo) THEN ...
```

GET data retrieval is not constrained by filters except for security filters (see **Help**'s *How to: Set Security Filters*). If there is a matching record in the table, GET will retrieve it.

FIND functions

The FIND family of functions is the general purpose data retrieval function in C/AL. It is much more flexible than GET, therefore more widely used. GET has the advantage of being faster as it operates only on an unfiltered direct access via the Primary Key, looking for a single uniquely keyed entry. There are two forms of FIND in C/AL, one a remnant from a previous database structure and the other designed specifically to work efficiently with SQL Server. Both are supported and you will find both in standard code.

The older version of FIND function has the following syntax:

```
[BooleanValue :=] RecordName.FIND ( [Which] ).
```

The newer SQL Server specific members of the FIND family have slightly different syntax, as we shall see shortly.

Just as with the GET function, assigning the FIND function result to a Boolean value is optional. But in almost all of the cases, FIND is embedded in a condition that controls subsequent processing appropriately. Either way, it is important to structure your code to handle the instance where the FIND is not successful.

FIND differs from GET in several important ways:

- FIND operates under the limits of whatever filters are applied on the subject field.

- FIND presents the data in the sequence of the key which is currently selected by default or by C/AL code.

- When FIND is used, the index used for the data reading is controlled by the SQL Server Query Analyzer.

- Different variations of the FIND function are designed specifically for use in different situations. This allows coding to be optimized for better SQL Server performance. All the FIND functions are described further in the **Help** section *C/AL Database Functions and Performance on SQL Server*.

Following are the various forms of FIND:

- FIND('-'): Finds the first record in a table that satisfies the defined filter and current key.

- FINDFIRST: Finds the first record in a table that satisfies the defined filter and defined key choice. Conceptually equivalent to the FIND('-') for a single record read, but better for SQL Server when a filter or range is applied.

- FIND('+'): Finds the last record in a table that satisfies the defined filter and defined key choice. Often not an efficient option for SQL Server as it reads a set of records when many times only a single record is needed. The exception is when a table is to be processed in reverse order. Then it is appropriate to use FIND('+') with SQL Server.

- FINDLAST: Finds the last record in a table that satisfies the defined filter and current key. Conceptually equivalent to the FIND('+') but often much better for SQL Server as it reads a single record, not a set of records.

- FINDSET: The efficient way to read a set of records from SQL Server for sequential processing within a specified filter and range. FINDSET allows defining the standard size of the read record cache as a setup parameter, but normally defaults to reading 50 records (table rows) for the first server call. The syntax includes two optional parameters:

```
FINDSET([ForUpdate][, UpdateKey]);
```

The first parameter controls whether or not the read is in preparation for an update and the second parameter is TRUE when the first parameter is TRUE and the update is of key fields.

FIND ([Which]) options and the SQL Server alternates

Let's review the options of the FIND function using the syntax:

```
[BooleanValue :=] RecordName.FIND ( [Which] )
```

The [Which] parameter allows the specification of which record is searched for relative to the defined key values. The defined key values are the set of values currently in the fields of the active key in the memory-resident record of table RecordName.

The following table lists the Which parameter options and prerequisites:

FIND "which" parameter	FIND action	Search and primary key value prerequisite before FIND
=	Match the search key values exactly	All must be specified
>	Read the next record with key values larger than the search key values	All must be specified
<	Read the next record with key values smaller than the search key values	All must be specified
>=	Read the first record found with key values equal to or larger than the search key values	All must be specified
<=	Read the next record with key values equal to or smaller than the search key values	All must be specified
-	Read the first record in the selected set. If used with SQL Server, reads a set of records	No requirement
+	Read the last record in the selected set. If used with SQL Server, reads a set of records	No requirement

This second table lists the FIND options which are specific to SQL Server:

FIND(xxxx) options	FIND action	Search and primary key value prerequisite before FIND
FINDFIRST	Read the first record in a table based on the current key and filter. Used only for access to a single record, not in a read loop.	All must be specified
FINDLAST	Read the last record in a table based on the current key and filter. Used only for access to a single record, not in a read loop.	All must be specified
FINDSET	Read the record set specified. Syntax is Record.FINDSET([ForUpdate][,UpdateKey]) Set ForUpdate = True if data to be updated Set ForUpdate = True and UpdateKey = True if a key field is to be updated If no parameter specified, both default to False	All must be specified

For both tables, the results always respect applied filters.

The FIND('-') function is sometimes used as the first step of reading a set of data such as reading all the sales invoices for a single customer. In such a case, the NEXT function is used to trigger all the data reads after the sequence is initiated with a FIND('-'). Generally FINDSET should be used rather than FIND('-'), however FINDSET only works for reading forward, not in reverse.

One form of the typical C/SIDE database read loop is as follows:

```
IF MyData.FIND('-') THEN
 REPEAT
 Processing logic here
UNTIL MyData.NEXT = 0;
```

The same processing logic using the FINDSET function is as follows:

```
IF MyData.FINDSET THEN
 REPEAT
 Processing logic here
UNTIL MyData.NEXT = 0;
```

We will discuss the REPEAT-UNTIL control structure in more detail in the next chapter. Essentially, it does what it says; "repeat the following logic until the defined condition is true". In the case of the FIND-NEXT read loop, the NEXT function provides both the definition of how the read loop will advance through the table and will exit.

When `DataTable.NEXT = 0`, that means there are no more records to be read. We have reached the end of the available data, based on the filters and other conditions that apply to our reading process.

The specific syntax of the `NEXT` function is `DataTable.NEXT(Step)`. `DataTable` is the name of the table being read. Step defines the number of records NAV will move forward (or backward) per read. The default Step is 1, meaning NAV moves ahead one record at a time, reading every record. A Step of 0 works the same as a step of 1. If the Step is set to 2, NAV will move ahead two records at a time and the process will only be presented with every other record.

`Step` can also be negative, in which case NAV moves backwards through the table. This would allow you to do a `FIND('+')` for the end of the table, then a `NEXT(-1)` to read backwards through the data. This is very useful if, for example, you need to read a table sorted ascending by date and want to access the most recent entries first.

Conditional statements

Conditional statements are the heart of process flow structure and control.

The BEGIN–END compound statement

In C/AL, there are instances where the syntax only allows for use of a single statement. But a design may require the execution of several (or many) code statements.

C/AL provides at least two ways to address this need. One method is to have the single statement be call to a function that contains multiple statements.

However, inline coding is often more efficient to run and to understand. So C/AL provides a syntax structure to define a **Compound Statement** or **Block of code**. A compound statement containing any number of statements can be used in place of a single code statement.

A compound statement is enclosed by the reserved words `BEGIN` and `END`. The compound statement structure looks like this:

```
BEGIN
    <Statement 1>;
    <Statement 2>;
    ..
    <Statement n>;
END
```

The C/AL code contained within a `BEGIN` – `END` block should be indented, as shown previously, to make it obvious that it is a block of code.

The IF–THEN–ELSE statement

IF is the basic conditional statement of most programming languages. It operates in C/AL similarly to how it works in other languages. The basic structure is: IF a conditional expression is true, THEN execute Statement-1 ELSE (if condition not true) execute Statement-2. The ELSE portion is optional. The syntax is:

```
IF <Condition> THEN <Statement-1> [ ELSE <Statement-2> ]
```

Note that the statements within the IF do not have terminating semicolons unless they are contained in a BEGIN - END framework. IF statements can be nested so that conditionals are dependent on the evaluation of other conditionals. Obviously one needs to be careful with such constructs, because it is easy to end up with convoluted code structures that are difficult to debug and difficult for the developer following you to understand. In the next chapter, we will review the CASE statement which can make some complicated conditionals much easier to format and to understand.

As we work with NAV C/AL code, we will see that often the <Condition> is really an expression built around a standard C/AL function. This approach is frequently used when the standard syntax for the function is "Boolean value, function expression". Some examples are as follows:

- IF Customer.FIND('-') THEN... ELSE...
- IF CONFIRM('OK to update?',TRUE) THEN... ELSE...
- IF TempData.INSERT THEN... ELSE...
- IF Customer.CALCFIELDS(Balance,Balance(LCY)) THEN...

Indenting code

Since we have just discussed BEGIN-END compound statements and IF conditional statements, which also are compound (that is, containing multiple expressions), this seems a good time to discuss indenting code.

In C/AL, the standard practice for indenting subordinate, contained, or continued lines is relatively simple. Always indent such lines by two characters except where there are left and right parentheses to be aligned.

 To indent a block of code by two characters at a time, select it and click on the *Tab* key. To remove the indentation one character at a time, select the code and click on *Shift + Tab*.

In the following examples, the parentheses are not required in all the instances, but they don't cause any problem and can make the code easier to read:

Some examples are:

```
IF (A <> B) THEN
    A := A + Count1
ELSE
    B := B + Count2;
```

Or:

```
IF (A <> B) THEN
    A := A + Count1;
```

Or:

```
IF (A <> B)THEN
BEGIN
    A := A + Count1;
    B := A + Count2;
    IF (C > (A * B)) THEN
      C := A * B;
END
ELSE
    B := B + Count2;
```

Some simple coding modifications

Now we're going to add some C/AL code to objects we've created for our WDTU application.

Adding field validation to a table

In *Chapter 4, Pages – the User's Interactive Interface*, we created Table 50010 – Radio Show Fan. Now we've decided that we want to be able to use this list for promotional activities such as having drawings for concert tickets. Of course we want to send the tickets to the winners at their mailing addresses. We didn't include those fields originally in our table design, so must add them now. To keep our design consistent with the standard product, we will model those fields after the equivalent ones in Table 18 – Customer. Our updated Table 50010 will look like the following:

Part of modeling our Table 50010 – Radio Show Fan fields on those in Table 18 – Customer is faithfully copying the applicable properties. For example, the **TableRelation** property for the **Post Code** field in Table 18 contains the following, which we should include for the **Post Code** in Table 50010.

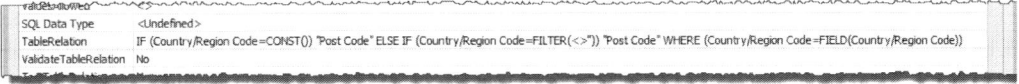

When a Radio Show Fan record is added or the **Post Code** field is changed, we would like to update the appropriate address information. Let's start with some code in a Validation trigger of our table.

Since we modeled the address fields for our Fan record on the standard Customer table, let's look at the Customer table to see how **Post Code** validation is handled there. We can access that code through the Table Designer via **Object Designer** | **Table** | select **Table 18 - Customer** | **Design** | select **Field 91 - Post Code** | F9. We see the following:

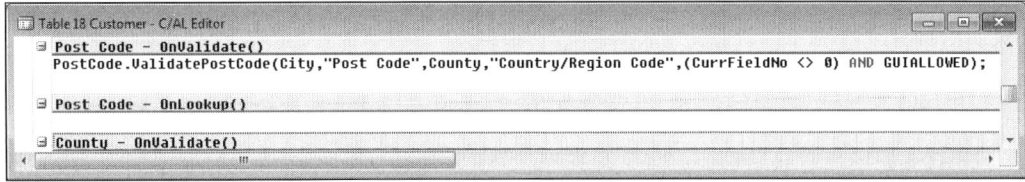

Looking at this C/AL code, we can see that the **OnValidate** trigger contains a call to a function in another object identified as PostCode. To find out what object PostCode actually is, we need to look in the **C/AL Globals** (which we have sometimes referred to in this book as Working Storage):

Now we see that PostCode is a reference to the **Record** (that is, a table) **PostCode**. This is sort of like a treasure hunt at a birthday party. Now we follow that clue to the next stop, the Post Code table and the ValidatePostCode function that is used in the Customer Post Code validation trigger. To learn as much as we can about how this function works, how we should call it, and what information is available from the Post Code table (table 225), we will look at several things:

- The Post Code table field list
- The C/AL code for the function in which we are interested
- The list of functions available in the Post Code table
- The calling and return parameters for the ValidatePostCode function

Screenshots for all those areas are as follows:

First, the field list in **Table 225 Post Code**:

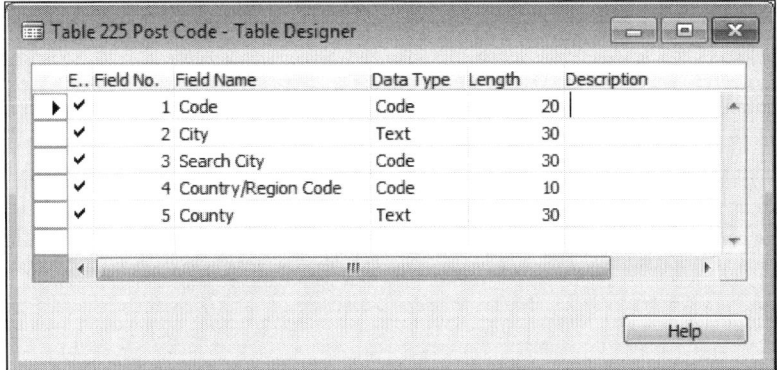

Next, the C/AL code for the **ValidatePostCode** function:

Now, the list of callable functions available within the Post Code table (this isn't critical information but helps us see the whole picture of the structure):

Finally, a look at the calling **Parameters** for the **ValidatePostCode** function:

And the **Return Value** for the **ValidatePostCode** function:

Doing some analysis of what we have dissected, we can see the **ValidatePostCode** function call uses five calling **Parameters**. There is no **Return Value**. The function avoids the need for a **Return Value** by passing four of the parameters "by reference" (not "by value") as you can tell by the checkmark in the **Var** column. The function code updates the parameters which reference data elements in the calling object. This interpretation is reinforced by studying the **ValidatePostCode** function C/AL code as well.

We conclude that we can just copy the code from the **Post Code OnValidate** trigger in the Customer table into the equivalent trigger in our Fan table. This will give us the Post Code maintenance we want. The result looks like the following screenshot (the variable CurrFieldNo is apparently a System-Defined Variable leftover from previous versions representing the integer number of the currently active field; it is not documented in Help):

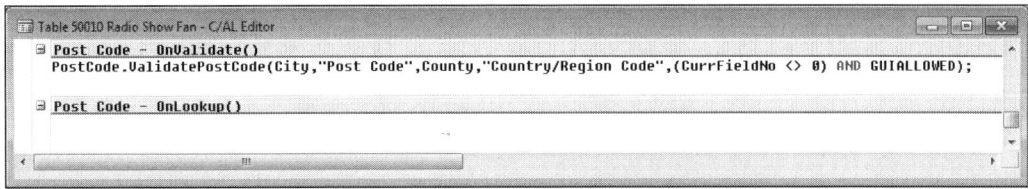

If you press *F11* at this point, you will get an error message indicating that the variable **PostCode** has not been defined:

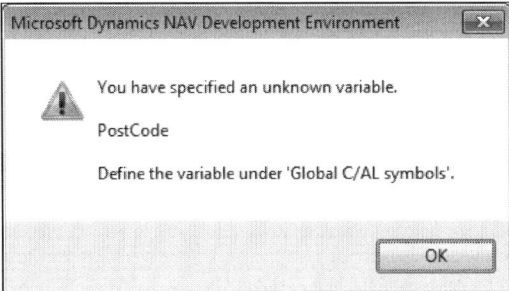

Obviously, we need to attend to this. The answer is shown in the next screenshot in the form of the **PostCode** Global Variable definition:

After we save this change (by simply moving focus from the new line of code to another line on the form or closing the form), press *F11* again. We should get no reaction other than a brief cursor blink when the object is compiled.

Because we haven't created a page for maintenance of Table 50010, we will test our work by running the table. All we need to do is move to the **Post Code** field, click on it and choose an entry from the displayed list of codes. The result should be the population of the **Post Code** field, the **Country/Region Code** field and the **City** field. If we fill in the new data fields for some Fan records, our **Radio Show Fan** table could look like the following:

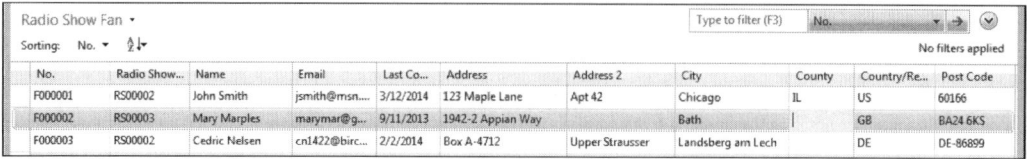

We've accomplished our goal. The way we've done it may seem disappointing. It didn't feel like we really designed a solution or wrote any code. What we did was find where in NAV the same problem was already solved, figured out how that solution worked, cloned it into our object, and we were done.

Obviously this approach doesn't work every time. But every time it does work is a small triumph of efficiency. The structure of the solution is totally consistent with the standard product, we have re-used existing code constructs, have minimized the debugging effort and chances of production problems. In addition, our modifications are likely to work even if the standard base application function changes in a future version.

Adding code to a report

Most reports require some embedded logic to process user selected Options, calculate values or access data in related tables. To illustrate some possibilities, we will extend our WDTU application to add a new report.

To support promotions giving away posters, concert tickets, and so on, we must further enhance the Radio Show Fan table and create a new report to generate mailing information from it. Our first step is to create a **New** report in the C/SIDE Report Designer, define the data fields we want to include for mailings (including a Global variable of CountryName), then **Save** and **Compile** the result as **Report 50002 Fan Promotion List**.

Layout the new report heading

Next we will begin the design of the report layout in the Visual Studio Report Designer. From the C/SIDE RD, we click on **View | Layout** to open VS RD ready to begin work on our layout. We'll begin by defining a report header.

Right-click in the shaded part of the layout work area (in the middle of the screen display) and select **Add Page Header**. On the left side of the menu at the top, click on **View | View Report Data** (or *Ctrl + Alt + D*) to display **ReportData** including the **DataSetResult**. Depending on what information we want to appear in the header, we might use fields from various parts of the **ReportData**. In our example, we drag in a **Text Box** from the **Toolbox** and placed it in the upper-left corner. The **Text Box** was then filled by typing in a report name. Most of the other header fields were brought in from the **Report Data Built-in Fields** section. We used **Execution Time**, **Page Number**, and **User ID** fields. We added another **Text Box** for the word Page in front of the **Page Number**.

Entering text data directly into the VS RD layout is only appropriate for beginners or for reports that are for very short-term use. Good report design practice requires that such values are defined in the C/SIDE RD, where multilanguage is supported and where such fields should be maintained. In the C/SIDE RD, those values can be entered and maintained in the Report Label Designer accessed via **View | Labels**.

In the process of working on this sample report, you might want another set of data and a different layout. Feel free to design your header to suit your own preferences.

Save and test

At this point, it's time to save and test what we've done so far. Click on menu option **Build** | **Build Solution** (or *F6*) to check if the layout will compile. Then click on **File** | **Exit** (or *Alt* + *F4*) to exit VS RD. Save the report layout changes, exit the C/SIDE RD, save, and compile your report object.

This first test is very simple (assuming it works). Run **Report 50002**. The Report Request Page will appear in the RoleTailored client. Click on **Preview** to see the Report display onscreen. The layout shown in the preceding screenshot will result in the following report page:

Lookup Related table data

Once we have a successful test of the report (heading only), we'll move on to laying out the body of the report. As we think through the data we want to include in a mailing address (Name, Address, Address 2, City, County (State), Country Name, Post Code), we realize that our table data includes Country Code, not Country Name. So we will look up the Country Name from the **Country/Region** table (Table 9). Let's take care of that now.

We'll add a couple of Global Variables to our report. One of them will allow us to access the **Country/Region** table and the other will act as a holding place for the Country Name data we get from that table.

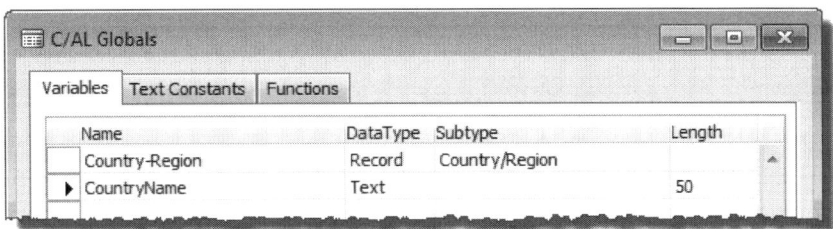

Each time we read a **Radio Show Fan** record, we'll look up the Country Name for that fan and store it in **CountryName**.

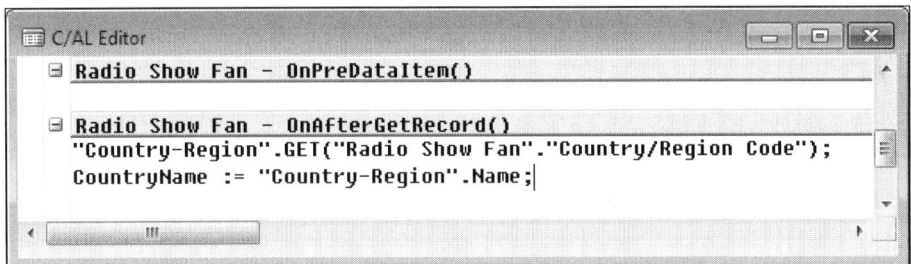

While what we've done will probably run most of the time, how could it be made better? For one thing, shouldn't we handle the situation where there is no Country/Region Code in the fan record? And do we really need to move the country name to a Global variable instead of simply reporting it directly from the **Country/Region** record?

Both of these issues could be handled better. Look up the GET function in the Help to see what should be done in terms of error handling. And, after you work through the report as we're doing it here, enhance it by eliminating use of the **CountryName** Global variable. For now, let's just move on to completing an initial version of our report by creating the rest of our report layout in the VS RD.

Layout the new report body

Open the report layout in the VS RD. From the **Toolbox**, we'll grab a Table and drag it into the layout work area for the report body. The Table starts with only three columns. After positioning the Table to the top left of the body, we will add four more columns to accommodate the seven data fields we want to include for each mailing address.

We will drag a data field from the **DataSet_Result** into each of the Data Row Text Boxes (the bottom row). In the top row, captions will appear. Where we want the displayed captions to be different than what fills in automatically, we'll type in what we want.

In future reports, we'll define labels in the C/SIDE RD **Report Label Designer**. In fact, that's how we got the **CountryCaption** and **StateCaption** you see in the preceding and following screenshot:

Save and test

After we **Build, Save, Exit, Update, Save**, and **Compile**, it's time to do another test **Run** of our report in process. If we simply **Preview** without doing any filtering, we should see all of our test data address information (complete with Country Name):

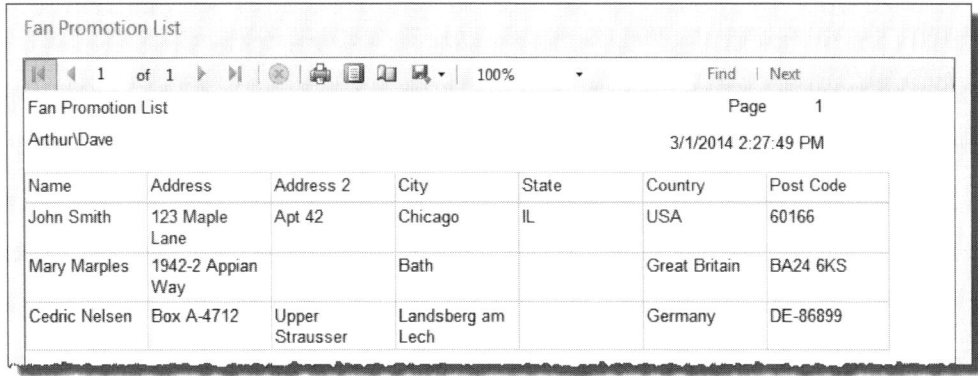

Handling user-entered selection criteria

Part of our report design includes allowing the user to choose fans based on some simple demographic data based on age and gender. We'll need to add two more fields to our Radio Show Fan table definition, one for **Gender** and the other for **Birth Date**, from which we can calculate the fan's age.

This back and forth process of updating first one object, then a different one, then yet another, is typical of the NAV development process much of the time. Exceptions are those cases where either the task is so simple you think of everything the first time through or the cases where you create a completely documented, full-featured design before any development starts.

An advantage to the more flexible approach we are following is it allows you to view (and share with others) intermediate versions of the application as it is developed. Design issues can be addressed as they come up and overlooked features can be considered mid-stream. Two downsides are the very real possibility of scope creep (the project growing uncontrollably) and poorly organized code. Scope creep can be controlled by good project management. If the first pass through results in poorly organized code, then a thoughtful refactoring is appropriate, cleaning up the code while retaining the design.

In order for the user to choose which Fan demographics will be used to filter the Fan data for a particular promotion, we will have to create a Request Page for entry of the desired criteria. This, in turn, requires the definition of a set of Global Variables to support the Request Page data entry fields and as working variables for the age calculation and Fan selection. We've decided that if a Fan fits any of the individual criteria, we will include them. This makes our logic simpler. Our final Global Variable list looks like this:

Defining the Request Page

Now let's define the Request Page. Open up Report **50002** in the C/SIDE Report Designer, click on **View | Request Page** and make the entries necessary to describe the page layout.

Finishing the processing code

Next we will create the C/AL code to calculate a Fan's age (in years) based on their Birth Date and the current WORKDATE. The logic is simple—subtract the Birth Date from the WORKDATE. This gives a number of days. So we divide by 365 (not worrying about Leap Years) and round down to integer years (if someone is 25 years, 10 months, and 2 days, we will just consider them 25). In the code following, we did the division as though the result were a decimal field. But our math is integer, we could have used the simpler expression: **FanAge := ((WORKDATE - "Birth Date") DIV 365);**

Finally, we'll write the code to check each Fan record data against our selection criteria, determining if we want to include that fan in our output data (`SelectThisFan` set to `True`). This code will select all the fans who fit any of the checked criteria; there is no combination logic here. Following is our commented C/AL code for Report 50002:

```
C/AL Editor

⊟ Radio Show Fan - OnPreDataItem()

⊟ Radio Show Fan - OnAfterGetRecord()
    //Look up the Country Name using the Code
    "Country-Region".GET("Radio Show Fan"."Country/Region Code")
    CountryName := "Country-Region".Name;

    //Calculate the Fan's age
    FanAge := ROUND(((WORKDATE - "Birth Date")/365),1.0,'<');

    //Select Fans to receive Promotion material
    SelectThisFan := FALSE;
    IF (Age12orLess) AND (FanAge <= 12) THEN
      SelectThisFan := TRUE;
    IF ("Age13-18") AND (FanAge > 12) AND (FanAge < 19) THEN
      SelectThisFan := TRUE;
    IF ("Age19-34") AND (FanAge > 18) AND (FanAge < 35) THEN
      SelectThisFan := TRUE;
    IF ("Age35-50") AND (FanAge > 34) AND (FanAge < 51) THEN
      SelectThisFan := TRUE;
    IF (AgeOver50) AND (FanAge > 50) THEN
      SelectThisFan := TRUE;
    IF (Male) AND (Gender = Gender::Male) THEN
      SelectThisFan := TRUE;
    IF (Female) AND (Gender = Gender::Female) THEN
      SelectThisFan := TRUE;
    //IF Fan not selected, skip this Fan record
    IF SelectThisFan <> TRUE THEN CurrReport.SKIP;

⊟ Radio Show Fan - OnPostDataItem()
```

After this version of the report is successfully tested, enhance it. Make the report support choosing any of the options (as it is now) or, at user option, choose a combination of age range plus gender. Hint: Add additional checkboxes to allow the user to control which set of logic will be applied. You should also change the code to use CASE statements (rather IF statements). CASE statements often provide a view of the logic that is easier to understand.

Test the completed report

After we **Save** and **Compile** our report, we'll **Run** it again. Now we get an expanded Request Option Page. After we've check-marked a couple of the selection criteria, as shown here:

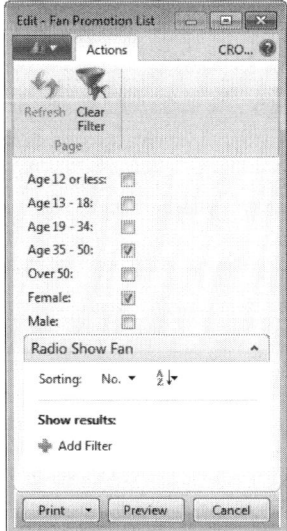

Now **Preview** our report. Using the sample data previously illustrated, our report output shows two records, one selected on the basis of Gender and the other on Age.

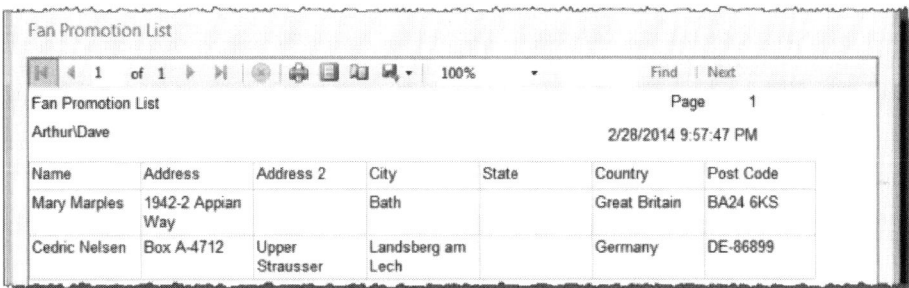

Output to Excel

An easy way to get the data to a mailing list is now to output it to Excel, where we can easily manipulate it into a variety of formats without further programming.

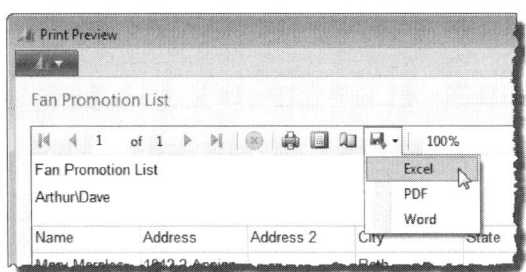

Here's what that output looks like in Excel:

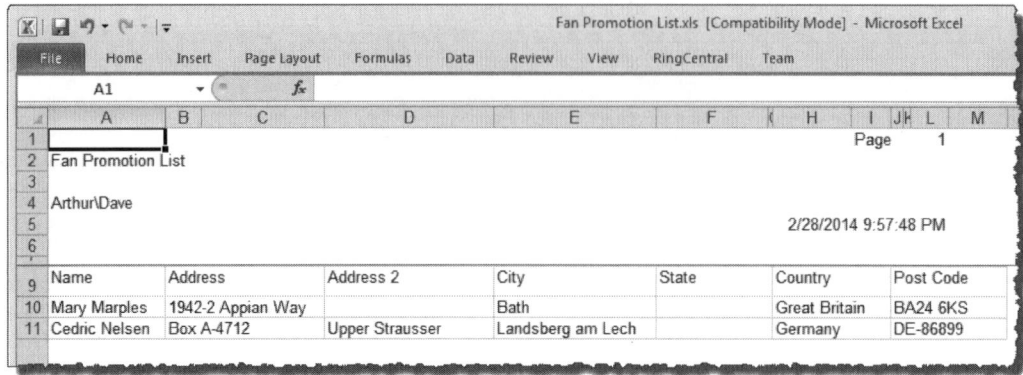

At this point we have our report that runs and is useful. It can be enhanced to support more complex selection criteria. As usual, there are a number of different ways to accomplish essentially the same result. Some of those paths would be significantly different for the developer, but nearly invisible to the user. Some might not even matter to the next developer who has to work on this report. What is important is that the result works reliably, provides the desired output, operates with reasonable speed, and does not cost too much to create or maintain. If all those goals are met, most of the other differences are usually not very important.

Summary

> *Language is a process of free creation; its laws and principles are fixed, but the manner in which the principles of generation are used is free and infinitely varied...*
>
> *– Noam Chomsky*

In this chapter, we covered Object Designer navigation, along with navigation of the individual Designers (Table, Page, Report, and so on). We covered a number of C/AL language areas, including functions and how they may be used, variables of various types (both development and system), basic C/AL syntax, expressions and operators. Some of the essential C/AL functions that we covered included user dialogs, SETRANGE filtering, GET, variations of FIND, BEGIN-END for code structures, plus IF-THEN for basic process flow control. Finally, we got some hands-on experience by adding validation code to a table and creating a new report that included embedded C/AL code and a Request Page. In the next chapter, we will expand our exploration and practice the use of C/AL. We will learn about additional C/AL functions, flow control structures, input/output functions, and filtering.

Review questions

1. All NAV objects can contain C/AL code. True or False?

2. All NAV development work starts from the Object Designer. True or False?

3. What object type has a Wizard to "jump start" development:

   a. Page

   b. XMLport

   c. Table

   d. Report

4. If an object type has a Wizard, you must start with the Wizard before proceeding to the object Designer form. True or False?

5. In what formats can objects be exported? Choose two:

   a. fob

   b. text

   c. .NET

   d. XML

   e. gif

6. Which object export format should be used to transmit updates to client sites?

   a. fob

   b. text

   c. .NET

7. Object numbers and names are so flexible that you can (and should) choose your own approach to numbering and naming. True or False?

8. Whenever possible, the controlling logic for managing data should be resident within the tables. True or False?

9. Which setting defines how parameters are passed to functions, whether a parameter is passed by reference or by value? Choose that setting identity:

    a. DataType

    b. Subtype

    c. Var

    d. Value

10. When an ERROR statement is executed, the user is given the choice to terminate processing, causing rollback, or to ignore the error and continue processing. True or False?

11. Choice of the proper version of the FIND statement can make a significant difference in processing speed. True or False?

12. When a new function is needed, it is always better to create one in your custom code than to call an existing function that exists in standard code. True or False?

13. Properties on objects, controls, fields, etc. are only used for controlling output display attributes. True or False?

14. When you are working in the Object Designer, changing C/AL code, the Object Designer automatically backs up your work every few minutes so you don't have to do so. True or False?

15. C/AL code cannot be inserted into the RDLC generated by the Visual Studio Report Designer. True or False?

16. Which of the following are not Relational Operators? Choose two.

    a. <

    b. MOD

    c. IN

    d. OR

    e. =

17. When a CONFIRM function is used, a user response is required. True or False?

18. Filter Wildcards include which three of the following?

    a. ?

    b. ::

    c. *

    d. ^

    e. @

19. All C/AL Assignment statements include the symbol :=. True or False?

20. C/AL code must be indented properly to work properly. True or False?

7
Intermediate C/AL

Any fool can write code that a computer can understand. Good programmers write code that humans can understand.
— Martin Fowler

Knowing how things work is the basis for appreciation, and is thus a source of civilized delight.
— William Safire

In the previous chapter, we learned enough C/AL to create a basic, operational set of code. In this chapter, we will learn about more C/AL functions and pick up a few good habits along the way. If you are getting started as a professional NAV Developer, the C/AL functions represent a significant portion of the knowledge that you will need on a day-to-day basis. If you are a manager or consultant needing to know what NAV can do for your business or your customer, an understanding of these functions will help you too.

Our goal is to competently manage I/O, create moderately complex program logic structures, and understand data filtering and sorting as handled in NAV and C/AL. Since the functions and features in C/AL are designed for business and financial applications, we can do a surprising amount of ERP work in NAV with a relatively small number of language constructs.

Keep in mind that anything discussed in this chapter relates only indirectly to those portions of NAV objects which contain no C/AL; for example, MenuSuites and Visual Studio Report Designer report layouts. This chapter's goals are to:

- Review some C/AL development basics
- Learn about a variety of useful (and widely used) C/AL functions
- Better understand filtering
- Apply some of what we've learned to expand our WDTU application

Some C/AL development tools

All internal NAV logic development is done in C/AL and all C/AL development is done in C/SIDE. Some user interface design is done by means of the Visual Studio Report Designer. And it is possible to have integrated .NET objects filter, format, or otherwise manipulate data for user presentation.

C/AL Symbol Menu

As an Integrated Development Environment, C/SIDE contains a number of tools designed to make our C/AL development effort easier. One of these is the C/AL Symbol Menu. When we are in one of the Object Designers where C/AL code is supported, the C/AL Symbol Menu can be accessed via either the menu option, **View | C/AL Symbol Menu**, or by pressing *F5*.

The default three-column display has variables and object categories in the left column. If the entry in the left column is an object or a variable of function type, then the center column contains subcategories for the highlighted left-column entry. The right column contains the set of functions that are a part of the highlighted center-column entry. In a few cases (such as BLOB fields), additional information is displayed in the columns further to the right. These columns are accessed through the arrows displayed just below the rightmost display column, as shown in the following screenshot:

The C/AL Symbol Menu is a very useful multipurpose tool for the developer. We can use it as a quick reference to see what C/AL functions are available to us, to see the syntax of those functions, to access the **Help** screen for those functions, and to view what other systems would refer to as the **symbol table**. We can also use the C/AL Symbol Menu as a source of variable names or function structures to paste into our code.

Use of the C/AL Symbol Menu for reference purposes is very helpful when we are starting as a C/AL developer as well as the experienced developer. It is a guide to the inventory of available code tools with some especially handy built-in programming aids.

The first such aid is the display of the highlighted function's syntax shown at the bottom left of the screen. We have also quick and focused access to **Developer and IT Pro Help** to further study the highlighted function and its syntax. When we focus on an entry in the right (third) column and press *F1*, we will be taken directly to the **Help** screen for that function. If the focus is on the left or center column, pressing *F1* may just bring up the general **Developer and IT Pro Help** screen rather than a specific entry (or it may bring up an entry somewhat related to the focus location).

The second use of the C/AL Symbol Menu is as a symbol table. The symbol table for our object is visible in the left column of the **C/AL Symbol Menu** screen. The displayed symbol set (that is, variable set) is context sensitive. It will include all system-defined symbols, all our **Global** symbols, and the **Local** symbols from the function that had focus at the time we had accessed the C/AL Symbol Menu. Though it would be useful, there is no way within the Symbol Menu to see all Local variables in one view. The Local symbols will be at the top of the list, but we have to know the name of the first Global symbol to determine the scope of a particular variable (that is, if an entry appears in the symbol list before the first Global, it is a Local variable, otherwise it's Global).

The third use for the C/AL Symbol Menu is as a code template with a paste function option available. This function will be enabled if we have accessed **C/AL Symbol Menu** from **C/AL Editor**. Paste is initiated by clicking on either the **Apply** button or the **OK** button. In both the cases, the element with focus will be pasted into our code. Clicking on **Apply** will leave the Symbol Menu open and clicking on **OK** will close it (double-clicking on the element has the same effect as clicking on **OK**).

If the element with focus is a simple variable, that variable will be pasted into our code. If the element is a function whose syntax appears at the lower-left side of the screen, the result of the paste action (that is, **Apply**, **OK**, or double-click) depends on whether the **Paste Arguments** checkbox (just below the leftmost column) is checked or not. If the **Paste Arguments** checkbox is not checked, only the function itself will be pasted into our code. If the **Paste Arguments** checkbox is checked (as shown in the preceding screenshot), the complete syntax string, as shown, will be pasted into our code. This can be a very convenient way to create a template to help us enter the correct parameters with the correct syntactical punctuation more quickly.

When we are in the C/AL Symbol Menu, we can focus on a column, click on a letter, and jump to the next field in sequence in the column starting with that letter. This acts as a limited search substitute, sort of an assisted browsing.

Internal documentation

When we are creating or modifying software, we should always document what we have done. It is often difficult for developers to spend much time (that is, money) on documentation because most don't enjoy doing it and the benefits are uncertain. A reasonable goal is to provide enough documentation so that a knowledgeable person following us can understand what we have done as well as the reasons for doing it.

If we choose good variable names, the C/AL code will tend to be self-documenting. If we lay our code out neatly using indentation consistently and localizing logical elements in functions, the flow of our code should be easy to read. We should also include comments describing the functional reason for the change. This will help the next person in this code not only to be able to follow the logic of the code, but to understand the business reasons for that code.

In case of a brand-new function, a simple statement of purpose is often all that is necessary. In case of a modification, it is extremely useful to have comments providing a functional definition of what the change is intended to accomplish, as well as a description of what has been changed. If there is external documentation of the change, including a design specification, the comments in the code should refer back to this external documentation.

In any case, the primary focus should be on the functional reason for the change, not just the technical explanation. Any good programmer can study the code and understand what is changed, but without the documentation describing why the change was made, the task of the next person to maintain or upgrade that code will be made much more difficult.

The following screenshot shows the documentation is for a brand-new report. The comments are in the **Documentation** section, where there are no format rules, except for those we impose. This is a new report, which we created in *Chapter 6, Introduction to C/SIDE and C/AL*. The comment is coded to indicate the organization making the change (in this case **CDS**) and a sequence number for this change. In this case, we are using a two-digit number (**06**) for the change, plus the version number of the change, **00**, hence we start with **CDS.06.00**, followed by the date of the change. Some organizations also would include some identifier for the developer in the **Documentation** section comments.

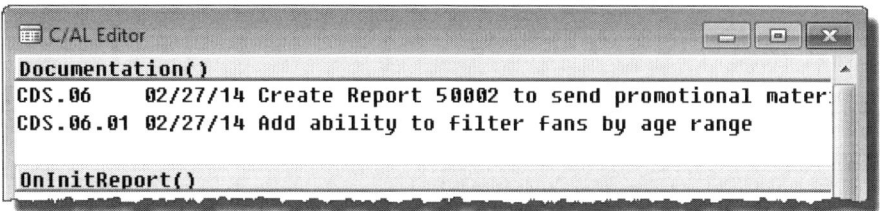

We can make up our own standard format that will identify the source and date of the work, but we should have a standard and use it. When we add a new data element to an existing table, the **Description** property should receive the same modification identifier that we would place in the code comments.

When we make a subsequent change to an object, we should document that change in the Documentation trigger and also in the code, as described earlier.

Inline comments can be done in two ways. The most visible way is to use a //
character sequence (two forward slashes). The text that follows the slashes on that
line will be treated as a comment by the compiler; it will be ignored. If the comment
spans multiple physical lines, each line of the comment must also be preceded by
two forward slashes.

In the following screenshot, we have used // to place comments inline to identify
a change:

Here we have made the modification version number **01**, resulting in a change
version code of **CDS.07.01**. In the following code, modifications are highlighted
by bracketing the additional code with comment lines containing the modification
identifier, and **start** and **end** text indicators. Published standards do not include
the dashed lines shown here, but doing something that makes comments stand
out makes it easier to spot modifications when we are visually scanning code.

The second way to place a comment within the code is to surround the comment
with a matched pair of braces ({ }). Because braces are less visible than the slashes,
we should use // when our comment is relatively short. If we decide to use { },
it's a good idea to insert a // comment at least at the beginning and end of the
material inside the braces, to make the comments more visible. Some experienced
developers recommend using // on all removed code lines, to make the deletions
easier to spot later.

For example, have a look at the following code:

```
{//CDS.07.02 start deletion -------------
//CDS.07.02 Replace validation with a call to an external function
...miscellaneous C/AL validation code
//CDS.07.02 end deletion ------------ }
```

When we delete code (make it inoperative), we should leave the original statements in place but commented out so that the old code is inoperative (an exception to this may apply if a source code control system is in use which tracks all changes). The same concept applies when we change the existing code; leave the original code in place commented out, with the new version being inserted as shown in the following screenshot:

```
    IF WORKDATE > "Due Date" THEN
       EXIT('Unfavorable')
 END ELSE
 //CDS07.12  ---start----------
 //Revise date exclusion to match accounting period structure
 //  IF "Closed at Date" > "Due Date" THEN
   IF "Closed at Date" >= "Due Date" THEN
      EXIT('Attention');
 //CDS07.12  --- end ----------
 EXIT('');
```

When we make such changes, we don't want to forget to also update the object version numbers located in the **Version List** field on the **Object Designer** screen.

From our previous experience, we know that the format of the internal documentation is not what's critical. What is critical is that the documentation exists, is consistent in format and accurately describes the changes that have occurred. The internal documentation should be a complement to external documentation which defines the original functional requirements, validation specifications, and recommended operating procedures.

Validation functions

C/AL includes a number of utility functions designed to facilitate data validation or initialization. Some of these functions are:

- TESTFIELD
- FIELDERROR
- INIT
- VALIDATE

TESTFIELD

The TESTFIELD function is widely used in standard NAV code. With TESTFIELD, we can test a variable value and issue an error message in a single statement, if the test fails. The syntax is as follows:

```
Record.TESTFIELD (Field, [Value])
```

If Value is specified and the field does not contain that value, the process terminates with an error condition and the associated error message is issued.

If no Value is specified, the condition evaluated is to check for field contents of zero or blank. If the field is zero or blank, this is an error.

The advantage of TESTFIELD is ease of use and consistency in code and in the message displayed. The disadvantage is the error message is not as informative as we might provide as a careful developer.

The following screenshot of the TESTFIELD usage is from **Table 18 - Customer**. This code checks to make sure the Sales Order field, Status, is equal to the option value Open before allowing the value of the Sell-to Customer No. field to be entered.

```
TESTFIELD(State,Status::Open);
```

A screenshot of the error message, generated when attempting to change the value of the Sell-to Customer No. field when Status is not equal to the option value Open, is as follows:

Status must be equal to 'Open' in Sales Header: Document Type=Order, No.=104009. Current value is 'Released... 1 \ 2

FIELDERROR

Another function very similar to the TESTFIELD function is FIELDERROR. But where TESTFIELD performs a test and terminates with either an error or an OK result, FIELDERROR presumes that the test was already performed and the field failed the test. FIELDERROR is designed to display an error message and then terminate the process. This approach is followed in much of the NAV logic, especially in the Posting Codeunits (for example, Codeunits 12, 80, 90). The syntax is as follows:

```
TableName.FIELDERROR(FieldName[,OptionalMsgText]);
```

If we include our own message text by defining a Text Constant in the **C/AL Globals | Text Constants** tab (so the code can be multilingual), we will have:

```
Text001    must be greater than Start Time
```

The following code references the Text Constant:

```
IF Rec."End Time" <= "Start Time" THEN
   Rec.FIELDERROR("End Time",Text001);
```

The result is an error message from FIELDERROR like that shown in the following screenshot:

> ❌ End Time must be greater than Start Time in Radio Show No.='RS00006'. (Select Refresh to discard errors)

The following screenshot shows an error message that simply identifies the data field. It does not reference a message text, but only displays the primary record key information.

> ❌ End Time must not be 7:10:00 AM in Playlist Line Playlist No.='1112',Line No.='10000'.

Because the error message begins with the name of the field, we need to be careful that our Text Constant is structured to make the resulting error message easy to read. The **Refresh** action referred to by the instructions means the *F5* key.

If we don't include our own message text, the default message comes in two flavors. The first instance is the case where the referenced field is not empty, where the error message presumes that the error is due to a wrong value, as shown in the preceding screenshot. In the case where the referenced data field is empty, the error message logic presumes the field should not be empty, as shown in the following screenshot:

> ❌ You must specify End Time in Playlist Line Playlist No.='1112',Line No.='10000'.

INIT

The INIT function initializes a record in preparation for its use, typically in the course of building a new entry for a table. The syntax is:

```
Record.INIT;
```

All the data fields in the record are initialized as follows:

- The fields which have an InitValue property defined are initialized to the specified value
- The fields which do not have a defined InitValue are initialized to the default value for their data type
- The primary key fields are not automatically initialized. If they contain values, those will remain. If new values are desired, they must be assigned in code.

VALIDATE

The syntax of the VALIDATE function is as follows:

```
Record.VALIDATE ( Field [, Value] )
```

VALIDATE will fire the OnValidate trigger of Record.Field. If we have specified the Value parameter, it is assigned to the field and the field validations are invoked.

If we don't specify Value, the field validations are invoked using the field value that already exists in the field. This function allows us to easily centralize our code design around the table, one of NAV's strengths.

For example, if we were to code changing Item."Base Unit of Measure" to another unit of measure, the code should make sure the change is valid. We should get an error if the new unit of measure has any quantity other than 1 (because this is a requirement of that field). Making the unit of measure change with a simple assignment statement would not catch a quantity error.

Following are two forms of using VALIDATE that give the same end result:

- ```
  Item.VALIDATE("Base Unit of Measure",'Box');
  ```
- ```
  Item."Base Unit of Measure" := 'Box';
  Item.VALIDATE("Base Unit of Measure");
  ```

Date and Time functions

NAV provides a considerable number of Date and Time functions. We will cover a number of these functions that are more commonly used, especially in the context of accounting date sensitive activity. These are as follows:

- TODAY, TIME, and CURRENTDATETIME
- WORKDATE
- DATE2DMY, DATE2DWY, DMY2DATE, DWY2DATE and CALCDATE

TODAY, TIME, and CURRENTDATETIME functions

TODAY retrieves the current system date as set in the operating system. TIME retrieves the current system time as set in the operating system. CURRENTDATETIME retrieves the current date and time in the DATETIME format, which is stored in UTC international time (formerly referenced as GMT or Greenwich Mean Time) and then displayed in local time. If we are using the Windows client, these use the time on the NAV Client. If your system operates in multiple time zones at one time, you should enter a search value of time zone in **Microsoft Dynamics NAV Help** to review the several references on how to deal with multiple time zones.

The syntax for each of these follows:

```
DateField := TODAY;
TimeField := TIME;
DateTimeField := CURRENTDATETIME;
```

These are often used for date- and time-stamping transactions or for entering the default values in fields of the appropriate data type. For data entry purposes, the current system date can be entered by simply entering a letter T or the word TODAY in the date entry field (this is not a case-sensitive entry). NAV will automatically convert that entry to the current system date.

The undefined date in NAV 2013 is represented by the earliest valid DATETIME in SQL Server, which is January 1, 1753 00:00:00:000. The undefined date in NAV is represented as 0D (zero D, as in Days), with subsequent dates handled through December 31, 9999. A date outside this range will result in a runtime error.

The Microsoft Dynamics NAV undefined time (0T) is represented by the same value as an undefined date (0D). If a two-digit year is entered or stored and has a value between 30 and 99, it is assumed to be in the 1900s. If the two-digit date is between 00 and 29, then it is treated as a 2000s date.

WORKDATE function

Many standard NAV routines default dates to **Work Date** rather than to the system date. When a user logs in to the system, the Work Date is initially set equal to the system date. But, at any time, the operator can set the Work Date to any date by accessing the Application Menu, clicking on **Set Work Date…**, and then entering the new Work Date.

The user can also click on the Work Date displayed in the status bar at the bottom of the RTC. The following screenshot shows the **Set Work Date** screen:

For data entry purposes, the current Work Date can be entered by the operator by simply entering a letter w, W, or the word WORKDATE in the date entry field. NAV will automatically convert that entry to the current Work Date.

The syntax for getting the current `WorkDate` value from within C/AL code is as follows:

```
DateField := WORKDATE;
```

The syntax for setting the `WorkDate` to a new date from within C/AL code is as follows:

```
WORKDATE(newdate);
```

DATE2DMY function

`DATE2DMY` allows us to extract the sections of a date (Day of the month, Month, and Year) from a Date field. The syntax is as follows:

```
IntegerVariable := DATE2DMY ( DateField, ExtractionChoice )
```

The `IntegerVariable` and `DateField` fields are just what their names imply. The `ExtractionChoice` parameter allows us to choose which value (Day, Month, or Year) will be assigned to the `IntegerVariable`. The following table provides the `DATE2DMY` extraction choices:

DATE2DMY extraction choice	Integer value result
1	Two-digit day (1 to 31)
2	Two-digit month (1 to 12)
3	Four-digit year

DATE2DWY function

`DATE2DWY` allows us to extract the sections of a date (Day of the week, Week of the year, and Year) from a Date field in exactly the same fashion as `DATE2DMY`. The `ExtractionChoice` parameter allows us to choose which value (Day, Week, or Year) will be assigned to the `IntegerVariable`, as shown in the following table:

DATE2DWY extraction choice	Integer value result
1	Two-digit day (1 to 7 for Monday to Sunday)
2	Two-digit week (1 to 53)
3	Four-digit year

DMY2DATE and DWY2DATE functions

DMY2DATE allows us to create a date from integer values (or defaults) representing the day of the month, month of the year, and the four-digit year. If an optional parameter (MonthValue or YearValue) is not specified, the corresponding value from the system date is used. The syntax is as follows:

```
DateVariable := DMY2DATE ( DayValue [, MonthValue] [, YearValue] )
```

The only way to have the function use Work Date values for Month and Year is to extract those values and then use them explicitly. An example is as follows:

```
DateVariable := DMY2DATE(22,DATE2MDY(WORKDATE,2),DATE2MDY(WORKDATE,3))
```

 This example also illustrates how expressions can be built up of nested expressions and functions. We have WORKDATE within DATE2MDY within DMY2DATE.

DWY2DATE operates similarly to DMY2DATE; allowing us to create a date from integer values representing the day of the week (from 1 to 7 representing Monday to Sunday), week of the year (from 1 to 53) followed by the four-digit year. The syntax is as follows:

```
DateVariable := DWY2DATE ( DayValue [, WeekValue] [, YearValue] )
```

An interesting result can occur for week 53 because it can span two years. By default, such a week is assigned to the year in which it has four or more days. In that case the year of the result will vary depending on the day of the week in the parameters (in other words the year of the result may be one year greater than the year specified in the parameters).

CALCDATE function

CALCDATE allows us to calculate a date value assigned to a Date data type variable. The calculation is based on a Date Expression applied to a Base Date (Reference Date). If we don't specify a value for BaseDateValue, the current system date is used as the default date. We can specify the BaseDateValue either in the form of a variable of data type Date or as a Date constant.

The syntax for CALCDATE is as follows:

```
DateVariable := CALCDATE ( DateExpression [, BaseDateValue])
```

There are a number of ways in which we can build a DateExpression. The rules for the CALCDATE function DateExpression are similar to the rules for **DateFormula** described in *Chapter 3, Data Types and Fields*.

If there is a CW, CM, CP, CQ, or CY (Current Week, Current Month, Current Period, Current Quarter, Current Year) parameter in an expression, then they will be evaluated based on the BaseDateValue. If we have more than one of these in our expression, the results are unpredictable. Any such expression should be thoroughly tested before releasing to users.

If our Date Expression is stored in a DateFormula variable (or a Text or Code variable with the **DateFormula** property set to **Yes**), the Date Expression will be language independent. Also, if we create our own Date Expression in the form of a string constant within our inline C/AL code, surrounding the constant with < > delimiters as part of the string, that will make the constant language independent. Otherwise, the Date Expression constant will be language dependent.

Regardless of how we have constructed our DateExpression, it is important to test it carefully and thoroughly before moving on. Incorrect syntax will result in a runtime error. One easy way to test is by using a Report whose sole task is to evaluate our expression and display the result. If we want to try different Base Dates, we can use the Request Page, accept the Base Date as input, then calculate and display the DateVariable in the OnValidate trigger.

Some sample CALCDATE expression evaluations are as follows:

- ('<CM>',031014D) will yield 03/31/2014, that is, the last day of the Current Month for the date 3/10/2014.

- ('<-WD2>',031314D) will yield 03/11/2014, that is, the Weekday 2 (the prior Tuesday) before the date 3/13/2014.

- ('<CM+1D>',BaseDate) where BaseDate equals 03/10/14, will yield 04/01/2014, that is, the last day of the month of the Base Date plus one day (the first day of the month following the Base Date).

Data conversion and formatting functions

Some data type conversions are handled in the normal process flow by NAV without any particular attention on part of the Developer; for example, Code to Text, Char to Text, and so on. Some data type conversions can only be handled through C/AL functions. Formatting is included because it can also include a data type conversion. Rounding does not perform a data type conversion but does result in a change in format (the number of decimal places). These C/AL functions are:

- ROUND

- FORMAT

- EVALUATE

ROUND

The ROUND function allows us to control the rounding precision for a decimal expression. The syntax for the ROUND function is as follows:

```
DecimalResult := ROUND (Number [, Precision] [, Direction] )
```

Here Number is what is being rounded, Precision spells out the number of digits of decimal precision, and Direction indicates whether to round up, round down, or round to the nearest number. The following table shows some examples of Precision values:

Precision value	Rounding effect
100	To a multiple of 100
1	To an integer format
.01	To two decimal places (the US default)
0.01	Same as .01
.0001	To four decimal places

If no Precision value is specified, the Rounding default is controlled by a value set in **General Ledger Setup** in the **Appln.Rounding Precision** field in the **Application** tab. If no value is specified, Rounding will default to two decimal places. If the precision value is (for example) .04 rather than .01, the Rounding will be done to multiples of 4 at the number of decimal places specified.

The options available for the Direction value are shown in the following table:

Direction value (a text value)	Rounding effect
'='	Round to the nearest (mathematically correct and the default)
'>'	Round up
'<'	Round down

The following statement would result in a DecimalValue containing 1234.567:

```
DecimalValue := ROUND (1234.56789,0.001,'<')
```

The following statements would each result in a DecimalValue containing 1234.568:

```
DecimalValue := ROUND (1234.56789,0.001,'=')
DecimalValue := ROUND (1234.56789,0.001,'>')
```

FORMAT function

The FORMAT function provides for the conversion of an expression of any data type (integer, decimal, date, option, time, Boolean) into a formatted string. The syntax is as follows:

```
StringField := FORMAT( ExpressionToFormat [, OutputLength]
    [, FormatString or FormatNumber])
```

The formatted output of the ExpressionToFormat will be assigned to the output StringField. The optional parameters control the conversion according to a complex set of rules. These rules can be found in the **Developer and IT Pro Help** file for the FORMAT function and the FORMAT property. Whenever possible, we should always apply FORMAT in its simpler form. The best way to determine the likely results of a FORMAT expression is to test it through a range of the values to be formatted. We should make sure that we include the extremes of the range of possible values in our testing.

The optional OutputLength parameter can be zero (which is the default), a positive integer, or a negative integer. The typical OutputLength value is either zero, in which case, the defined format is fully applied, or it is a figure designed to control the maximum character length and padding of the formatted string result.

The last optional parameter has two mutually exclusive sets of choices. One set, represented by an integer FormatNumber, allows the choice of a particular predefined (standard) format, of which there are four to nine choices depending on the ExpressionToFormat data type. The format parameter of the number 9 is used for XMLport data exporting. Use of the optional number 9 parameter will convert C/SIDE format data types into XML standard data types. The other set of choices allows us to build our own format expression.

The **Developer and IT Pro Help** information for the FORMAT property provides a relatively complete description of the available tools from which we can build our own format expression. The FORMAT property Help also provides a complete list of the predefined format choices as well as a good list of example formats and formatted data results.

> A FORMAT function which cannot be executed will result in a runtime error that will terminate execution of the process. Thus, to avoid production crashes, we will want to place a high importance on thoroughly testing any code where FORMAT is used.

EVALUATE function

The EVALUATE function is essentially the reverse of the FORMAT function, allowing conversion of a string value into the defined data type. The syntax of the EVALUATE function is as follows:

```
[ BooleanVariable := ] EVALUATE ( ResultVariable,
                         StringToBeConverted [, 9]
```

The handling of a runtime error can be done by specifying BooleanVariable or including EVALUATE in an expression to deal with an error (such as an IF statement). The ResultVariable data type will determine what data conversion the EVALUATE function will attempt. The format of the data in StringToBeConverted must be compatible with the data type of ResultVariable otherwise a runtime error will occur.

The optional parameter, number 9, is used for XMLport data exporting only. Use of the optional number 9 parameter will convert C/SIDE format data types into XML standard data types. This deals with the fact that several equivalent C/SIDE-XML data types are represented differently at the base system level (that is, "under the covers"). The C/SIDE data types include decimal, Boolean, datetime, date, time, integer and duration.

FlowField SumIndexField functions

In *Chapter 3, Data Types and Fields*, we discussed SumIndexFields and FlowFields in the context of table, field, and key definition. To recap briefly, SumIndexFields are defined in the screen where table keys are defined. They allow very rapid calculation of values in filtered data. In most ERP and accounting software systems, the calculation of group totals, periodic totals and such, require reading all of the data to be totaled.

SIFT allows a NAV system to respond almost instantly with totals in any area where the SumIndexField was defined. In fact, use of SIFT totals combined with NAV's retention of detailed data supports totally flexible ad hoc queries of the form "What were our sales for red widgets between November, 15 and December, 24?" And the answer is returned almost instantly! SumIndexFields are the basis of FlowFields which have a **Method** of Sum or Average; such a FlowField must refer to a data element that is defined as a SumIndexField.

When we access a record that has a SumIndexField defined, there is no visible evidence of the data sum that SumIndexField represents. When we access a record that contains FlowFields, the FlowFields are empty virtual data elements until they are calculated. When a FlowField is displayed in a page or report, it is automatically calculated by NAV; the developer doesn't need to do so. But in any other scenario, the developer is responsible for calculating FlowFields (using the CALCFIELDS function).

FlowFields are one of the key areas where NAV systems are subject to significant processing bottlenecks. Even with the improved NAV 2013 design, it is still critical that the Table Keys used for SumIndexField definition are designed with efficient processing in mind. Sometimes, as part of a performance tuning effort, it's necessary to revise or add new keys to improve FlowField performance.

 Even though we can manage indexes in SQL Server independently of the NAV key definitions, having two different definitions of keys for a single table will make our system more difficult to support in the long run because the SQL Server resident changes aren't always readily visible to the NAV developer.

In addition to being careful about the SIFT-key structure design, it is also important not to define any SumIndexFields that are not necessary. Each additional SumIndexField adds additional processing requirements and thus adds to the processing load of the system. Including SumIndexFields in a List page is almost always a bad idea, because each instance must be calculated as it is displayed.

The functions covered here include CALCFIELDS, SETAUTOCALCFIELDS, and CALCSUMS.

CALCFIELDS function

The syntax for CALCFIELDS is as follows:

```
[BooleanField := ] Record.CALCFIELDS ( FlowField1 [, FlowField2] ,…)
```

Executing the CALCFIELDS function will cause all the specified FlowFields to be calculated. Specification of the BooleanField allows us to handle any runtime error that may occur. Any runtime errors for CALCFIELDS usually result from a coding error or a change in a table key structure.

The FlowField calculation takes into account the filters (including FlowFilters) that are currently applied to the Record. After the CALCFIELDS execution, the included FlowFields can be used similarly to any other data fields. The CALCFIELDS must be executed for each cycle through the subject table.

Whenever the contents of a BLOB field are to be used, CALCFIELDS is used to load the contents of the BLOB field from the database into memory.

When the following conditions are true, CALCFIELDS uses SIFT data.

- The NAV key contains the fields used in the filters defined for the FlowField
- The SumIndexFields on the operative key contain the fields provided as parameters for calculation
- The **MaintainSIFTIndex** property on the key is set to **Yes** (this is the default setting)

If all these conditions are not true and a CALCFIELDS is invoked, we will not get a runtime error as in previous NAV version, but SQL Server will calculate the requested total(s) the hard way, by reading all the necessary records. This could be very slow and inefficient and should not be used for frequently processed routines or large data sets.

SETAUTOCALCFIELDS function

The syntax for SETAUTOCALCFIELDS is:

```
[BooleanField := ] Record.SETAUTOCALCFIELDS
         ( FlowField1 [, FlowField2] [, FlowField3]...)
```

When SETAUTOCALCFIELDS is inserted in code in front of record retrieval, the specified FlowFields are automatically calculated as the record is read. This is more efficient than performing a CALCFIELDS on the FlowFields after the record has been read.

If we want to end the automatic FlowField calculation on a record, call the function without any parameters:

```
[BooleanField := ] Record.SETAUTOCALCFIELDS()
```

Automatic FlowField calculation equivalent to SETAUTOCALCFIELDS is automatically set on for the system record variables Rec and xRec.

CALCSUMS function

The CALCSUMS function is conceptually similar to CALCFIELDS for the calculation of Sums only. But CALCFIELDS operates on FlowFields and CALCSUMS operates directly on the record where the SumIndexFields are defined for the keys. This difference means that we must specify the proper key plus any filters to apply when using CALCSUMS (the applicable key and filters to apply are already defined in the properties for FlowFields).

The syntax for CALCSUMS is as follows:

```
[ BooleanField := ] Record.CALCSUMS ( SumIndexField1
[,SumIndexField2] ,...)
```

Prior to this statement, we should specify a key that has the SumIndexFields defined. Before executing the CALCSUMS function, we also need to specify any filters that we want to apply to the Record from which the sums are to be calculated. The SumIndexField calculations take into account the filters that are currently applied to the Record.

Executing the CALCSUMS function will cause the specified SumIndexField totals to be calculated. Specification of the BooleanField allows us to handle any runtime error that may occur. Runtime errors for CALCSUMS usually result from a coding error or a change in a table key structure.

Before the execution of CALCSUMS, SumIndexFields contain only the data from the individual record that was read. After the CALCSUMS execution, the included SumIndexFields contain the totals that were calculated by the CALCSUMS function (these totals are only in memory, not on the disk). These totals can then be used the same as data in any field, but if we want to access the individual record's original data for that field, we must either save a copy of the record before executing the CALCSUMS or we must re-read the record. The CALCSUMS must be executed for each read cycle through the subject table.

CALCFIELDS and CALCSUMS comparison

In the Sales Header record, there are FlowFields defined for Amount and "Amount Including VAT". These FlowFields are all based on Sums of entries in the Sales Line table. The CalcFormula for Amount is Sum("Sales Line".Amount WHERE (Document Type=FIELD(Document Type),Document No.=FIELD(No.))). Remember, Amount must be a SumIndexField assigned to a Sales Line key that contains the fields on which we will filter (in this case Document Type and Document No.). To calculate a TotalOrderAmount value while referencing the Sales Header table, the code can be as simple as:

```
"Sales Header".CALCFIELDS (Amount);

TotalOrderAmount := "Sales Header".Amount;
```

To calculate the same value from code directly referencing the Sales Line table, the required code is similar to the following (assuming a Sales Header record has already been read):

```
"Sales Line".SETRANGE("Document Type","Sales Header"."Document Type");
"Sales Line".SETRANGE("Document No.","Sales Header"."No.");
"Sales Line".CALCSUMS(Amount);
TotalOrderAmount := "Sales Line".Amount;
```

Flow control

Process flow control functions are the functions that execute the decision making and resultant logic branches in executable code. IF-THEN-ELSE, discussed in *Chapter 6, Introduction to C/SIDE and C/AL*, is also a member of this class of functions. Here we will discuss the following:

- REPEAT-UNTIL

- WHILE-DO

- FOR-TO and FOR-DOWNTO

- CASE-ELSE

- WITH-DO

- QUIT, BREAK, EXIT, and SKIP

REPEAT-UNTIL

REPEAT-UNTIL allows us to create a repetitive code loop which *repeats* a block of code *until* a specific conditional expression evaluates to TRUE. In that sense, REPEAT-UNTIL defines a block of code, operating somewhat like the BEGIN-END compound statement structure which we covered in *Chapter 6, Introduction to C/SIDE and C/AL*. REPEAT tells the system to keep reprocessing the block of code, while the UNTIL serves as the exit doorman, checking if the conditions for ending the processing are true. Because the exit condition is not evaluated until the end of the loop, a REPEAT-UNTIL structure will always process at least once through the contained code.

REPEAT-UNTIL is very important in NAV because it is often part of the data input cycle with the FIND-NEXT structure, which will be covered shortly.

Here is an example of the REPEAT-UNTIL structure to process data in the 10-element array CustSales:

```
LoopCount := 0;
REPEAT
 LoopCount := LoopCount + 1;
 TotCustSales := TotCustSales + CustSales[LoopCount];
UNTIL LoopCount = 10;
```

WHILE-DO

A WHILE-DO control structure allows us to create a repetitive code loop which will *do* (execute) a block of code *while* a specific conditional expression evaluates to TRUE. WHILE-DO is different from REPEAT-UNTIL, because it may need a BEGIN-END structure to define the block of code to be executed repetitively and it has different timing for the evaluation of the exit condition.

The syntax of the WHILE-DO control structure is as follows:

```
WHILE <Condition> DO <Statement>
```

The Condition can be any Boolean expression which evaluates to TRUE or FALSE. The Statement can be simple or the most complex compound BEGIN-END statement. Most WHILE-DO loops will be based on a BEGIN-END block of code. The Condition will be evaluated at the beginning of the loop. When it evaluates to FALSE, the loop will terminate. Thus a WHILE-DO loop can exit without processing.

A WHILE-DO structure to process data in the 10-element array CustSales follows:

```
LoopCount := 0;
WHILE LoopCount < 10
DO BEGIN
 LoopCount := LoopCount + 1;
 TotCustSales := TotCustSales + CustSales[LoopCount];
END;
```

In NAV, REPEAT-UNTIL is much more frequently used than WHILE-DO.

FOR-TO or FOR-DOWNTO

The syntax for a FOR-TO control statement is:

```
FOR <Control Variable> := <Start Number> TO <End Number> DO
<Statement>
```

The syntax for a FOR-DOWNTO control statement is:

```
FOR <Control Variable> := <Start Number> DOWNTO <End Number> DO
<Statement>
```

A FOR control structure is used when we wish to execute a block of code a specific number of times.

The `Control Variable` is an Integer variable. `Start Number` is the beginning count for the `FOR` loop and `End Number` is the final count for the loop. If we wrote the statement: `FOR LoopCount := 5 TO 7 DO [block of code]` then `[block of code]` would be executed three times.

`FOR-TO` increments the `Control Variable`. `FOR-DOWNTO` decrements the `Control Variable`.

We must be careful not to manipulate the `Control Variable` in the middle of our loop. Doing so will likely yield unpredictable results.

CASE-ELSE statement

The `CASE-ELSE` statement is a conditional expression very similar to `IF-THEN-ELSE` except that it allows for more than two choices of outcomes for the evaluation of the controlling expression. The syntax of the `CASE-ELSE` statement is as follows:

```
CASE <ExpressionToBeEvaluated> OF
  <Value Set 1> : <Action Statement 1>;
  <Value Set 2> : <Action Statement 2>;
  <Value Set 3> : <Action Statement 3>;
  . . .
  . . .
  <Value Set n> : <Action Statement n>;
  [ELSE <Action Statement n + 1>;
END;
```

The `ExpressionToBeEvaluated` must not be a record. The data type of the `Value Set` must be able to be automatically converted to the data type of the `ExpressionToBeEvaluated`. Each `Value Set` must be an expression, a set of values or a range of values. The following example illustrates a typical instance of a `CASE-ELSE` statement:

```
CASE Customer."Salesperson Code" OF
  '2','5','9': Customer."Territory Code" := 'EAST';
  '16'..'20': Customer."Territory Code" := 'WEST';
  '3': Customer."Territory Code" := 'NORTH';
  '27'..'38': Customer."Territory Code" := 'SOUTH';
  ELSE Customer."Territory Code" := 'FOREIGN';
END;
```

In the preceding example, we see several alternatives for the Value Set. The first line (EAST) Value Set contains a list of values. If Salesperson Code is equal to '2', '5', or '9', the value EAST will be assigned to Customer."Territory Code". The second line (WEST) Value Set is a range, any value from '16' through '20'. The third line (NORTH) Value Set is just a single value ('3'). If we look through the standard NAV code, we will see that a single value is the most frequently used CASE structure in NAV. In the fourth line of our example (SOUTH), the Value Set is again a range ('27'..'38'). If nothing in any Value Set matches ExpressionToBeEvaluated, the ELSE clause will be executed.

An example of an IF-THEN-ELSE statement equivalent to the preceding CASE-ELSE statement is as follows:

```
IF Customer."Salesperson Code" IN ['2','5','9'] THEN
  Customer."Territory Code" := 'EAST'
    ELSE IF Customer."Salesperson Code" IN ['16'..'20'] THEN
      Customer."Territory Code" := 'WEST'
    ELSE IF Customer."Salesperson Code" = '3' THEN
      Customer."Territory Code" := 'NORTH'
    ELSE IF Customer."Salesperson Code" IN ['27'..'38'] THEN
      Customer."Territory Code" := 'SOUTH'
    ELSE Customer."Territory Code" := 'FOREIGN';
```

The following is slightly less intuitive example of the CASE-ELSE statement. In this instance, ExpressionToBeEvaluated is a simple TRUE and the Value Set statements are all conditional expressions. The first line containing a Value Set expression that evaluates to TRUE will be the line whose Action Statement is executed. The rules of execution and flow in this instance are the same as the previous example.

```
CASE TRUE OF Salesline.Quantity < 0:
 BEGIN
  CLEAR(Salesline."Line Discount %");
  CredTot := CredTot - Salesline.Quantity;
 END;
  Salesline.Quantity > QtyBreak[1]:
   Salesline."Line Discount %" := DiscLevel[1];
  Salesline.Quantity > QtyBreak[2]:
   Salesline."Line Discount %" := DiscLevel[2];
  Salesline.Quantity > QtyBreak[3]:
   Salesline."Line Discount %" := DiscLevel[3];
  Salesline.Quantity > QtyBreak[4]:
   Salesline."Line Discount %" := DiscLevel[4];
 ELSE
  CLEAR(Salesline."Line Discount %");
 END;
```

WITH-DO statement

When we are writing code referring to fields within a record, the most specific syntax for field references is the fully qualified reference [`RecordName.FieldName`]. When referring to the **City** field in the **Customer** record, use the reference `Customer.City`.

In many C/AL instances, the record name qualifier is implicit because the compiler assumes a default record qualifier based on code context. This happens automatically for variables within a page bounded to a table. The bound table becomes the implicit record qualifier for fields referenced in the Page object. In a Table object, the table is the implicit record qualifier for fields referenced in the C/AL in that object. In Report and XMLport objects, the DataItem record is the implicit record qualifier for the fields referenced within the triggers of that DataItem such as `OnAfterGetRecord` and `OnAfterImportRecord`.

In all other C/AL code, the only way to have an implicit record qualifier is to use the `WITH-DO` statement. `WITH-DO` is widely used in the base product in Codeunits and processing Reports. The `WITH-DO` syntax is:

```
WITH <RecordQualifier> DO <Statement>
```

Typically, the `DO` portion of this statement will be followed by a `BEGIN-END` code block, allowing for a compound statement. The scope of the `WITH-DO` statement is terminated by the end of the `DO` statement.

When we execute a `WITH-DO` statement, `RecordQualifier` becomes the implicit record qualifier used by the compiler until the end of that statement or until that qualifier is overridden by a nested `WITH-DO` statement. A fully qualified syntax would require the following form:

```
Customer.Address := '189 Maple Avenue';
Customer.City := 'Chicago';
```

The `WITH-DO` syntax takes advantage of the implicit record qualification making the code easier to write, and hopefully easier to read, for example:

```
WITH Customer DO
BEGIN
 Address := '189 Maple Avenue';
 City := 'Chicago';
END;
```

Nested WITH-DO statements are legal code, but are not used in standard NAV. They are also not recommended because they can easily confuse the developer, resulting in bugs. The same comments apply to nesting a WITH-DO statement within a function where there is an automatic implicit record qualifier, such as in a table, Report, or XMLport.

Of course, wherever the references to record variables other than the implicit one occur within the scope of a WITH-DO, we must include the specific qualifiers. This is particularly important when there are variables with the same name (for example, City) in multiple tables that might be referenced in the same set of C/AL logic.

Some developers maintain that it is always better to use fully qualified variable names to reduce the possibility of inadvertent reference errors. This approach also eliminates any possible misinterpretation of variable references by the following maintenance developer.

QUIT, BREAK, EXIT, and SKIP functions

This group of C/AL functions also controls the process flow. Each acts to interrupt the flow in different places and with different results. To get a full appreciation for how these functions are used, we need to review them in place in code in NAV 2013.

QUIT function

The QUIT function is the ultimate processing interrupt for Report or XMLport objects. When a QUIT function is executed, processing immediately terminates even for the OnPostObject triggers. No database changes are committed. QUIT is often used in reports to terminate processing when the report logic determines that no useful output will be generated by further processing.

The syntax of the QUIT function is:

```
CurrReport.QUIT;
CurrXMLport.QUIT;
```

BREAK function

The BREAK function terminates the DataItem in which it occurs. BREAK can only be used in DataItem triggers in Reports and XMLports. BREAK can be used to terminate the sequence of processing one DataItem segment of a report while allowing subsequent DataItem processing to continue.

The BREAK syntax is one of the following:

```
CurrReport.BREAK;
CurrXMLport.BREAK;
```

EXIT function

EXIT is used to end the processing within a C/AL trigger. EXIT works the same whether it is executed within a loop or not. EXIT can be used to end the processing of the trigger or to pass a return value from a local function. A return value cannot be used for system defined triggers or local functions that don't have a return value defined. If EXIT is used without a return value, a default return value of zero is returned. The syntax for EXIT is:

```
EXIT([<ReturnValue>])
```

SKIP function

When executed, the SKIP function will skip the remainder of the processing in the current record cycle of the current trigger. Unlike BREAK, it does not terminate the DataItem processing completely. It can be used only in the OnAfterGetRecord trigger of a Report or XMLport object. In reports, when the results of processing in the OnAfterGetRecord trigger are determined not to be useful for output, the SKIP function is used to terminate that single iteration of the trigger without interfering with any subsequent processing.

The SKIP syntax is one of the following:

```
CurrReport.SKIP;
CurrXMLport.SKIP;
```

Input and Output functions

In the previous chapter, we learned about the basics of the FIND function. We learned about FIND('-') to read from the beginning of a selected set of records, FINDSET to read a selected set of records and FIND('+') to begin reading at the far end of the selected set of records. Now we will review additional functions that are generally used with FIND functions in typical production code. While designing the code by using the MODIFY and DELETE record functions, we need to consider the possible interactions with other users on the system. There might be someone else modifying and deleting records in the same table which our application is updating.

We may want to utilize the LOCKTABLE function to gain total control of the data briefly, while updating the data. We can find more information on LOCKTABLE in either the **Developer and IT Pro Help** or the MSDN online **C/SIDE Reference Guide** help. The SQL Server database supports Record Level Locking. There are a number of factors that we should consider when coding data locking in our processes. It is worthwhile reading all of the MSDN **C/SIDE Reference Guide** material found by a search on LOCKTABLE, particularly **Locking in Microsoft SQL Server** (http://msdn. microsoft.com/en-us/library/dd301365.aspx).

NEXT function with FIND or FINDSET

The syntax defined for the NEXT function is:

```
IntegerValue := Record.NEXT ( ReadStepSize )
```

The full assignment statement format is rarely used to set an IntegerValue. In addition, there is no documentation for the usage of a non-zero IntegerValue. When IntegerValue goes to zero, it means that a NEXT record was not found.

If the ReadStepSize value is negative, the table will be read in reverse; if ReadStepSize is positive (the default), the table will be read forward. The size of the value in ReadStepSize controls which records should be read. For example, if ReadStepSize is 2 or -2, every second record will be read. If ReadStepSize is 10 or -10, then every tenth record will be read. The default value is 1, in which case every record will be read and the read direction will be forward.

In a typical data read loop, the first read is a FIND or FINDSET function followed by a REPEAT-UNTIL loop. The exit condition is the expression UNTIL Record.NEXT = 0;. The C/AL for FINDSET and FIND('-') are structured alike.

The full C/AL syntax for this typical loop looks like the following:

```
IF CustRec.FIND('-') THEN
REPEAT
 Block of C/AL logic
UNTIL CustRec.NEXT = 0;
```

INSERT function

The purpose of the INSERT function is to add new records to a table. The syntax for the INSERT function is as follows:

```
[BooleanValue :=] Record.INSERT ( [ TriggerControlBoolean ] )
```

If `BooleanValue` is not used and the `INSERT` function fails (for example, if the insertion would result in a duplicate Primary Key), the process will terminate with an error. Generally, we should handle a detected error in code by using the `BooleanValue` and supplying our own error handling logic rather than allowing a default termination.

The `TriggerControlBoolean` value controls whether or not the table's `OnInsert` trigger fires when the `INSERT` occurs. The default value is `FALSE`. If we let the default `FALSE` control, we run the risk of not performing error checking that the table's designer assumed would be run when a new record was added.

When we are reading a table and also need to insert records into that table, to be safe the `INSERT` action should be done to a separate instance of the table, using either a global or local variable. If we insert into the table we are reading, we run the risk of reading the new records as part of our processing (likely a very confusing action). We also run the risk of changing the sequence of our processing unexpectedly due to the introduction of new records into our data set. While the database access methods are continually improved by Microsoft and this warning may be overcautious, it is better to be safe than sorry.

MODIFY function

The purpose of the `MODIFY` function is to modify (that is, update) the existing data records. The syntax for `MODIFY` is:

```
[BooleanValue :=] Record.MODIFY ( [ TriggerControlBoolean ] )
```

If `BooleanValue` is not used and `MODIFY` fails (for example, if another process changes the record after it was read by this process), the process will terminate with an error statement. The code should either handle a detected error or gracefully terminate the process. The `TriggerControlBoolean` value controls whether or not the table's `OnModify` trigger fires when this `MODIFY` occurs. The default value is `FALSE`. `MODIFY` cannot be used to cause a change in a Primary Key field. In that case, the `RENAME` function must be used.

In NAV 2013, there is improved checking to ensure a `MODIFY` function is executed using the current version of the data record by making sure another process hasn't modified and committed the record after it was read by this process. The program should refresh the record using the `GET` function, then change any values, then call the `MODIFY` function.

Rec and xRec

In Table and Page objects, the system automatically provides us with the system variables Rec and xRec. Until a record has been updated by MODIFY, Rec represents the current record data in process and xRec represents the record data before it was modified. By comparing field values in Rec and xRec, we can determine if changes have been made to the record in the current process cycle. The Rec and xRec records have all the same fields in the same structure as the table to which they relate.

DELETE function

The purpose of the DELETE function is to delete existing data records. The syntax for DELETE is as follows:

```
[BooleanValue :=] Record.DELETE ( [ TriggerControlBoolean ] )
```

When DELETE fails and the BooleanValue is not used, the process will terminate with an error statement. Our code should handle any detected error or terminate the process, as appropriate.

The TriggerControlBoolean value is TRUE or FALSE, and it controls whether or not the table's OnDelete trigger fires when this DELETE occurs. The default value is FALSE. If we let the default FALSE prevail, we run the risk of not performing error checking that the table's designer assumed would be run when a record was deleted.

In NAV 2013, there is improved checking to make sure a DELETE function is using the current version of the record, making sure another process hasn't modified and committed the record after it was read by this process. Therefore, before the DELETE function is called, the program should refresh the record using the GET function.

MODIFYALL function

MODIFYALL is the high-volume version of the MODIFY function. If we have a group of records in which we wish to modify one field in all of them to the same new value, we should use MODIFYALL. MODIFYALL is controlled by the filters that apply at the time of invoking. The other choice for doing a mass modification would be to have a FIND-NEXT loop in which we modified each record one at a time. The advantage of MODIFYALL is that it allows us, as developers, and the system to optimize code for the volume update. Any system optimization will be a function of what SQL statements are generated by the C/AL compiler.

The syntax for MODIFYALL is as follows:

```
Record.MODIFYALL (FieldToBeModified,NewValue
    [,TriggerControlBoolean ] )
```

The `TriggerControlBoolean` value, a `TRUE` or `FALSE` entry, controls whether or not the table's `OnModify` trigger fires when this `MODIFY` occurs. The default value is `FALSE`. The `OnValidate` trigger for the field being modified is never executed when a `MODIFYALL` is being executed. In a typical situation, a filter or series of filters would be applied to a table followed by the `MODIFYALL` function. A simple example where we are going to reassign all the `Territory Codes` for a particular `Salesperson` to `NORTH` is as follows:

```
CustRec.RESET;
CustRec.SETRANGE(«Salesperson Code»,'DAS');
CustRec.MODIFYALL("Territory Code",'NORTH',TRUE);
```

DELETEALL function

`DELETEALL` is the high-volume version of the `DELETE` function. If we have a group of records that we wish delete, use `DELETEALL`. The other choice would be to have a `FIND-NEXT` loop in which we delete each record one at a time. The advantage of the `DELETEALL` is that it allows the developer and the system to optimize code for the volume deletion. Any system optimization will be a function of what SQL statements are generated by the C/AL compiler.

The syntax for `DELETEALL` is as follows:

```
Record.DELETEALL ( [,TriggerControlBoolean] )
```

The `TriggerControlBoolean` value, a `TRUE` or `FALSE` entry, controls whether or not the table's `OnDelete` trigger fires when this `DELETE` occurs. The default value is `FALSE`. If the `TriggerControlBoolean` value is `TRUE`, then the `OnDelete` trigger will fire for each record deleted. In that case, there is little or no speed advantage for `DELETEALL` versus the use of a `FIND-DELETE-NEXT` loop.

In a typical situation, a filter or series of filters would be applied to a table followed by the `DELETEALL` function, similar to the preceding example. Like `MODIFYALL`, `DELETEALL` respects the filters that have been set and does not do any referential integrity error checking.

Filtering

Few other systems have filtering implemented as comprehensively as NAV nor do they have it tied to the detailed retention of historical data. The result of NAV's features is that even the most basic implementation of NAV includes very powerful data analysis capabilities available to the end user.

As developers, we should appreciate the fact that we cannot anticipate every need of any user, let alone anticipate all the needs of all our users. We know we should give the user as much freedom as we can to allow them to selectively extract and review data from their system. Wherever feasible, the user should be given the opportunity to apply their own filters so that they can determine the optimum selection of data for their particular situation. On the other hand, freedom, here as everywhere, is a double-edged sword. With the freedom to decide just how to segment one's data, comes the responsibility for figuring out what constitutes a good segmentation to address the problem at hand.

As experienced application software designers and developers, presumably we have considerable insight into good ways to analyze and present the data. On that basis, it may be appropriate for us to provide some predefined selections. In some cases, constraints of the data structure allow only a limited set of options make sense. In such a case, we should provide specific accesses to data (pages and/or reports). But we should allow more sophisticated users to access and manipulate the data flexibly on their own.

When applying filters by using any of the options, be very conscious of the table key that will be active when the filter takes effect. In a table containing a lot of data, filtering on a field that is not very high in (near the front of) the currently active key may result in a poor (or very poor) response time for the user. In the same context, in a system suffering from a poor response time during processing, we should first investigate the relationships of active keys to applied filters.

Both SETCURRENTKEY and SETRANGE functions are important in the context of data filtering. Both were reviewed in *Chapter 6, Introduction to C/SIDE and C/AL*, so we won't review them again here.

SETFILTER function

SETFILTER allows us to define and apply any Filter expression that could be created manually, including various combinations of ranges, C/AL operators, and even wild cards. SETFILTER syntax is as follows:

```
Record.SETFILTER ( Field, FilterString [, FilterValue1], . . . ] );
```

SETFILTER also can be applied to Query objects with similar syntax:

```
Query.SETFILTER ( ColumnName, FilterString
     [, FilterValue1], . . . ] );
```

FilterString can be a literal such as '1000..20000' or 'A*|B*|C*', but this is not good practice. Optionally, you can use variable tokens in the form of %1, %2, %3, and so forth, representing variables (but not operators) FilterValue1, FilterValue2, and so forth to be substituted in the filter string at runtime. This construct allows you to create filters whose data values can be defined dynamically at runtime. A new SETFILTER replaces any previous filtering in the same filtergroup (discussed in a couple of pages) on that field or column prior to setting the new filter.

A pair of SETFILTER examples is as follows:

- CustRec.SETFILTER("Salesperson Code",'KKS'|'RAM'|'CDS');
- CustRec.SETFILTER("Salesperson Code",'%1|%2|%3',SPC1, SPC2,SPC3);

If SPC1 equals 'KKS', SPC2 equals 'RAM', and SPC3 equals 'CDS', these two examples would have the same result. Obviously the second option allows flexibility not provided by the first option because the variables could be assigned other values.

COPYFILTER and COPYFILTERS functions

These functions allow copying the filters of a single field or all the filters on a record (table) and applying those filters to another record. The syntax follows:

```
FromRecord.COPYFILTER(FromField, ToRecord.ToField)
```

The From and To fields must be of the same data type. The From and To tables do not have to be the same layout.

```
ToRecord.COPYFILTERS(FromRecord)
```

 The COPYFILTER field based function begins with the FromRecord variable while that of COPYFILTERS record based function begins with the ToRecord variable. The ToRecord and FromRecord variables must be different instances of the same table.

GETFILTER and GETFILTERS functions

These functions allow us to retrieve the filters on a single field or all the filters on a record (table) and assign the result to a text variable. The syntaxes are as follows:

- ResultString := FilteredRecord.GETFILTER(FilteredField)
- ResultString := FilteredRecord.GETFILTERS

Similar functions exist for Query Objects. These syntaxes are:

- `ResultString := FilteredQuery.GETFILTER(FilteredColumn)`
- `ResultString := FilteredQuery.GETFILTERS`

The text contents of the `ResultString` will contain an identifier for each filtered field and the currently applied value of the filter. `GETFILTERS` is often used to retrieve the filters on a table and print them as part of a report heading. The `ResultString` will look similar to the following:

Customer:.No.: 10000..999999, Balance: >0

FILTERGROUP function

The `FILTERGROUP` function can change or retrieve the filtergroup that is applied to a table. A filtergroup contains a set of filters that have been applied to the table previously by `SETFILTER` or `SETRANGE` functions or as table properties defined in an object. The `FILTERGROUP` syntax is:

```
[CurrentGroupInteger ] := Record.FILTERGROUP ([NewGroupInteger])
```

Using just the `Record,FILTERGROUP([NewFilterGroupInteger])` portion sets the active filtergroup.

Filtergroups can also be used to filter Query DataItems. All the currently defined filtergroups are active and apply in combination (are logically ANDed,—yielding a logical intersection of the sets). The only way to eliminate the effect of a filtergroup is to remove the filters in a group.

The default filtergroup for NAV is 0 (zero). Users have access to the filters in this filtergroup. Other filtergroups, numbered up through 6, have assigned NAV uses. We should not redefine the use of any of these filtergroups but use higher numbers for any custom filtergroups in our code.

See the **Developer and IT Pro Help** for `FILTERGROUP function` and `Understanding Query Filters` for more information.

One use of a filtergroup would be to assign a filter which the user cannot see is present or change. The code could change the filtergroup, set a special filter, and then return the active filtergroup to its original state. For example, look at the following code:

```
Rec.FILTERGROUP(42);
Rec.SETFILTER(Customer."Salesperson Code",MySalespersonID);
Rec.FILTERGROUP(0);
```

This could be used to apply special application-specific permissions to a particular system function, such as filtering out access to customers by salesperson so that each salesperson can only examine data for their own customers.

MARK function

A mark on a record is an indicator that disappears when the current session ends and which is only visible to the process, that is, setting the mark. The MARK function sets the mark. The syntax is as follows:

```
[BooleanValue := ] Record.MARK ( [SetMarkBoolean] )
```

If the optional BooleanValue and assignment operator (:=) is present, the MARK function will give us the current Mark status (TRUE or FALSE) of the Record. If the optional SetMarkBoolean parameter is present, the Record will be marked (or unmarked) according to that value (TRUE or FALSE). The default value for SetMarkBoolean is FALSE. The MARK functions should be used carefully and only when a simpler solution is not readily available. Marking records can cause significant performance problems on large data sets, so we should use this feature sparingly.

CLEARMARKS function

CLEARMARKS clears all the marks from the specified record (that is, from the particular instance of the table in this instance of the object). The syntax is as follows:

```
Record.CLEARMARKS
```

MARKEDONLY function

MARKEDONLY is a special filtering function that can apply a mark-based filter.

The syntax for MARKEDONLY is as follows:

```
[BooleanValue := ] Record.MARKEDONLY
    ( [SeeMarkedRecordsOnlyBoolean] )
```

If the optional BooleanValue parameter is defined, it will be assigned a value TRUE or FALSE to tell us whether or not the special MARKEDONLY filter is active. Omitting the BooleanValue parameter, MARKEDONLY will set the special filter depending on the value of SeeMarkedRecordsOnlyBoolean. If that value is TRUE, it will filter to show only marked records; if that value is FALSE, it will remove the marked filter and show all records. The default value for SeeMarkedRecordsOnlyBoolean is FALSE.

Though it may not seem logical, there is no option to see only the unmarked records.

RESET function

The RESET function allows us to reset (clear) all filters that are currently applied to a record. RESET also sets the current key back to the Primary Key, removes any marks, and clears all internal variables in the current instance of the record. Filters in FILTERGROUP 1 are not reset. The syntax is as follows:

```
FilteredRecord.RESET;
```

InterObject communication

There are several ways for communicating between objects during NAV processing.

Communication via data

The most widely used and simplest communication method is through data tables. For example, the **No. Series** table is the central control for all document numbers. Each object that assigns numbers to a document (for example, Order, Invoice, Shipment, and so on) uses Codeunit 396, **NoSeriesManagement**, to access the **No. Series** table for the next number to use, and then update the **No. Series** table so that the next object needing to assign a number to the same type of document will have the updated information.

Communication through function parameters

When an object calls a function in another object, information is generally passed through the calling and return parameters. The calling and return parameter specifications were defined when the function was originally developed. The generic syntax for a function call is as follows:

```
[ReturnValue := ] FunctionName ( [ Parameter1 ] [ ,Parameter2 ] ,…)
```

The rules for including or omitting the various optional fields are specific to the local variables defined for each individual function. As developers, when we design the function, we define the rules and thereby determine just how communications with the function will be handled. It is obviously important to define complete and consistent parameter passing rules prior to beginning a development project.

Communication via object calls

Sometimes we need to create an object which in turn calls other objects. We may simply want to allow the user to run a series of processes and reports but only enter the controlling parameters once. Our user interface object will be responsible for invoking the subordinate objects after having communicated setup and filter parameters.

There is a significant set of standard functions designed for various modes and circumstances of invoking other objects. Examples of these functions are SETTABLEVIEW, SETRECORD, and GETRECORD (there are others as well). There are also instances where we will need to build our own data passing function.

In order to properly manage these relatively complex processes, we need to be familiar with the various versions of RUN and RUNMODAL functions. We will also need to understand the meaning and effect of a single instance or multiple instances of an object. Briefly, key differences between invoking a page or report object from within another object via RUN versus RUNMODAL are as follows:

- RUN will clear the instance of the invoked object every time the object completes, which means that all of the internal variables are initialized. This clearing behavior does not apply to a Codeunit object; state will be maintained across multiple calls to RUN.

- RUNMODAL does not clear the instance of the invoked object, so internal global variables are not re-initialized each time the object is called. The object can be re-initialized by using CLEAR(Object).

- RUNMODAL does not allow any other object to be active in the same user session while it is running, whereas RUN does.

Covering these topics in more detail is too advanced for this book, but once you have mastered the material covered here, you should study the information in the **Developer and IT Pro Help** relative to this topic.

Enhancing the WDTU application

Now that we have some more tools with which to work, let's enhance our WDTU application. This time our goal is to implement functionality to allow the Program Manager to plan the Playlist schedules for Radio Shows. The process, from the user's point of view, will be essentially as follows:

1. Call up the Playlist document page which displays Header, Details and a FactBox data entry workspaces.

2. Enter Playlist Header, drawing on the Radio Show for data.

3. Enter Playlist Lines, drawing on the Resource table for DJ data, the Radio Show table for News or Weather or Sports shows, and on the Item table for Music, PSAs and Advertisements.

4. The FactBox will display the Required program element fields from Radio Show/Playlist Header. These will include News (Yes or No), Weather (Yes or No), Sports (Yes or No), Number of required PSAs, and Advertisements.

5. The FactBox will also track each of the five possible required elements.

Since this development effort is an exercise to learn more about developing NAV applications, we also have some specific NAV C/AL components we want to use so we can learn more about them. Among these are the following:

- Create a CASE statement as well as a multipart `IF` statement for contrast

- Add code to the **OnValidate** trigger of fields in a table

- Implement a lookup into a related table to access needed data

- Cause FlowFields to be processed for display

- Implement a Factbox (to display Radio Show requirements for News, Sports, Weather, PSAs, and Ads)

- Create a new function, passing a parameter in and getting results passed back

As with any application enhancement, there will be a number of auxiliary tasks we'll have to accomplish to get the job done. These include adding some new fields to one or more tables. Not surprisingly, adding new data fields often leads to adding the new fields to one or more pages for maintenance or display. We'll have to create some test data in order to test our modifications. It's not unusual in the course of an enhancement to also find that a few other changes are needed to support the new functionality.

Modifying table fields

Since in NAV we want the tables to be the core of the design and to host as much of the processing as makes sense, we will start our enhancement work with table modifications.

The first table modification is to add the data fields to the Playlist Header to support the definition and tracking of various program segment requirements. In the Radio Show table, each show has requirements defined for specific numbers of PSAs and Advertisements, and for the presence of News, Sports, and Weather spots. The Playlist Header needs this requirements information stored along with the associated counts for this show instance for PSAs and Ads. We are going to obtain the News, Sports and Weather line counts by means of a function call.

Since the Playlist Line includes an **Option** field which identifies the PSA and Advertisement records, we use a **FlowField** to calculate the counts for each of those line types. We construct the **FlowField** definition starting in the **Properties** form of the field.

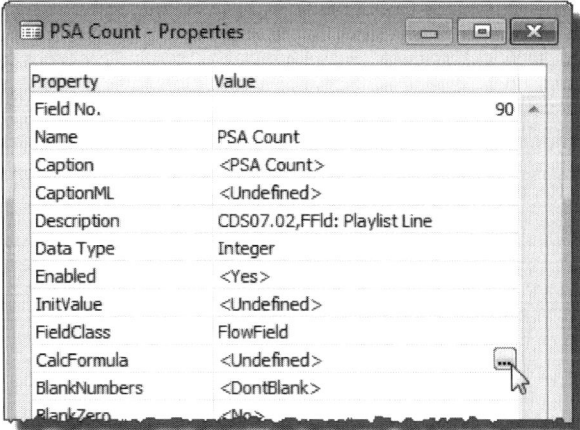

When we click on the **CalcFormula** line ellipses, the **Calculation Formula** screen appears.

In this case, the method we want to use is **Count**. Then, when we click on the **Table Filter** ellipses, we will have the opportunity to enter the components defining the filters that should be applied to the Playlist Line to isolate the records that we want to count.

When we complete the **Table Filter** definition and click on the **OK** button, we will return to the **Calculation Formula** screen with the **Table Filter** field filled in (if we just click on *Esc*, the data we entered will not be saved).

Again, click on the **OK** button to return to the **Properties** screen.

Go through the same sequence for the Ad Count field.

The only change we want to make to the Playlist Line table now is to be sure the Duration field is not editable. We do this so the Start Time and End Time scheduling defines Duration rather than the other way around. Making the Duration field non-editable is done by simply setting the field's **Editable** property to No.

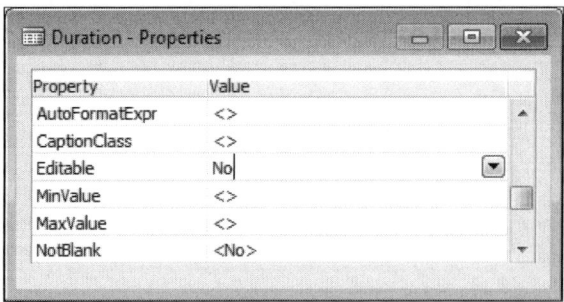

Adding validation logic

We need validation logic for both our Playlist tables, Header and Line.

Playlist Header Validations

The Playlist Header data fields are:

- **No.**: This is the ID number for this instance of a radio show; it's user defined

- **Radio Show No.**: This is chosen from the Radio Show table

- **Description**: This is displayed via a FlowField from the Radio Show table

- **Posting Date**: This shows the scheduled broadcast date

- **Start Time**: This shows the scheduled broadcast start time

- **End Time**: This shows the scheduled broadcast end time

- **Duration**: This is the length of the show; it's displayed via a FlowField from the Radio Show table

- **PSAs Required and Ads Required**: This shows how many PSAs and Ads are required during the show; this value is copied from the Radio Show table, but is editable by the user

- **News Required, Sports Required and Weather Required**: This tells whether or not each of these program segments are required during the show; it's copied from the Radio Show table, but is editable by the user

When the user chooses the Radio Show to be scheduled, we want the five different feature requirements fields in the Playlist Header to be filled in.

```
Table 50002 Playlist Header - C/AL Editor                    [ _ ][ □ ][ X ]

⊟ No. - OnLookup()


⊟ Radio Show No. - OnValidate()
  IF RadioShow.GET("Radio Show No.") THEN
  BEGIN
    "PSAs Required" := RadioShow."PSA Required Qty.";
    "Ads Required" := RadioShow."Advertisement Required Qty.";
    "News Required" := RadioShow."News Required";
    "Sports Required" := RadioShow."Sports Required";
    "Weather Required" := RadioShow."Weather Required";
  END;


⊟ Radio Show No. - OnLookup()
```

Even though the `Radio Show No.` was entered in the data field, our validation code needs to read the Radio Show record (here defined as the Global variable `RadioShow`). Once we have read the Radio Show record, we can assign all five show feature requirements fields from the Radio Show record into the Playlist Header record.

Then, because two fields in the Playlist Header record are Lookup FlowFields, we need to update the page after entry of the `Radio Show No.` value. The update is done via a `CurrPage.UPDATE` command, as shown in the following screenshot:

The next Validation we need is to calculate the show `End Time` as soon as the `Start Time` has been entered. The calculation is simple—add the length of the show to the `Start Time`. Because we have defined the `Duration` field in the Playlist Header to be a Lookup reference to the source field in the Radio Show record, to calculate with that field would require using a `CALCFIELDS` function first, so instead, we'll obtain the show length from the Radio Show record.

This is one of those situations we sometimes encounter when developing a modification. We now see that it might be better to have the Playlist Header `Duration` field be a **Normal** data field rather than a **FlowField**. If this is the only place where we will use `Duration` from the Playlist Header for calculation or assignment, then the current design is fine. But otherwise, we might decide to change the `Duration` field to a **Normal** field and assign `Run Time` from Radio Show to it at the same time the several requirements fields are assigned. For the purposes of our WDTU scenario, we will stick with what we already have.

Creating the Playlist Subform page

In *Chapter 2*, *Tables*, a homework assignment was to create Page 50003 Playlist, a Document page. We should have used the Page Wizard to create that page, giving us something like this:

Another necessary part of a Document page is the Subform page. Our Subform page can be created using the Page Wizard to create a ListPart based on Table **50003 Playlist Line**. After you finish the Wizard, save and compile the page as **50004 Playlist Subform**. The result will look like that in the following screenshot:

To make the Document work the way we are used to having NAV Document forms work, we need to set some properties for this new page. See the green arrow highlighted properties in the following screenshot:

We have set the **DelayedInsert**, **MultipleNewLines**, and **AutoSplitKey** properties all to Yes. These settings will allow the Playlist Lines to not be saved until the primary key fields are all entered (**DelayedInsert**), will support simple sequential entry of data lines (**MultipleNewLines**), and will support the easy insertion of new entries between two existing lines (**AutoSplitKey**).

Finally, we need to connect our new Playlist Subform Listpart Page 50004 to the Playlist Document Page 50003 to give us a basic, complete Document page. All we need to do to accomplish that is add a new line to Page 50003 as shown here:

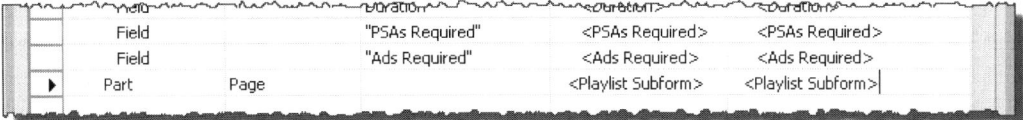

The last step in this phase of our development is to set the Page Part property **SubPageLink** to automatically filter the contents of the Subform page to only be the lines that are child elements of the parent record showing in the card-like portion of the Document page (at the top).

Playlist Line validations

The Playlist Line data fields are:

- **Playlist No.**: This is the automatically assigned link to the **No.** field in the parent Playlist record (the automatic assignment is based on the Playlist Subform page properties, which we'll take care of when working on the Playlist pages)

- **Line No.**: This is an automatically assigned number (based on page properties) of the rightmost field in the Playlist Line primary key

- **Type**: This is a user selected option defining if this entry is a Resource (such as an announcer), a Show (such as a News show), or an Item (such as a recording to play)

- **No.**: This is the ID number of the selected entry in its parent table

- **DataFormat**: This is the information from the Item table for a show or recording

- **Description**: This is assigned from the parent table, but can be edited by the user

- **Duration**, **Start Time**, and **End Time**: This is the information about a show or recording indicating the length and its position within the schedule of this Radio Show

The source of contents of the **No.**, **DataFormat**, **Description**, and time-related fields of the record depend on the **Type** field. If the **Type** value is **Resource**, the fields are filled in from the Resource table; for Item, from the Item table; for Show, from the Radio Show table. To support this, our **OnValidate** code looks like the Type entry and uses a CASE statement to choose which set of actions to take.

First, we will build the basic CASE statement, as shown in the following screenshot, and compile it. That way we make sure we've got all the components of the structure in place and only need to fill in the logic for each of the option choices.

Use of the C/AL Symbol Menu makes it much easier to find the correct field names for each of the variables we want to select to assign to the Playlist Line record fields.

Once the C/AL Symbol Menu is displayed, first we select the source object or variable in the left column. In this case, that's the **Resource** table. Then select the subcategory in the middle column. We want a list of the fields in the **Resource** table, so we select **FieldName**. Then, in the third column, a list of **Resource FieldNames** is displayed. We select **Name** to be assigned to the **Playlist Line Description** field. When we double-click on the desired **FieldName**, it will be inserted at the point of focus in the C/AL Editor.

When we are all done constructing the CASE statement, it should look like this:

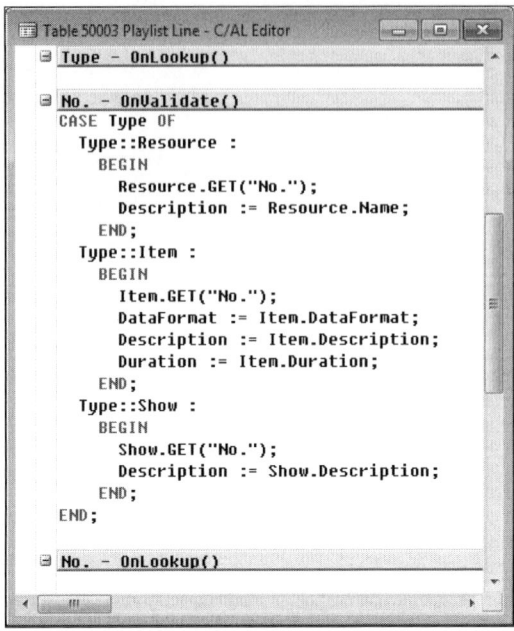

The last set of **OnValidate** code we need to add is to calculate the End Time from the supplied Start Time and Duration (or Start Time from the End Time and Duration).

Obviously, the design could be expanded to have the Duration value be user editable along with an appropriate change in the C/AL logic. After our initial work on the Playlist functionality is completed, making that change would be a good exercise for you as would the addition of "housekeeping" commands to clear out fields that are not used by the assigned record **Type** (such as clearing the **DataFormat** field for a Show record).

Creating a function

For this application, we want our FactBox to display information relating to the specific Radio Show we are scheduling. The information to be displayed includes the five show segment requirements and the status of fulfillment (counts) of those requirements by the data entered to date. The requirements come from Playlist Header fields—PSAs Required, Ads Required, News Required, Sports Required, and Weather Required. The counts come from summing up data in the Playline Line records for a show. They are the PSA Count, Ad Count, News Count, Sports Count, and Weather Count.

Because the Playlist Line contains an option field (DataFormat) that identifies PSA and Ad records, these counts can be obtained through simple FlowField property definitions. For the other three counts, we must read through the Playlist Lines and total up each of the counts. To accomplish that, we'll create a function which we can call from the FactBox page. Since our new function is local to the Playlist Header and Playlist Lines tables, we will define the function in the Playlist Header (table 50002).

The first step in defining the function is to enter its name in the **Functions** tab of the **Globals** screen for the object. Open the object, Table 50002, by clicking on **Table | Design**, then click on **View | C/AL Globals**, and then click on the **Functions** tab.

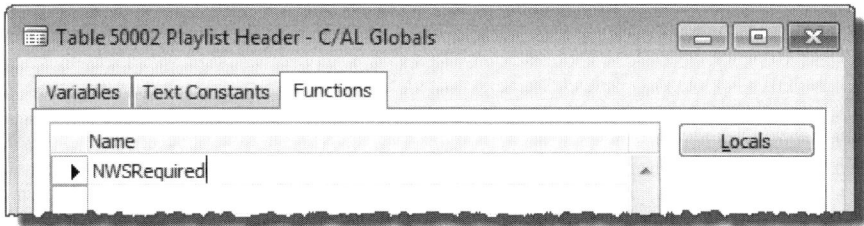

Then, after clicking on the **Locals** button and viewing the **Parameters** tab, we can enter the parameters we want to pass to the function. In this case, we want the parameter to be passed by value, not be reference, so we do not check the **Var** checkbox on the **Parameter** line. For more information about parameter passing, look at the **Help** sections—*C/AL Function Calls* and *How to: Add a Function to a Codeunit*. The name of the parameter is local to the function.

Since we want a single function that will serve to count Playlist Lines that are News, Weather, or Sports, the parameter we pass in will be an option code of News, Weather, or Sports. The **Option Subtype** sequence must be the same as those in the **Type** field in the **Playlist Lines** table, otherwise we will have **Options** mismatching.

The return value we want back from this function is an Integer type. Again, the variable name is local.

The logic of our counting process must be along the lines of the following pseudocode:

1. Filter the Playlist Line table for the Radio Show we are scheduling and for segment entries (Playlist Line) that represent shows.

2. Look up the Radio Show record for each of those records.

3. Using the data from the Radio Show record, look up the Radio Show Type code.

4. In the Radio Show Type record, use the News, Weather, Sports fields to determine which Playlist Line counter should be incremented.

Based on this logic, we must have **Local Variables** defined for the three tables Playlist Line, Radio Show, and Radio Show Type. The following shows those **Local Variables**.

Translating the pseudocode we just reviewed into C/AL, our function looks like this:

```
Weather Count - OnLookup()

NWSRequired(NWSCategory : ' ',News,Weather,Sports') TypeCount : Integer
  PlaylistLine.RESET;
  PlaylistLine.SETRANGE("Playlist No.",Rec."No.");
  PlaylistLine.SETRANGE(Type,PlaylistLine.Type::Show);
  IF PlaylistLine.FINDSET(FALSE,FALSE) THEN REPEAT
    IF RadioShow.GET(PlaylistLine."No.") THEN
      IF RadioShowType.GET(RadioShow.Type) THEN BEGIN
        CASE NWSCategory OF
          NWSCategory::News :
            BEGIN
              IF RadioShowType."Is News" THEN
                TypeCount += 1;
            END;
          NWSCategory::Weather :
            BEGIN
              IF RadioShowType."Is Weather" THEN
                TypeCount += 1;
            END;
          NWSCategory::Sports :
            BEGIN
              IF RadioShowType."Is Sports" THEN
                TypeCount += 1;
            END;
        END;
      END;
  UNTIL PlaylistLine.NEXT = 0;
```

Creating a FactBox page

All the hard work is now done. We just have to define a FactBox page and add it to the Playlist page. We can create a FactBox page using the New Page Wizard to define a CardPart.

Our FactBox is to contain the fields from the Playlist Header that relate to the five required show segments, including the **PSA Count** and **Ad Count** fields.

Once we exit the Page Wizard into the Page Designer, we will have a page layout that looks like the following:

At this point we need to put in place the logic to take advantage of the **NWSRequired** function that we created earlier. This function is designed to return the count of the segment type identified in the calling parameter. Since a line on a page can be an expression, we can simply code the function calls right on the page lines, with an appropriate caption defined, as you can see in the following screenshot. The only other task has been to define a Global variable, **NWSCategory**, which is defined as an **Option** with the choices of **News**, **Weather**, and **Sports**. This variable is used for the calling parameter.

One final development step is required. We must connect the new FactBox CardPart to the Playlist Document. All that is required is to define the FactBox Area and add our FactBox as an element in that area.

Properties for the FactBox Pagepart are shown in the following:

Multiple FactBoxes can be part of a primary page. If you look at Page 21 – Customer Card, you will see a FactBox Area with eight FactBoxes.

The end result of our development effort is shown when we **Run** Page 50000 – Playlist with some sample test data (which we entered by running the various tables).

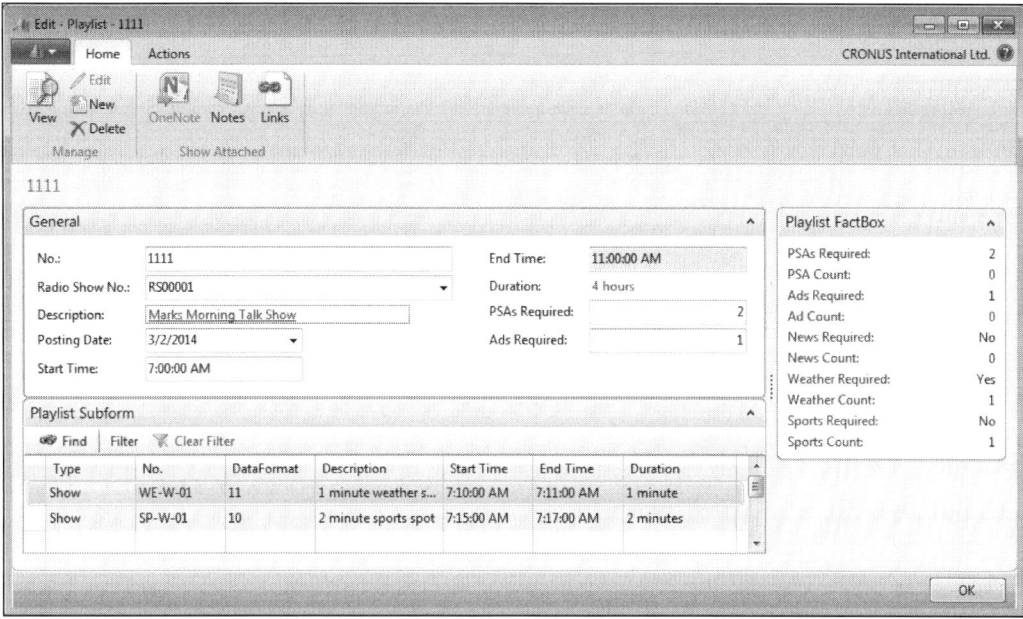

Summary

In this chapter, we covered a number of practical tools and topics regarding C/AL coding and development. We started with reviewing methods and then we dived into a long list of functions that you will need on a frequent basis.

We covered a variety of selected data-centric functions, including some for computation and validation, some for data conversion, and others for date handling. Next, we reviewed functions that affect the flow of logic and the flow of data, including FlowFields and SIFT, Processing Flow Control, Input and Output, and Filtering. Finally we put a number of these to work in an enhancement for our WDTU application.

In the next chapter, we will move from the details of the functions to the broader view of C/AL development integration into the standard NAV code, and debugging techniques.

Review questions

1. Documentation cannot be integrated into in-line C/AL code. True or False?

2. The TESTFIELD function can be used to assign new values to a variable. True or False?

3. The C/AL Symbol Menu can be used for several of the following purposes. Choose three:

   a. Find applicable functions

   b. Paste highlighted entries directly into code

   c. Test coded functions

   d. Use entries as a template for function syntax and arguments

   e. Translate text constants into a support language

4. The VALIDATE function can be used to assign new values to a variable. True or False?

5. The WORKDATE value can be set to a different value from the system date. True or False?

6. Which three of the following are valid date related NAV functions?

   a. DATE2DWY

   b. CALCDATE

   c. DMY2DATE

   d. DATE2NUM

7. An Average FlowField requires which two of the following:

   a. A record key

   b. SQL Server database

   c. A SumIndexField

   d. A Decimal variable

8. Which of the following functions should be used within a report
   `OnAfterGetRecord` trigger to end processing just for a single iteration
   of the trigger? Choose one:

    a. `EXIT`

    b. `BREAK`

    c. `QUIT`

    d. `SKIP`

9. Which of the following formats of `MODIFY` will cause the table's `OnModify`
   trigger to fire? Choose one:

    a. `MODIFY`

    b. `MODIFY(TRUE)`

    c. `MODIFY(RUN)`

    d. `MODIFY(READY)`

10. `SETRANGE` is often used to clear all filtering from a single field. True or False?

11. `RESET` is used to clear the current sort key setting from a record.
    True or False?

12. Which of the following is not a valid C/AL flow control combination?
    Choose one:

    a. `REPEAT-UNTIL`

    b. `DO-UNTIL`

    c. `CASE-ELSE`

    d. `IF-THEN`

13. Which functions can be used to cause FlowFields to be calculated?
    Choose two:

    a. `CALCSUMS`

    b. `CALCFIELDS`

    c. `SETAUTOCALCFIELDS`

    d. `SUMFLOWFIELD`

14. The `REPEAT - UNTIL` looping structure is most often used to control data
    reading processes. True or False?

15. A `CASE` statement structure should never be used in place of a nested `IF`
    statement structure. True or False?

16. A `FILTERGROUP` function should not be used in custom code. True or False?

8
Advanced NAV
Development Tools

It is a far better to adapt the technology to the user than to force the user to adapt to the technology. — *Larry Marine*

Design must reflect the practical and esthetic in business but above all.. good design must primarily serve people. — *Thomas J. Watson, Sr.*

Because NAV is extremely flexible and suitable for addressing many problem types, there are a lot of choices for advanced NAV topics. We'll try to cover those which will be most helpful in the effort of putting together a complete implementation.

First we will review the overall structure of NAV as an application software system aiming for a basic understanding of the process flow of the system along with some of the utility functions built into the standard product. Before designing modifications for NAV, it is important to have a good understanding of the structural "style" of the software, so that our enhancements are designed for a better fit.

Second, we will review some special components of the NAV system that allow us to accomplish more at less cost. These resources include features such as Web Services that we can build on, and tools such as the new Debugger that help us be more efficient and effective in our construction processes. Fortunately, NAV has an excellent supply of such tools.

NAV process flow

Primary data such as sales orders, purchase orders, production orders, and financial transactions flow through the NAV system as follows:

- **Initial setup**: Essential Master data, reference data, control, and setup data is entered. Much of this preparation is done when the system (or a new application) is prepared for production use.

- **Transaction entry**: Transactions are entered into Documents and then transferred as part of a Posting sequence into a `Journal` table, or data may be entered directly into a `Journal` table. Data is preliminarily validated as it is entered with master and auxiliary data tables being referenced as appropriate. Entry can be via manual keying, an automated transaction generation process, or an import function which brings in transaction data from another system.

- **Validation**: Provides for additional data validation processing of a set of one or more transactions, often in batches, prior to submitting it to Posting.

- **Posting**: Posts a Journal Batch, which includes completing transaction data validation, adding entries to one or more Ledgers, perhaps also a register and document history.

- **Utilization**: Access the data via Pages, Queries, and/or Reports including those that feed Web Services and other consumers of data. At this point, total flexibility exists. Whatever tools are appropriate for users' needs should be used, whether internal to NAV or external (external tools are often referred to as Business Intelligence or BI tools). NAV's built in capabilities for data manipulation, extraction, and presentation should not be overlooked.

- **Maintenance**: Continued maintenance of all NAV data as appropriate.

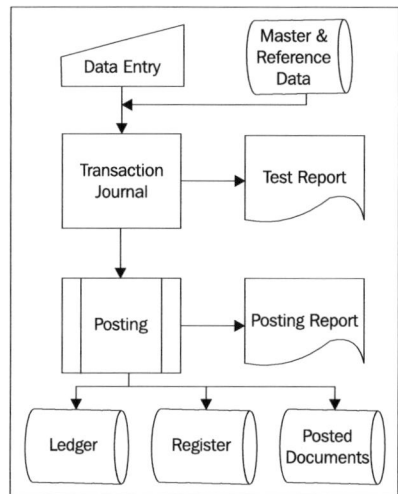

The preceding diagram provides a simplified picture of the flow of application data through a NAV system. Many of the transaction types have additional reporting, multiple ledgers to update, even auxiliary processing. But this represents the basic data flow in NAV whenever a Journal and a Ledger table are involved.

When we enhance an existing NAV functional area (such as Jobs or Service Management), we may need to enhance related process flow elements by adding new fields to journals, ledgers, posted documents, and so on. It's always a good idea to add new fields rather than changing the use of standard fields. It makes debugging, maintenance and upgrading all easier.

When we create a new functional area, we will likely need to replicate the standard NAV process flow in some form for the new application's data. For example, for our WDTU application, we handle the entry of Playlists in the same fashion as a Journal is entered. A day's Playlists would be similar to a Journal Batch in another application. When a day's shows have been broadcasted, the Playlist will be posted into the Radio Show Ledger as a permanent record of the broadcasts.

Initial setup and data preparation

Data must be maintained as new Master data becomes available, as various system operating parameters change, and so on. The standard approach for NAV data entry allows records to be entered that have just enough information to define the primary key fields, but not necessarily enough to support processing. This allows a great deal of flexibility in the timing and responsibility for entry and completeness of new data. This approach applies to both, setup data entry and ongoing production transaction data entry.

This system design philosophy allows initial and incomplete data entry by one person, with validation and completion to be handled later by someone else. Often data comes into an organization on a piecemeal basis.

For example, a sales person might initialize a new customer entry with name, address, and phone number, saving the entry with just the data entered to which they have access. At this point, there is not enough information recorded to process orders for this new customer. At a later time, someone in the accounting department can set up posting groups, payment terms, and other control data that should not be controlled by the sales department. With this additional data, the new customer record is ready for production use.

The NAV data entry approach allows the system to be updated on an incremental basis as the data arrives, providing an operational flexibility that many systems lack. The other side of this flexibility is added responsibility for the users to insure that partially updated information is completed on a timely fashion. For the customer who can't deal with that responsibility, it may be necessary to create special procedures or even system customizations which enforce the necessary discipline.

Transaction entry

Transactions are entered into a `Journal` table. Data is preliminarily validated as it is entered; master and auxiliary data tables are referenced as appropriate. Validations are based on the evaluation of the individual transaction data plus the related Master records and associated reference tables (for example, lookups being satisfied, application or system setup parameter constraints being met, and so on).

Testing and posting the Journal Batch

Any additional validations that need to be done to ensure the integrity and completeness of the transaction data prior to being posted are done either in pre-post routines or directly in the course of the Posting processes. The actual posting of a Journal Batch occurs when the transaction data has been completely validated. Depending on the specific application, when Journal transactions don't pass muster during this final validation stage, either the individual transaction is bypassed while acceptable transactions are posted, or the entire Journal Batch is rejected until the identified problem is resolved.

The Posting process adds entries to one or more Ledgers, and sometimes to a document history table. When a Journal Entry is posted to a Ledger, it becomes a part of the permanent accounting record. Most data cannot be changed or deleted once it resides in a Ledger.

Register tables may also be updated during Posting, recording the ID number ranges of ledger entries posted, when posted, and in what batches. This adds to the transparency of the NAV application system for audits and analysis.

In general, NAV follows the standard accounting practice of requiring Ledger revisions to be made by Posting reversing entries, rather than by deletion of problem entries. The overall result is that NAV is a very auditable system, a key requirement for a variety of government, legal, and certification requirements for information systems.

Utilizing and maintaining the data

The data in a NAV system can be accessed via Pages, Queries, and/or Reports, providing total flexibility. Whatever tools are available to the developer or the user, and are appropriate, should be used. There are some very good tools in NAV for data manipulation, extraction, and presentation. Among other things, these include the SIFT/Flowfield functionality, the pervasive filtering capability (including the ability to apply filters to subordinate data structures), and the Navigate function. NAV includes the ability to create page parts for graphing, with a wide variety of predefined graph page parts included as part of the standard distribution. We can also create our own chart parts using tools delivered with the system or available from Web blogs.

The NAV database design approach could be referred to as a "rational normalization". NAV isn't constrained by a rigid normalized data structure, where any data element appears only once. The NAV data structure is normalized so long as that principle doesn't get in the way of processing speed. Where processing speed or ease of use for the user is improved by duplicating data across tables, NAV does so. In addition, the duplication of master file data into transactions allows for one-time modification of that data when appropriate (such as a ship-to address in a Sales Order). That data duplication often greatly simplifies data access for analysis.

Data maintenance

As with any database-oriented application software, ongoing maintenance of Master data, reference data, and setup and control data is required. In NAV, maintenance of data uses many of the same data preparation tools that were initially used to set up the system.

Role Center pages

One of the key features of NAV 2013 is the Role Tailored user experience centered around Role Centers tied to user work roles. The Role Tailored approach provides a single point of access into the system for each user through their assigned Role Center. The user's Role Center acts as their home page. Their Role Center focuses on the tasks needed to support its users' jobs throughout the day. Primary tasks are front and center, while the Action Ribbon and Departments Menu provide easy access only a click or two away to other functions.

The standard NAV 2013 distribution from Microsoft includes 21 different Role Center pages, identified for user roles such as Bookkeeper, Sales Manager, Shop Supervisor, Purchasing Agent, and so on. Some localized NAV distributions may have additional Role Center pages included. It is critical to realize that the Role Centers supplied out of the box are not generally intended to be used directly out of the box. According to the Help section, *Working with Role Centers*, only 3 of the 21 supplied Role Centers have been fully configured. These three are:

- 9004 – Bookkeeper
- 9005 – Sales Manager
- 9006 – Order Processor

The 21 Role Centers should be used as templates or models for custom Role Centers tailored to the specific work role requirements of the individual customer implementation.

One of the critical tasks of implementing a new system will be to analyze the work flow and responsibilities of the system's intended users and configure Role Centers to fit the users. In some cases, the supplied Role Centers can be used with minimal tailoring. Sometimes, it will be necessary to create complete new Role Centers. Even then, we will often be able to start with a copy of an existing Role Center Page, which we will modify as required. In any case, it is important to understand the structure of the Role Center Page and how it is built.

Role Center structure

The following screenshot shows Page 9006 – Order Processor Role Center:

The components of the Role Center highlighted in the preceding screenshot are:

1. Action Ribbon
2. Navigation Pane
3. Activity Pane
4. Cue Group Actions (in Cue Groups)
5. Cues (in Cue Groups)
6. Page Parts
7. User's Outlook
8. System Parts

A general representation of the structure of a Role Center Page is shown in the following outline:

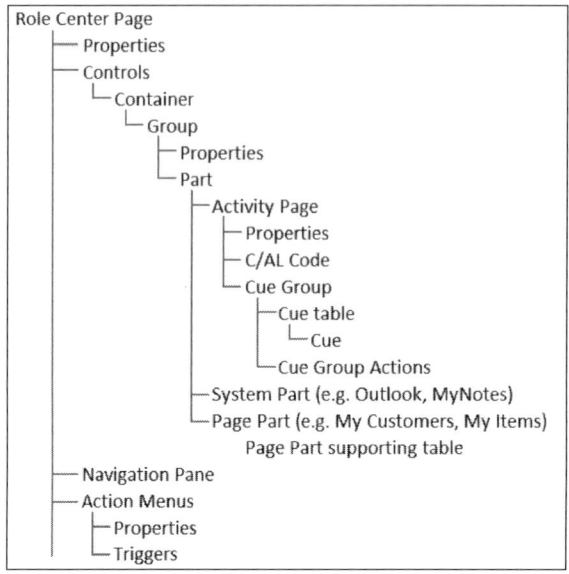

```
Role Center Page
        ── Properties
        ── Controls
                └─ Container
                        └─ Group
                                ├─ Properties
                                └─ Part
                                        ├─ Activity Page
                                        │       ├─ Properties
                                        │       ├─ C/AL Code
                                        │       └─ Cue Group
                                        │               ├─ Cue table
                                        │               │       └─ Cue
                                        │               └─ Cue Group Actions
                                        ├─ System Part (e.g. Outlook, MyNotes)
                                        └─ Page Part (e.g. My Customers, My Items)
                                                Page Part supporting table
        ── Navigation Pane
        ── Action Menus
                ├─ Properties
                └─ Triggers
```

We need to understand the construction of a Role Center page so that we are prepared to modify an existing Role Center or create a new one. First we'll take a look at Page 9006 – Order Processor Role Center in the Page Designer.

Page 9006 Order Processor Role Center - Page Designer

E..	Type	SubType	SourceExpr	Name	Caption
⊟	Container	RoleCenterArea		<Control1900000008>	<Control1900000008>
⊟	Group	Group		<Control1900724808>	<Control1900724808>
	Part	Page		<SO Processor Activities>	<SO Processor Activities>
	Part	System		<Outlook>	<Outlook>
⊟	Group	Group		<Control1900724708>	<Control1900724708>
	Part	Page		<Trailing Sales Orders ...	<Trailing Sales Orders Chart>
	Part	Page		<My Job Queue>	<My Job Queue>
	Part	Page		<My Customers>	<My Customers>
	Part	Page		<My Items>	<My Items>
	Part	Page		<Connect Online>	<Connect Online>
▶	Part	System		<MyNotes>	<MyNotes>

Preview   Help

The Role Center page layout should look familiar, because it's very similar in structure to the pages we've designed previously. What's specific to a Role Center page? There is a Container control of the **RoleCenterArea** SubType. This is required for a Role Center page. There are two Group Controls which represent the two columns (left and right) of the Role Center page display. Each group contains several parts which show up individually in the Role Center display.

Role Center page properties are accessed by highlighting the first blank line on the Page Designer form (the line below all of the defined controls), then clicking on the **Properties** icon, or we could right-click and choose the **Properties** option, or click on **View | Properties** or press *Shift + F4*. Note that the **PageType** is RoleCenter, and there is no **Source Table**.

Role Center activities page

Since the Group Control has no underlying code or settings, we'll examine the first Part Control's properties. The **PagePartId** property is SO Processor Activities.

Cue Groups and Cues

Now we'll focus on Page **9060 – SO Processor Activities**. Designing that page, we see the following layout. Comparing the controls we see here to those of the Role Center, we can see this Page Part is the source of the **Activities** section of the Role Center Page. There are three **CueGroup** Controls – `For Release`, `Sales Orders Released Not Shipped` and `Returns`. In each **CueGroup**, there are the **Field Controls** for the individual **Cues**.

An individual Cue is displayed as an iconic shortcut to a filtered list. The size of the stack of papers in the Cue icon represents the number of records in that list. The actual number of entries is also displayed as part of the icon (see the **Sales Orders - Open** example in following screenshot). The purpose of a Cue is to provide a focus on and single click access to a specific user task. The set of Cues is intended to represent the full set of primary activities for a user, based on their work Role.

Cue source table

In the Properties of the SO Processor Activities page, we see this is a **PageType** of `CardPart` tied to **SourceTable** `Sales Cue`.

Next we want to **Design** the referenced table, **Sales Cue**, to see how it is constructed. There we see a simply structured table, with an integer field for each of the Cues that were displayed in the Role Center we are analyzing. There is also a key field and two fields identified as Date Filters.

When we display the properties of one of these integer fields, **Sales Orders - Open**, we find it is a `FlowField` providing a Count of the `Sales Orders` with a `Status` of `Open`:

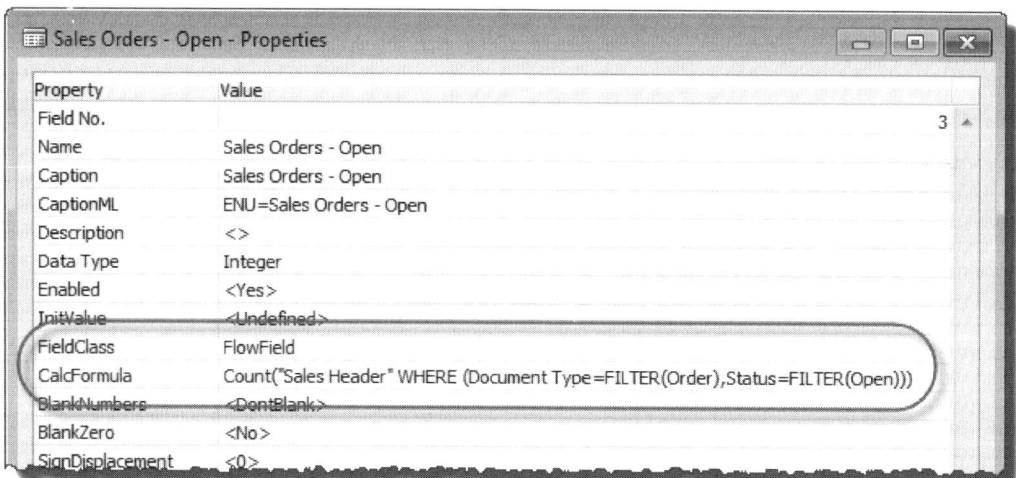

If we inspect each of the other integer fields in this table, we will find a similar FlowField setup. Each is defined to fit the specific Cue to which it's tied. If we think about what the Cues show (a count) and how FlowFields work (a calculation based on a range of data records), we can see this is a simple, direct method of providing the information necessary to support Cue displays. Clicking on the Cue (the count) then opens up the list of records being counted.

The following screenshot shows the list of Cue tables. Each of the Cue tables contains a series of FlowFields that support a set of Cues. Obviously, some Cue tables service more than one of the Role Center pages.

Cue Group Actions

Another set of Role Center page components to analyze are the **Cue Group Actions**. While the Cues are the primary tasks that are presented to the user, the Cue Group Actions are a related secondary set of tasks displayed to the right of the Cues.

Cue Group Actions are defined in the Role Center essentially the same way as Actions are defined in other page types. As the name implies, Cue Group Actions are associated with a Control with the **SubType** CueGroup. If we right- click on the CueGroup Control, one of the options available is **Control Actions** (as shown in the following screenshot):

When we choose **Control Actions**, the **Action Designer** form will be displayed showing the two CueGroup actions in the For Release CueGroup in the SO Processor Role Center page. If we open the **Properties** window we will see the "New" functionality is accomplished by setting the **RunPageMode** property to Create.

System Part

Now that we have covered the components of the **Activities** portion of the Role Center page, let's take a look at the other components.

Returning to Page 9006 in the **Page Designer**, we will examine the **Properties** of the next Part Control. This Page Part is the one that incorporates a view of the users' Outlook data into the Role Center. Looking at this control's properties, we see a **PartType** of system and a **SystemPartID** of Outlook. The Outlook Page Part can only appear in the left column of the Role Center page.

Page Parts

Now let's look at the second Group in Page 9006, the Group that defines the right-hand column appearing in the Role Center page. There are five Page Parts and a System Part defined.

Page Parts not visible

If we look again at the display of the Role Center page generated by this layout, we will see a chart (**Trailing Sales Orders**), followed by two ListParts (**My Customers** and **My Items**), in turn followed by the System Part (**My Notifications**).

The two Page Parts, **My Job Queue** and **Connect Online**, do not appear. These two Page Parts have been defined by the developer with the **Visible** property equal to FALSE, which causes them not to display unless the Role Center Page is customized by the user (or an administrator or by a developer) and the part added to the visible part list.

Page Part Charts

The first Page **Part** in the second **Group** provides for a Chart to display using the Chart Control Add-in included in NAV 2013. The Chart Control Add-in is documented in the **Developer and IT Pro Help** in the *Displaying Charts Using the Chart Control Add-in* section. In the Page 9006, the Page Part **Trailing Sales Orders Chart** invokes Page 760 of the same name. Looking at Page 760 in the Page Designer, we see the following layout:

The properties of the **Field** named **Business Chart** look like the following:

Note that the property **ControlAddIn** contains the necessary information to access the Chart Control Add-in. This property provides access to the screen, shown in the following screenshot, where the Client Add-ins are listed that are available for use in our NAV system. An Add-in is a Microsoft .NET Framework assembly (a module external to NAV but registered with the system) that lets us add customer functionality to a NAV Windows Client.

Page Parts for user data

The next three Page Parts in Role Center Page 9006 all provide data that is specific to the individual user. They track "My" data, information important to the user who is logged in. If we design any one of the pages, we can open the page properties to find out what table the page is tied to. Then, viewing any of these tables in the Table Designer, we will see that a highly ranked field is user ID. An example is the My Item table.

The user ID allows the data to be filtered to present user specific information to each user. In some cases, this data can be updated directly in the Role Center Page Part, for example in My Customers and My Items. In other cases, such as My Job Queue, the data is updated elsewhere and is viewed only in the Role Center Page Part. If our users needed to track other information in a similar manner, such as My Service Contracts, we could readily plagiarize the approach used in the standard Page Parts.

Continuing with the last Control in Page 9006, we see another **PartType** of System, in this case one for the **SystemPartID** of MyNotes. System Part options for the right-hand column include MyNotes, Notes, or RecordLinks (or None).

Navigation Pane and Action Menus

The last major Role Center Page components we're going to review are the **Navigation Pane** and the **Action Ribbon**. Even though there are two major parts of the Role Center Page that provide access to action choices, they both are defined in the **Action Designer** section of the **Page Designer**.

The display of Action Controls in a Role Center page is dependent on a combination of the definition of the controls in the Action Designer, certain properties of the page, and configuration/personalization of the page. Many of the default Role Centers provided with the product are configured as examples of possibilities of what can be done. Even if one of the default Role Centers seems to fit our customer's requirements exactly, we should create a copy of that Role Center page as another page object and reconfigure it. That way we can document how that page was set up and make any necessary tweaks.

We're going to start with Role Center Page 9006, because it is used as the default Role Center and is used in so many other examples. Copy Page 9006 into Page 50020 - Order Processor RC WDTU using the sequence **Object Designer | Page | Design | File |Save As...** and with a new page object ID 50020 and object Name WDTU Role Center.

Once we have the new page saved, in order to use this page as a Role Center we must create a Profile for the page. This is done within the Role Tailored Client and is typically a System Administrator task. Invoke the RTC and click on the **Departments** menu button in the Navigator Pane. Then click on **Administrator: Application Setup | Role Tailored Client | Lists: Profiles**. Click on the **New** icon and create a new profile like this one.

For the purpose of easy access to this Role Center for testing, we could also checkmark the **Default Role Center** box. Then, when we invoke the RTC, our test Role Center will be the one that displays (if no other profile is assigned to this user). Another approach to testing is to assign our User ID to use this Profile.

When we are doing development work on a Role Center, we can run the Role Center as a page from the C/SIDE Object Designer in the same way as other pages. However, the Role Center page will launch as a task page on top of whatever Role Center is configured for the active user. The Navigation Pane of the Role Center being modified will not be active and can't be tested with this approach. In order to test all of the aspects of the Role Center page, we must launch it as the assigned Role Center for the active user.

Other methods for running a Role Center for test purposes are these available from the mibuso.com NAV forum (`http://mibuso.com/dlinfo.asp?FileID=1194` and `http://mibuso.com/dlinfo.asp?FileID=1051`) or the one described in the Help section *Starting the Windows Client at the Command Prompt*. The guidance on use of Command Prompt initiation of the RTC is helpful in several other areas as well.

A major area where action choices are presented in a Role Center (and also in other page types) is in the ribbon. The ribbon for the standard Page 9006 - Order Processor Role Center, as delivered from Microsoft, looks like the following:

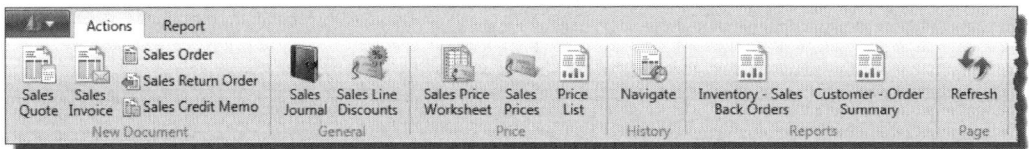

After we have created our Role Center copy, the ribbon for Page 50020 – Order Processor RC WDTU looks like the following:

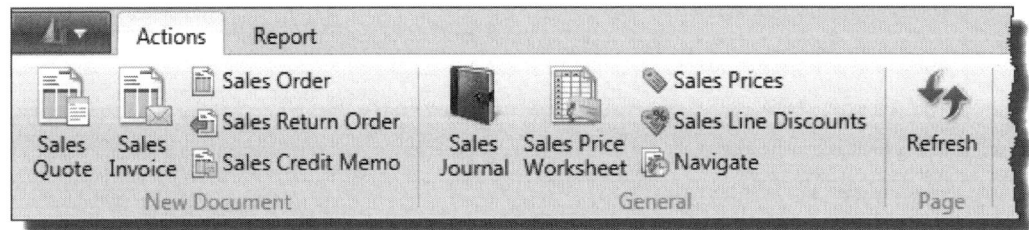

When we compare the available actions in the two ribbon images, we see most the same actions, but displayed quite a bit differently. Two of the report actions available in the standard ribbon don't show up in the Page 50020 ribbon, but if we take a look at the report tab on the ribbon, we'll see that they are available there.

If we made the same kind of analysis of other default Role Centers, we would find similar results. The appearance of the ribbon changes, losing detail, when the page is copied to another object number. As it turns out, the default Role Centers have been configured by Microsoft as part of the effort to show good examples of Role Center ribbon design. This is a good reason for starting with a fresh copy of our Role Centers when designing for our customer.

Action Designer

The actions for a page are defined and maintained in the **Action Designer**. The **Action Designer** is accessed from within the **Page Designer**. Open our new Page **50020 - WDTU Role Center** in the **Page Designer**, then either press *Ctrl + Alt + F4* or **View | Page Actions** to open the **Action Designer** to view the current set of actions defined for this page.

For our newly created Page 50020, cloned from Page 9006, the Action Designer contents look like the following:

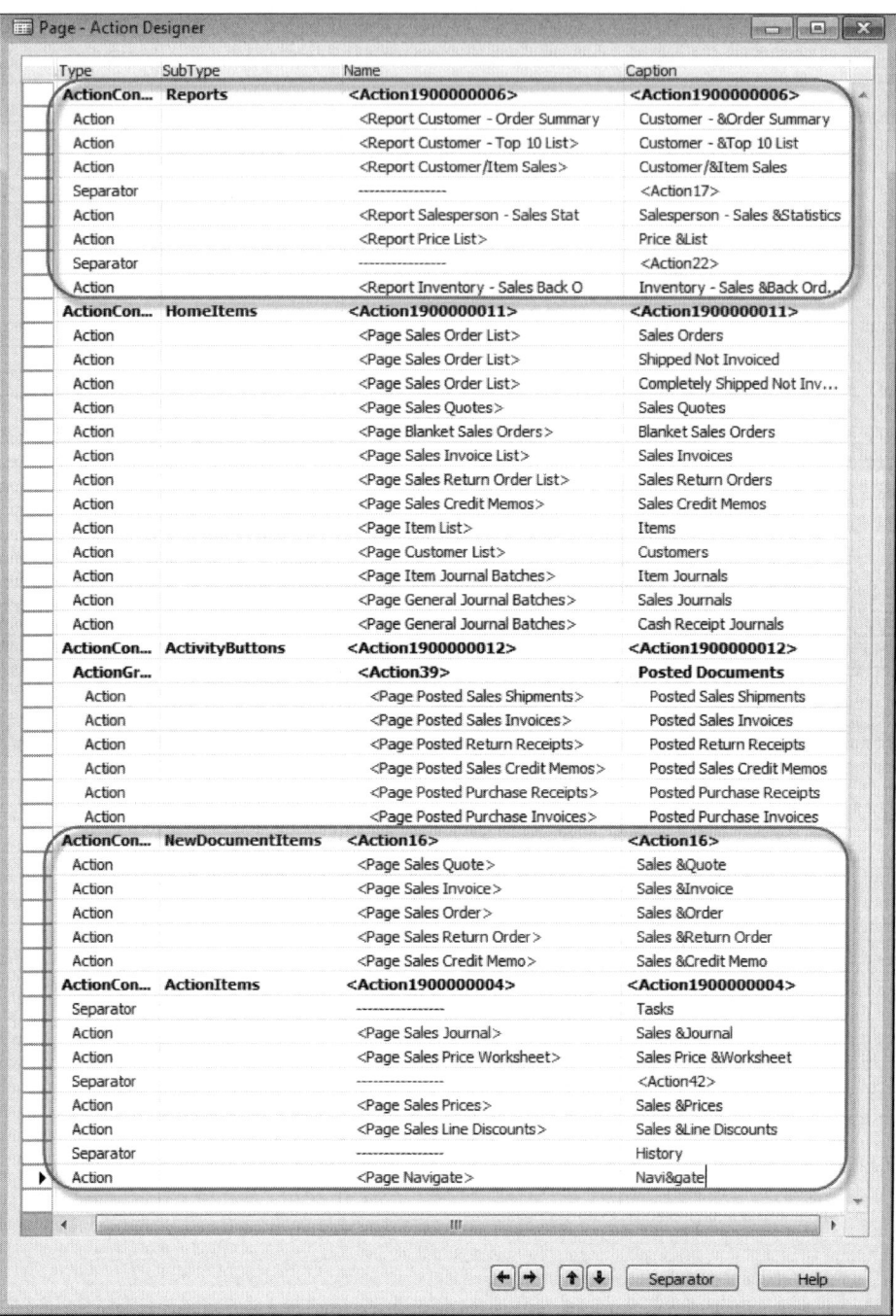

The actions enclosed in the green rectangles are the ones that are assigned to the ribbon. Whether or not they actually are displayed, how and where they are displayed is controlled by a combination of factors:

- The structure of the controls within the action list
- The properties of the individual actions
- The customizations that have been applied by a developer, administrator, or the user.

The first column of each action control is the **Type**. In hierarchical order, the action control entries can be ActionContainer, Action Group, Action, or Separator. The specific **SubType** of each **ActionContainer** entry determines the area, Ribbon, or Navigation Pane, in which the subordinate groups of actions will appear.

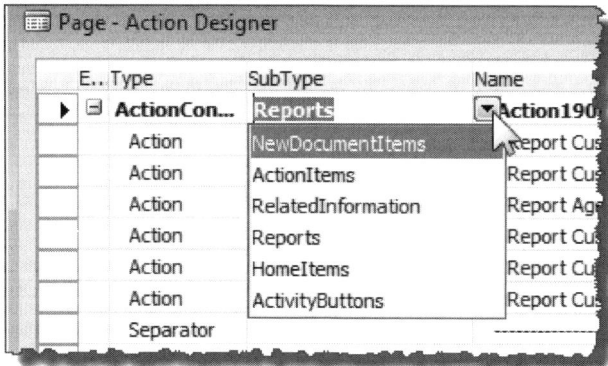

If the **SubType** is HomeItems or ActivityButtons (SubTypes that can only be used in Role Center pages), the indented subordinate actions will appear in the Navigation Pane. All the other SubTypes (NewDocumentItems, ActionItems, and Reports) will cause their subordinate actions to appear in the Role Center Ribbon. These three SubTypes are not limited to use in Role Center pages. The **SubType** RelatedInformation is not intended for use in Role Center pages, but for use in other page types.

An ActionGroup control provides a grouping of actions which will appear as a category in the ribbon. This is one way of defining a category to display in the ribbon. For actions to appear within the category on the ribbon, these Action controls must follow the ActionGroup and be indented. If an ActionGroup is indented within a parent ActionGroup, it will generate a drop-down list of actions.

The other type of action control is the Separator. In NAV 2009 page menus, the separator controls displayed a dashed line between logical sets of actions. In the NAV 2013 Action Ribbon, the separator controls don't appear to do anything.

If we compare the control entries in the preceding Action Designer screenshot to the action icons that display in the screenshot of the unmodified Page 50020 ribbon, we see the following:

- The action control entries of the `NewDocumentItems` and `ActionItems` `ActionContainers` appear on the Actions tab of the ribbon. ActionItems is intended for task related functions. NewDocumentItems is intended for those actions that cause a new document to be opened.

- All the control entries in the `NewDocumentItems` `ActionContainer` appear in the New Document Items Category in the Action Ribbon.

- The control entries in the `ActionItems` `ActionContainer` appear in the **General** Category of the ribbon.

- One action, **Refresh**, is a default action that is automatically generated and assigned to the **Page** Category.

- All the control entries in the `Reports` `ActionContainer` are in the General Category on the Reports tab of the Action Ribbon.

Creating a WDTU Role Center Ribbon

If we were creating a role center to be used in a real production environment, we would likely be defining a new Activities Page, new Cues, a new or modified Cue table, new FactBoxes, and so on. But since our primary purpose here is learning, we're going to take the shortcut of piggybacking on the existing role center and simply add our WDTU actions to the foundation of that role existing center.

There are several steps to be taken to define our WDTU Role Center Ribbon. The same end result, from the user's point of view, can be achieved using different approaches. We can also perform the development steps in different sequences. For the WDTU ribbon work, we will use the Developer tools.

The steps we need to follow for our WDTU actions are:

1. Define one or more new ribbon categories for the WDTU actions.
2. Create the WDTU action controls in the Action Designer.
3. Assign the WDTU action controls to the appropriate ribbon categories.
4. Finalize any look and feel items.

Because some of the original Order Processor Role Center ribbon layout disappeared when we cloned Page 9006 to Page 50020, we will also recreate that layout. For this part of our ribbon definition effort, because we want to learn more ways to accomplish implementation goals, we will use the Configuration/Personalization tools.

The steps needed to replicate the Page 9006 ribbon layout are:

1. Define the needed ribbon categories.
2. Assign the action controls to the appropriate categories.
3. Finalize any look and feel items.

The normal sequence of defining an Action Ribbon is to complete the work which utilizes development tools, then proceed with the work which can be done by an implementer or system administrator (or even an authorized user). So we will work on the WDTU portion of the Action Ribbon first, then the work of replicating the original layout.

Let's add the following functions to the WDTU portion of the Action Ribbon:

- Radio Show List page
- Playlist page
- Radio Show Types page
- Playlist Item Rates page
- Item List (filtered for Playlist Items) page
- Record Labels page

We'll put the first two items in a category named WDTU Operations and the other four items in a category named WDTU Data Maintenance.

Promoted Actions Categories

There are at least two ways available to set up the categories. One involves assigning values to the Page Property **PromotedActionCategoriesML** (which appears to be originally intended to support NAV's MultiLanguage capabilities rather than Ribbon layout customization).

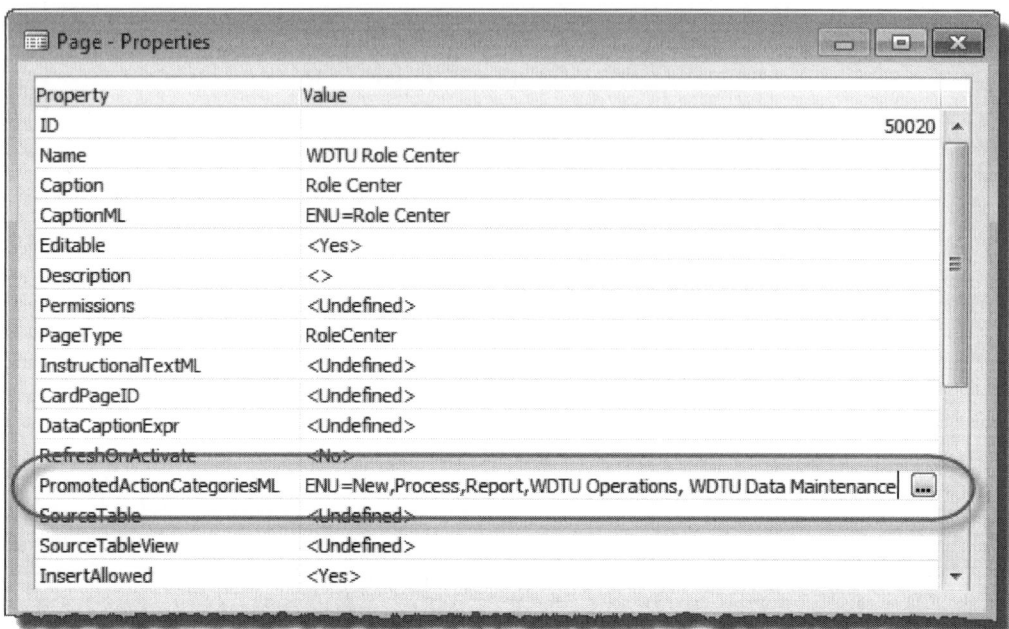

There are 10 **PromotedActionCategoriesML** slots available. The first three are assigned categories by default of New, Process, and Report, but can be renamed (the default names are retained in this example). The category slots must be referred to by their default names (New, Process, Report, Category4, Category5, ..., Category10) when referred to in code. In the standard product the CategoryN names are used in a number of pages. Category4, for example, is used in Pages **88 Job Card**, **950 Time Sheet**, **5900 Service Order**, and others. Category4 and Category5 both are used in Pages **1027 Job WIP Cockpit** and **8629 Config. Wizard**. Category4, Category5, and Category6 are all used in Page **9500 Debugger**.

Individual actions are assigned to appear in a specific category through the action's properties. **Promoted** is set to `Yes`, the **PromotedCategory** is (in this case) set to `Category4` which has been assigned to display as **WDTU Operations**. Note that the **Image** property was also assigned; as a general rule, an image should be assigned for all action controls to indicate functionality to the user.

Let's do the same thing for one of our WDTU Maintenance actions, the Radio Show Types page. We'll set **Promoted** to `Yes`, the **PromotedCategory** to `Category5`, and the **Image** to `Entry`. The Ribbon resulting from the two actions being **Promoted** and assigned looks like the following screenshot. Using this method of defining and assigning Categories causes a new **Home** tab to be added to the ribbon.

Action Groups

Another way of defining Categories and assigning actions to them is through the use of ActionGroups. This approach seems quite a bit simpler. All we have to do is make the proper `ActionGroup` entries in the **Action Designer** with the appropriate `Action` entries indented under them as shown in the following screenshot:

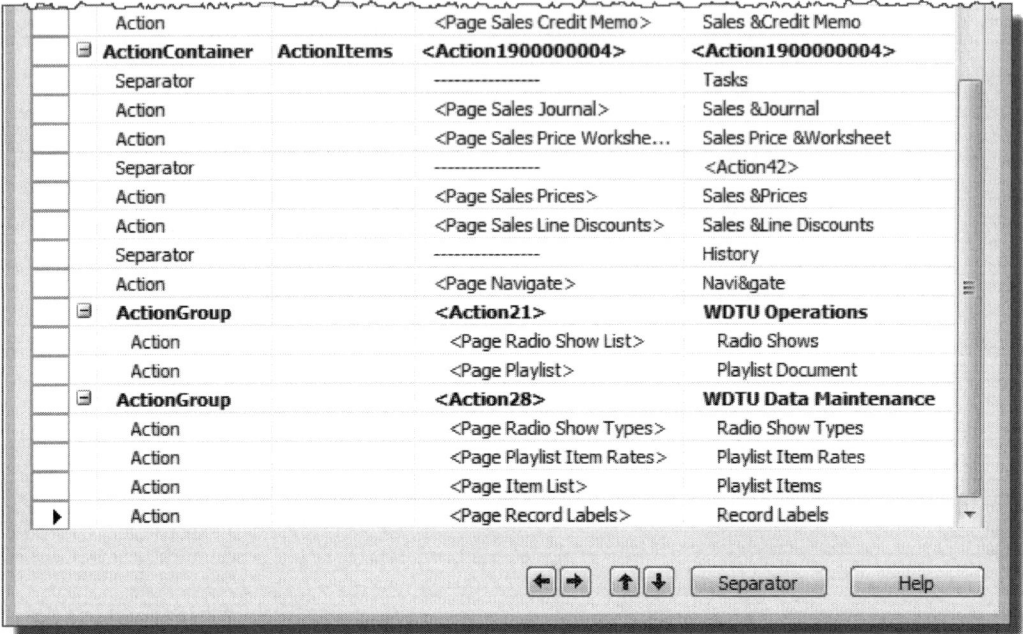

The resulting Ribbon looks like the following. Note that the WDTU categories and actions appear this time on the Actions tab and there is no Home tab.

Configuration/Personalization

The procedures and interface tools we use to do Configuration are also used by users to do Personalization. Both terms refer to revising the display contents and format of a Role Center as it appears to one or more users. As it says in the Help section *Walkthrough: Configuring the Order Processor Role Center*.

> The difference between configuration and personalization is configuring a Role Center changes the user interface for all users who have that profile, whereas personalizing a Role Center only changes the user interface for a single user.

We could replace the WDTU Category assignments we just made using ActionGroups by defining Categories and assigning actions using Configuration. The result would look exactly the same to our users. But instead, let's use Configuration to quickly restore the layout of the actions that were in Role Center Page 9006. We can run page 9006 to see what that layout is (or reference the earlier snapshot of the Page 9006 ribbon).

A couple of important points:

- Configuration is tied to a specific Profile. Other profiles using the same Role Center page do not see the same Configuration layout.

- Configuration can only be done by the Owner of a Profile. When we created our WDTU Test Profile, we did not assign an owner so that will have to be done now.

- Profile setup can be accessed in the RTC in **Departments** | **Administration** | **Application Setup** | **Role Tailored Client** | **Profiles**. This can also be found by entering the word Profile in the RTC Search box. The Owner ID for a Profile can be updated there by an Administrator with sufficient Permissions.

A Role Center ribbon is configured by opening the Role Tailored Client in Configuration mode with the focus on the Profile we want to configure. Personalization doesn't require this step. This is done from the DOS Command prompt using a command line essentially similar to:

```
"C:\Program Files (x86)\Microsoft Dynamics NAV\70\
RoleTailored Client\Microsoft.Dynamics.Nav.Client.exe"
 -configure -profile:"WDTU Test"
```

For additional information refer to the Help section *How to: Open the Microsoft Dynamics NAV Windows Client in Configuration Mode*.

Once the Role Center displays, click on the arrowhead to the right of the Microsoft Dynamics icon (*1* in the following screenshot), then on **Customize** option (*2* in the following screenshot), followed by the **Customize Ribbon** option (*3* in the following screenshot).

That will take us to this screen:

As we can see, using the Customize Ribbon screen we can Create Groups (referred to as Categories elsewhere), add new actions to those available on the ribbon, remove actions (make them not visible), reorganize ribbon entries, even create new tabs, or rename existing items. In sum, everything that we've done so far to customize the Role Center Ribbon can be done through this screen. The big difference is that Customization (a general term encompassing both Configuration and Personalization) is specific to a single Profile, while the other modifications will apply to all profiles.

As part of our Personalizing, we might use the **Move Up** and **Move Down** options to rearrange the actions on the ribbon, moving the WDTU actions to the left. When we are done configuring the ribbon for the WDTU Test Profile, it might look like the following:

Navigation Pane

The Navigation Pane is the menu list that makes up the leftmost column on a Role Center. A Navigation Pane can have two or more buttons. The required two buttons are Home and Departments.

Navigation Home Button

The basic contents of the Home button for a Role Center are defined in the **Action Designer** in the `ActionContainer` of **SubType** `HomeItems`.

In addition to the action controls defined in the Action Designer, the Navigation Pane Home menu list includes all the Cue entries that appear in the Activities Pane of the Role Center. We can see the combined sets of action options in the following screenshot. Note that there are a number of indented (nested) options within groups such as **Sales Orders, Sales Quotes** and **Sales Credit Memos**. These groups have been set up using the same type of Configuration tools we just used for the ribbon.

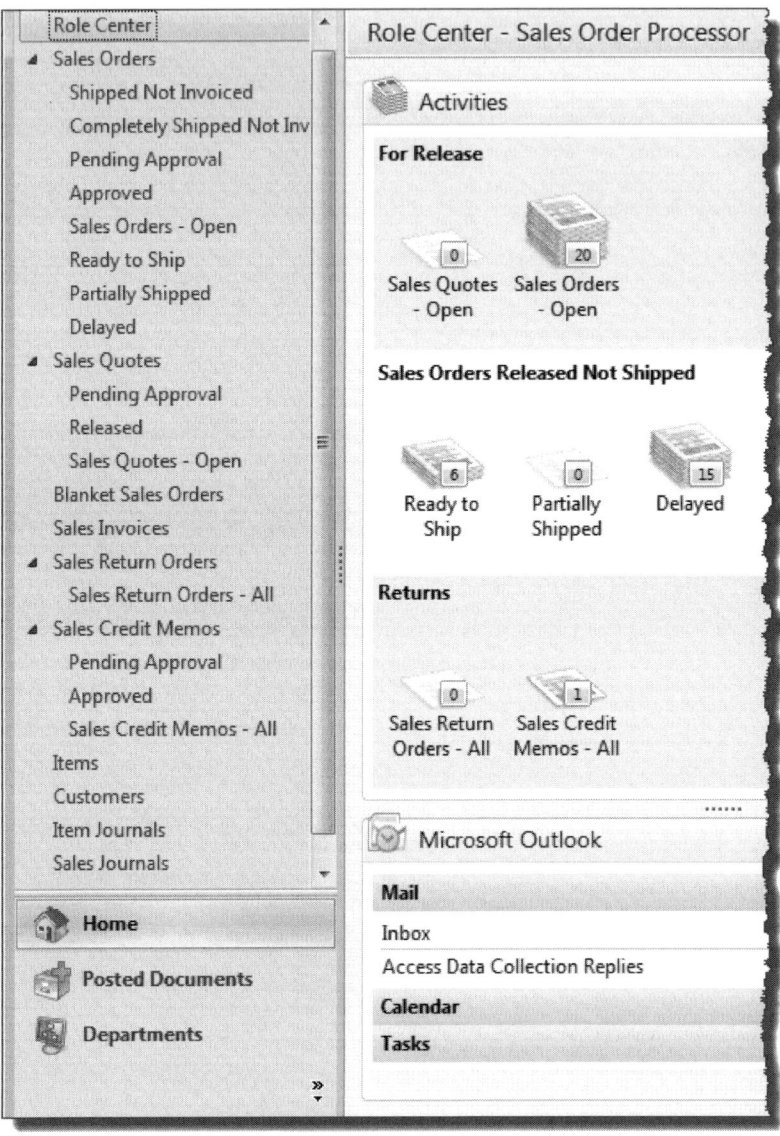

We can access the Configuration/Personalization tools either through the arrow next to the Microsoft Dynamics logo or through the chevron at the bottom right of the Navigation Pane (below the buttons).

Navigation Departments Button

The other required Navigation Pane button, the Departments button, has its menu entries generated based on the contents of the MenuSuite object. If we click on the Departments button, a screen like the following will be displayed:

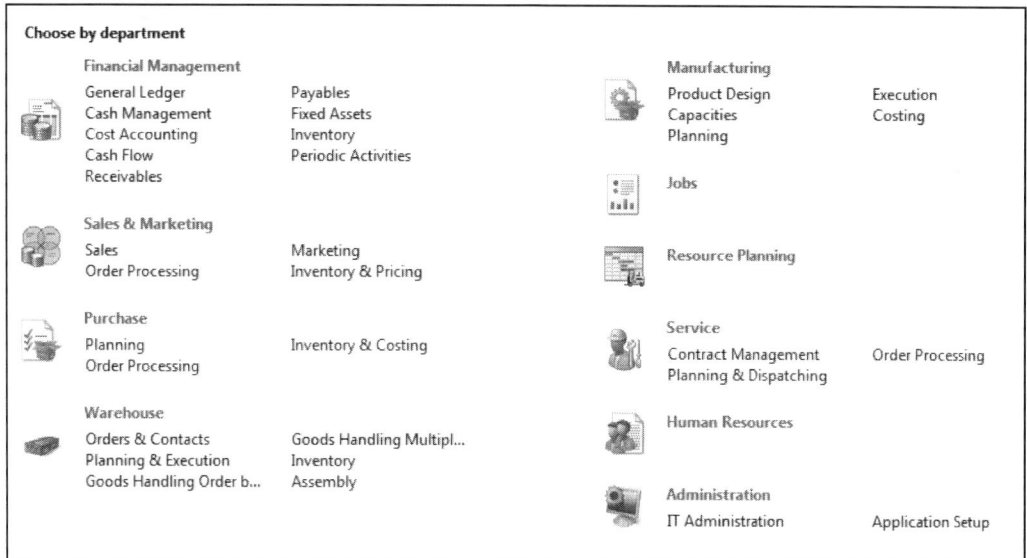

Other Navigation Buttons

Other Navigation Pane buttons can be defined and populated by means of
`ActionGroup` entries with the `ActionContainer ActivityButtons` in the **Action
Designer** as shown in the following screenshot:

Navigation Pane buttons can also be added, renamed, repopulated and made
not visible through the **Customize Navigation Pane...** option in the page
Customization submenu.

XMLports

XML is **eXtensible Markup Language**, a structured text format developed to
describe data to be shared by dissimilar systems. XML has become a default standard
for communications between systems. To make handling XML-formatted data
simpler and more error resistant, NAV provides XMLports, a data import/export
object. In addition to processing XML-formatted data, XMLports can also handle a
wide variety of other text file formats (including CSV files, generic flat files, and so
on). XML formatted data is text based, with each piece of information structured in
one of two basic formats, Elements or Attributes. An Element is the overall logical
unit of information while an Attribute is a property of an Element. Thus, they are
formatted as:

- `<Tag>element value</Tag>` (an Element format)
- `<Tag AttribName = "attribute data value">` (an Attribute format)

Elements can be nested, but must not overlap. Element and Attribute names are case-sensitive. Names cannot start with a number, punctuation character, or the letters "xml" (or XML) and cannot contain spaces.

An Attribute value must always be enclosed in single or double quotation marks. Some references suggest that Elements should be used for data and Attributes for metadata. Complex data structures are built up of combinations of these two formats.

Consider the following example:

```
<Table Name='Sample XML format'>
    <Record>
        <DataItem1>12345</DataItem1>
        <DataItem2>23456</DataItem2>
    </Record>
    <Record>
        <DataItem1>987</DataItem1>
    </Record>
    <Record>
        <DataItem1>22233</DataItem1>
        <DataItem2>7766</DataItem2>
    </Record>
</Table>
```

In this case, we have a set of data identified as a `Table` with an attribute of `Name` equal to `'Sample XML format'`, which contains three `Records`, each `Record` containing data in one or two fields named `DataItem1` and `DataItem2`. The data is in a clearly structured text format so it can be read and processed by any system prepared to read this particular XML format. If the field tags are well designed, the data is easily interpretable by humans as well. The key to successful exchange of data using XML is the sharing and common interpretation of the format between the transmitter and recipient.

XML is a standard format in the sense that the data structure options are clearly defined. But it is very flexible in the sense that the identifying tag names in `<  >` brackets and the related data structures that can be defined and handled are totally open ended. The specific structure and the labels are whatever the communicating parties decide they should be. The "rules" of XML only determine how the basic syntax shall operate.

XML data structures can be as simple as a flat file consisting of a set of identically formatted records or as complex as an sales order structure with headers containing a variety of data items, combined with associated detail lines containing their own variety of data items. An XML data structure can be as complicated as the application requires.

XML standards are maintained by the W3C whose website is at www.w3.org. There are many other useful web sites for basic XML information.

XMLport components

Although in theory XMLports can operate in both an import and an export mode, in practice, individual XMLports objects tend to be dedicated to either import or export. This allows the internal logic to be simpler. XMLports utilize a process of looping through and processing data similar to that of Report objects.

The components of XMLports are:

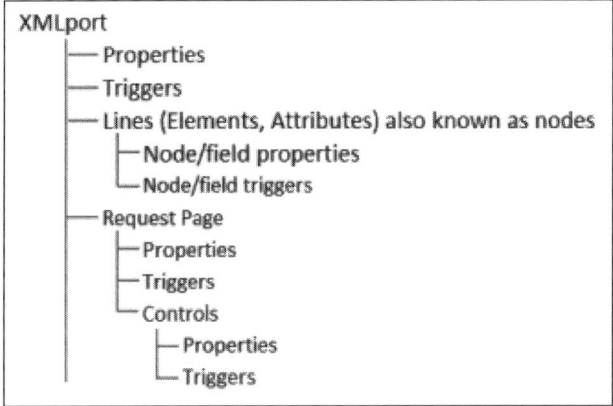

XMLport properties

XMLport properties are shown in the following screenshot of the **Properties** of the XMLport object **9170**:

Descriptions of the individual properties are as follows:

- **ID**: The unique XMLport object number.

- **Name**: The name by which this XMLport is referred to within C/AL code.

- **Caption**: The name that is displayed for this XMLport; it defaults to the contents of the **Name** property.

- **CaptionML**: The **Caption** translation for a defined alternative language.

- **Direction**: This defines whether this XMLport can only `Import`, `Export`, or `<Both>`; the default is `<Both>`.

- **DefaultFieldsValidation**: This defines the default value (**Yes** or **No**) for the **FieldValidate** property for individual XMLport data fields. The default for this field is Yes, which would in turn set the default for individual field **FieldValidate** properties to Yes.

- **Encoding (or TextEncoding)**: This defines the character encoding option to be used, UTF-8 (ASCII compatible) or UTF-16 (not ASCII compatible) or ISO-8859-2 (for certain European languages written in Latin characters). UTF-16 is the default. This is inserted into the heading of the XML document.

- The **TextEncoding** option is only available if the **Format** property is Fixed Text or Variable Text. In this case, a character coding option of MS-DOS is available and is the default.

- **XMLVersionNo**: This defines to which version of XML the document conforms, Version 1.0 or 1.1. The default is Version <1.0>. This is inserted into the heading of the XML document.

- **Format/Evaluate**: This can be C/SIDE Format/Evaluate (the default) or XML Format Evaluate. This property defines whether the external text data is (for imports) or will be (for exports) XML data types or C/SIDE data types. Default processing for all fields in each case will be appropriate to the defined data type. If the external data does not fit in either of these categories, then the XML data fields must be processed through a temporary table.

  The temporary table processing approach reads the external data into text data fields with data conversion logic done in C/AL into data types that can then be stored in the NAV database. Very limited additional information on this is available in the online **Help** in Temporary Property (XMLports).

- **UseDefaultNamespace** and **DefaultNamespace**: These properties are provided to support compatibility with other systems which require the XML document to be in a specific namespace, such as use of a web service as a reference within Visual Studio. **UseDefaultNamespace** defaults to **No**. A default namespace in the form of **URN** (**Uniform Resource Name** or, in this case, a **Namespace Identifier**) concluding with the object number of the XMLport is supplied for the **DefaultNamespace** property. This property is only active if the **Format** property is XML.

- **InlineSchema**: This property defaults to **No**. An inline schema allows the XML schema document (an XSD) to be embedded within the XML document. This can be used by setting the property to **Yes** when exporting an XML document, which will add the schema to that exported document. This property is only active if the **Format** property is XML.

- **UseLax**: This property defaults to **No**. Some systems may add information to the XML document, which is not defined in the XSD schema used by the XMLport. When this property is set to **Yes**, that extraneous material will be ignored, rather than resulting in an error. This property is only active if the **Format** property is XML.

- **Format**: This property has the options of XML, Variable Text, or Fixed Text. It defaults to XML. This property controls the import/export data format that the XMLport will process. Choosing **XML** means that the processing will only deal with a properly formatted XML file. Choosing **Variable Text** means that the processing will only deal with a file formatted with delimiters set up as defined in the **FieldDelimiter**, **FieldSeparator**, **RecordSeparator**, and **TableSeparator** properties (such as **CSV** files). Choosing **Fixed Text** means that the each individual element and attribute must have its Width property set to a value greater than 0 (zero) and the data to be processed must be formatted accordingly.

- **FileName**: This can be filled with the predefined path and name of a specific external text data file to be either the source (for **Import**) or target (for **Export**) for the run of the XMLport or this property can be set dynamically. Only one file at a time can be opened, but the file in use can be changed during the execution of the XMLport (not often done).

- **FieldDelimiter**: This applies to **Variable Text** format external files only. It defaults to **<">** — double quotes, the standard for so-called "comma-delimited" text files. This property supplies the string that will be used as the starting delimiter for each data field in the text file. If this is an **Import**, then the XMLport will look for this string, and then use the string following as data until the next **FieldDelimiter** string is found, terminating the data string. If this is an **Export**, the XMLport will insert this string at the beginning and end of each data field contents string.

- **FieldSeparator**: This applies to **VariableText** format external files only. Defaults to **<,>** — a comma, the standard for so-called "comma delimited" text files. This property supplies the string that will be used as the delimiter between each data field in the text file (looked for on **Imports** or inserted on **Exports**). See the Help for this property for more information.

- **RecordSeparator**: This applies to **VariableText** or **FixedText** format external files only. This defines the string that will be used as the delimiter at the end of each data record in the text file. If this is an **Import**, the XMLport will look for this string to mark the end of each data record. If this is an **Export**, the XMLport will append this string at the end of each data record output. The default is **<<NewLine>>**, which represents any combination of CR (carriage return — ASCII value 13) and LF (line feed — ASCII value 10) characters. See the Help for this property for more information.

- **TableSeparator**: This applies to **VariableText** or **FixedText** format external files only. This defines the string that will be used as the delimiter at the end of each Data Item (for example, each text file). The default is **<<NewLine><NewLine>>**. See the Help for this property for more information.

- **UseRequestForm**: This determines whether a Request Page should be displayed to allow the user choice of Sort Sequence, entry of filters, and other requested control information. The options are **Yes** and **No**. The default is **<Yes>**. An XMLport Request Page has only the **OK** and **Cancel** options.

- **TransactionType**: This property identifies the XMLport processing Server Transaction Type as **Browse**, **Snapshot**, **UpdateNoLocks**, or **Update**. This is an advanced and seldom-used property. For more information, we can refer to the Help files and SQL Server documentation.

- **Permissions**: This property provides report-specific setting of permissions, which are rights to access data, subdivided into **Read**, **Insert**, **Modify**, and **Delete**. This allows the developer to define permissions that override the user-by-user permissions security setup.

XMLport triggers

The XMLport has a very limited set of triggers.

- **Documentation()** is executed for documentation comments.

- **OnInitXMLport()** is executed once when the XMLport is loaded before the table views and filters have been set.

- **OnPreXMLport()** is executed once after the table views and filters have been set. These can be reset here.

- **OnPostXMLport()** is executed once after all the data is processed, if the XMLport completes normally.

XMLport data lines

An XMLport can contain any number of data lines. The data lines are laid out in a strict hierarchical structure, with the elements and attributes mapping exactly, one for one, in the order of the data fields in the external text file, the XML document.

XMLports should not be run directly from a Navigation Pane action command (due to conflicts with NAV UX standards), but can be run either from ribbon actions on a Role Center or other page or by means of an object containing the necessary C/AL code. When running from another object (as opposed to from an action menu entry), C/AL code calls the XMLport to stream data either to or from an appropriately formatted file (XML document or other text format). This code is typically written in a Codeunit but can be placed in any object that can contain C/AL code.

The following example is code to execute an exporting XMLport and save the resulting file from the NAV service tier to the client machine.

```
XMLfile.CREATE(TEMPORARYPATH + 'RadioShowExport.xml');
XMLfile.CREATEOUTSTREAM(OutStreamObj);
XMLPORT.EXPORT(50000,OutStreamObj);
FromFileName := XMLfile.NAME;
ToFileName := 'RadioShowExport.xml';
XMLfile.CLOSE;

//Need to call DOWNLOAD to move the xml file
//from the service tier to the client machine
DOWNLOAD(FromFileName,'Downloading File...','C:','Xml file(*.xml)|*.
xml',ToFileName);

//Make sure to clean up the temporary file from the
//service tier
ERASE(FromFileName);
```

Two text variables (the "from" file name and "to" file name), a file variable, and an OutStream object variable are required to support the preceding code. The data variables are defined as shown in the following screenshot:

XMLport line properties

The XMLport line properties which are active on a line depend on the contents of the **SourceType** property. The first four properties listed are common to all three **SourceType** values (**Text**, **Table**, or **Field**) and the other properties specific to each are listed below the screenshots showing all the properties for each **SourceType**.

- **Indentation**: This indicates at what subordinate level in the hierarchy of the XMLport this entry exists. Indentation **0** is the primary level, parent to all higher numbered levels. Indentation **1** is a child of indentation **0**, indentation **2** is a child of **1**, and so forth. Only one indentation **0** is allowed in an XMLport , so often we will want to define the Level 0 line to be a simple text element line. This allows the definition of multiple Tables at Indentation level 1.

- **NodeName**: This defines the Node Name that will be used in the XML document to identify the data associated with this position in the XML document. No spaces are allowed in a **NodeName**; we can use underscores, dashes, and periods but no other special characters.

- **NodeType**: This defines if this data item is an **Element** or an **Attribute**.

- **SourceType**: This defines the type of data this field corresponds to in the NAV database. The choices are **Text**, **Table**, and **Field**. Text means that the value in the **SourceField** property will act as a Global variable and, typically must be dealt with by embedded C/AL code. Table means that the value in the **SourceField** property will refer to an NAV table. Field means that the value in the **SourceField** property will refer to an NAV field within the parent table previously defined as an element.

SourceType as Text

The following screenshot shows the properties for **SourceType** as **Text**:

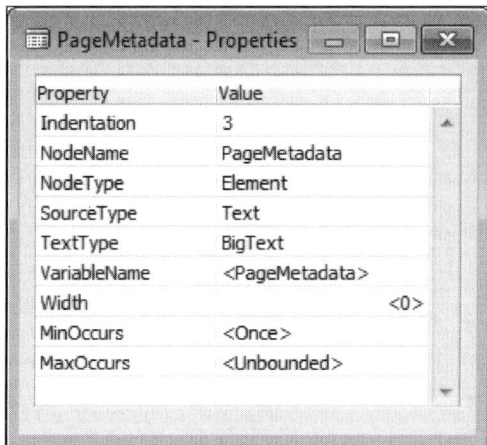

The description of the Text-specific properties is as follows:

- **TextType**: This defines the NAV Data Type as **Text** or **BigText**. **Text** is the default
- **VariableName**: This contains the name of the Global variable, which can be referenced by C/AL code

The **Width**, **MinOccurs**, and **MaxOccurs** properties are discussed later in this chapter.

SourceType as Table

The following screenshot shows the properties for **SourceType** as `Table`:

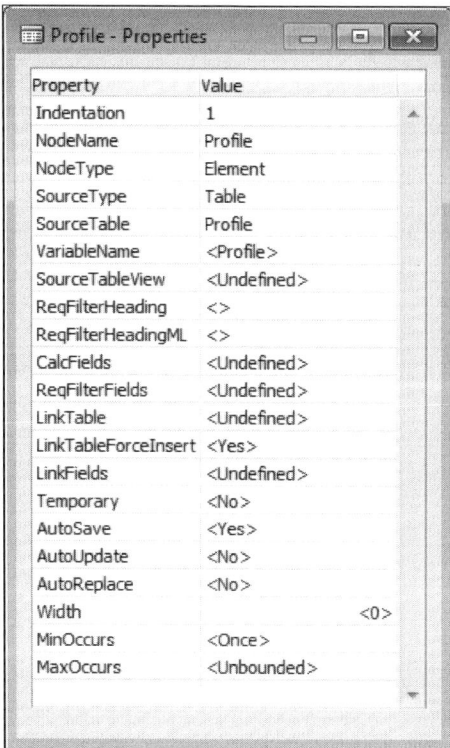

The descriptions of the table-specific properties are as follows:

- **SourceTable**: This defines the NAV table being referenced.
- **VariableName**: This defines the name to be used in C/AL code for the NAV table. This is the functional equivalent to definition of a Global variable.
- **SourceTableView**: This enables the developer to define a view by choosing a key and sort order or by applying filters on the table.
- **ReqFilterHeading** and **ReqFilterHeadingML**: These fields allow the definition of the name of the Request Page filter definition tab that applies to this table.
- **CalcFields**: This lists the FlowFields in the table that are to be automatically calculated.
- **ReqFilterFields**: This lists the fields that will initially display on the Request page filter definition tab.
- **LinkTable**: This allows the linking of a field in a higher-level item to a key field in a lower-level item. If, for example, we were exporting all of the Purchase Orders for a Vendor, we might Link the **Buy-From Vendor No.** in a Purchase Header to the **No.** in a Vendor record. The **LinkTable** in this case would be Vendor and **LinkField** would be No.; therefore **LinkTable** and **LinkFields** work together. Use of the **LinkTable** and **LinkFields** operates the same as applying a filter on the higher-level table data so that only records relating to the defined lower-level table and field are processed. See the Help for more detail.
- **LinkTableForceInsert**: This can be set to force insertion of the linked table data and execution of the related **OnAfterInitRecord()** trigger. This property is tied to the **LinkTable** and **LinkFields** properties. It also applies to **Import**.
- **LinkFields**: This defines the fields involved in a table + field linkage.
- **Temporary**: This defaults to No. If this property is set to Yes, it allows the creation of a Temporary table in working storage. Data imported into this table can then be evaluated, edited, and manipulated before being written out to the database. This Temporary table has the same capabilities and limitations as a Temporary table defined as a Global variable.
- **AutoSave**: If set to Yes (the default), an imported record will be automatically saved to the table. Either **AutoUpdate** or **AutoReplace** must also be set to Yes.

- **AutoUpdate**: If a record exists in the table with a matching primary key, all the data fields are initialized, and then all the data from the incoming record is copied into the table record.

- **AutoReplace**: If a record exists in the table with a matching primary key, the populated data fields in the incoming record are copied into the table record; all the other fields in the target record are left undisturbed. This provides a means to update a table by importing records with a limited number of data fields filled in.

The **Width**, **MinOccurs**, and **MaxOccurs** properties are discussed later in this chapter.

SourceType as Field

The following screenshot shows the properties for **SourceType** as `Field`:

The description of the Field-specific properties is as follows:

- **SourceField**: This defines the data field being referenced. It may be a field in any defined table.

- **FieldValidate**: This applies to Import only. If this property is `Yes`, then whenever the field is imported into the database, the **OnValidate()** trigger of the field will be executed.

- **AutoCalcField**: This applies to Export and FlowField Data fields only. If this property is set to Yes, the field will be calculated before it is retrieved from the database. Otherwise, a FlowField would export as an empty field.

The details of the **Width**, **MinOccurs**, and **MaxOccurs** properties follow in the next section.

Element or Attribute

An **Element** data item may appear many times but an **Attribute** data item may only appear at most once; the occurrence control properties differ based on the **NodeType**.

NodeType of Element

The Element-specific properties are as follows:

- **Width**: When the XMLport **Format** property is Fixed Text, then this field is used to define the fixed width of this element's field.
- **MinOccurs**: This defines the minimum number of times this data item can occur in the XML document. This property can be Zero or Once (the default).
- **MaxOccurs**: This defines the maximum number of times this data item can occur in the XML document. This property can be Once or Unbounded. Unbounded (the default) means any number of times.

NodeType of Attribute

The Attribute-specific property is as follows:

- **Occurrence**: This is either Required (the default) or Optional, depending on the text file being imported

XMLport line triggers

The XMLport line triggers are shown in the following screenshot for the three line Source types — **Profiles** (Text), **Profile** (Table), and **ID** (Field).

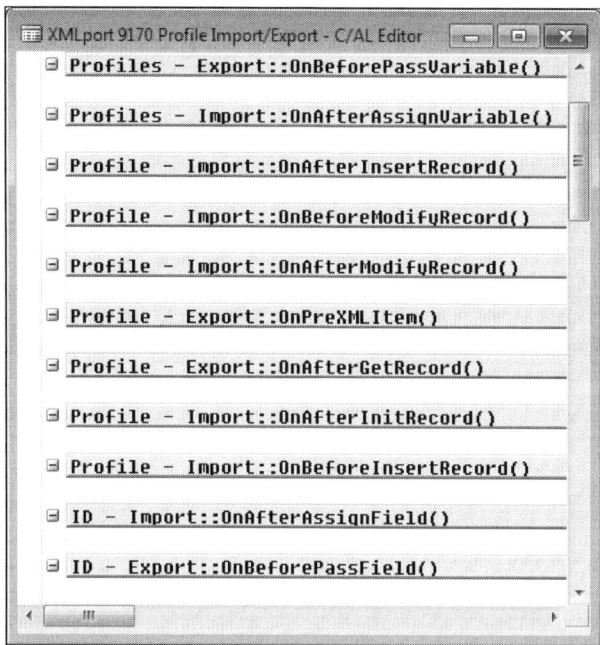

As we can see in the screenshot, there are different XMLport triggers depending whether **DataType** is Text, Table, or Field.

DataType as Text

The triggers for DataType as Text are:

- **Export::onBeforePassVariable()**, for **Export** only. This trigger is typically used for manipulation of the text variable.

- **Import::OnAfterAssignVariable()**, for **Import** only. This trigger gives us access to the imported value in text format.

DataType as Table

The triggers for DataType as Table are as follows:

- **Import::OnAfterInsertRecord()**, for **Import** only: This trigger is typically used when the data is being imported into Temporary tables. This is where we would put the C/AL code to build and insert records for the permanent database table(s).

- **Import::OnBeforeModifyRecord()**, for **Import** only: For use when AutoSave is Yes, to update the imported data before saving it.

- **Import::OnAfterModifyRecord()**, for **Import** only: For use when AutoSave is Yes, to update the data after updating.

- **Export::OnPreXMLItem()**, for **Export** only: This trigger is typically used for setting filters and initializing before finding and processing the first database record.

- **Export::OnAfterGetRecord()**, for **Export** only: This trigger allows access to the data after the record is retrieved from the NAV database. This trigger is typically used to allow manipulation of table fields being exported.

- **Import::OnAfterInitRecord()**, for **Import** only: This trigger is typically used to check whether or not a record should be processed further or to manipulate the data.

- **Import::OnBeforeInsertRecord()**, for **Import** only: This is another place where we can manipulate data before it is inserted into the target table. This trigger is executed after the **OnAfterInitRecord()** trigger.

DataType as Field

The triggers for DataType as Field are as follows:

- **Import::OnAfterAssignField()**, for **Import** only. This trigger provides access to the imported data value for evaluation or manipulation before outputting to the database.

- **Export::OnBeforePassField()**, for **Export** only. This trigger provides access to the data field value just before the data is exported.

XMLport Request Page

XMLports can also have a Request Page to allow the user to enter Option control information and filter the data being processed. Default filter fields that will appear on the Request Page are defined in the Properties form for the table XMLport line.

Any desired options that are to be available to the user as part of the Request Page must be defined in the **Request Options Page Designer**. This Designer is accessed from the XMLport Designer through **View | Request Page**. The definition of the contents and layout of the Request Options Page is done essentially the same way as other pages are done. As with any other filter setup screen, the user has complete control of what fields are used for filtering and what filters are applied.

Web services

Web services is an industry standard software interface which allows software applications to interoperate using standard interface specifications along with standard communications services and protocols. When NAV publishes some web services, those functions can be accessed and utilized by properly programmed software residing anywhere on the Web. This software does not need to be directly compatible with C/SIDE or even .NET, it just needs to obey web services conventions and have security access to the NAV Web Services.

Some benefits of NAV Web Services are:

- Very simple to publish (that is, to expose a web service to a consuming program outside of NAV)
- Provides managed access to NAV data while respecting and enforcing NAV rules, logic, and design that already exists
- Uses Windows Authentication and respects NAV data constraints
- Supports SSL—Secure Socket Layer
- Supports both the SOAP interface (cannot access Query objects) and the OData interface (cannot access Codeunit objects)

Disadvantages of NAV Web Services include:

- Allowing access to a system from the Web requires a much higher level of security
- The NAV objects that are published generally need to be designed (or at least customized) to properly interface with this very different user interface
- Access from the Web complicates the system administrator's job of managing loads on the system

There are several factors that should be considered in judging the appropriateness of an application being considered for web services integration. Some of these are:

- What is the degree to which the functionality of the standard RTC interface is needed? Web services application should not try to replicate what would normally be done with a full client, but should be used for limited, focused functionality.

- What is the amount of data to be exchanged? Generally, web services are used remotely. Even if it is used locally, there are additional levels of security handshaking and inter-system communications required. These involve additional processing overhead. Web services should be used for low data volume applications.

- How public is the user set? For security reasons, the user set for direct connection to our NAV system should generally be limited to known users, not the general public. Web services should not be used to provide Internet exposure to the customer's NAV system, but rather for **intranet** access.

Because web services are intended for use by low-intensity users, there are separate license options available with lower costs per user than the full-client license. This can make the cost of providing web services-based access quite reasonable, especially if by doing so, we increase the ability of our customer to provide better service to their clients and to realize increased profits.

Exposing a web service

Three types of NAV objects can be published as Web services — Pages, Queries and Codeunits. The essential purposes are:

- Pages provide access to the associated primary table. Use Card Pages for table access unless we have a specific reason for using another page type.

- Codeunits provide access to the functions contained within each Codeunit.

- Queries provide rapid, efficient access to data in a format that is especially compatible with a variety of other Microsoft products as well as products from other vendors.

When a Page has no special constraints, either via properties or permissions, there will normally be ten methods available. They are:

- Create: Creates a single record (similar to a NAV INSERT)
- CreateMultiple: Creates a set of records (passed argument must be an array)
- Read: Reads a single record (similar to a NAV GET)
- ReadMultiple: Reads a filtered set of records, paged. Page size is a parameter
- Update: Updates a single record (similar to a NAV MODIFY)
- UpdateMultiple: Updates a set of records (passed argument must be an array)
- Delete: Deletes a single record
- IsUpdated: Checks if the record has been updated since it was read
- ReadByRecID: Reads a record based on the record ID
- GetRecIDFromKey: Gets a record ID based on the record key

Whatever constraints have been set in the page that we have published will be inherited by the associated web services. For example, if we publish a page that has the **Editable** property set to No, only the Read, ReadMultiple, and IsUpdated methods will be available as web services. The other five methods will have been suppressed by virtue of the Editable = No property.

A codeunit that has been published as a web service has its functions made available to for access. A query published as a web service provides access to a service metadata (EDMX) document or an AtomPub Document. To learn more about using queries published as web services, refer to the information published in the **Developer and IT Pro Help** in the system or in MSDN.

Publishing a web service

Publishing a web service is one of the easiest things we will ever do in NAV. But, as stated earlier, that doesn't mean we will be able to simply publish existing objects without creating versions specifically tailor for use with Web Services. However, for the moment, let's just go through the basic publishing process.

The point of access is the Departments menu through **Navigation Pane | Departments | Administration | IT Administration | General | Web Services**. The web services page displays as shown in the following screenshot.

The first column allows us to specify whether the object is a Page, Codeunit, or Query. That is followed by the Object ID and then the **Service Name**. Finally, the **Published** flag must be checked. At that point the web services for that object have been published.

Determining what was published

Once an object has been published, we may want to see exactly what is available as a web service. Since web services are intended to be accessed from the Web, in the address bar of our browser, we will enter the following (all as one string):

```
http://<Server>:<WebServicePort>/<ServerInstance>/WS/
<CompanyName>/services
```

Example URL addresses are:

```
http://localhost:7047/DynamicsNAV/WS/Services
http://Arthur:7047/DynamicsNAV/WS/CRONUS_International_Ltd

/Services
```

 The company name is optional and case-sensitive.

When the correct address string is entered, our browser will display a screen similar to the following screenshot. This is in an XML format of a data structure called **Web Services Description Language (WSDL)**:

In this case, we can see that we have two NAV Services available — Codeunit/ Radio_Show_Management and Page/Radio_Show_Card.

To see the methods (that is, the NAV functions) that have been exposed as web services by publishing these two objects, we can enter other similar URLs in our browser address bar. To see the web services exposed by our codeunit, we change the URL used earlier to replace the word Services with Codeunit/Radio_Show_ Management. We do have to include the company name in the URL that lists the method's WSDL.

To see the OData services, change the URL to one in the following form:

```
http://<Server>:<WebServicePort>/<ServerInstance>/OData
```

From that entry in our browser, we get information about what's available as OData. OData is structured like XML, but OData provides the full metadata (structural definition) of the associated data in the same file as the data. This allows OData to be consumed without the requirement of a lot of back and forth technical pre-planning communications.

The actual consumption (meaning "use of") of a web service is also fairly simple, but that process occurs outside of NAV in any of a wide variety of off-the-shelf or custom applications not part of this book's focus. Examples are readily available in Help, the MSDN library, the NAV forums, and elsewhere.

Tools that can be used to consume NAV Web Services include, among others, Microsoft InfoPath, Microsoft Excel, Microsoft SharePoint, applications written in C#, other .NET languages, open source PHP, and a myriad of other application development tools. Remember, web services are a standard interface for dissimilar systems.

As with any other enhancement to the system functionality, serious thought needs to be given to the design of what data is to be exchanged and what functions within NAV 2013 should be invoked for the application to work properly. In many cases, we will want to provide some simple routines to perform standard NAV processing or validation tasks without exposing the full complexity of NAV internals as web services.

Perhaps we want to provide just two or three functions from a Codeunit that contains many additional functions. Or we want to expose a function that is contained within a Report object. In each of these instances and others, it will be necessary to create a basic library of C/AL functions, perhaps in a codeunit that can be published as web services.

Use of web services carries with it issues that must be dealt with in any production environment. In additional to delivering the required application functionality, there are security, access, and communications issues that need to be addressed. While outside the scope of this text, these are nevertheless critical to the implementation of a successful application solution.

XMLport – web services integration example

WDTU subscribes to a service that compiles listenership data. That data is provided to subscribers in the form of XML files. The agency that provides the service has agreed to push that XML data directly to a web service exposed by our NAV 2013 system. This approach will allow WDTU to have access to the latest listenership data as soon as it is released by the agency.

WDTU must provide access to the XMLport that fits the incoming XML file format. The handshaking response expected by the agency computer from our web service is a fixed XML file with one element (Station ID) and an attribute of said element (Frequency).

The first step is to build our XMLport. We access the XMLport designer through the **Object Designer** | **XMLport button** | **New** button. Define the new XMLport lines as shown in the following screenshot:

After we have the lines entered, we will press *Alt + F* and click on **Save As…**. Fill in the **Save As** screen as shown and click on **OK** to save and compile the XMLport without exiting the XMLport Designer.

Highlight the blank line at the bottom of the XMLport Designer screen and press *Shift + F4* (or click on the **Properties** icon, or right click and then click on **Properties**) to display the XMLport properties screen.

Set the **Format/Evaluate** property to XML Format/Evaluate. This allows Visual Studio to automatically understand the data types (integer, decimal, and so on) involved. Set **UseDefaultNamespace** to Yes, and the **DefaultNamespace** to urn:Microsoft-dynamics-nav/xmlports/RatingsImport.

Even though we are using the XMLport as an import only object, make sure the **Direction** property stays at <Both>. When the value is set to either Import or Export, it is not possible to use the XMLport as a **Var** (by reference) parameter in the codeunit function which we will expose as a web service.

The XMLport 50006 Properties screen with these changes in place is as follows:

After we close the **Properties** screen for the XMLport, highlight the **Root Element** line and display its properties. Set the **MaxOccurs** property to Once as shown in the following screenshot:

Close the **Root Properties**, highlight the **Ratings Data Table Element** and access its **Properties** screen. Set **MinOccurs** to Zero and make sure **MaxOccurs** remains at the default value of <Unbounded> as shown in the following screenshot. Once that is done, close the **RatingsData – Properties** screen. Because our XMLport matches the incoming data format from the listenership ratings agency, no C/AL code is necessary in this XMLport. Exit the **XMLport Designer** and save and compile **XMLport 50006**.

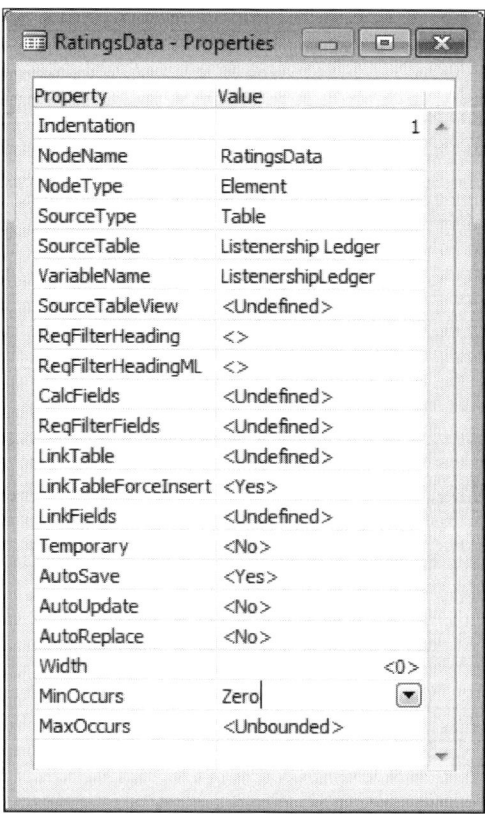

Now that we have our XMLport constructed, it's time to build the codeunit that will be published as a web service. Go to the **Object Designer** | **Codeunit button** | **New button**. Then click on the menu option **View** | **C/AL Globals** | **Functions** tab. Enter the new **Function** name of `ImportRatings` and click on the **Locals** button.

In the **C/AL Locals** screen, enter the single parameter `RatingsXML`, **DataType** of `XMLport`, and a **SubType** of `Ratings Import`. Make sure the **Var** column on the left is checked. The **C/AL Locals** screen should then look like the following:

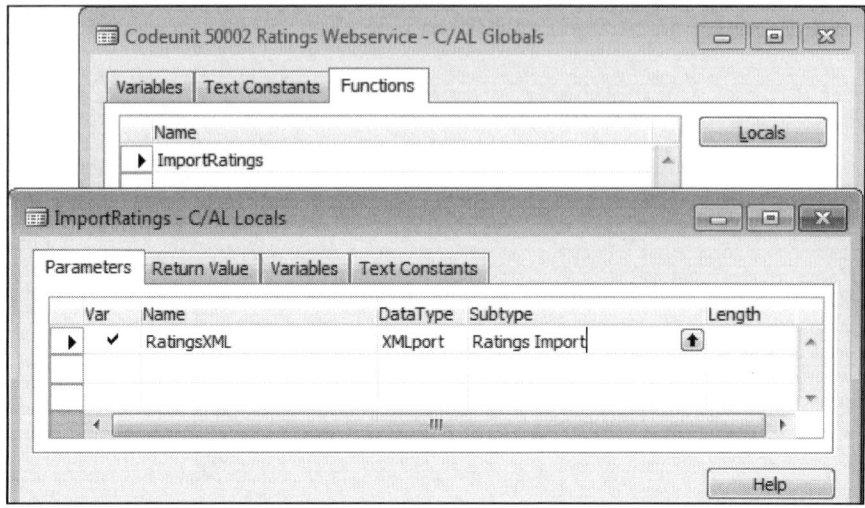

Finally, click on the **Return Value** tab and set the **Return Type** to `Text` and the **Length** to `250`. Exit the **C/AL Locals** and **C/AL Globals** screens, returning to the **Codeunit C/AL Editor** screen. Before proceeding further, let's save our work. Just as in the **XMLport Designer**, we can save our work without exiting the Designer by clicking on **File | Save As…** , then entering the designer object number (**50002**) and name (**Ratings Webservice**).

We only need two lines of C/AL code in the codeunit. The first line's task is to import the XML utilizing the XMLport parameter to cause the XMLport to process. The second line of code's purpose to send the required text response back to the external system, with the response formatted as XML data. The code looks similar to the one shown in the following screenshot of the **C/AL Editor**:

Exit **Codeunit 50002**, and compile and save it. Now we want to publish the codeunit we just created.

Open the Role Tailored Client, navigate to **Departments | Administration | IT Administration | General | Web Services** (or just search for Web Services using the Search box) and invoke the **Web Services** page. Enter the **Object Type** of Codeunit, **Object ID** of 50002, **Service Name** of WDTU Ratings, and check the **Published** checkbox.

Now, to test what we've done, we need to open a browser and enter a URL in the following format:

    <CompanyName>/services

For example, http://<Server>:<SOAPWebServicePort>/<ServerInstance>/WS/. More specifically:

    http://localhost:7047/DynamicsNAV70/WS/CRONUS International Ltd/
    Codeunit/WDTU_Ratings

We should see a result in our browser screen that looks like the following, notifying that we can connect with our web service and that our XMLport contains all the fields for the data we plan to import.

Summary

In this chapter, we reviewed some of the more advanced NAV 2013 tools and techniques. By now we should have an admiration for the power and flexibility of NAV 2013. Many of these subject areas require more study and hands-on practice by you. We spent a lot of time on Role Center construction because that is the heart of the Role Tailored Experience. Much of what you learn about Role Center design and construction can be applied across the board in role tailoring other components. We went through XMLports and Web Services, then showed how the two capabilities can be combined to provide a simple, but powerful, method of interfacing with external systems. By now, you should be just about ready to begin your own development project. In the next chapter, we will cover the debugger, extensibility (adding non-C/AL controls to pages) and some additional topics.

Review questions

1. In NAV, data can be entered into Journals, edited and then Posted to the Ledgers or, if the user is very careful, can be entered directly into the Ledger. True or False?

2. Role Center pages can contain actions in the Cue Groups, in the Navigation Pane, and in the Action Ribbon. True or False?

3. The Action items for the Departments button come from what source? Choose one:

    a. Action Menu entries

    b. Cue Group definitions

    c. MenuSuite objects

    d. Navigation Pane objects

4. Once a Role Center layout has been defined by the Developer, it cannot be changed by the users. True or False?

5. In the Role Tailored Client, XMLports can be used to process XML formatted files as well as other text file formats. True or False?

6. XMLports must be run from a Codeunit object in the Role Tailored Client. True or False?

7. Software external to NAV that accesses NAV Web Services must be dot NET compatible. True or False?

8. Action Ribbons can be modified in which of the following ways. Choose three:

    a. C/Side changes in the Action Designer

    b. Dynamic C/AL code Configuration

    c. Implementer/Administrator Configuration

    d. User Personalization

    e. Application of a profile template

9. XMLports cannot contain C/AL code. All data manipulation must occur outside of the XMLport object. True or False?

10. Web services are an industry standard interface defined by the World Wide Web Consortium. True or False?

11. An action can appear in multiple places in a Role Center, for example, in the Home button of the Navigation Pane, in the Action Ribbon and in a Cue Group. True or False?

12. Role Centers can have several components. Choose two:

    a. Activity Pane

    b. Browser Part

    c. Cues

    d. Report Review Pane

13. Web Services are a good tool for publishing NAV to be used as a public retail sales system on the web. True or False?

14. A Cue is a shortcut to a filtered list supported by a field in a Cue table. True or False?

15. New System Parts can be created by a NAV developer using C/SIDE tools. True or False?

16. Most implementations should be able to install the Role Centers that provided as part of the standard system with little or no configuration changes. True or False?

17. All Web Service data interfaces require the use of XML data files. True or False?

18. An XMLport can only deal with a single Table. True or False?

19. The default **PromotedActionCategoriesML** includes which two of the following?

    a. Page

    b. Report

    c. Standard

    d. New

9
Develop, Debug, Deliver

The greatest challenge to any thinker is stating the problem in a way that will allow a solution.   *– Bertrand Russell*

A little knowledge that acts is worth infinitely more than much knowledge that is idle.   *– Kahlil Gibran*

Each new version of NAV includes new features and capabilities. NAV 2013 is no exception to this. It is our task to understand how to apply these new features, use them intelligently in our designs, and develop with both their strengths and limitations in mind. The new features in NAV 2013 include new ways to debug our work and new ways to deliver information to our users. Our goal in the end is not only to provide workman-like results but, if possible, to delight our users with the quality of the experience and the ease of use of our products.

In this chapter, we will:

- Review NAV objects that contain functions we can use directly or as templates in our solutions
- Review some of the primary NAV C/SIDE tools that help us debug our solutions
- Learn about the way we can enhance our solutions using external controls integrated into NAV
- Discuss design, development and delivery issues that need to be addressed in most projects.

Creating new C/AL routines

Now that we have a good overall picture of how we enable users to access the tools we create, we are ready to start creating our own NAV C/AL routines. It is important that we learn our way around the NAV C/AL code in the standard product first. You may recall the advice in a previous chapter that the new code we create should be visually and logically compatible with what already exists. If we think of our new code as a guest being hosted by the original system, we will be doing what any thoughtful guest does—fit smoothly into the host's environment.

An equally important aspect of becoming familiar with the existing code is to increase the likelihood that we can take advantage of the features and components of the standard product to address some of our application requirements. There are at least two types of existing NAV C/AL code of which we should make use whenever appropriate.

One group is the callable functions that are used liberally throughout NAV. Once we know about these, we can use them in our logic whenever they fit. There is no documentation for most of these functions, so we must either learn about them here or by doing our homework, studying NAV code. The second group includes the many code snippets we can copy when we face a problem similar to something the NAV developers have already addressed.

The code snippets differ from the callable functions in two ways. First, they are not structured as coherent and callable entities. Second, they are likely to only apply to our problem as a model, code that must be modified to fit the situation (for example, changing variable names, adding or removing constraints, and so on).

Callable functions

Most of the callable functions in NAV are designed to handle a very specific set of data or conditions and have no general-purpose use (for example, the routines for updating Check Ledger entries during a posting process are likely to apply only to that specific function). If we are making modifications to a particular application area within NAV, we may find functions that we can utilize, either as is or as models for our new functions.

There are quite a few functions within NAV that are relatively general purpose. They either act on data that is common in many different situations (for example, dates) or they perform processing tasks that are common to many situations (for example, provide access to an external file). We will review a few such functions in detail, and list a number of others worth studying. If nothing else, these functions are useful as guides for "here is how NAV does it". The various parameters in these explanations are named to assist with our learning, not named the same as in the NAV code (though all structure, data types, and other technical specs match the NAV code).

If we are going to use one of these functions, we must take care to clearly understand how it operates. In each case, we will study the function and test with it before assuming we understand how it works. There is no documentation for these functions, so their proper use is totally up to us. If we need a customization, that must be done by making a copy of the target function and then modifying the copy.

Codeunit 358 – Date Filter-Calc

This codeunit is a good example of how well designed, well written code has long-term utility. If we look at the Object Designer information for this codeunit, we will see that it originated in NAV (Navision) V3.00 in 2001. That doesn't mean it is out of date; that means it was well thought out and complete.

Codeunit 358 contains two functions we can use in our code to create filters based on the Accounting Period Calendar. The first is `CreateFiscalYearFilter`. If we are calling this from an object that has Codeunit 358 defined as a Global variable named `DateFilterCalc`, our call would use the following syntax:

```
DateFilterCalc,CreateFiscalYearFilter
        (Filter,Name,BaseDate,NextStep)
```

The calling parameters are `Filter` (text, length 30), `Name` (text, length 30), `BaseDate` (date), and `NextStep` (integer).

The second such function is `CreateAccountingPeriodFilter` that has the following syntax:

```
DateFilterCalc.CreateAccountingPeriodFilter
        (Filter,Name,BaseDate,NextStep)
```

The calling parameters are `Filter` (text, length 30), `Name` (text, length 30), `BaseDate` (date), and `NextStep` (integer).

In the following screenshot, from Page 151 – Customer Statistics, we can see how NAV calls these functions. Page 152 – Vendor Statistics, Page 223 – Resource Statistics, and a number of other Master table statistics forms also use this set of functions.

```
OnAfterGetRecord()
IF CurrentDate <> WORKDATE THEN BEGIN
  CurrentDate := WORKDATE;
  DateFilterCalc.CreateAccountingPeriodFilter(CustDateFilter[1],CustDateName[1],CurrentDate,0);
  DateFilterCalc.CreateFiscalYearFilter(CustDateFilter[2],CustDateName[2],CurrentDate,0);
  DateFilterCalc.CreateFiscalYearFilter(CustDateFilter[3],CustDateName[3],CurrentDate,-1);
END;
```

In the following screenshot, NAV uses the filters stored in the CustDateFilter array to constrain the calculation of a series of FlowFields for the Customer Statistics page.

```
FOR i := 1 TO 4 DO BEGIN
  SETFILTER("Date Filter",CustDateFilter[i]);
  CALCFIELDS(
    "Sales (LCY)","Profit (LCY)","Inv. Discounts (LCY)","Inv. Amounts (LCY)","Pmt. Discounts (LCY)",
    "Pmt. Disc. Tolerance (LCY)","Pmt. Tolerance (LCY)",
    "Fin. Charge Memo Amounts (LCY)","Cr. Memo Amounts (LCY)","Payments (LCY)",
    "Reminder Amounts (LCY)","Refunds (LCY)","Other Amounts (LCY)");
```

When one of these functions is called, the Filter and Name parameters are updated within the function, so we can use them as return parameters, allowing the function to return a workable filter and a name for that filter. The filter is calculated from the BaseDate and NextStep we supply.

The returned filter is supplied back in the format of a range filter string, 'startdate.. enddate' (for example, 01/01/14..12/31/14). If we call CreateFiscalYear, the Filter will be for the range of a fiscal year, as defined by the system's Accounting Period table. If we call CreateAccountingPeriodFilter, the Filter will be for the range of a fiscal period, as defined by the same table.

The dates of the Period or Year filter returned are tied to the BaseDate parameter, which can be any legal date. The NextStep parameter says which period or year to use, depending on which function is called. A NextStep = 0 says use the period or year containing the BaseDate, NextStep = 1 says use the next period or year into the future, and NextStep = -2 says use the period or year before last (go back two periods or years).

The Name value returned is also derived from the Accounting Period table. If the call is to the CreateAccountingPeriodFilter, then Name will contain the appropriate Accounting Period Name. If the call is to the CreateFiscalYearFilter, then Name will contain 'Fiscal Year yyyy', where yyyy will be the four-digit numeric year.

Codeunit 359 – Period Form Management

This codeunit contains three functions that can be used for date handling. They are `FindDate`, `NextDate`, and `CreatePeriodFormat`:

- `FindDate` function
    - ○ Calling Parameters (`SearchString` (text, length 3), `Calendar` (Date table), `PeriodType` (Option, integer))
    - ○ Returns DateFound Boolean

    `FindDate(SearchString,CalendarRec,PeriodType)`

This function is often used in pages to assist with the date calculation. The purpose of this function is to find a date in the virtual Date table based on the parameters passed in. The search starts with an initial record in the Calendar table. If we pass in a record that has already been initialized by positioning the table a date, that will be the base date, otherwise the Work Date will be used.

The `PeriodType` is an Option field with the option value choices of day, week, month, quarter, year, accounting period. For ease of coding, we could call the function with the integer equivalent (0, 1, 2, 3, 4, 5) or set up our own equivalent Option variable. In general, it's a much better practice to set up an Option variable because the Option strings make the code self-documenting.

The `SearchString` allows us to pass in a logical control string containing =, >, <, <=, >=, and so on. `FindDate` will find the first date starting with the initialized `Calendar` date that satisfies the `SearchString` logic instruction and fits the `PeriodType` defined. For example, if the `PeriodType` is day and the date 01/25/14 is used along with the `SearchString` of >, then the date 01/26/14 will be returned in the `Calendar`.

- `NextDate` function
    - ○ Calling Parameters (`NextStep` (integer), `Calendar` (Date table), `PeriodType` (Option, integer))
    - ○ Returns an Integer

    `IntegerVariable:= NextDate(NextStep,CalendarRec,PeriodType)`

NextDate will find the next date record in the Calendar table that satisfies the calling parameters. The Calendar and PeriodType calling parameters for FindDate have the same definition as they do for the FindDate function. However, for this function to be really useful, the Calendar must be initialized before calling NextDate — otherwise, the function will calculate the appropriate next date from day 0. The NextStep parameter allows us to define the number of periods of PeriodType to move, so as to obtain the desired next date. For example, if we start with a Calendar table positioned on 01/25/14, a PeriodType of quarter (that is 3), and a NextStep of 2, the NextDate will move forward two quarters and return with Calendar focused on Quarter, 7/1/14 to 9/30/14.

- CreatePeriodFormat function
    - Calling Parameters (PeriodType (Option, integer), Date (date))
    - Returns Text, length 10:

```
FormattedDate:= CreatePeriodFormat(PeriodType,DateData)
```

CreatePeriodFormat allows us to supply a date and specify which of its format options we want via PeriodType. The function's return value is a ten-character formatted text value; for example, mm/dd/yy or ww/yyyy or mon/yyyy or qtr/yyyy or yyyy.

Codeunit 365 – Format Address

The functions in the Format Address codeunit do the obvious, they format addresses in a variety of situations. The address data in any master record (Customer, Vendor, Sales Order Sell-to, Sales Order Ship-to, Employee, and so on.) may contain embedded blank lines. For example, the Address 2 line may be empty. When we print out the address information on a document or report, it will look better if there are no blank lines. These functions take care of such tasks.

In addition, NAV provides setup options for multiple formats of City – Post Code – County – Country combinations. The Format Address functions format addresses according to what was chosen in the setup or was been defined in the Countries/Regions page for different Postal areas.

There are over 60 data-specific functions in the Format Address codeunit. Each data-specific function allows us to pass a record parameter for the record containing the raw address data (such as a Customer record, a Vendor Record, a Sales Order, and so on.) plus a parameter of a one-dimensional Text array with 8 elements of length upto 90 characters. Each function extracts the address data from its specific master record format and stores it in the array. The function then passes that data to a general-purpose function, which does the actual work of re-sequencing according to the various setup rules and compressing the data by removing blank lines.

The following are examples of function call format for the functions for `Company` and the `Sales Ship-to` addresses. In each case `AddressArray` is Text, Length 90, and one-dimensional with 8 elements.

- `"Format Address".Company(AddressArray,CompanyRec);`
- `"Format Address".SalesHeaderShipTo(AddressArray,`
  `SalesHeaderRec);`

The function's processed result is returned in the `AddressArray` parameter.

In addition to the data-specific functions in the `Format Address` codeunit, we can also directly utilize the more general-purpose functions contained there. If we add a new address structure as part of an enhancement, we may want to create our own data-specific address formatting function in our custom codeunit. But we should design our function to call the general-purpose functions that already exist (and are already debugged).

The primary general-purpose address formatting function (the one we are most likely to call directly) is `FormatAddr`. This is the function that does most of the work in this codeunit. The syntax for the `FormatAddr` function is as follows:

```
FormatAddr(AddressArray,Name,Name2,ContactName,Address1,Address2,
          City,PostCode,County,CountryCode)
```

The calling parameters of `AddressArray`, `Name`, `Name2` and `ContactName` are all Text, length 90. `Address1`, `Address2`, `City`, and `County` are all Text, length 50. `PostCode` and `CountryCode` are Code, length 20 and length 10, respectively.

Our data is passed into the function in the individual `Address` fields. The results are passed back in the `AddressArray` parameter for us to use.

There are two other functions in the `Format Address` codeunit that can be called directly. They are `FormatPostCodeCity` and `GeneratePostCodeCity`. The `FormatPostCodeCity` function serves the purpose of finding the applicable setup rule for `PostCode` + `City` + `County` + `Country` formatting. It then calls the `GeneratePostCodeCity` function, which does the actual formatting.

Codeunit 396 – NoSeriesManagement

Throughout NAV, master records (Customer, Vendor, Item, and so on.) and activity documents (Sales Order, Purchase Order, Warehouse Transfer Orders, and so on) are controlled by the unique identification number assigned to each one. This unique identification number is assigned through a call to a function within the NoSeriesManagement codeunit. That function is InitSeries. The calling format for InitSeries is as follows:

```
NoSeriesManagement.InitSeries(WhichNumberSeriesToUse,
LastDataRecNumberSeriesCode, SeriesDateToApply, NumberToUse,
NumberSeriesUsed)
```

The parameter WhichNumberSeriesToUse is generally defined on a **Numbers** tab in the Setup record for the applicable application area. The LastDataRecNumberSeriesCode tells the function what Number Series was used for the previous record in this table. The SeriesDateToApply parameter allows the function to assign ID numbers in a date-dependent fashion. The NumberToUse and the NumberSeriesUsed are return parameters.

The following screenshot shows an example for Table 18 - Customer:

```
Table 18 Customer - C/AL Editor
OnInsert()
  IF "No." = '' THEN BEGIN
    SalesSetup.GET;
    SalesSetup.TESTFIELD("Customer Nos.");
    NoSeriesMgt.InitSeries(SalesSetup."Customer Nos.",xRec."No. Series",0D,"No.","No. Series");
  END;
```

This screenshot shows a second example. It's for Table 36 - Sales Header:

```
Table 36 Sales Header - C/AL Editor
OnInsert()
  IF "No." = '' THEN BEGIN
    TestNoSeries;
    NoSeriesMgt.InitSeries(GetNoSeriesCode,xRec."No. Series","Posting Date","No.","No. Series");
  END;
```

With the exception of GetNextNo (used in assigning unique identifying numbers to each of a series of transactions) and possibly TestManual (used to test if manual numbering is allowed), we are not likely to use other functions in the NoSeriesManagement codeunit. The other functions are principally used either by the InitSeries function or other NAV routines whose job it is to maintain Number Series control information and data.

Function models to review and use

It is very helpful when we're creating new code to have a model that works that we can study (or clone). This is especially true in NAV where there is little or no "how to" documentation available for the many different functions we use. One of the more challenging aspects of learning to develop in the NAV environment is learning how to address issues in the "NAV way". Learning the "NAV way" is very beneficial, because there is no better place to learn the strengths and subtle features of the product than to study the code written by the developers who are part of the inner circle.

> If there is a choice, don't add custom functions to the standard NAV Codeunits. Well segregated customizations in clearly identified custom objects make both maintenance and upgrades easier. When we build our function modeled on NAV functions, the new code should be in a customer licensed codeunit.

A list of objects that contain functions we may find useful for use in our code or as models follows. We find these useful for studying how "it's" done in NAV ("it" obviously varies depending on the function's purpose).

- Codeunit 1 – Application Management: A library of utility functions widely used in the system
- Codeunits 11, 12, 13, 21, 22, 23, 80, 81, 82, 90, 91, 92 – the Posting sequences for Sales, Purchases, General Ledger, Item Ledger; these control the posting of journal data into the various ledgers
- Codeunit 228 – Test Report-Print: Functions for printing Test Reports for user review prior to Posting data
- Codeunit 229 – Print Documents: Functions for printing Document formatted reports
- Codeunits 397, 400 – Mail: Functions for interfacing with Outlook and SMTP mail
- Codeunit 408 – Dimension Management: Don't write your own; use these
- Codeunit 419 – 3-tier File Management: Functions including BLOB tasks, file uploading and downloading
- Codeunits 802 – Online Map interfacing
- Codeunit 5054 – Word Management: Interfaces to Microsoft Word
- Codeunit 5063 – Archive Management: Storing copies of processed documents
- Codeunits 5300 thru 5313 – More Outlook interfacing
- Codeunits 5813 thru 5819 – Undo functions

- Codeunit 6224 – XML DOM Management for XML structure handling
- Table 330 – Currency Exchange Rate: Contains some of the key currency conversion functions
- Table 370 – Excel Buffer: Excel interfacing
- Page 344 – Navigate: Home of the unique and powerful Navigate feature

Management codeunits

There are approximately 100 codeunits with the word "Management" or "Mgt" as part of their description name (filter the codeunits using `*Management*|*Mgt*`). Each of these codeunits contains functions in which the purpose is the management of some specific aspect of NAV data. Many are very specific to a narrow range of data. Some are more general, because they contain functions we can reuse in another application area (for example, Codeunit 396 – `NoSeriesManagement`).

When we are working on an enhancement in a particular functional area, it is extremely important to check the Management codeunits utilized in that area. We may be able to use some functions directly. This will have the benefit of reducing the code we have to create and debug. Of course, when a new version is released, we will have to check to see if the functions on which we relied have changed in a way that affects our code.

If we can't use the existing material as is, we may find functions we can use as models for tasks in the area of our enhancement. And, even if that is not true, by researching and studying the existing code, we will learn more about how data is structured and processes flow in the standard system.

Multi-language system

The NAV system is designed as a multi-language system, meaning it can interface with users in many languages. The base product is distributed with American English as the primary language, but each local version comes with one or more other languages ready for use. Since the system can be set up to operate from a single database displaying user interfaces in several different languages, NAV is particularly suitable for firms operating from a central system serving users in multiple countries. NAV is used by businesses all over the world, operating in dozens of different languages. It is important to note that when the application language is changed, that has no effect on the data in the database. The data is not multi-language unless we provide that functionality by means of our own enhancements or data structure.

The basic elements that support the multi-language feature include:

- Multi-language Captioning properties (for example, **CaptionML**) supporting definitions of alternative language captions for all fields, action labels, titles, and so on.

- Application Management codeunit logic that allows language choice at login.

- `fin.stx` files supplied by NAV, which are language specific and contain texts used by C/SIDE for various menus such as File, Edit, View, Tools, and so on. (`fin.stx` cannot be modified except by Microsoft).

- The Text Constants property **ConstantValueML** supporting definition of alternative language messages.

Before embarking on creating modifications that need to be multi-language enabled, review all the available documentation on the topic (search Help on the word "language"). It's wise to do some small-scale testing to ensure we understand what is required, and that our approach will work (such testing is required for any significant enhancement).

Multi-currency system

NAV was one of the first ERP systems to fully implement a multi-currency system. Transactions can start in one currency and finish in another. For example, we can create the order in US dollars and accept payment for the invoice in Euros. For this reason, where there are money values, they are generally stored in the local currency (referenced as **LCY**) as defined in the setup. There is a set of currency conversion tools built into the applications and there are standard (by practice) code structures to support and utilize those tools. Two examples of code segments from the `Sales Line` table illustrating handling of money fields follow:

```
GetSalesHeader;
IF SalesHeader."Currency Code" <> '' THEN BEGIN
  Currency.TESTFIELD("Unit-Amount Rounding Precision");
  "Unit Cost" :=
    ROUND(
      CurrExchRate.ExchangeAmtLCYToFCY(
        GetDate,SalesHeader."Currency Code",
        "Unit Cost (LCY)",SalesHeader."Currency Factor"),
      Currency."Unit-Amount Rounding Precision")
END ELSE
  "Unit Cost" := "Unit Cost (LCY)";
```

In both cases, there's a function call to ROUND and use of the currency-specific **Currency."Amount Rounding Precision"** control value.

```
"Line Discount Amount" :=
   ROUND(
      ROUND(Quantity * "Unit Price",Currency."Amount Rounding Precision") *
      "Line Discount %" / 100,Currency."Amount Rounding Precision");
```

As we can see, before creating any modification that has money fields, we must familiarize ourselves with the NAV currency conversion feature, the code that supports it and the related setups. A good place to start is the C/AL code in Table 37 – Sales Line, Table 39 – Purchase Line, and Table 330 – Currency Exchange Rate.

Navigate

Navigate is an under-appreciated tool for both the user and for the developer. Our focus here is on its value to the developer. Navigate (Page 344) finds and displays the counts and types of all the associated entries for a particular posting transaction. The term "associated", in this case, is defined as those entries having the same **Document Number** and **Posting Date**. This is a handy tool for the developer as it can show the results of posting activity and provide the tools to drill into the detail of all those results. If we add new transactions and Ledgers as part of an enhancement, our Navigate function should cover those too.

Navigate can be called from the **Navigate** action, which appears in a number of places in the Departments Tasks menu and Role Center ribbons. From anywhere within NAV, the easiest way to find Navigate is to enter the word navigate into the Search box (see the following screenshot).

If we invoke the Navigate page using the menu action item, we must enter the **Posting Date** and **Document Number** for the entries we wish to find. Alternately, we can enter a **Business Contact Type** (Vendor or Customer), a **Business Contact No.** (Vendor No. or Customer No.), and optionally, an **External Document No**. There are occasions when this option is useful, but the **Posting Date + Document No**. option is more frequently useful.

Instead of seeking out a Navigate page and entering the critical data fields, it is much easier to call Navigate from a **Navigate** action on a page showing data. In this case, we just highlight a record and click on **Navigate** to search for all the related entries. In the following screenshot, a **General Ledger Entry** is highlighted:

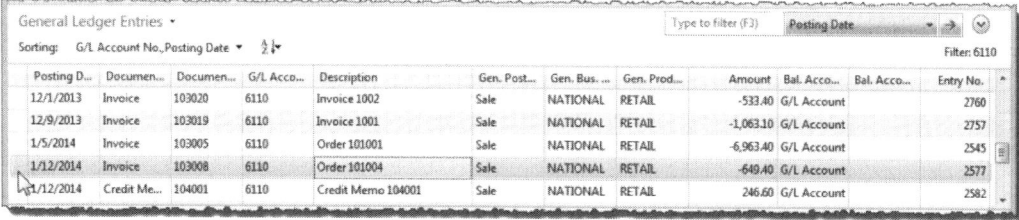

After clicking on the **Navigate** action, the page will pop up, filled in similar to the following:

Had we accessed the **Navigate** page through one of the menu entries we found via **Search** (*Ctrl + F3*), we would have filled in the **Document No**. and **Posting Date** fields and clicked on **Find**. As we can see here, the **Navigate** page shows a list of related, posted entries (one of which will include the entry we highlighted when we invoked the Navigate function). If we highlight one of the lines in the **Table Name** list at the bottom of the page, then click on the **Show** icon at the top of the page, we will see an appropriately formatted display of the chosen entries.

If we highlight the **G/L Entry** table entries and click on **Show**, we would see a result like the following screenshot. Note that all the **G/L Entry** are displayed for the same **Posting Date** and **Document No.**, matching those specified at the top of the **Navigate** page.

Modifying for Navigate

If our modification creates a new table that will contain posted data and the records contain both Document No. and Posting Date fields, we can include this new table in the **Navigate** function.

The C/AL Code for **Posting Date + Document No.** Navigate functionality is found in the `FindRecords` and `FindExtRecords` functions of Page 344 – Navigate. The following screenshot shows the segment of the Navigate CASE statement code for the `Check Ledger Entry` table:

```
IF CheckLedgEntry.READPERMISSION THEN BEGIN
  CheckLedgEntry.RESET;
  CheckLedgEntry.SETCURRENTKEY("Document No.","Posting Date");
  CheckLedgEntry.SETFILTER("Document No.",DocNoFilter);
  CheckLedgEntry.SETFILTER("Posting Date",PostingDateFilter);
  InsertIntoDocEntry(
    DATABASE::"Check Ledger Entry",0,CheckLedgEntry.TABLECAPTION,CheckLedgEntry.COUNT);
END;
```

The code checks READPERMISSION. If that permission is enabled for this table, then the appropriate filtering is applied. Next, there is a call to the InsertIntoDocEntry function, which fills the temporary table that is displayed in the **Navigate** page. If we wish to add a new table to the Navigate function, we must replicate this functionality for our new table.

In addition, we must add the code that will call up the appropriate page to display the records that Navigate finds. This code should be inserted in the ShowRecords function trigger of the **Navigate** page, modeling on the applicable section of code in this function (chose the code set that best fits our new tables). Making a change like this, when appropriate, will not only provide a powerful tool for our users, but also provide a powerful tool for us as developers.

Debugging in NAV 2013

In general, the processes and tools we use for debugging can serve multiple purposes. The most immediate purpose is always that of identifying the causes of errors and then resolving those errors. There are two categories of production errors (which may also occur during development) and NAV 2013's brand new Debugger module is very well suited to addressing both of these. The new debugger smoothly integrates developing in the Development Environment and testing in the Role Tailored Client.

The first category is the type that causes an error condition that terminates processing. In this case, the immediate goal is to find the cause and fix it as quickly as possible. The new debugger is an excellent tool for this purpose. The second category is the type that, while running to completion successfully, gives erroneous results.

We often find that debugging techniques can be used to help us better understand how NAV processes work. We may be working on the design of (or determination of the need for) a modification or we may simply want to learn more about how a particular function is used or outcome is accomplished in the standard NAV routines. It would be more appropriate to call these efforts analysis or self-education, rather than debugging, even though the processes we use to dissect the code and view what it's doing are very similar. In the course of these efforts, sometimes less sophisticated approaches are useful in understanding what's going on. We'll quickly review some of those alternate approaches before studying use of the new NAV 2013 Debugger.

Text Exports of Objects

Using a developer license, we are allowed to export objects into text files, where they can use a text editor to examine or even manipulate the result. Let us take a look at an object that has been exported into text and imported into a text editor (we use CodeWright, which is now ancient history but still sold by Embarcadero—it can be tailored for various code syntaxes—ours is tailored for C/AL). We will use one of the tables that are part of our WDTU development, the `Radio Show Type` table, **50001** as shown in the following screenshot:

```
OBJECT Table 50001 Radio Show Type
{
  OBJECT-PROPERTIES
  {
    Date=05/08/12;
    Time=[ 1:59:50 PM];
    Modified=Yes;
    Version List=CDS02;
  }
  PROPERTIES
  {
    LookupPageID=Page50002;
    DrillDownPageID=Page50002;
  }
  FIELDS
  {
    { 10  ;   ;Code              ;Code10        }
    { 20  ;   ;Description       ;Text30        }
    { 30  ;   ;Is Weather        ;Boolean       }
    { 40  ;   ;Is Sports         ;Boolean       }
    { 50  ;   ;Is News           ;Boolean       }
  }
  KEYS
  {
    {    ;Code                              ;Clustered=Yes }
  }
  FIELDGROUPS
  {
  }
  CODE
  {

    BEGIN
    END.
  }
}
```

The general structure of all exported objects is similar, with differences that we would expect for the different objects. This particular table contains no C/AL-coded logic, as these statements would be visible in the text listing. We can see by looking at this table object that we could easily search for instances of the string `Code` throughout the text export of the entire system, but it would be more difficult to look for references to the **Radio Show Types** except by page ID, `Page50002`. While we can find the instances of `Code` with our text editor, it would be quite difficult to differentiate those instances that relate to the **Radio Show Type** table from those in any other table. This includes those that have nothing to do with our WDTU system enhancement, as well as those simply defined in an object as Global Variables.

If we are determined to use a text editor to find all instances of `"Radio Show Type"`. `Code`, we can do the following:

- Rename the field in question to something unique. C/SIDE will rename all the references to this field to this new name.

- Export all the sources to text followed by using our text editor (or even Microsoft Word) to find the new, unique name.

- Either return the field in the database to the original name or work in a temporary copy of the database, which we will then discard. Otherwise, we will have quite a mess.

One task that needs to be done occasionally is to renumber an object or to change an internal object reference that refers to a no longer existing element. The C/SIDE editor may not let us do that easily or, in some cases, not at all. In such a case, the best answer may be to export the object into text, make the change there and then import it back in as modified. Be careful. When we import a text object, C/SIDE does not check to see if the incoming object is valid. C/SIDE makes that check when we import a compiled `fob` object. If we must do object renumbering, we should use the functionality built into Mergetool (available at `www.mergetool.com`). Many years ago, Mergetool was the recommended Upgrade support tool for Navision and once again it's the best answer.

There are occasions when it is very helpful to simply view an object "flattened out" in text format. In a report or XMLport where we may have combinations of logic and properties, the only way to see everything at once is in text format. We can use any text editor we like, Notepad or Word or one of the visual programming editors; the exported object is just text. We need to cope with the fact that when we export a large number of objects in one pass, they all end up in the same text file. That makes the exported file relatively difficult to use. The solution is to split that file into individual text files, named logically, one for each NAV object. There are several freeware tools to do just that, available from the NAV forums on the Internet.

Two excellent NAV forums are www.mibuso.com and www.dynamicsuser.net.

Dialog function debugging techniques

Sometimes the simpler methods are more productive than the more sophisticated tools, because we can set up and test quickly, resolve the issue (or answer a question), and move on. All the simpler methods involve using one of the C/AL DIALOG functions such as MESSAGE, CONFIRM, DIALOG, or ERROR. All of these have the advantage of working well in the RTC environment. However, we should remember that none of these techniques conform to the **Testing Best Practices** in the **Testing the Application** Help. These should only be used when a quick, one-time approach is needed or when recommended testing practices simply won't provide the information needed and one of these techniques will do so.

Debugging with MESSAGE and CONFIRM

The simplest debug method is to insert MESSAGE statements at key points in our logic. It is very simple and, if structured properly, provides us with a simple "trace" of the code logic path. We can number our messages to differentiate them and display any data (in small amounts) as part of a message.

```
MESSAGE('This is Test 4 for %1',Customer."No.");
```

The disadvantage is that MESSAGE statements do not display until processing either terminates or is interrupted for user interaction. If we force a user interaction at some point, then our accumulated messages will appear prior to the interaction. The simplest way to force user interaction is to issue a CONFIRM message in the format as follows:

```
IF CONFIRM ('Test 1',TRUE) THEN;
```

If we want to do a simple trace but want every message to be displayed as it is generated (that is, have the tracking process move at a very measured pace), we could use CONFIRM statements for all the messages. We then have to respond to each one before our program will move on, but sometimes that is what we want.

Debugging with DIALOG

Another tool that is useful for progress tracking is the DIALOG function. DIALOG is usually set up to display a window with a small number of variable values. As processing progresses, the values are displayed in real time. Some ways we might use this:

- Simply tracking progress of processing through a volume of data. This is the same reason we would provide a DIALOG display for the benefit of the user. The act of displaying slows down processing somewhat, so we may want to update the DIALOG display occasionally, not on every record.

- Displaying indicators when processing reaches certain stages. This can be used as a very basic trace with the indicators showing the path taken so we may gauge the relative speed of progress through several steps.

- We might have a six-step process to analyze. We could define six tracking variables and display all of them in the DIALOG. We would initialize each variable with values dependent on what we are tracking, such as A1, B2000, C300000, and so on. At each process step, update and display the current state of one or all of the variables. This can be a very helpful guide for how our process is operating. To slow things down, we could put a SLEEP(100) or SLEEP(500) after the DIALOG statement (the number is milliseconds of delay).

Debugging with text output

We can build a very handy debugging tool by outputting the values of critical variables or other informative indicators of progress either to an external text file or to a table created for this purpose. We need to either do this in single user mode or make it multiuser. That might be as simple as including the User ID on every entry.

This technique allows us to run a considerable volume of test data through the system, tracking some important elements while collecting data on the variable values, progress through various sections of code, and so on. We can even timestamp our output records so that we can use this method to look for processing speed problems.

Following the test run, we can analyze the results of our test more quickly than if we were using displayed information. We can focus on just the items that appear most informative and ignore the rest. This type of debugging is fairly easy to set up and to refine, as we identify the variables or code segments of most interest. We can combine this approach with the following approach using the ERROR statement if we output to an external text file, then close it before invoking the ERROR statement, so that its contents are retained following the termination of the test run.

Debugging with ERROR

One of the challenges of testing is maintaining repeatability. Quite often we need to test several times using the same data, but the test changes the data. If we have a small database, we can always back up the database and start with a fresh copy each time. But that can be inefficient and, if the database is large, impractical. If we are using the built-in NAV Test functions, we can roll back any database changes so the tests are totally repeatable. Another alternative is to conclude our test with an ERROR function to test and retest with exactly the same data.

The ERROR function forces a runtime error status, which means the database is not updated (it is rolled back to the status at the beginning of the process). This works well when our debugging information is provided by using the Debugger or by use of any of the DIALOG functions just mentioned prior to the execution of the ERROR function. If we are using MESSAGE to generate debugging information, we could execute a CONFIRM immediately prior to the ERROR statement and be assured that all of the messages are displayed. Obviously this method won't work well when our testing validation is dependent on checking results using Navigate or our test is a multistep process such as order entry, review, and posting. In this latter case, only use of the built-in Test functions (creating Test Runner Codeunits) will be adequate. But in some situations, use of the ERROR function is a very handy technique for repeating a test with minimal effort.

When testing just the posting of an item, it often works well to place the test-concluding ERROR function just before the point in the applicable Posting codeunit where the process would otherwise be completed successfully. We must make sure there aren't any COMMIT statements included in the code being tested.

The new NAV 2013 Debugger

As defined in the Help **Debugging** (which should be studied), debugging is the process of finding and correcting errors. In NAV 2013, a brand new Debugger has been added, providing a much improved, more powerful tool for debugging. The user interface for the NAV 2013 Debugger is written in C/AL. The Debugger objects can be identified by filtering in the Object Designer, **All** objects, on *Debug*. Reviewing the structure of the Debugger objects in C/SIDE may help us better understand its inner workings.

The new Debugger can be activated in multiple different ways including from within the Development Environment, from within the RTC, from a command line and by means of a C/AL function. The latter two options attach to a session at the same time as they activate. The best choice for activation method depends on the specific situation and the debugging technique being utilized by the developer.

Only a user who has SUPER permissions for all companies is allowed to activate the debugger. The user permissions setup should have an empty Company field as shown in the following screenshot:

Activating the Debugger

Activating the Debugger from the Development Environment is a simple matter of clicking on **Tools | Debugger | Debug Sessions...** (or *Shift + Ctrl + F11*). The initial page that displays when the Debugger is activated will look like the following (typically with each session having a different User ID). Multiple sessions can be debugged in parallel.

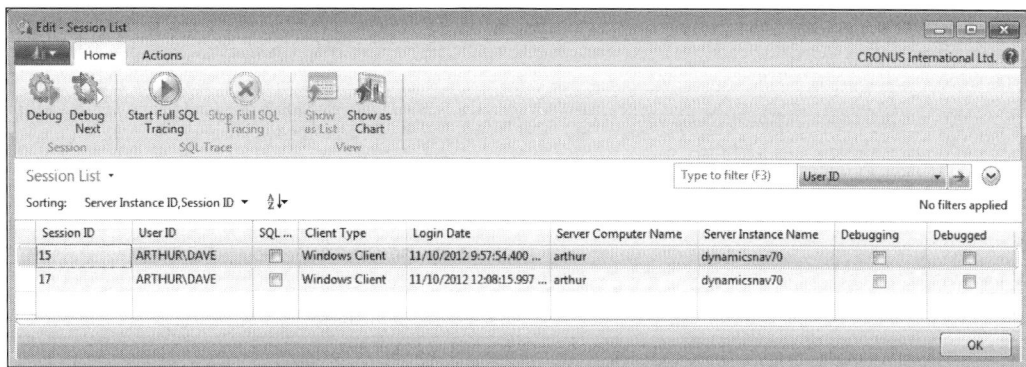

If we activate the Debugger any of the methods that do not specify a session, this screen will appear. The Debugger can also be activated from within the RTC as follows:

1. Enter `Sessions` in the Search box.

2. Select the link displayed (**Administration/IT Administration/General**).

3. In the **General** section, click on **Sessions**.

We can also get to this same point by clicking on the **Departments** button in the Navigation pane. Then click on **IT Administration | General**, followed by **Sessions** in the **Tasks** section.

Once we click on **Sessions**, we may receive the message shown in the following screenshot. If so, choose the **Allow for this client session** option.

However we activate it, the Debugger runs as a separate independent session that can be attached to an operating session. The Help **Activating the Debugger** describes activating the Debugger to debug a Web Service. The Help **Configuring NAS Services** has information about using the Debugger with a NAS Service.

Attaching the Debugger to a Session

From the **Edit - Session** list screen, we have two options for attaching the
Debugger session to a session. One way is to highlight a Session and then click
on the **Debug** icon.

The other way is to click on the **Debug Next** icon, then initiate a new Session. The
Debugger will be attached to the new Session.

When we click on **Debug Next**, an empty **View - Debugger** page will open, awaiting the event that will cause a break in processing and the subsequent display of Code detail, Watched variables, the Call Stack.

Creating break events

Once the Debugger is activated and attached to a session, some break event must occur to cause the debug trace and associated data display to begin. Break events include (but are not limited to):

- An error occurs that would cause the object execution to be terminated
- A previously set **Breakpoint** is reached during processing
- The record is read when the **Break on Record Changes Break Rule** is active
- The Break icon in the Running Code group is clicked in the ribbon of the **View – Debugger** page
- A Breakpoint Condition, which has been set in the Breakpoints group in the ribbon of the **View - Debugger** page, is satisfied during processing

Of the preceding events, the two most common methods of starting up a debug trace are the first two, an error or reaching a previously set breakpoint. If, for example, an error condition is discovered in an operating object, the debugging process can be initiated by:

1. Activating the debugger.
2. Attaching the debugger session to the session where the error will occur.
3. Running the process where the error occurs.

When the error occurs, the page parts (Code, Watches, and Call Stack) in the debug window will be populated and we can proceed to investigate variable values, review code, and so forth.

Breakpoints are stopping points in an object that have been set by the developer. Breakpoints can be set in a variety of ways, including in the Development Environment, in the **View - Debugger Code** page, and in the **Edit – Debugger Breakpoint List**.

While the latter two locations for setting breakpoints may be very useful while we are in the middle of a debugging session, those breakpoints only display while the Debugger is active. Once we exit the debugging session, those breakpoints that were set in the Debugger will disappear from view, while the breakpoints that were set from within the applicable C/SIDE Designer will remain visible until removed.

The result may be somewhat confusing because when we can only see all of the breakpoints when we are in the Debugger. If we try to set a breakpoint in the Development Environment and a breakpoint has already been set on that line of code while in the Debugger, we will get an error message.

For this reason, it may be better practice to set all our planned testing breakpoints in the Development Environment. When we set breakpoints within the Debugger, we should clear them before ending our test session. Otherwise we may later run into breakpoints we didn't remember existed and which we can't see in the Designers.

Active breakpoints are represented in code by a filled in circle. Disabled breakpoints are represented by an empty circle. Examples of these breakpoints are shown in the code in the following screenshot:

```
OnInsert()
  IF "No." = '' THEN BEGIN
    SalesSetup.GET;
    SalesSetup.TESTFIELD("Customer Nos.");
    NoSeriesMgt.InitSeries(SalesSetup."Custome
  END;
  IF "Invoice Disc. Code" = '' THEN
    "Invoice Disc. Code" := "No.";
```

When viewing C/AL code in a Designer, breakpoints can be set, disabled, or removed by pressing the *F9* key. When viewing C/AL code in the **Code** window of the Debugger, breakpoints can only be set or removed by pressing the *F9* key or clicking on the **Toggle** icon. Other Debugger breakpoint controls are shown in the following screenshot:

The Debugger window

The ribbon actions in the Debugger window are as follows:

- **Step Into**: Designed to trace into a function
- **Step Over**: Designed to execute a function without stopping, then break
- **Step Out**: Designed to complete the current function without stopping, then break
- **Continue**: Continue until the next break

- **Break**: Break at the next statement
- **Stop**: Stop the current activity but leave the debugging session active
- **Toggle**: Set or clear a breakpoint at the current line
- **Set/Clear Condition**: Set or clear a conditional (based on C/AL expression) breakpoint at the current line
- **Disable All**: disables all checkpoints in the attached session
- **Break Rules**: Displays the following screen:

The Debugger Break Rules are as follows:

- ◦ **Break On Error** default is on.
- ◦ If **Break On Record Changes** is on when a debug session is attached to an operating session, the debugging will start immediately.
- ◦ **Skip Codeunit 1** default is on allowing all the Codeunit 1 processing to normally be processed without tracing.

- **Breakpoints**: Displays a list of the active breakpoints and provides action options to enable, disable or delete breakpoints individually or in total.

- **Variables**: Displays the Debugger Variable List where we can examine the status of all variables that are in scope. Additional variables can be added to the Watch list here.

Variables can be removed from the Watch list in the Debugger **Watches** page part.

The **Last Error** Debugger ribbon action displays the last error message shown by the session being debugged.

There are several valuable Help sections on use of the Debugger, including:

- *Debugging*
- *Debugger Keyboard Shortcuts*
- *Breakpoints* (this one is especially good)

- *Closing the Debugger*
- *How to: Add Variables to the Watches FactBox*
- *How to: Debug a Background Session*
- *How to: Manage Breakpoints from the Development Environment*
- *How to: Set Conditional Breakpoints*
- *Walkthrough: Debugging the Microsoft Dynamics NAV Windows Client*

Changing the code while debugging

While a debugger session is active, we can open the object being debugged in an appropriate Designer, change the object, save and recompile it. The revised object will immediately be available to other sessions on the system. However, the version of the object that is being executed and in view in the debugger is the old version of the object, not the changed one. Furthermore, if we refresh the view of the code in the Debugger **Code** window, the new version will be displayed while the old version continues to be executed, leaving potential for significant confusion. Therefore, it's best not to change an object and continue to debug it without starting a new session.

C/SIDE Test-driven development

NAV 2013 includes an enhanced C/AL Testability feature set designed to support C/AL test-driven development. **Test-driven development** is an approach where the application tests are defined prior to the development of the application code. In an ideal situation, the code supporting application tests is written prior to, or at least at the same time as, the code implementing the target application function written.

Advantages of test-driven development include:

- Designing testing processes in conjunction with functional design
- Finding bugs at an earlier stage
- Preventing bugs reaching production
- Enabling regression testing, preventing changes introducing bugs into previously validated routines

The C/AL Testability feature provides test specific types of Codeunits—**Test Codeunits** and **Test Running Codeunits**. Test Codeunits contain Test methods, UI handlers, and C/AL code to support Test methods, including the **AssertError** function. Test Runner Codeunits are used to invoke Test Codeunits, for test execution management, automation and integration. Test Runner Codeunits have two special triggers, each of which run in separate transactions, so the test execution state and results can be tracked.

- **OnBeforeTestRun** is called before each test. It allows defining, via a Boolean, whether or not the test should be executed.

- **OnAfterTestRun** is called when each test completes and the test results are available. This allows the test results to be logged, or otherwise processed via C/AL code.

Among the ultimate goals of the C/AL Testability feature are:

- The ability to run suites of application tests both in automated mode and in regression tests:
    - **Automated** means that a defined series of tests could be run and the results recorded, all without user intervention.
    - **Regression testing** means that the test can be run repeatedly as part of a new testing pass to make sure that features previously tested are still in working order.

- The ability to design tests in an "atomic" way, matching the granularity of the application code. In this way, the test functions can be focused and simplified. This allows for relatively easy construction of a suite of tests and, in some cases, reuse of Test Codeunits (or at least reuse of the structure of previously created Test Codeunits).

- The ability to develop and run the Test and Test Runner Codeunits within the familiar C/SIDE environment. The code for developing these testing codeunits is C/AL.

- The **TestIsolation** property of TestRunner Codeunits allows tests to be run, then all database changes are rolled back so that no changes are committed. After a test series in this mode, the database is the same after the test as it was before the test.

- Once the testing codeunits have been developed, the actual testing process should be simple and fast in order to run and evaluate results.

Both positive and negative testing are supported. **Positive testing** looks for a specific result, a correct answer. **Negative testing** checks that errors are presented when expected, especially when data or parameters are out of range. The testing structure is designed to support the logging of test results, both failures and success, to tables for review, reporting and analysis.

A function property defines functions within Test Codeunits to be either `Test` or `TestHandler` or `Normal`. Another function property, **TestMethodType**, allows the definition of a variety of Test Function types to be defined. **TestMethodType** property options include the following, which are designed to handle User Interface events without the need for a user to intervene:

- **MessageHandler**: Handles the `MESSAGE` statement
- **ConfirmHandler**: Handles `CONFIRM` dialogs
- **StrMenuHandler**: Handles `STRMENU` menu dialogs
- **PageHandler**: Handles Pages that are not run modally
- **ModalPageHandler**: Handles Pages that are run modally
- **ReportHandler**: Handles Reports

C/SIDE Test Driven Development approach should proceed along the following lines:

- Define an application function specification
- Define the application technical specification
- Define the testing technical specification including both Positive and Negative tests
- Develop Test and Test Running codeunits (frequently only one or a few Test Running codeunits will be required)
- Develop Application objects
- As soon as feasible, begin running Application object tests by means of the Test Running codeunits, and logging test results for historical and analytical purposes
- Continue the development—testing cycle, updating the tests and the application as appropriate throughout the process
- At the end of successful completion of development and testing, retain all the Test and Test Running codeunits for use in regression testing the next time the application must be modified or upgraded

On PartnerSource, there is now available a full set of 7,000 to 9,000 regression tests written using the NAV 2013 Testability tools. The number of tests that applies to a specific situation depends on the local version and specific features involved. To access the download, search on **testability** and download the **Application Test Toolset for Microsoft Dynamics NAV 2013**. Make sure your license is updated too.

Included in the supplement are the regression tests and various tools for managing and executing tests built on top of the testability features released with Microsoft Dynamics NAV 2013. Also included is a coverage tool and guidance documentation for creating our own tests and integrating those with the Microsoft provided tests. This allows us to do full regression testing for large modifications and ISV solutions.

Other Interfaces

Some NAV systems must communicate with other software or even with hardware. Sometimes that communication is *Inside-Out* (that is, initiated by NAV), sometimes it is *Outside-In* (that is, initiated by the outside connection). It's not unusual for system-to-system communications to be a two-way street, a meeting of peers. To supply, receive, or exchange information with other systems (hardware or software), we need at least a basic understanding of the interface tools that are part of NAV.

 Because of NAV's unique data structures and the critical business logic embedded therein, it is very risky for an external system to access NAV data directly via SQL Server without using C/AL based routines as an intermediary.

NAV has a number of other methods of interfacing with the world outside its database. We will review those very briefly here. To learn more about these, we should begin by reviewing the applicable material in the online **Developer and IT Pro Help** material plus any documentation available with the software distribution. We should also study sample code, especially that in the standard system as represented by the Cronus Demonstration Database. And, of course, we should take advantage of any other resources available including the NAV-oriented Internet forums and blogs.

Automation Controller

One option for NAV interfacing is by connection to COM Automation servers. A key group of Automation servers are the Microsoft Office products. Automation components can be instantiated, accessed, and manipulated from within NAV objects using C/AL code. Data can be transferred back and forth between the NAV database and COM Automation components.

Only non-visual controls are supported via this interface (that doesn't mean we couldn't figure out a work-around, just that they aren't supported). The Client Add-in feature, discussed later in this chapter, provides visual interface capability through another integration approach.

We cannot use an Automation Controller defined COM component as a control on an NAV Page object. Only client side automation objects are supported. This is because the NAV server tier operates in 64-bit mode and many COM objects are not compatible with 64-bit operating systems. Instead of server side automation objects, use Microsoft .NET interoperability functionality (for more information search Help on "interoperability").

Some common uses of Automation Controller interfaces are to:

- Populate Word template documents to create more attractive communications with customers, vendors, and prospects (for example, past due notices, purchase orders, promotional letters)
- Move data to Excel spreadsheets for manipulation (for example, last year's sales data to create this year's projections)
- Move data to and from Excel spreadsheets for manipulation (for example, last year's financial results out and next year's budgets back in)
- Use Excel's graphing capabilities to enhance management reports
- Access to and use of ActiveX Data Objects (ADO) Library objects to support access to and from external databases and their associated systems

It will also be helpful to review the information on this topic in the following Help sections:

- *COM Overview*
- *Best Practices for Using Automation With the Microsoft Dynamics NAV Windows Client*
- *Automation Data Type*
- *Using COM Technologies in Microsoft Dynamics NAV*

Linked data sources

The two table properties, **LinkedObject** and **LinkedInTransaction**, are available for NAV tables. Use of these properties in the prescribed fashion allows data access, including views, in linked server data sources such as Excel, Access, other instances of SQL Server, and even an Oracle database. For additional information, see the Help sections *Linked Objects* and *Accessing Objects in Other Databases or on Linked Servers*.

NAV Application Server (NAS)

Microsoft Dynamics NAV Application Server (NAS) is a middle-tier server component that executes business logic without a user interface or user interaction. In NAV 2013, NAS is one of the client services that runs in the Microsoft Dynamics NAV Server.

The NAS is essentially an automated user client. Because NAS is essentially a non-UI version of the standard NAV client module, NAS can access all of NAV's business rules.

Error messages that are generated by an NAS process are logged in the Event Viewer.

NAS operates essentially the same as any other NAV Windows client. If it is set up to run the JobQueue, it processes requests in the queue one at a time, in the same manner as the GUI client. Therefore, as developers, we need to limit the number of concurrent calls to an NAS instance as the queue should remain short to allow timely communications between interfaces. In NAV 2013, multiple background sessions can be started from client sessions. This provides new opportunities for NAV automation for the creative designer/developer.

Client Add-ins

The NAV 2013 Client Add-in API (also known as Client Extensibility) provides the capability to extend the Role Tailored Client for Windows (only) through the integration of external, non-NAV controls. The Client Add-in API uses .NET interfaces as the binding mechanism between a control add-in and the NAV framework. Different interfaces and base classes are available to use, or a custom interface can be created. Controls can be designed to raise events that call on the **OnControlAddin** trigger on the page field control that hosts the add-in. They can also add events and methods that can be called from within C/AL.

Contrary to the limitations on other integration options, Client Add-ins can be graphical and appear on the RTC display as part of or mingled with the native NAV controls. The following are a few simple examples of how Client Add-ins might be used to extend RTC UI behavior:

- A NAV text control that looks normal but offers a special behavior when we double click on it the field's contents display in a popup screen.

- A dashboard made up of several dials or gauges showing the percentage of chosen resources relative to target limits or goals. The dials are defined to support click and drill into the underlying NAV detail data.

- An integrated sales call mapping function displays customer locations on a map and creates a sequenced call list with pertinent sales data from the NAV database.

- Interactive visualization of a workflow or flow of goods in a process, showing the number of entries at each stage, supporting filtering to display selected sets of entries.

Client Add-in construction

Some Client Add-ins will be created, packaged, and distributed by ISV Partners who specialize in an application area. When enhancing a system for a customer's specific application, we may decide to create a special purpose add-in.

As with any API, there is a defined approach that we must use to create a Client Add-in to interface with the NAV Windows RTC. So long as the code within the add-in is well-behaved .NET code, we have a great deal of flexibility in the structure of the code within the add-in. The control can be one we create, a standard WinForms control or one that we've acquired from a third party.

Once we have the .NET control we're going to use for our application, we need to build the add-in structure which envelopes the control. The most logical toolsets for building add-ins are any version of Visual Studio 2005, 2008 or 2010 or one of the free downloadable tools such as Visual Studio Express for C#. By the time you are reading this, it is likely that VS 2012 will also be supported.

The **Developer and IT Pro Help** in NAV 2013 contains many Help sections covering a wide variety of topics relating to Client Add-ins. Here's a partial list:

- *Binding a Windows Client Control Add-in to the Database*
- *Client Extensibility API Overview*
- *Client Extensibility Overview*
- *Developing Windows Client Control Add-ins*
- *Exposing Events and Calling Respective C/AL Triggers from a Windows Client Control Add-in*
- *Exposing Methods and Properties in a Windows Client Control Add-in*
- *Extending the Windows Client Using Control Add-ins*
- *How to: Create a Window Client Control Add-in*
- *How to: Determine the Public Key Token of the Windows Client Control Add-in*
- *How to: Install a Windows Client Control Add-in Assembly*
- *How to: Register a Windows Client Control Add-in*

- *Installing and Configuring Windows Client Control Add-ins on Pages*
- *Walkthrough: Creating and Using a Window Client Control Add-in*
- *Windows Client Control Add-in Overview*

Also take a look at **Christian's Blog** on MSDN at `http://blogs.msdn.com/b/cabeln/` (Christian is responsible for the development of the Client Add-in capability).

WDTU Client Add-in

Let's create a Client Add-in for WDTU. We want to add an MP3 player to the Playlist page to allow the user to preview songs on the Playlist. This is what it will look like when we're done.

To accomplish this, we will create a Visual Studio 2010 .NET assembly (.dll) utilizing the Windows Media Player.

To start, we are going to open Visual Studio 2010 and create a New Project. For a template, select **Visual C# - Windows Class Library**. Make sure the .NET Framework selected is 3.5 or higher. Name the solution **WDTUplayer**, and place in a directory we can access later (we'll use C:\Temp\). Check the **Create directory for solution** checkbox.

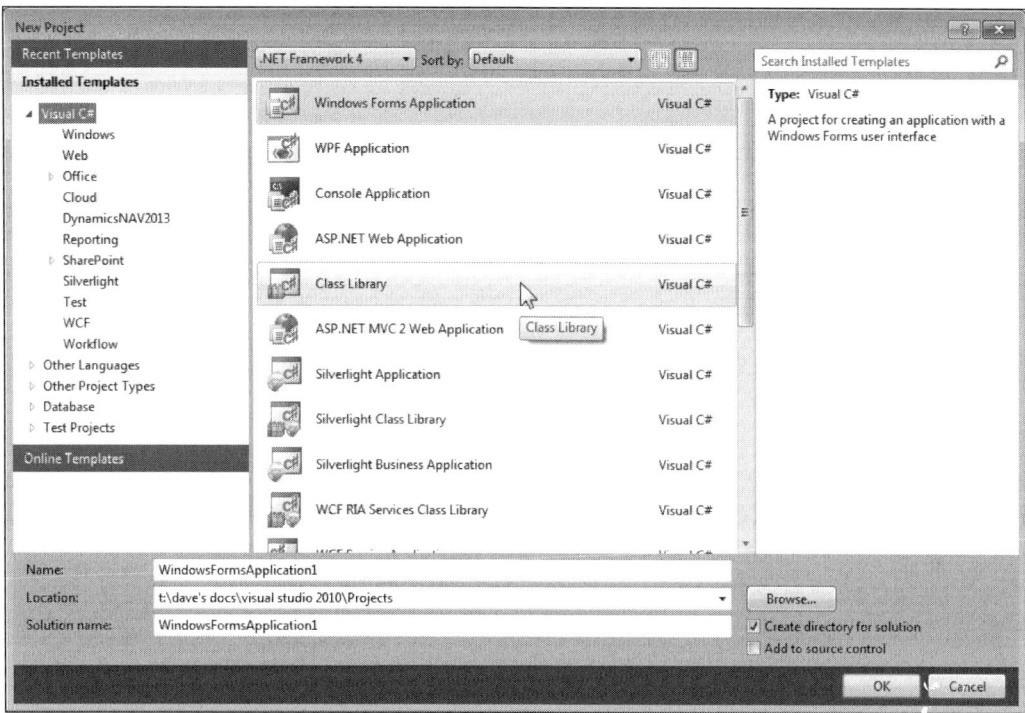

In order to access the `.dll` in NAV we need to create a **Strong Key Name (SNK)**. To do this in Visual Studio, go to the menu for **Project** and select **Properties**.

Select the **Signing** tab and checkmark the **Sign the Assembly** option.

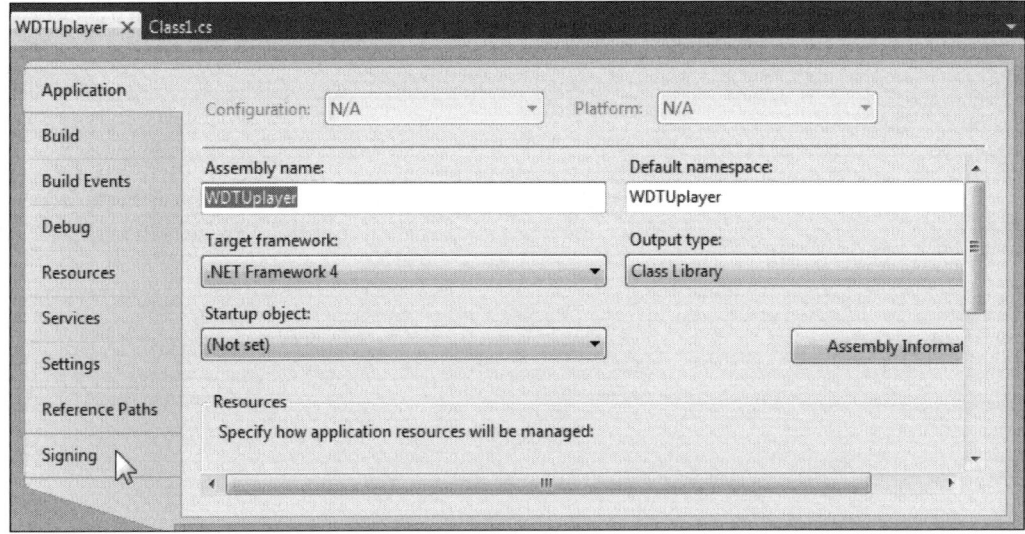

Select **<New...>** from the **Choose a strong name key file** dropdown box, and fill in a file name such as `WDTUplayer.snk`. Creating the SNK before adding any controls or other objects to the project allows those additional elements to inherit the SNK.

Go to the **Project** menu option and select **Add New Item** (*Ctrl + Shift + A*) and select **Windows Form**. The new Windows Form object will be added to our Form design layout screen. Right-click on the form and select **Properties** (or **View | Properties**). Review the form properties and set the ones defined in the following tables:

Property	Value
AutoScaleMode	None
AutoSize	True
FormBorderStyle	None
Locked	True
Padding	0,0,0,0
MaximizeBox	False

Property	Value
MaximumSize	0,0
MinimizeBox	False
MinimumSize	0,0
Size	276,47
Text	WDTU MP3 Player

Next we need to make the Windows Media Player (a COM object) available in the Toolbox. To add it in, Windows Media Player must be installed on our machine (it typically is). Click on **View | Toolbox** (or *Ctrl + W/Ctrl + X*) and scroll to the **General** group.

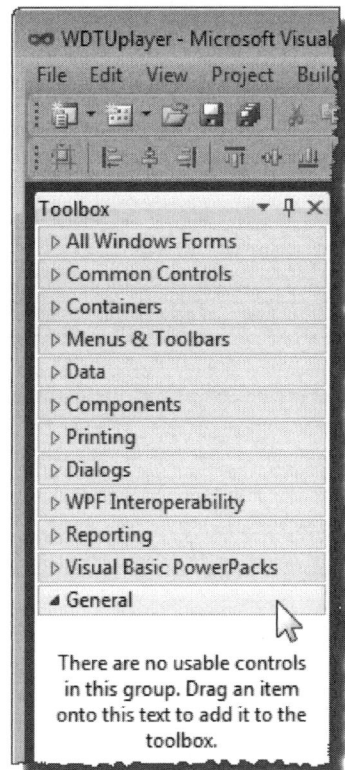

Right-click on **General** and select the **Choose Items** option. In the **Choose Toolbox Items** form select the **COM Components** tab and scroll down to **Windows Media Player**. Check the checkbox and click on **OK**.

The **Windows Media Player** control will now be available in the **Toolbox | General** tab.

Select the **Windows Media Player** control and drop it into the form that we added earlier. Right-click on the **Windows Media Player** control and then click on **Properties**. Uncheck **Auto Start** and check **Stretch to fit**.

Close the **Windows Media Player Properties** window, click on **View | Properties Window** (or *Ctrl + W/Ctrl + P*) and set properties as shown in the following table:

Property	Value
Name	WDTU_MP3_Player
Anchor	Top, Bottom, Left, Right
fullScreen	False
Location	0,0
Margin	0,0,0,0
Locked	True
Size	275, 45
stretchToFit	False
windowlessVideo	False

Click on **View | Solution Explorer** (or *Ctrl + W/Ctrl + S*) to make the **Solution Explorer** display (typically it will already be visible on our screen). In the **Solution Explorer**, click on the **References** option, then right-click to select **Add Reference**.

Add **Microsoft.Dynamics.Framework.UI.Extensiblity**, usually found in `C:\Program Files (x86)\Microsoft Dynamics NAV\70\RoleTailored Client\`.

To get to the code behind `Form1.cs`, in the **Solution Designer** window, right-click to select **View Code** or double-click on the form image in the main window. Once we are viewing the code, make code changes to make our code look like the following:

```
using System;
using System.Collections.Generic;
using System.ComponentModel;
using System.Data;
using System.Drawing;
using System.Linq;
using System.Text;
using System.Windows.Forms;

namespace WDTUplayer
{
    public partial class Form1 : Form
    {
```

```
        //string to put value from NAV into
        string MoviePath;

        public Form1()
        {
            //Make sure not a null string -
            //will error if not initalized
            MoviePath = "";
            InitializeComponent();
        }

        //Function called from Class to set URL path string
        public void SetMoviePath(string pMoviePath)
        {
            MoviePath = pMoviePath;
        }

        //Default function for NAVMediaPlayer control on form
        //where the URL can be dynamically set from NAV
        private void WDTU_MP3_Player_Enter(object sender, EventArgs e)
        {
            WDTU_MP3_Player.settings.autoStart = false;
            WDTU_MP3_Player.URL = MoviePath;
        }

    }
}
```

In the `Class1.cs` object, the code needs to be created as follows:

```
using System;
using System.Collections.Generic;
using System.ComponentModel;
using System.Linq;
using System.Text;
using Microsoft.Dynamics.Framework.UI.Extensibility;
using Microsoft.Dynamics.Framework.UI.Extensibility.WinForms;
using System.Windows.Forms;
using System.Drawing;

namespace WDTUplayer
{
    [ControlAddInExport("Cronus.DynamicsNAV.WDTU_MP3")]
    [Description("WDTU MP3 Player")]

    public class WDTU : StringControlAddInBase
    {
        //Create form instance to pass value from NAV
        Form1 WMPForm = new Form1();
```

```
              //Initialize the form
              protected override Control CreateControl()
              {
                  WMPForm.TopLevel = false;
                  WMPForm.Visible = true;
                  return WMPForm;
              }

              // This is the function that receives from NAV (set)
              // and sends back to NAV (get) the string value from
              // the SourceExp property on the NAV page field with
              // the ControlAddIn assigned to it
              public override string Value
              {
                  get
                  {
                      return base.Value;
                  }
                  set
                  {
                      base.Value = value;
                      WMPForm.SetMoviePath(base.Value);
                      //Function in form
                  }

              }
          }
      }
```

Note the statement defining `public override string` Value. This is the override of the `Value` property in the `Class1.cs` object that retrieves the value passed from NAV (`set`) and passes the value from the .NET assembly back to NAV (`get`). Because we defined the **WMPForm** variable as the Form object, we can pass the value retrieved from NAV (the field value linked in the CardPart page we will create to hold our Client Add-in).

Save all the objects and go to the **Build** menu and select **Build WDTUPlayer**. Locate and copy the following files from our Visual Studio Project folder.

- `WDTUplayer.dll`
- `Interop.WMPLib.dll`
- `AxInterop.WMPLib.dll`

Client Add-ins are each placed in their own directory within the directory `C:\Program Files (x86)\Microsoft Dynamics NAV\70\`. The default location is `RoleTailored Client\Add-ins`.

We'll create directory **WDTU_mp3** in that location and place our three files there.

From the **Start Menu**, run the **Visual Studio Command Prompt** (VSCP).

When the Visual Studio Command Prompt screen is displayed, enter the following command:

```
sn -T "C:\Temp\WDTUplayer\WDTUplayer\bin\Debug\WDTUplayer.dll"
```

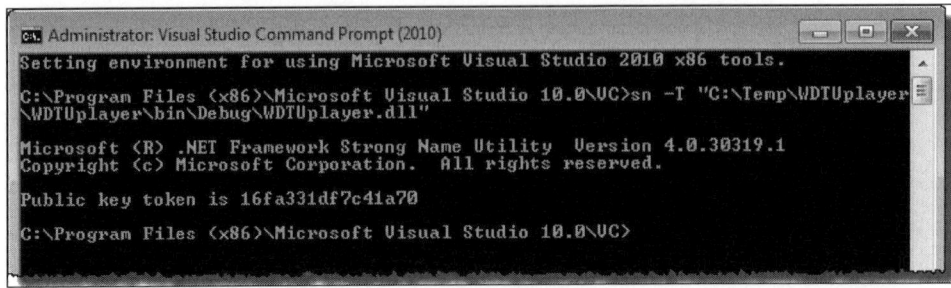

The **Public key token** is 16fa331df7c41a70 (yours may be different).

Exit the Visual Studio Command screen and open the NAV 2013 Development Environment. Click on the **Object Designer** button **Tables**, find **Table 2000000069 - Client Add-in**, then **Run** the table. Enter the control add-in name, public key token, a version (we decide what version), and a description.

Now that our Client Add-in is registered in NAV, we will create a CardPart to display a control containing our new Media Player Add-in control (which links the .NET .dll element to a field in NAV).

Click on **Page | New** in the Development Environment. Enter Item for the Table, and select **Create a page using a wizard:** and **CardPart** for the page type.

On the next tab only select a single field, **MP3 File Location**. This is the value we wish to pass to the .NET assembly.

Click on **Finish** and save the Page as `50010 - WDTU MP3 Player`. Click on the field **MP3 File Location** and view the properties. Scroll down to **ControlAddIn** and perform a lookup to select the **Cronus.DynamicsNAV.WDTU_MP3**. The public key token will also be populated. Set the **ShowCaption** property to `No`.

Save and close the page Design **Page 50003 - Playlist**. Open the properties of the subform control for the Playlist Subform and copy the control ID.

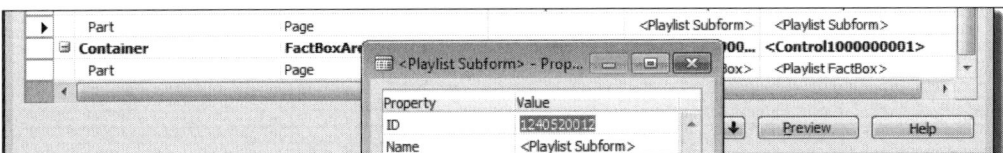

We need to assign this to the WDTU MP3 Player CardPart to link the CardPart to the SubForm lines. In the Page Designer for Playlist page, add the CardPart as a FactBox under the PlaylistFactbox.

Display the properties for this new Page Part control and fill in the properties as shown in the following screenshot:

Now we will test our work. Of course, in order to test, we have to have test data set up to match what we've designed in our software. We must have items that represent MP3 files and that contain the location of those MP3 files. Plus, the MP3 files must exist in the defined location. We should set up at least a couple of test items and associated MP3 files so we can enjoy the results of our work.

Once we have a minimal amount of test data set up, **Run** the **Playlist** page (**50003**). If all is well, the WDTU MP3 player should play the MP3 from the defined file location for each item in the playlist subpage. If it doesn't work, then this will be an opportunity to experiment some more with the NAV 2013 Debugger.

Client Add-in comments

In order to take advantage of the Client Add-in capabilities, we need to develop some minimal Visual Studio development skills and probably some .NET programming skills. Care will have to be taken when designing add-ins that their User Interface style complements, rather than clashing with, the UI standards of the NAV RTC.

Client Add-ins are a major extension of the Dynamics NAV system. This feature allows ISVs to create and sell libraries of new controls and new control-based micro-applications. It allows vertically focused Partners to create of versions of NAV that are much more tailored to their specific industries. This feature allows the integration of third party products, software, and hardware, at an entirely new level.

The Client Add-in feature is very powerful. Learn it, use it, and both you and your users will benefit.

Customizing Help

An auxiliary toolkit that is available to help us deliver better solutions to our customers is the Microsoft Dynamics NAV 2013 Help Toolkit. The Toolkit can be downloaded from PartnerSource. Once installed on our development system, this toolkit allows us to create customized Help for the application customizations that we deliver. We can also download the sources for the standard Help files, both W1 and localized.

Part of the Help Toolkit is the *Help Toolkit Help Guide*. Once we have downloaded and unzipped the Help Toolkit, we will find it useful to immediately find the file `NAV_HelpGuide.chm` and double-click on it to see the Help contents. In this Help file are instructions on installing and using the Help Toolkit. Reading through the installation instructions, perhaps even printing them off for handy reference, will make installing the toolkit much easier.

A sample display of a portion of the Table of Contents of the Help Toolkit is shown in the following screenshot. The *Getting Started* section contains the installation and configuration instructions. We can see that the Help for the Toolkit includes information on the tasks involved in creating customized Help for our application.

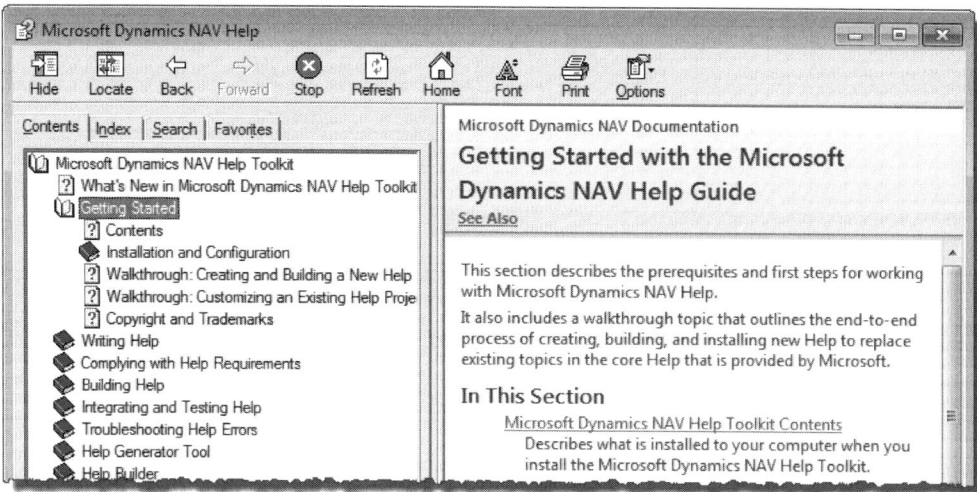

Before we begin our first Help customization effort, we should use this material as a tutorial. A good place to start is the section entitled *Walkthrough: Creating and Building a New Help Project*.

Developing customized Help is similar in many ways to developing customizations to the application software. The top-level style of new material should be essentially similar to the original product material. If the customizations are too different from the base material, it will create operational challenges for the users and, in turn, training and support challenges for the Partner.

Help customizations should be designed to make it as easy as possible to port them to new versions of the product when upgrading occurs. Similar to software development, whenever possible Help revisions should be done on a copy of the original Help topic, leaving the original unchanged. For example, if the Customer Card is modified, make the Help changes in a copy of the Customer Card Help.

We should take advantage of the Help Toolkit to make it easier for our customers, our users, and therefore easier (and more profitable) for us.

NAV development projects – some general guidance

Now that we understand the basic workings of the NAV C/SIDE development environment and C/AL, we'll review the process of software design for NAV enhancements and modifications.

When we start a new project, the goals and constraints for the project must be defined. The degree to which we meet these will determine our successes. Some examples:

- What are the functional requirements and what flexibility exists within these?
- What are the user interface standards?
- What are the coding standards?
- What are the calendar and financial budgets?
- What existing capabilities within NAV will be used?

Knowledge is key

Designing for NAV requires more forethought and knowledge of the operating details of the application than was needed with traditional models of ERP systems. As we have seen, NAV has unique data structure tools (SIFT and FlowFields), quite a number of NAV-specific functions that make it easier to program business applications, and a data structure (journal, ledger, and so on) which is inherently an accounting structure. The learning curve to become expert in the way NAV works is not easy. NAV has a unique structure and Microsoft provides very little product documentation other than the embedded Help. The NAV books published by Packt Publishing can be of great help.

Data-focused design

Any new application design must begin with certain basic analysis and design tasks. That is just as applicable whether our design is for new functionality to be integrated into NAV or is for an enhancement/expansion of existing NAV capabilities.

First, determine what underlying data is required. What will it take to construct the information the users need to see? What level of detail and in what structural format must the data be stored so that it may be quickly and completely retrieved? Once we have defined the inputs that are required, we must identify the sources of this material. Some may be input manually, some may be forwarded from other systems, some may be derived from historical accumulations of data, and some will be derived from combinations of all these, and more. In any case, every component of the information needed must have a clearly defined point of origin, schedule of arrival, and format.

Defining the needed data views

Define how the data should be presented. How does it need to be "sliced and diced"? What levels of detail and summary? What sequences and segmentations? What visual formats? What media will be used? Will the users be local or remote? Ultimately many other issues also need to be considered in the full design, including user interface specifications, data and access security, accounting standards and controls, and so on. Because there are a wide variety of tools available to extract and manipulate NAV data, we can start relatively simply and expand as appropriate later. The most important thing is to assure that we have all the critical data elements identified and then captured.

Designing the data tables

Data table definition includes the data fields, the keys to control the sequence of data access and to ensure rapid processing, frequently used totals (which are likely to be set up as **SumIndex Fields**), references to lookup tables for allowed values, and relationships to other primary data tables. We not only need to do a good job of designing the primary tables, but also all those supporting tables containing "lookup" and "setup" data. When integrating a customization, we must consider the effects of the new components on the existing processing as well as how the existing processing ties into our new work. These connections are often the finishing touch that makes the new functionality operate in a truly seamlessly integrated fashion with the original system.

Designing the user data access interface

Design the pages and reports to be used to display or interrogate the data. Define what keys are to be used or available to the users (though the SQL Server database supports sorting data without predefined NAV C/AL keys). Define what fields will be allowed to be visible, what are the totaling fields, how the totaling will be accomplished (for example, FlowFields or on-the-fly processing), and what dynamic display options will be available. Define what type of filtering will be needed. Some filtering needs may be beyond the ability of the built-in filtering function and may require auxiliary code functions. Determine whether external data analysis tools will be needed and will therefore need to be interfaced. Design considerations at this stage often result in returning to the previous data structure definition stage to add additional data fields, keys, SIFT fields, or references to other tables.

Designing the data validation

Define exactly how the data must be validated before it is accepted upon entry into a table. There are likely to be multiple levels of validation. There will be a minimum level, which defines the minimum set of information required before a new record is accepted.

Subsequent levels of validation may exist for particular subsets of data, which are in turn tied to specific optional uses of the table. For example, in the base NAV system, if the manufacturing functionality is not being used, the manufacturing-related fields in the Item Master table do not need to be filled in. But if they are filled in, they must satisfy certain validation criteria.

As mentioned earlier, the sum total of all the validations that are applied to data when it is entered into a table may not be sufficient to completely validate the data. Depending on the use of the data, there may be additional validations performed during processing, reporting, or inquiries.

Data design review and revision

Perform these three steps (table design, user access, data validation) for the permanent data (Masters and Ledgers) and then for the transactions (Journals). Once all the supporting tables and references have been defined for the permanent data tables, there are not likely to be many new definitions required for the Journal tables. If any significant new supporting tables or new table relationships are identified during the design of Journal tables, we should go back and re-examine the earlier definitions. Why? Because there is a high likelihood that this new requirement should have been defined for the permanent data and was overlooked.

Designing the Posting processes

First define the final data validations, then define and design all the ledger and auxiliary tables (for example, Registers, Posted Document tables, and so on). At this point, we are determining what the permanent content of the Posted data will be. If we identify any new supporting table or table reference requirements at this point, we should go back to the first step to make sure that this requirement didn't need to be in the design definition.

Whatever variations in data are permitted to be Posted must be acceptable in the final, permanent instance of the data. Any information or relationships that are necessary in the final Posted data must be ensured to be present before Posting is allowed to proceed.

Part of the Posting design is to determine whether data records will be accepted or rejected individually or in complete batches. If the latter, we must define what constitutes a Batch; if the former, it is likely that the makeup of a Posting Batch will be flexible.

Designing the supporting processes

Design the processes necessary to validate, process, extract, and format data for the desired output. In earlier steps, these processes can be defined as "black boxes" with specified inputs and required outputs, but without overdue regard for the details of the internal processes. This allows us to work on the several preceding definition and design steps without being sidetracked into the inner workings of the output-related processes.

These processes are the cogs and gears of the functional application. They are necessary, but often not pretty. By leaving design of these processes in the application design as late as possible, we increase the likelihood that we will be able to create common routines and to standardize how similar tasks are handled across a variety of parent processes. At this point, we may identify opportunities or requirements for improvement in material defined in a previous design step. In that case, we should return to that step relative to the newly identified issue. In turn, we should also review the effect of such changes for each subsequent step's area of focus.

Double-check everything

Do one last review of all the defined reference, setup, and other control tables to make sure that the primary tables and all defined processes have all the information available when needed. This is a final design quality control step.

It is important to realize that returning to a previous step to address a previously unidentified issue is not a failure of the process, it is a success. An appropriate quote used in one form or another by construction people the world over is *Measure twice, cut once*. It is much cheaper and more efficient to find and fix design issues during the design phase rather than after the system is in testing or, worse yet, in production (it's less painful too).

Design for efficiency

Whenever we are designing a new modification, we not only need to design to address the defined needs, but also to provide a solution that processes efficiently. An inefficient solution carries unnecessary ongoing costs. Many of the things that we can do to design an efficient solution are relatively simple.

- Properly configure system and workstation software (this is often overlooked)
- Make sure networks can handle the expected load (and then some more)
- Have enough server memory to avoid using virtual memory (disk)
- Most of all, do everything reasonable to minimize disk I/O

Disk I/O

The slowest thing in any computer system is the disk I/O. Disk I/O almost always takes more time than any other system processing activity. When we begin concentrating our design efforts on efficiency, focus first on minimizing disk I/O.

The most critical elements are the design of the keys, the number of keys, the design of the SIFT fields, the number of SIFT fields, the design of the filters, and the frequency of accesses of data (especially FlowFields). If our system is going to have five or ten users, processing a few thousand order lines per day and is not heavily modified, we probably won't have much trouble. But if we are installing a system with one or more of the following attributes, any of which can have a significant effect on the amount of disk I/O, we will need to be very careful with our design and implementation.

- Large concurrent user count
- High transaction volumes, especially in data being Posted
- Large stored data volumes, especially that resulting from customizations or setup option choices
- Significant modifications
- Very complex business rules

Locking

One important aspect of the design of an integrated system such as NAV that is often overlooked until it rears its ugly head after the system goes into production is the issue of "**Locking**". Locking occurs when one process has control of a data element, record, or group of records (in other words, part or all of a table) for the purpose of updating the data within the range of the locked data and, at the same time, another process requests the use of some portion of that data but finds it to be locked by the first process.

In the worst case, a "**deadlock**", there is a design flaw; each process has data locked that the other process needs and neither process can proceed. One of our jobs, as developers or implementers, is to minimize the locking problems and eliminate any deadlocks.

Locking interference between processes in an asynchronous processing environment is inevitable. There are always going to be points in the system where one process instance locks out another one momentarily. The secret to success is to minimize the frequency of these and the time length of each lock. Locking becomes a problem when the locks are held too long and the other locked-out processes are unreasonably delayed.

One might ask *What is an unreasonably delay?* For the most of the part, a delay becomes unreasonable when the users can tell that it's happening. If the users see stopped processes or experience counter-intuitive processing time lengths (that is, a process that seems like it should take 10 seconds actually takes two minutes), then the delays will seem unreasonable. Of course, the ultimate unreasonable delay is the one that does not allow the required work to get done in the available time.

The obvious question is how to avoid locking problems. The best solution is simply to speed up the processing. That will reduce the number of lock conflicts that arise. Important recommendations for speed include:

- Restrict the number of active keys, especially on the SQL Server
- Restrict the number of active SIFT fields, eliminating them when feasible
- Carefully review the keys, not necessarily using the "factory default" options
- Making sure that all disk access code is SQL Server optimized

Some additional steps that can be taken to minimize locking problems are:

- Always process tables in the same relative order.

- When a common set of tables will be accessed and updated, lock a "standard" master table first (for example, when working on Orders, always lock the Order Header table first).

- Shift long-running processes to off-hours or even separate databases.

In special cases, the following techniques can be used (if done very, very carefully).

- Process data in small quantities (for example, process 10 records or one order, then COMMIT, which releases the lock). This approach should be very cautiously applied.

- In long process loops, process a SLEEP command in combination with an appropriate COMMIT command to allow other processes to gain control (see the preceding caution).

Refer to the documentation with the system distribution and on the NAV forums.

Updating and upgrading

One must differentiate between "updating" a system and "upgrading" a system. In general, most of the NAV development work we will do is modifying individual NAV systems to provide tailored functions for end-user firms. Some of those modifications will be created as part of an initial system configuration and implementation before the NAV system is in production use. Other such modifications will be targeted at a system that is in day to day production to bring the system up to date with changes in business process or external requirements. We'll refer to these system changes as "updating".

"Upgrading" is when we implement a new version of the base C/AL application code distributed by Microsoft and port all the previously existing modifications into that new version. First we'll discuss updating, and then we'll discuss upgrading

Design for updating

Any time we are updating a production system by applying modifications to it, a considerable amount of care is required. Many of the disciplines that should be followed in such an instance are the same for a NAV system as for any other production application system. But some disciplines are specific to NAV and the C/SIDE environment.

Customization project recommendations

Some of these recommendations may seem patently obvious. That might be a measure of our experience and our own common sense. Even so, it is surprising the number of projects that go sour because one (or many) of the following are not considered in the process of developing modifications:

- One modification at a time
- Design thoroughly before coding

- Design the testing in parallel with the modification
- Use the C/AL Testability feature extensively
- Multistage testing:
    ◦ Cronus for individual objects
    ◦ Special test database for functional tests
    ◦ Copy of production database for final testing as appropriate
    ◦ Setups and implementation
- Testing full features:
    ◦ User interface tests
    ◦ System load tests
    ◦ User Training
- Document and deliver in a pre-defined, organized manner
- Follow up, wrap up, and move on

One change at a time

It is important to make changes to objects in a very well organized and tightly controlled manner. In most situations, only one developer at a time will make changes to an object. If an object needs to be changed for multiple purposes, the first set of changes should be fully tested (at least through development testing stage) before the object is released to be modified for a second purpose.

If the project is so large and complex or deadlines are so tight that this "one modification at a time" approach is not feasible, we should consider use of a software development version control system. Because most version control systems don't interface smoothly with C/SIDE, some significant effort is required. One notable exception is the iFacto ReVision Source Code Control system, specifically designed to work with Dynamics NAV (see `www.ifacto.be/en/revision`).

Similarly, we should only be working on one functional change at a time. As developers, we might be working on changes in two different systems in parallel, but we shouldn't be working on multiple changes in a single system simultaneously. It's challenging enough to keep all the aspects of a single modification to a system under control without having incomplete pieces of several tasks, all floating around in the same system.

If multiple changes need to be made simultaneously to a single system, one approach is to assign multiple developers, each with their own components to address. Another approach is for each developer to work on their own copy of the development database, with a project librarian assigned to resolve overlapping updates. We should learn from the past. In mainframe development environments, having multiple developers working on the same system at the same time was common. Coordination issues were addressed as a standard part of the project management process. Applicable techniques are well-documented in professional literature. Similar solutions would still apply.

Testing

As we know, there is no substitute for complete and thorough testing. Fortunately, NAV provides useful tools, which we have already discussed, to help us to be more efficient than we might be in some other environment. In addition to the built-in testing tools, there are also some testing techniques that are NAV specific.

Database testing approaches

If our modifications are not tied to previous modifications and specific customer data, then we may be able to use the Cronus database as a test platform. This works well when we target a database that is not heavily modified in the area on which we are currently working. As the Cronus database is small, we will not get lost in large data volumes. Most of the master tables are populated, so we don't have to create and populate this information. Setups are done and generally contain reasonably generic information.

If we are operating with an unmodified version of Cronus, we have the advantage that our test is not affected by other pre-existing modifications. The disadvantage, of course, is that we are not testing in a wholly realistic situation. Because the data volume in Cronus is so small, we are not likely to detect a potential performance problem.

Even when our modification is targeted at a highly modified system where those other modifications will affect what we are doing, it's often useful to test a version of our modification initially in Cronus. This may allow us to determine if our change has internal integrity before we move on to testing in the context of the fully modified copy of the production system.

If the target database for our modifications is an active customer database, there is no substitute for doing complete and final testing in a copy of the production database using a copy of the customer's license. This way, we will be testing the compatibility of our work with the production setup, the full set of existing modifications, and of course, live data content and volumes. The only way to get a good feeling for possible performance issues is to test in a copy of the production database.

 Final testing should always be done using the customer's license.

Testing in production

While it is always a good idea to thoroughly test before adding our changes to the production system, sometimes we can safely do our testing inside the production environment. If the modifications consist of functions that do not change any data and can be tested without affecting any ongoing production activity, it may be feasible to test within the production system.

Examples of modifications that may be able to be tested in the live production system can range from a simple inquiry page or a new analysis report or export of data that is to be processed outside the system to a completely new subsystem that does not change any existing data. There are also situations where the only changes to the existing system are the addition of fields to existing tables. In such a case, we may be able to test just a part of the modification outside production (we'll discuss that mode of testing a little later), and then implement the table changes to complete the rest of the testing in the context of the production system.

Finally, we can use the Testing functions to control tests so that any changes to the database are rolled back at the conclusion of the testing. This approach allows for testing inside a production database with less fear of corrupting live data.

Using a testing database

From a testing point of view, the most realistic testing environment is a copy of actual production database. There are often apparently good excuses why it is just too difficult to test using a copy of the actual production database.

 Don't give in to excuses—use a testing copy of the production database!

Remember, when we implement our modifications, they are going to receive the "test by fire" in the environment of production. We need to do everything within reason to assure success. Let's review some of the potential problems involved in testing with a copy of the production database and how to cope with them:

- *It's too big*—is not a good argument relative to disk space. Disk space is so inexpensive that we can almost always afford plenty of disk space for testing. We should also make every possible useful intermediate stage backup. Staying organized and making lots of backups may be time consuming, but done well and done correctly, it is less expensive to restore from a backup than to recover from being disorganized or having to redo a major testing process. This is one of the many places where appropriate use of the C/AL Testability tools can be very helpful by allowing various approaches to repetitive testing

- *It's too big*—is a meaningful argument if we are doing file processing of some of the larger files (for example, Item Ledger, Value Entry, and so on). But NAV's filtering capabilities are so strong that we should relatively easily be able to carve out manageable size test data groups with which to work.

- *There's no data that's useful*—might be true. But it would be just as true for a test database unless it were created expressly for this set of tests. By definition, whatever data is in a copy of the production database is what we will encounter when we eventually implement the enhancements on which we are working. If we build useful test data within the context of a copy of the production database, our tests will be much more realistic and, therefore, of better quality. In addition, the act of building workable test data will help to define what will be needed to set up the production system to utilize the new enhancements.

- *Production data will get in the way*—may be true. If this is especially true, perhaps, the database must be preprocessed in some way to begin testing or testing must begin with some other database such as Cronus or a special testing-only mockup. As stated earlier, all the issues that exist in the production database must be dealt with when we put the enhancements into production. Therefore, we should test in that environment. Overcoming such challenges will prepare us to do a better job at the critical time of going live with the newly modified objects.

- *We need to test repeatedly from the same baseline* or *We must do regression testing*—both are good points, but don't have much to do with the type of database we're using for the testing. Both the cases are addressed by properly managing the setup of our test data and keeping incremental backups of our pre-test and post-test data at every step of the way. SQL Server tools can assist in this effort. In addition, the C/AL Testability Tools are explicitly designed to support regression testing.

Remember, doing the testing job well is much less expensive than implementing a buggy modification.

Testing techniques

As experienced developers, we are already familiar with good testing practices. Even so, it never hurts to be reminded about some of the more critical habits to maintain.

Any modification greater than trivial should be tested in one way or another by at least two people. The people assigned should not be a part of the team who created the design or code of the modification. It would be best if one of the testers is an experienced user because users seem to have a knack (for obvious reasons) of understanding how the modification operates compared to how the rest of the system acts in the course of day-to-day work. This helps us to obtain meaningful feedback on the user interface before going into production.

One of the testing goals is to supply unexpected data and make sure that the modification can deal with it properly. Unfortunately, those who were involved in creating the design will have a very difficult time being creative in supplying the unexpected. Users often enter data the designer or programmer didn't expect. For that reason, testing by experienced users is beneficial.

The C/AL Testability Tools provide features to support testing how system functions deal with problem data. If possible, it would be good to have users help to define test data, and then use the Testability Tools to ensure the modifications properly handle the data.

After we cover the mainstream issues (whatever it is that the modification is intended to accomplish) we need to make sure our testing covers all boundary conditions. Boundary conditions are the data items that are exactly equal to the maximum or minimum or other range limit. More specifically, boundaries are the points at which input data values change from valid to invalid. Boundary condition checking in the code is where programmer logic often goes astray. Testing at these points is very effective for uncovering data-related errors.

Deliverables

Create useful documentation and keep good records of testing processes and results. Testing scripts, both human-oriented and C/AL Testability Tool-based, should be retained for future reference. Document the purpose of the modifications from a business point of view. Add a brief, but complete, technical explanation of what must be done from a functional design and coding point of view to accomplish the business purpose. Record briefly the testing that was done. The scope of the record keeping should be directly proportional to the business value of the modification being made and the potential cost of not having good records. All such investments are a form of insurance and preventative medicine. We hope they won't be needed but we have to allow for the possibility they will be needed.

More complex modifications will be delivered and installed by experienced implementers, maybe even by the developers themselves. Small NAV modifications may be transmitted electronically to the customer site for installation by a skilled super-user. Any time this is done, all the proper and normal actions must occur, including those actions regarding backup before importing changes, user instruction (preferably written) on what to expect from the change, and written instruction on how to correctly apply the change. As responsible developers, whenever we supply objects for installation by others, we must make sure that we always supply `.fob` format files (compiled objects), not text objects. This is because the import process for text objects simply does not have the same safeguards as does the import process for compiled objects.

Finishing the project

Bring projects to conclusion, don't let them drag on through inaction and inattention—open issues get forgotten and then don't get addressed. Get it done, wrap it up, and then review what went well and what didn't go well, both for remediation and for application to future projects.

Set up ongoing support services as appropriate and move on to the next project. With the flexibility of the Role Tailored Client allowing page layout changes by both super users (configuration) and users (personalization), the challenge of User support has increased. No longer can the support person expect to know what display the user is viewing today.

Consequently, support services will almost certainly require the capability for the support person to view the user's display. Without that, it will be much more difficult, time consuming, and frustrating for the two-way support personnel—user communication to take place. If it doesn't already exist, this capability will have to be added to the Partner's support organization tool set and practices. There may be communications and security issues that need to be addressed at both the support service and the user site.

Plan for upgrading

The ability to upgrade a customized system is a very important feature of NAV. Most other complex business application systems are very difficult to customize at the database-structure and process-flow levels. NAV readily offers this capability. This is a significant difference between NAV and the competitive products in the market.

Complementing the ability to be customized is the ability to upgrade a customized NAV system. While not a trivial task, at least it is possible with NAV. In many other systems, the only reasonable path to an upgrade is often to discard the old version and re-implement with the new version, recreating all customizations.

We may say, *Why should a developer care about upgrades?* There are at least two good reasons we should care about upgrades. First, because our design and coding of our modifications can have a considerable impact on the amount of effort require to upgrade a system. Second, because as skilled developers doing NAV customizations, we might well be asked to be involved in an upgrade project. Since the ability to upgrade is important and because we are likely to be involved one way or another, we will review a number of factors that relate to upgrades.

Benefits of upgrading

Just so we are on common ground about why upgrading is important to both the client and the NAV Partner, the following is a brief list of some of the benefits available from an upgrade.

- Easier support of a more current version
- Access to new features and capabilities
- Continued access to fixes and regulatory updates
- Improvements in speed, security, reliability, and user interface
- Assured continuation of support availability
- Compatibility with necessary infrastructure changes, such as new operating system versions
- Opportunity to do needed training, data cleaning, and process improvement
- Opportunity to resolve old problems, to do postponed "housekeeping", create a known system reference point

This list is not complete and not every benefit will be realized in any one situation.

Coding considerations

The most challenging and most important part of an upgrade is porting code and data modifications from the older version of a system to the new version. When the new version has major design or data structure changes in an area that we have customized, it is quite possible that our modification structure will have to be re-designed and perhaps even be re-coded from scratch.

On the other hand, many times the changes in the new product version of NAV don't affect much existing code, at least in terms of the base logic. If modifications are done properly, it's often not too difficult to port custom code from the older version into the new version. By applying what some refer to as "low-impact coding" techniques, we can make the upgrade job easier and thereby less costly.

Good documentation

In the earlier chapters, we discussed some documentation practices that are good to follow when making C/AL modifications. Here is a brief list of practices that should be followed.

- Identify every project with its own unique project tag
- Use the project tag in all documentation relating to the modification
- Include a brief but complete description of the functional purpose of the modification in a related `Documentation()` trigger
- Include a description of the modifications to each object in the `Documentation()` trigger of that object, including changes to properties, Global and Local variables, functions, and so on
- Add the project tag to the version code of all modified objects
- Bracket all C/AL code changes with inline comments so that they can be easily identified
- Retain all replaced code within comments, using `//` or `{ }`
- Identify all new table fields with the project tag

Low-impact coding

We have already discussed most of these practices in other chapters but will review them here in the context of coding to make it easier to upgrade. We won't be able to follow each of these, but will have to choose the degree to which we can implement low-impact code and which options to choose:

- Separate and isolate new code
- Create functions for significant amounts of new code that can be accessed using single code line function calls
- Either add independent Codeunits as repositories of modification functions or, if that is overkill, place the modification functions within the modified objects
- Add new data fields; don't change the usage of existing fields
- When the functionality is new, add new tables rather than modifying existing tables
- For minor changes, modify the existing pages, or copy and change the clone pages
- Copy and then modify the copies of Reports and XMLports rather than modifying the original versions in place
- Don't change field names in objects; just change captions and labels as necessary

In any modification, we will have conflicting priorities regarding doing today's job in the easiest and least expensive way versus doing the best we can do to plan for the future. The right decision is never a black and white choice, but must be guided by subjective guidelines as to which choice is really in the customer's best interest.

Supporting material

With every NAV system distribution there have been some reference guides. These are minimal in NAV 2013. There are previously published guides available, but sometimes we have to search for them. Some were distributed with previous versions of the product but not with the latest version. Some are posted at various locations on PartnerSource or another Microsoft website. Some may be available on one of the forums or from a blog.

Be a regular visitor to websites for more information and advice on C/AL, NAV, and other related topics. The websites `dynamicsuser.net` and `www.mibuso.com` are especially comprehensive and well attended. Other smaller or more specialized sites also exist. Some of those available as of the writing of this book are:

- Microsoft Dynamics NAV Team Blog: `blogs.msdn.com/nav/`
- Clausl's Dynamics NAV Blog: `http://www.mibuso.com/blogs/clausl`
- Christian's Blog: `blogs.msdn.com/b/cabeln/`
- Freddy's Blog: `blogs.msdn.com/b/freddyk/`
- Kine's info: `msmvps.com/blogs/kine/`
- Waldo's Blog: `www.waldo.be/`
- Mark Brummel's Blog: `dynamicsuser.net/blogs/mark_brummel/`

There are a number of other good blogs available. Look for them and review them regularly. The good ideas posted by the members of the NAV community in their blogs and on the NAV forums are generously shared freely and often.

Finally, there are a number of books focusing on various aspects of Dynamics NAV published by Packt Publishing (`www.packtpub.com`). Even the books that are about older versions of NAV have a lot of good information about developing with the NAV tools and applying NAV's functionality in a wide variety of application environments.

Summary

We have covered many topics in this book with the goal of helping you to become productive in C/AL development with Dynamics NAV 2013. Hopefully you've found your time spent with us to be a good investment. From this point on, your assignments are to continue exploring and learning, enjoy working with NAV, C/SIDE, and C/AL, and to treat others as you would have them treat you.

> *The only real failure in life is not to be true to the best one knows.* — Buddha

Review questions

1. Which of the following defines the Client Add-in feature? Choose one:

    a. The ability to add a new client of your own design to NAV 2013

    b. A tool to provide for extending the Role Tailored Client User Interface behavior

    c. A special calculator feature for the RTC client

    d. A new method for mapping Customers to Contacts

2. The Help files for NAV cannot be customized by Partner or ISV developers. True or False?

3. Custom C/AL code is not allowed to call functions that exist in the base Microsoft created NAV objects. True or False?

4. When planning a new NAV development project, it is good to focus the design on the data structure, required data accesses, validation and maintenance. True or False?

5. The developer cannot affect the way that "Locking" occurs in a NAV database. True or False?

6. Which of the following provides access to several libraries of functions for various purposes widely used throughout the NAV system? Choose one:

    a. Codeunit 412 – Common Dialog Management

    b. Codeunit 408 – Dimension Management

    c. Codeunit 396 – NoSeriesManagement

    d. Codeunit 1 – Application Management

7. Customized NAV systems cannot be upgraded to new versions. True or False?

8. Which of the following are good coding practices? Choose three:

    a. Careful naming

    b. Good documentation

    c. Liberal use of wildcards

    d. Design for ease of upgrading

9. NAV's multi-language capability allows for an installation to have multiple languages active at one time. True or False?

10. The Navigate feature can be used for which of the following? Choose three:

    a. Auditing by a professional accountant

    b. User analysis of data processing

    c. Reversing posting errors

    d. Debugging

11. You can enhance the Navigate function to include new tables that have been added to the system as part of an enhancement. True or False?

12. The NAV 2013 Debugger runs as a separate session. True or False?

13. The C/Side Testing tools allow the implementation of regression tests. True or False?

14. NAV does not support linked SQL Server databases. True or False?

15. Client Add-ins must be written in what language? Choose one:

    a. C#

    b. VB.NET

    c. Any .NET language

    d. C/AL.NET

16. The NAV 2013 Debugger allows the value of Watched Variables to be changed in the middle of a debugging session. True or False?

17. The C/Side Testing tools support which of the following? Choose four:

    a. Positive testing

    b. Negative testing

    c. Automated testing

    d. C# test viewing

    e. TestIsolation (roll-back) testing

18. COM object integration is not supported by NAV 2013. True or False?

19. NAV 2013 includes a flexible multi-currency feature that allows transactions to begin in one currency and conclude in a different currency. True or False?

20. NAV 2013 modifications should always be delivered to customers in the form of text files. True or False?

A
Answers to Review Questions

Chapter 1, An Introduction to NAV 2013

Question Number	Answers
1.	a, b, d, e
2.	a, c, d
3.	Table, Page, Report, Codeunit, XMLport, Query, MenuSuite
4.	True
5.	True
6.	d
7.	False
8.	False
9.	a – 4, b – 5, c – 1, d – 3, e - 2
10.	a, d
11.	b
12.	d
13.	True
14.	False
15.	b
16.	False

Question Number	Answers
17.	False
18.	b, d
19.	False
20.	False

Chapter 2, Tables

Question Number	Answers
1.	a, d
2.	False (up to 500 data fields)
3.	False (it's 50000 to 99999)
4.	a, d
5.	False
6.	False
7.	True
8.	True
9.	True
10.	False
11.	a, c, d
12.	a, c, d
13.	True
14.	False
15.	c
16.	False

Chapter 3, Data Types and Fields

Question Number	Answers
1.	False (the maximum is 30 characters)
2.	b
3.	c
4.	c

Question Number	Answers
5.	b, d
6.	True
7.	a, c, e
8.	False
9.	True
10.	False
11.	True
12.	False
13.	False
14.	c
15.	True

Chapter 4, Pages – the User's Interactive Interface

Question Number	Answers
1.	False
2.	False
3.	b, d
4.	True
5.	c
6.	True
7.	b, d
8.	False (it will default to the original property definition, but can be changed)
9.	a, c
10.	False
11.	False
12.	False
13.	a, c, e
14.	False
15.	False

Chapter 5, Queries and Reports

Question Number	Answers
1.	False
2.	False
3.	True
4.	b
5.	True
6.	True
7.	True
8.	a, c
9.	False
10.	a, b, c
11.	True
12.	False
13.	a, c, d
14.	False
15.	True
16.	a, c
17.	False
18.	b, c

Chapter 6, Introduction to C/SIDE and C/AL

Question Number	Answers
1.	False
2.	True
3.	a
4.	False
5.	a, b
6.	a
7.	True
8.	True

Question Number	Answers
9.	c
10.	False
11.	True
12.	False
13.	False
14.	False
15.	True
16.	b, d
17.	True
18.	a, c, e
19.	True
20.	False

Chapter 7, Intermediate C/AL

Question Number	Answers
1.	False
2.	False
3.	a, b, d
4.	True
5.	True
6.	a, b, c
7.	a, d (an Average FlowField gives a decimal result)
8.	d
9.	b
10.	True
11.	True
12.	b
13.	b, c
14.	True
15.	False
16.	False

Chapter 8, Advanced NAV Development Tools

Question Number	Answers
1.	False
2.	True
3.	c
4.	False
5.	True
6.	False
7.	False
8.	a, c, d
9.	False
10.	True
11.	True
12.	a, c
13.	False
14.	True
15.	False
16.	False
17.	True
18.	False
19.	b, d

Chapter 9, Develop, Debug, Deliver

Question Number	Answers
1.	b
2.	False
3.	False
4.	True
5.	False
6.	d
7.	False

Question Number	Answers
8.	a, b, d
9.	True
10.	a, b, d
11.	True
12.	True
13.	True
14.	False
15.	c
16.	False
17.	a, b, c, e
18.	False
19.	True
20.	False

Index

Y

Thank you for buying
Programming Microsoft Dynamics® NAV 2013

About Packt Publishing

Packt, pronounced 'packed', published its first book "Mastering phpMyAdmin for Effective MySQL Management" in April 2004 and subsequently continued to specialize in publishing highly focused books on specific technologies and solutions.

Our books and publications share the experiences of your fellow IT professionals in adapting and customizing today's systems, applications, and frameworks. Our solution based books give you the knowledge and power to customize the software and technologies you're using to get the job done. Packt books are more specific and less general than the IT books you have seen in the past. Our unique business model allows us to bring you more focused information, giving you more of what you need to know, and less of what you don't.

Packt is a modern, yet unique publishing company, which focuses on producing quality, cutting-edge books for communities of developers, administrators, and newbies alike. For more information, please visit our website: www.packtpub.com.

About Packt Enterprise

In 2010, Packt launched two new brands, Packt Enterprise and Packt Open Source, in order to continue its focus on specialization. This book is part of the Packt Enterprise brand, home to books published on enterprise software – software created by major vendors, including (but not limited to) IBM, Microsoft and Oracle, often for use in other corporations. Its titles will offer information relevant to a range of users of this software, including administrators, developers, architects, and end users.

Writing for Packt

We welcome all inquiries from people who are interested in authoring. Book proposals should be sent to author@packtpub.com. If your book idea is still at an early stage and you would like to discuss it first before writing a formal book proposal, contact us; one of our commissioning editors will get in touch with you.

We're not just looking for published authors; if you have strong technical skills but no writing experience, our experienced editors can help you develop a writing career, or simply get some additional reward for your expertise.

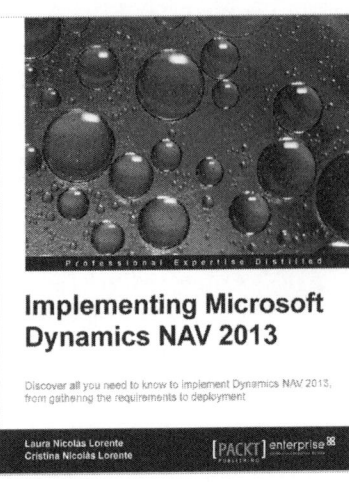

Implementing Microsoft Dynamics NAV 2013

ISBN: 978-1-849686-02-0   Paperback: 550 pages

Discover all you need to know to implement Dynamics NAV 2013, from gathering the requirements to deployment

1. Successfully handle your first Dynamics NAV 2013 implementation

2. Explore the new features that will help you provide more value to your customers

3. Full of illustrations and diagrams with clear step-by-step instructions and real-world tips extracted from years of experience

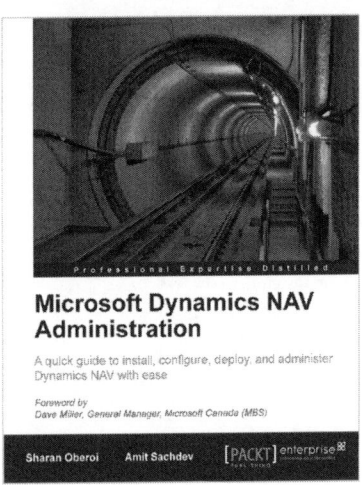

Microsoft Dynamics NAV Administration

ISBN: 978-1-847198-76-1   Paperback: 190 pages

A quick guide to install, configure, deploy, and administer Dynamics NAV with ease

1. Install, configure, deploy and administer Dynamics NAV with ease

2. Install Dynamics NAV Classic Client (Dynamics NAV C/SIDE), Dynamics NAV Role Tailored Client (RTC), and Dynamics NAV Classic Database Server on your computer to manage enterprise data

3. Connect Dynamics NAV clients to the Database Server in the earlier versions and also the latest Dynamics NAV 2009 version

Please check **www.PacktPub.com** for information on our titles

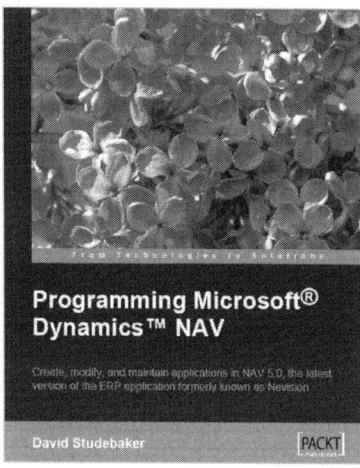

Programming Microsoft® Dynamics™ NAV

ISBN: 978-1-90481-174-9   Paperback: 480 pages

Create, modify, and maintain applications in NAV 5.0, the latest version of the ERP application formerly known as Navision

1. For experienced programmers with little or no previous knowledge of NAV development

2. Learn as quickly as possible to create, modify, and maintain NAV applications

3. Written for version 5.0 of NAV; applicable for all versions

Microsoft Dynamics Sure Step 2010

ISBN: 978-1-849681-10-0   Paperback: 360 pages

The smart guide to the successful delivery of Microsoft Dynamics Business Solutions

1. Learn how to effectively use Microsoft Dynamics Sure Step to implement the right Dynamics business solution with quality, on-time and on-budget results.

2. Leverage the Decision Accelerator offerings in Microsoft Dynamics Sure Step to create consistent selling motions while helping your customer ascertain the best solution to fit their requirements.

Please check **www.PacktPub.com** for information on our titles

Printed in Great Britain
by Amazon.co.uk, Ltd.,
Marston Gate.